The Black Gauntlet

THE BLACK GAUNTLET:

A TALE OF

Plantation Life in South Carolina.

BY

MRS. HENRY R. SCHOOLCRAFT,

WIFE OF THE INDIAN HISTORIAN, AND AUTHOR OF "AFRICAN LETTERS," ETC. ETC.

"Is there not some chosen curse,
Some hidden thunder in the stores of heav'n,
Red with uncommon wrath, to blast the man
Who owes his greatness to his country's ruin!"
Addison's Cato.

"For he was of that stubborn crew
Of errant saints whom all men grant
To be the true church militant;
Such as do build their faith upon
The holy text of pike and gun;
Decide all controversies by
Infallible artillery."
Butler's Hudibras.

PHILADELPHIA:
J. B. LIPPINCOTT & CO.
1860.

DEDICATION

TO

HENRY ROWE SCHOOLCRAFT, LL.D.

"Brutes find out where their talents lie;
A bear will not attempt to fly;
A founder'd horse will oft debate,
Before he tries a five-barr'd gate;
A dog by instinct turns aside,
Who sees the ditch too deep and wide.
But man we find the only creature
Who, led by folly, combats Nature;
And when she loudly cries—forbear,
With obstinacy fixes there;
And where his genius least inclines,
Absurdly bends his whole designs."

NE NA BAIM,* you have so repeatedly urged me to write sketches of character in Washington (the *omnium gatherum* of the world); and sketches of plantation life, in my own native State of South Carolina, where my ancestors have lived from its earliest settlement, that I have, for two months past, snatched every moment I could dutifully spare from my innumerable domestic cares, to comply with your wishes, by describing every-day life on the plantations. South Carolinians,

* Ne na baim, Indian word meaning my husband.

you know, are "old fogies," and consequently *they* do not believe with the Abolitionists, that *God* is a progressive being; but that throughout eternity *He* has been the same; perfect in wisdom, perfect in justice, and perfect in love to all his creatures; we cannot comprehend, therefore, the new-light doctrine, "That slavery is a sin;" for it seems quite incredible that God, through his servant Moses, should have ordered his own peculiar people (to whom he delivered his commandments under the thunderings of Sinai), to take their bondsmen from among the heathen nations around them, and keep them as an inheritance forever to their children's children, if slavery was a *crime* against the moral law. I have for twenty years studied the Bible with more intense interest than any other book; yet from Genesis to Revelation, I cannot find a sentence that holds out the idea, that slavery will ever cease while there are any heathen nations in this world; or, indeed, will ever cease in this present world at all; for in the final winding-up of all things, daguerreotyped to St. John in the Book of Revelation, we still find bondsmen alluded to in very many places.

Surely every Bible Christian is willing to let God Almighty be the expositor of *his own* laws; and even when He was made flesh, and dwelt among us thirty-three years, He never uttered one single word against slavery, though Jesus Christ rebuked all kinds of sin with the unsparing energy of Omnipotence itself.

I might, 'tis true, amuse my fancy like our daring, dashing, witty romancer, Mrs. Stowe, by imagining a millennial world, where all are born equal, where one man is not a dribbling idiot, and another a genius like Napoleon, Calhoun, or Webster; where one (and he a villain) does not roll in luxury, and fare sumptuously every day, while the wise and the good often have scarcely the wherewithal to keep from starvation; where bare-boned ghastly want, pain, frightful deformity, or decrepitude, does not number its millions as it does in every land we know anything about; where that insatiate monster Death does not stalk around day and night, slashing down with his cruelly relentless scythe, incomparable fathers and mothers, leaving their orphan children to be brought up for destruction by foreign selfishness; and the righteous who are the only salt of the earth, hurried away, too, the moment their influence and example seems indispensable to the wretched and morally decaying humanity around them; or I might even lash my sensibilities into fury, that neither the Old Testament nor the New; neither Moses, Jesus Christ, the Apostles, or our own historical experience for six thousand years, agrees with the Honorable Thomas Jefferson, that "All men are born free and equal." But of what practical use would all this castle-building be? It would fritter away the mind, not strengthen it, to bear with pious resignation the inequality that has caused so much heart-burning from the hour that the *first* son, of our *first* parents, killed his first brother, from envy of his superior vocation. The wheat and the tares, says inspiration itself, must grow together to the end of the world, when God will then separate them; and we poor animalcules might as well strive to prevent the return of day and night, as divorce what God hath joined together; and if Thomas Jefferson is right, we must search at once for an anti-slavery Bible, and an Abolition God, to make "all men equal;" and we must blot out the history of the whole human race, whose glaring inequality of mind, body, and condition, has been manifest to every observer, from the time that God created it between our first parents, and ordered Adam, in consequence of his superiority, to rule over Eve.

This primitive, radical inauguration of strength over weakness, has continued from that day to this, and will continue as long as this world lasts, for God has willed it so. Infinite wisdom; — not our impertinent speculations, governs the universe, and determines what is Right and Wrong *per se*. Our whole duty then is to bow to His revelation.

I do not, Ne na baim, own a slave, and I never again expect to be a slave-holder, though it is a high moral vocation to civilize and christianize the heathen, brought to our very doors in the South by the providence of God; — still, in the deepest recesses of my conscience, from the study of the Bible, and my own experience among Africans all my life, I am so satisfied that slavery is the school God has established for the conversion of barbarous nations, that were I an absolute Queen of these United States, my first missionary enterprise would be to send to Africa, to bring its heathen as *slaves* to this Christian land, and keep them in bondage until *compulsory* labor had tamed their beastliness, and civilization and Christianity had prepared them to return as missionaries of progress to their benighted black brethren.

God has placed a mark on the negro, as distinctive as that on Cain; and I do not believe there is a *white* man, woman, or child, on the face of the earth, who does not, in his deepest heart, regard the African an inferior race to his own. The fiat of the great God Almighty, the researches of ethnology, history, and experience, and our very instincts, teach us this fact; and I believe a refined Anglo-Saxon lady would sooner be burnt at the stake, than married to one of these black descendants of Ham.

Slavery is God's ordinance for one set of His rebellious creatures; and shall the clay say to the potter, Why hast thou made me thus? This world has been reeking with cruelty and injustice ever since Cain murdered Abel, because he thought God loved, and was too partial to him. But does the New-Light Abolitionist dream that, by a twist and a jerk, *he* can restore the lost image of God in man? Fie! fie! upon such monstrous infidel arrogance. Did Jesus Christ himself assume the power to make all men, *nolens volens*, righteous, in their laws, or in their practice? Slavery, during the thirty-three years he lived upon this earth, was more tyrannous than it has ever been since. Did he say a word against it as an institution? And the question is significantly asked in Scripture: When the Son of man cometh a second time to judge the world, will He find faith on the earth?

I grant that slavery, and marriage, and many other institutions of God, are used by Satan to culminate sin, and to torment the human heart; but shall we therefore abolish marriage, because it has been abused? and because innumerable wives have shed the bitterest tears possible to any of the descendants of Adam and Eve? I am certain that wives have suffered more intense, more hopeless anguish, from brutal, non-appreciative husbands, than any slave has ever experienced, since God first gave the command to his people to bring heathen nations into bondage to Christian nations; for the slave being made, by the mercy of his Creator, property, secures a more undying interest, in a selfish master's heart, than a wife, who can be so easily replaced, particularly when her husband begins to get tired of her; which is so often the case, that the newspapers report that in forty days one hundred and fifty divorces were granted in Kansas (where the Sharp's rifles were sent to shoot people into righteousness by exterminating them, and of course out of the evils of matrimony, by opening the widest door for its legal abrogation, by any individual who was incapable of adhesive affection or reverence for this ordinance of God.

In writing these sketches of South Carolina, Ne na baim, God knows that I have no ambition to be an author;—and nothing but my romantic veneration, that makes your wishes my law, could have induced me to take up my pen, other than as your amanuensis. For twelve years that you have been imprisoned at home by a stroke of paralysis, I have felt no earthly aspiration beyond the honor of helping you to complete your voluminous history of the Red race of this continent, by becoming your assiduous copyist and constant nurse; for, in the bodily afflictions that you have borne with the uncomplaining manliness, majesty, and serenity of Christianity, you have commanded the deepest moral appreciation and romance of a Southern woman's heart.

If, therefore, *your* criticism of my sketches induces you to think them at all worthy of publication, my ambition will be entirely satisfied; for every sentiment I have uttered I am willing to leave as a souvenir to my friends; for they are the mellowed convictions of my mind and heart.

You have made me read aloud to you so many books, that almost involuntarily I have acquired a habit of quoting from the best authors. Blot out, however, every line you disapprove; for your appreciation is all I crave. Indeed, I have felt desolate from earliest childhood; ever lamenting the loss of an incomparable father and mother, and loving sisters, and brothers, and friends, all snatched from me by inevitable destiny; so that, in this wide world, I have found *you*, Ne na baim, my only unchanging earthly hope. You are, therefore, my all — for the heart needs a home in this world as well as the next; and I could now be contented to live alone with *you*, surrounded with books, in a wigwam, in the Oke-fe-no-ke Swamp, among the birds, the flowers, and the wild beasts; for the rattlesnake and the tiger are not so malignantly insatiable as the poisoned tongue of suspicion, detraction, and envy — that neither you nor I have been shielded from, though living in the strictest retirement for half a score of years, and not intentionally standing in the sunlight of a human being; but humbly thanking God every day for that sublime blessing of *patience* under your severe afflictions, that has through you magnified the religious enthusiasm of Job, who from the depths of misery cried out, with his whole heart, "Though God slay me, I will still trust in Him."

"Many readers judge of the power of a book by the shock it gives to their feelings — as some savage tribes determine the power of muskets by their recoil; that being considered best that fairly prostrates the purchaser," says Longfellow.

THE

BLACK GAUNTLET.

CHAPTER I.

What constitutes a State?
Not high-raised battlements or labored mound,
Thick wall or moated gate;
Not cities proud with spires and turrets crowned;
Not bays and broad-armed ports,
Where, laughing at the storm, rich navies ride;
Not starred and spangled courts,
Where low-browed baseness wafts perfume to pride:
No! Men, high-minded men,
With powers as far above dull brutes endued,
In forest, brake, or den,
As beasts excel cold rocks and brambles rude;
Men, who their duties know,
But know their rights, and knowing dare maintain,
Prevent the long-aimed blow,
And crush the tyrant, while they rend the chain:
These constitute a State."

SIR W. JONES.

CAROLINA seems, from its earliest origin, to have been the pet of royalty. In 1660, Charles II. ascended the throne of England. The Protectorship and the Commonwealth, with its rigid state of social manners and opinions, was succeeded by its opposites in social, political, religious, and literary life.

The violent struggle that brought Charles I. to the scaffold, the marked era of the Protectorship and the Commonwealth, and the revolution that re-introduced a Stuart, had filled the kingdom with a numerous class of discontented persons, which had the effect of swelling the tide of emigration to the American colonies.

The adherents to the government of Charles now determined to apply to the Crown for the charter of a colony, to which his friends and favorites might freely migrate. Charles acceded to the petition, and in 1672 granted a charter for the large range of the Atlantic coast situated between Virginia and Florida, to which was given the name of Carolina. Causes led to delays in the execution of the charter, and in 1674 a renewed charter of the country was granted to certain nobles and gentlemen, which was of an almost sovereignly aristocratic character.

"Agreeably to the powers with which these proprietors were invested by their charter, they began to frame a system of laws, for the government of their Colony, in which arduons task they called in the great philosopher, John Locke, to their assistance. A model government, consisting of no less than a hundred and twenty different articles, was framed by this learned man, which they agreed to establish, and to the careful observance of which to bind themselves and their heirs forever." . . . "But there is danger of error, where speculative men of one country attempt to sketch out a plan of government for another, in a different climate and situation: so that although John Locke's great abilities and merit must be freely acknowledged, still his fine-spun system proved in effect useless and impracticable." . . . "Several attempts were afterwards made to amend these fundamental constitutions; but the inhabitants, satisfied that they were not applicable to *their* circumstances, would not themselves, or through their representatives in assembly, assent to them, as a body of laws." . . . "Whatever regulations the people found practical and useful, they adopted at the request of their governors; but still observed them on account of their *own* propriety and necessity, rather than as a system of laws imposed on them by British legislators."

Previous however to this experimental test, a residence in the Colony appeared very inviting, from Mr. John Locke's novel government of palatines, landgraves, and caciques. Locke's plan of government (says an old writer) for this Colony was, universal toleration in all religious matters: the only restriction in this respect being, that every person claiming the protection of that settlement should at the age of seventeen register himself in some particular communion. One of these early laws of Carolina reads thus: "No person above seventeen years of age shall have any benefit or protection of the law, or be capable of any place of honor or profit, who is not a member of some church or profession, having his name recorded in some one, and but one, religious record at a time." . . . "No person whatsoever shall speak any thing in their religious assembly irreverently or seditiously of the government, or governors, or state matters." . . .

"No agreement or assembly of men upon pretence of religion shall be accounted a church or profession, without these rules: —

"1. That there is a God.

"2. That God is to be publicly worshipped.

"3. That it is lawful and the duty of every man, being thereunto called by those that govern, to bear witness to the truth; and that every church or profession shall in their terms of communion set down the external way whereby they witness a truth, as in the presence of God, whether it be by laying on of hands or kissing the Bible," &c.

To civil liberty however our philosopher, John Locke, was not so favorable. "The code of Carolina gave to the proprietors, who founded the Colony, and to their heirs, not only all the rights of a monarch, but all the powers of legislation. The Court, which was composed of this sovereign body, and called the Palatine Court, was invested with the right of nominating to all employments and dignities, and even of conferring nobility, but with new and unprecedented titles." . . . "They were, for instance, to create in each county two caciques, each of whom was to be possessed of 24,000 acres of land; and a landgrave, who was to have 80,000." (There is a variety of differences in the accounts of historians of the number of acres these caciques and landgraves were to possess. Some of them, for instance Thompson's "Alcedo," make the number of acres 480,000 to the landgraves.)

The persons on whom these honors should be bestowed were to compose the Upper House, and their possessions were made inalienable. They had only the right of farming, or letting out a third part of them, at the most for three lives (perhaps thirty-one years.)

"The Lower House was composed of deputies from the several counties and towns. The number of this representative body was to be increased as the Colony grew more populous. No tenant was to pay more than about a shilling per acre, and even this rent was redeemable. All the inhabitants, however, both slaves and freemen, were under an obligation to take up arms, upon the first order from the Palatine Court.

"It was not long before the defects of this Constitution became apparent. The proprietary lords used every endeavor to establish an arbitrary government; and on the other hand, the colonists exerted themselves with great zeal to avoid servitude. In consequence of this struggle, the whole Province, distracted with tumults and dissensions, became incapable of any progress, though great things had been expected from its particular advantages of situation.

"Though a toleration in religious matters was a part of the original Constitution, dissensions arose likewise on this account.

"In 1705, Carteret, now Lord Granville, who, as the eldest of the proprietors, was sole Governor of the Colony, formed a design of obliging all the non-conformists to embrace the ceremonies of the Church of England; and this act of violence, though disavowed and rejected by the mother country, inflamed the minds of the people; and the government of Palatines, Landgraves, and Caciques (prepared by one of the most logical minds in England), after nearly half a century of turmoils, proved a perfect failure; and the Carolinians were only too glad to surrender the Proprietary Government into the hands of the king."

The following sketches embrace the family history of the descendants of one of the Palatines.

Mr. John Wyndham's paternal ancestors were among the earliest settlers on the waters of the Broad river (called by the French, Grande river). This part of the Atlantic coast had been opened to Spanish discovery early in the 16th century, and the name of *Chicora*, given to it by the Indians, was recognized. Cape St. Helena, and Broad river, with its celebrated island, Port Royal, had been known since the enterprise of Ribault. That officer, in 1572, built Fort Carolina, on the site where the town of Beaufort now stands. This ancient point of French discovery, had also been the first seat of English settlement under the Proprietary Government; although this germinating point of settlement was carried subsequently to the fertile banks of the Ashley and Cooper rivers. Here the City of Charleston was founded in 1680.

The refinement and chivalrous spirit that still distinguishes the oldest families in South Carolina, was introduced in the reign of Charles II., by the emigration of the cavaliers of England, who came out under the stimulant, as previously remarked, of grants of fertile lands, untrammelled religious opinion, and the love of enterprise in a new country.

Mr. Wyndham located himself on that part of the coast formerly occupied by the Yamasees, who in 1715 planned a massacre of all the white inhabitants. This was but a repetition of the terrible massacre of the

Virginia colonists under Opechanganough, in 1622; of the Susquehannocks, in Maryland, in 1612; of King Philip, of New England, in 1677; and of the Tuscaroras, in North Carolina, in 1711:—events which have done much to blunt Southern sympathy for this doomed race, up to the present day.

The waters of the Coosauhatchie and Combahee, flowed through portions of the country where Mr. Wyndham resided. The mounds near Pocataligo yet remain to attest the seat of the Yamasee dominions. This massacre, in South Carolina, broke out suddenly; for the Indians, with their usual stealthy cunning and secrecy, never betrayed a single hint of their bloody purpose, although it was planned a whole year before. Indications in their countenances of dissatisfaction, it is true, were observed, in consequence of which, Governor Craven sent Mr. Nairn to reside among them as Indian Agent, in order to test their fidelity, and redress their grievances, if they had any. But although the plot was then on the eve of execution, they lulled his every suspicion; and, after a satisfactory council with them, and partaking of their hospitalities, retired to rest, satisfied that his fears were unfounded.

Early the next morning, being the 13th of April, he was awakened by the war-whoop, and fell beneath their treacherous blows. He had a companion who escaped with a wound, and swam over the river to give the alarm; but this had no effect to save the immediately surrounding settlers, a hundred of whom were butchered with the tomahawk that day. Governor Craven, of Charleston, adopted the most stringent and prompt means to put down the savage outbreak; organizing a force of footmen (among whom were many slaves, who fought valiantly for their masters); and leading, himself, a body of volunteers, on horseback.

The result was, a hot and vengeful war; and, finally, the whole of the Indians, who were found in league with the Spaniards at St. Augustine, were driven from the territory.

"The Yamasees, after their defeat and expulsion, went directly to the Spanish territories in Florida, where they were received with bells ringing, and guns firing, as if they had come victoriously from the field; from which circumstance, together with the encouragement afterwards given to them to settle in Florida, there is too good reason to believe, that this horrid conspiracy was contrived by Spaniards, and carried on by their encouragement and assistance."

After passing the Savannah river, they were, at a subsequent period, attacked and subdued by the Appalachians, or Creeks; and the remainder of them adopted into that confederacy of tribes, under the name of Uchees. Thus the Colony was cleared of a most subtle foe. All that now remains to show that they ever inhabited the country, besides the names left in its geography, are the mounds, barrows, and banks of oyster-shells, marking the former sites of their villages, which are sometimes seen in our South Carolina cotton-fields at the present day.

CHAPTER II.

> "I saw young Harry with his beaver on,
> His cuisses on his thighs, gallantly arm'd,
> Rise from the ground like feather'd Mercury,
> And vaulted with such ease into his seat,
> As if an angel dropp'd down from the clouds
> To turn and wind a fiery Pegasus,
> And witch the world with noble horsemanship."
>
> SHAKSPEARE.

A GAY party of young ladies and gentlemen, sensibly dressed, were standing, laughing merrily, at old Mr. Wyndham's door, ready to mount their richly-caparisoned horses, for an excursion of pleasure nine miles off, where they expected to have their numbers reinforced by friends at an adjoining plantation (equestrian exercises being fashionable at this time, 1794, in South Carolina).

The extended hand of their several kneeling knights was the pedestal on which each Hebe placed her coquettishly-shod, tiny little foot, and with one impulse sprang into the saddle, and galloped off so truantly that it required considerable enterprise to overtake her. One of the most prominently graceful and self-possessed of these equestrians was a Miss Bloomfield, of Charleston, whose years perhaps numbered some seventeen summers, and whose height and bearing were equally majestic; for she had not only received every advantage of education from her grandfather, who had been a Bishop of the Church of England, but she early developed great inductive powers of mind, and was consequently too thoughtful to prove a general favorite among the young madcap fellows of this party, who were the direct descendants of the chivalrous, gay cavaliers of Charles the Second's reign.

Miss Bloomfield's strikingly-intellectual, large black eye, inclosed in a proportionally-ample socket (which is a rare perfection) — her pale, but at times speaking complexion — her chiselled features — her retiring, benevolent countenance, and yet occasional flashes of genuine humor — would have quivered an arrow of the deepest sensibility into the heart of a man of genius; but to others who could not, or would not, take the trouble to know her inner graces of adhesive affection, conscientiousness, and ambition to excel in all that was useful and morally elevating, she seemed stereotyped, if not repulsive; for she was born just about the time that the "Declaration of Independence" was declared against our mother country (England) by her American Colonies, and, no doubt, brought up in the school of such heroism * and self-denial as the patriotic women

---

* "The historian, Ramsay," says Mrs. Ellet, "bears heart-warm testimony to the patriotism of the South Carolina women who gloried in being called 'rebels,' and did their utmost to support the fortitude of their relatives in the Revolutionary War.

"The wife of Isaac Holmes, one of the patriots sent into exile at St. Augustine, sustained his firmness by her own resolution, to the moment when the guard separated him from his family, bidding him have no fears for those he left behind. Her

of the Revolution daily practised; her mind had been strengthened by the discipline of sorrow, and faith in that overruling Providence that carried us safely and triumphantly through that miraculous struggle, by furnishing us a *Washington* to lead our half-fed, half-clad,* undisciplined volunteers to battle and to victory, after a seven years' war.

---

parting injunction was, 'Waver not in your principles, but be true to your country.'

"When the sons of Rebecca Edwards were arrested as objects of retaliation, she encouraged them to persevere in devotion to the cause they had espoused; should they fall a sacrifice, a mother's blessing, and the approbation of their countrymen, would go with them to the last; but if fear of death ever prevailed on them to purchase safety by submission, they must forget she was their parent, for it would be her misery to look on them again."

* "During the Revolutionary War, General Andrew Pickens had a faithful African named Dick, who followed him throughout the war, and often fought by his side. This servant swam the Broad river twice, on a cold winter's night, to get to the camp of his master—mistaking the enemy's camp once. At the Cowpens, a wounded British officer, lying against a tree, asked Dick to bring him a little water. He brought it in his hat, and then immediately put out his knee, and asked to draw his boots. The officer said: 'Surely, boy, you will not take them before I die.' Dick replied: 'Him mighty fine, and massa need him mighty bad.'

"Garden relates a pleasant anecdote of the wit of Mrs. Elliott, of South Carolina, during the war. A British officer having ordered the plundering of her poultry-houses, she afterwards observed, straying about the premises, an old muscovy drake which had escaped the general search. She had him caught, and mounting a servant on horseback, ordered him to follow, and deliver the bird to the officer, with her compliments, as she concluded that in the hurry of departure it had been left altogether by accident."—*Mrs. Ellet's "Women of the Revolution."*

This mirthful party of beaux and belles continued their genial tramp from plantation to plantation, chatting volubly their numerous plans for a grand Christmas merry-making at Mr. Wyndham's affluent mansion, where the negroes Sambo, Robert, and Jack, who were enthusiastic and talented performers on the fiddle, should come in, with their violin, and tamborine, and banjo, and strike up electrifying music for their young master's guests to indulge in terpsichorean exercises during the whole jubilant season between the 25th of December and the first day of the new year.

Suddenly Miss Bloomfield's high-mettled charger took fright at the loud report of a gun, and rushed off at the top of his speed; and becoming more and more alarmed from the desperate pursuit of the frantic Jehues of the party, dashed into a cross-road after running a mile, and then into the woods; where, rushing against the veteran pine-trees, she would inevitably have been killed (for her terror had deprived her of all power over the reins), had not young Wyndham, distancing all others, caught her in his arms as she was reeling, in a fainting fit, out of the saddle.

Afflictions, however, seldom come single-handed; for no sooner had he run with his lovely burden to a neighboring spring, for a reviving draught, than that intolerably ubiquitous, meddlesome, mischief-making little wretch, nicknamed *Cupid*, who was accidentally on purpose romping in the woods in search of an adventure, quickly spied the romantic youth, stealing a kiss * before the other gallants could arrive at the spot.

* Poetical Idea.—A beautiful superstition prevails among the Seneca tribe of Indians. When an Indian maiden dies,

So, in revenge for this imprudent selfishness (as conventional sense might have assured him that such a smothering application could never restore a young lady from a fainting fit), Cupid hid himself in an ambush, and then taking deliberate aim, quivered his arrow so deeply in young Wyndham's heart, that none of the greatest, most scientific Esculapians, could, with all their surgical skill, extract it for seventeen years.*

---

they imprison a young bird until it first begins to try its power of song, and then, loading it with kisses and caresses, they loose its bonds over the grave, in the belief that it will not fold its wings nor close its eyes until it has flown to the spirit-land and delivered its precious burden of affection to the loved and lost. It is not unfrequent to see twenty or thirty birds let loose over one grave.

* "When all things have their trial, you shall find
Nothing is constant but a virtuous mind."

"That is not the most perfect beauty which in public would attract the greatest observation; nor even that which the statuary would admit to be a faultless piece of clay, kneaded up with blood. But that is true beauty, which has not only substance, but a spirit—a beauty that we must intimately know, justly to appreciate—a beauty lighted up in conversation, where the mind shines, as it were, through its casket, where, in the language of the poet, 'The eloquent blood spoke in her cheeks; and so distinctly wrought, that we might almost say her body thought.' An order and a mode of beauty which, the more we know, the more we accuse ourselves of not having discovered those thousand graces which bespeak that their owner had a soul. This is that beauty that never cloys, possessing charms as resistless as those of the fascinating Egyptian, for which Antony wisely paid the bauble of a world—a beauty, like the rising of his own Italian suns, always enchanting, never the same."—COLTON.

"Oh, who that has ever had rapture complete,
Would ask how we feel it, or why it is sweet;
How rays are confused, or how particles fly,
Through the medium refined of a glance or a sigh!
Is there one, who but once would not rather have known it,
Than written, with Harvey, whole volumes upon it?"

This now thoroughly sobered party of young people, waiting until Miss Bloomfield was entirely restored to her usual self-possession, assisted her to remount her capricious steed, and then wended their way homeward in a respectably modified canter.

("All talkers delight in getting hold of anything akin to a love story; not merely from a fondness for scandal, but because the most powerful and pleasurable of human feelings is in some measure awakened and excited thereby.")

No sooner, therefore, did they all dismount, than the girls, who had guessed the whole consequential effect of Miss B.'s gratitude to her preserver, and his much deeper excitement, from the stimulant of a *stolen* kiss,* rushed in, out of breath, to let old Mr. and Mrs. Wyndham know that their only, idolized son, was irretrievably committed to perpetrate a matrimonial speculation.

---

* "Oh kiss! which dost those ruddy gems impart,
Or gems or fruits, of new-found paradise:
Breathing all bliss, and sweet'ning to the heart;
Teaching dumb lips a nobler exercise.
A kiss! which souls, e'en souls, together ties
By links of love, and only nature's art:
How fain would I paint thee to all men's eyes,
Or of thy gifts, at least, shade out some part!".

SIR PHILIP SIDNEY.

Fathers and mothers almost always very calmly argue the almighty-dollar question, and then the aristocratic surroundings, and then the physical plausibility, and then the compatibility of the disposition, and last, not least, the moral responsibilities of their children's conjugal entanglements; but it so happened that Miss Bloomfield possessed every one of the temporalities — mental, moral, physical, and golden — necessary, in their esteem, to young people jogging on through life happily together. So they were perfectly delighted that Cupid, who loves a random shot, should have befriended them so unexpectedly by the certain promise of a charming daughter-in-law.

"There is a certain critical minute in every man's wooing, when his mistress may be won, which if he carelessly neglect to prosecute, he may wait long enough before he gain the like opportunity."

> "She is a woman, therefore may be woo'd:
> She is a woman, therefore may be won."

But the self-reliant, Quixotic young Wyndham was the last man to believe that "faint heart ever won fair lady"; so in an incredibly short time the twain were engaged to be married. And, as Miss Bloomfield's father and mother were both dead, the old Wyndhams wished the marriage to take place instanter at their own house; but this was not possible, without offending Miss Bloomfield's adopted parents in Charleston. So she returned to town, to make preparations for the wedding.

"Nothing shall assuage
Your love but marriage: for such is
The tying of two in wedlock, as is
The tuning of two lutes in one key: for
Striking the strings of the one, straws will stir
Upon the strings of the other; and in
Two minds link'd in love one cannot be
Delighted, but the other rejoiceth."

Young Wyndham was only nineteen, but his mind and person were most precociously developed, and the naturalness of his manly dignity was very charming. He had his father's great twelve-oared boat, named "Brandywine," gayly painted (for no steam conveyances were in vogue in Carolina then); and soon, every thing being in readiness, he sprang gayly into the boat, with the negroes, who were in the most joyous mood. (Indeed, no mother is more interested in her child's marriage, than all plantation servants are in those of their master's children.) His father and mother were too old to accompany him on such a hardy undertaking; but, with their whole-souled blessing, they repeated —

"Then waft him safe, ye winds,
O'er the deep and stormy brine;
And heaven protect the treasure
That freights the Brandywine."

Arriving safely at Charleston, the bridal ceremony was performed by the celebrated Dr. Furman, amidst a hundred whole-hearted friends; and the next day he arranged to return home in the Brandywine.

The oarsmen had their shining black skins set off to the greatest advantage, by the contrast of bright red woollen shirts, red woollen turbans, blue woollen coats, and white woollen pantaloons; and their eyes glistened with fun, at their young master's precocious experiment; so that when the bride arrived at the wharf, they advanced with great loyalty to welcome her as their new young mistress; and affectionately and proudly they lifted her into the boat, by two oarsmen crossing hands, so as to effect a sort of sedan chair. But at this particular moment of sentimental embarkation, a new obstacle presented itself in the person of the fashionable lady's maid, who for the first time got a glimpse of her mistress's stripling husband. Starting back in great wrath, she cried out: "Fur de *laud* sake, Miss Liza, wuffer you gone marry dis yere boy fur. I sway, I'se not a gwining one step, from this yere town, with that Buckra, de *debil* if I will." Nothing offends a *hobbledehoy* more, than to be suspected of too much youthfulness; so in a tone of gigantic command, Wyndham said, "Helmsman, put that woman in the boat," which these merry laughing fellows all nimbly ran to do in a single instant; and lady's maid, *Liddy*, now reclining under the awning with her young mistress, philosophized, no doubt, on the precociousness of the Southern boys.

A large company of congenial neighbors had been invited by the old Wyndhams, to repair to their palmetto grove, on a specified day, to welcome the bridal party home; and two hundred negroes, when they saw the boat in sight, and heard the jovial songs of the oarsmen, joined in the chorus from the shore, where they all were standing, to catch the first glimpse of their young master's blooming and majestically tall wife.

Friends had been busy for days previous, in arranging for the bride a matinée to be held in magnificent romantic arbors of laurel branches, and innumerably tinted evorgreens (for the goddesses, Feronia, and Flora, keep perpetual carnival in the South); and on the day of the marriage-feast, the sun shone so brilliantly, that Phæton must have borrowed the magnificent chariot of old Phœbus to drive tandem through the resplendent groen arches. Feronia encircled the grove with a hedge of living flowers and evergreens; and Ceres, and Flora, formed a splendid cornucopia, whose wide-spreading mouth, poured out in lavish luxuriance, the whole family of grains, fruits, and flowers, arranged on a grand towering grass-plat. Euterpe blew her numerous wind instruments, to convince the company that all discord is harmony misunderstood. Terpsichore, crowned with laurel, held in her hand a musical instrument in this favored palmetto grove, and Bacchus presented his choicest vintage.

Fortuna spread herself on this occasion, to expand her riches, in order to command all the edibles that the human stomach could appreciate in this feast of the god Cupid; and Fama blew her trumpet to puff the whole, against the advice of the Frenchman, who said, "Never talk to me at dinner, for I can't taste my meat;" all the senses were indulged at the same time.

The tables, formed in a circle around the garden, literally were groaning with the whole family of fish, flesh, and fowl, pies, cakes, and puddings, fruits and bouquets, nuts and wines; and last, not least, primitive

Holland Gin* (this mercurial unadulterated spirituous liquor being very much used in Carolina in the eighteenth century). It was, indeed, a feast worthy of the gods, for the innumerable bouquets had invited the gayest, most melodious wild birds to attend the rejoicing matinée and exchange their seraphic music for a sip of nectar from the lips of the blushing dewy roses. The groom and the bride, the friends and the relatives, all flitted around from bower to bower and from table to table, in this recherche garden, to partake of the turtle-soup and sheephead, shrimp pies and crab pies, and bird pies — the great saddles of venison, and wild goose, and apple sauces, and mammoth bivalves; and the cask of wine that had been housed in papa's cellar the day young Wyndham was born,† was now opened for the first time to be drank at his wedding.

* The population of South Carolina, perhaps statistics will inform us, consume quite as much ardent spirits now as it did thirty or forty years ago, but it is not so consecutively, or so gregariously and openly indulged in as formerly. The planters bought great hogsheads of whiskey for their negroes in those jolly old times, but *now* they substitute molasses instead. The field negroes rarely ever were known to be intoxicated, except two or three of them on holidays, when they are, for instance, allowed Christmas week to be merry and idle, and visit their friends sometimes a hundred miles off.

"The credulous hope of mutual minds is o'er,
The copious use of claret is forbid too,
So for a good old gentlemanly vice,
I think I must take up with avarice."

BYRON.

† It is a common practice in South Carolina for parents to put a cask of wine in the cellar the day their several children are born, which is not opened until their bridal morn.

After all the company had finished, the before-mentioned two hundred negroes, who had been keeping up a clatter of jokes at a respectable distance, were now invited to approach—and their young master and mistress helped them every one to what he or she, or the little darkie papoos, coveted on the tables.

Then handing each a glass of wine, they were called on for a toast to the bride and her rapturous husband. Screaming at the top of their stentorian voices, they sang out in chorus: —

"Lettle Miss bride, us wish you big joy:
Ebery year one gal and one boy."

United prayer from sincere hearts is generally answered by a kind Providence — for these sympathizing negroes lived to see this loving couple rejoicing in a beautiful family of nine children, all of whom they loved with a fealty known only in this cold world by the old homestead servants of the South.

Speaking of the enjoyment of life of the negro, Mr. Creecy says, in Louisiana, "All business men who expect to succeed should speak at least four languages, French, Spanish, German (English)." "Many," says he, "of the negroes speak three languages in such a manner as to defy you to tell which one of the three is their vernacular." "New Orleans is the heaven of the negroes, and in that city they are the happiest human beings that ever breathed the breath of life. They never know or feel the sufferings of cold or hunger; and they are scarcely ever compelled to *labor hard at any time* to procure food, clothing, and shelter. The diseases so fatal to strangers, they are in a great measure exempt from; and altogether they are, beyond doubt, the most comfortable and joyous of all God's creatures." "There are many free negroes in the city and State; some of them wealthy and the owners of numerous slaves; and strange as true, they are generally the *hardest* masters and mistresses." North of Rampart street, about its centre, is the celebrated Congo Square, well enclosed, containing five or perhaps six or more acres, well shaded, with gravelled walks and beautiful grass plats, devoted to negro dances and amusements. The Creoles of Louisiana — Spanish, French, and negroes — are Catholics with but few exceptions, and on Sabbath mornings the females and a few elderly males are punctual in attending to their religious duties. The holy mass is not neglected by those two classes, but the afternoons and evenings of the Lord's day are spent in amusements, fun, and frolic of every description — always with an eye to much sport and little expense.

The "haut ton" attend operas, theatres, masquerades, &c. The quadroons have their dashing fancy balls, dances, &c.; and the lower order of colored people and negroes, bond and free, assemble in great numbers in Congo Square (of course in the afternoons), in good weather, to enjoy themselves in their own peculiar manner. Groups of fifties and hundreds may be seen in different sections of the square, with banjos, tom-toms, violins, jawbones, triangles, and various other instruments, from which harsh or dulcet sounds may be extracted; and a variety indeed of queer, grotesque, fantastic, strange, and merry dancers are to be seen, to amuse and astonish, interest and excite, the risibles and wonder of "outside barbarians" unskilled in Creole or African manners and customs.

Sometimes much grace, and often surprising activity and long-continued rapid motions, are seen. The dancers are most fancifully dressed with fringes, ribbons, little bells, shells, and balls, jingling and flirting about the performer's arms and legs, who sing a second, or counter, to the music most sweetly—for all Africans have melody in their souls—and in all their movements, gyrations, and attitudinizing exhibitions the most perfect time is kept; making the beats with the feet, head, or hands, or all, as correctly as a well-regulated metronome. Young and old join in the sport and dances. One will continue the rapid jig till nature is exhausted —then a fresh disciple leaps before him or her, and "cuts out" the fatigued one, who sinks down gracefully on the grass, out of the way, and is fanned by an associate, with one hand, while water and refreshments are tendered by the other.

When a dancer, or danseuse, surpasses expectation, or is particularly brilliant in the execution of "flings" and "flourishings" of limb and body, shouts, huzzas, and clapping of hands follow, and numerous "piccallions" are thrown in the ring to the *performers* by (strange) spectators. All is hilarity, fun, and frolic. To witness such a scene is a certain cure for ennui, blue devils, mopes, horrors, and dyspepsia.

Hundreds of nurses, with children of all ages, attend; and many fathers and mothers, beaux and belles, are there to be found; there where no cares or sorrows intrude; where pains and heartaches are forgotten; where duns are unknown, and all earthly troubles cease to torment *pro tem.* Every stranger should visit Congo Square in its glory, once at least, and, my word for it, no one will ever regret or forget it. It is human nature to love to look on happy, joyous, and smiling faces, and there are no others to be seen. The gaieties continue till sunset; and at the "*gun fire*" the whole crowd disperse and disappear, and "the noise and confusion" in Congo Square is heard and seen no more until the next blessed "Dimanche."

"Order is heaven's first law; and this confest,
Some are, and must be, greater than the rest,
More rich, more wise; but who infers from hence
That such are happier, shocks all common sense.
Heaven to mankind impartial we confess,
If all are equal in their happiness:
But mutual wants this happiness increase,
All Nature's difference keeps all Nature's peace.
Condition, circumstance, is not the thing;
Bliss is the same, in subject or in king.
In who obtain defence, or who defend,
In him who is, or him who finds a friend;
Heaven breathes through every member of the whole,
One common blessing, as one common soul." — POPE.

"If men were all on an equality, the consequence would be that all must perish; for who would till the ground? who would sow it? who would plant? who would press wine?"

"So far is it from being true that men are naturally equal, that no two people can be a half an hour together, but one shall acquire an evident superiority over the other." — JOHNSON.

CHAPTER III.

"Honor and shame from no condition rise;
Act well your part, *there* all the honor lies.
Fortune in men has some small difference made,
One flaunts in rags, one flutters in brocade;
The cobbler apron'd, and the parson gown'd,
The friar hooded, and the monarch crown'd.
What differ more, you cry, than crown and cowl?
I'll tell thee, friend: a wise man and a fool.
You'll find if once the monarch acts the monk,
Or, cobbler-like, the parson will be drunk,
Worth makes the man, the want of it the fellow;
The rest is all but leather or prunella.
Stuck o'er with titles, and hung round with strings,
That thou may'st be by kings, or whores of kings,
Boast the pure blood of an illustrious race,
In quiet flow from Lucrece to Lucrece:
But by your fathers' worth if yours you rate,
Count me those only who were good and great.
Go! if your ancient, but ignoble blood
Has crept through scoundrels ever since the flood,
Go! and pretend your family is young;
Nor own your fathers have been fools so long.
What can ennoble sots, or slaves, or cowards?
Alas! not all the blood of all the Howards."

ON Mr. Wyndham's encircling peninsula home there were sixty or seventy field-negro houses, as every black family on a plantation is allowed a house by themselves, unless they choose to invite some other persons to live with them. These houses were all fronting the river, on a straight line from Mr. Wyndham's palatial mansion; and as negro houses are whitewashed twice a year, to promote health and keep the boards from rotting, and the windows painted green, they gave the plantation a most imposing, city-like appearance, to travellers passing up and down the river in front of his residence. Perhaps no poor on the face of God's earth are so comfortably housed, fed, and clad, as the Southern plantation negroes. They certainly have everything necessary to life and godliness; and are taught religion so carefully, that nothing prevents their being true lovers of God. Only compare their thoroughly ventilated, healthy houses, and their families around them, with the dens, and holes, and cellars, and tenements of the white poor of New York, and other great cities.

"Poor naked wretches, wheresoe'er you are,
That bide the pelting of this pitiless storm!
How shall your houseless heads, and unfed sides,
Your loop'd and window'd raggedness, defend you
From seasons such as these?"

"His raw-boned cheeks, through penury and pine,
Were shrunk into his jaws, as he did never dine."

"Speak gently, kindly to the poor;
Let no harsh term be heard;
They have enough they must endure,
Without an unkind word.'

This fertile, cultivated peninsula plantation of Mr. Wyndham's, was almost surrounded by rich islands, separated only by a small creek, that could be forded when the tide went down. Not a house had been built on them; and, as there was abundance of land, Mr. Wyndham allowed these islands to grow up into forests, for timber. The gentlemen in the *country*, in South Carolina, rear their houses on brick or stone pillars, some six feet from the ground; southern pitch-pine and oak are the materials for building, as these trees grow several hundred feet in height, and the fat, rosined wood is so strong, that it is almost incredible how long a house lasts that is built of it. Having no cellars and no basement rooms underneath, for there is little or no frost that can undermine the structure, the winds of heaven have free scope to blow off all the dampness, and miasma, and secret filth, so common in houses that have cellars, and that breed innumerable insects, very troublesome to the housekeeper.

The negro houses on the coast plantations are all built in the same way on pillars, and made of oak foundations, boarded up with pine boards. They are usually about fifteen feet square; have four windows, and a partition separating the sitting from the sleeping-room: they are only one story in height, and have a loft, that the negroes use for storing away their provisions. Every house has at the back of it a little spot for a garden, and poultry-coop, and pig-pen, paled in, if they choose to raise hogs, or plant vegetables, herbs, flowers, and trees. The brick chimneys are immense—some six or eight feet wide; for a negro never feels comfortable without a fire-place large enough to stretch his whole length across it, which they do every night until one o'clock, when they retire to their beds. They are allowed as much wood as they choose to bring out of the forests near by, and neither winter nor summer are they ever contented without a large fire in their chimneys.

Grecian mythology teaches us, "that Somnus was one of the infernal deities, and presided over sleep. His palace was a dark cave, where the sun never penetrates; at its entrance are a number of poppies, and somniferous herbs. The god himself is represented as asleep on a bed of feathers, with black curtains. The dreams stand by him; and Morpheus, as his principal minister, watches to prevent the noise from awaking him." The African, on the contrary, when he feels like taking a nap in the day-time, will select a spot where no motherly branches of a tree can screen him from the meridian sun; but he lies down in the fields, or near his house, with old Phœbus blazing in his eyes, and presently the flies swarming in his face; whose sharp, tiny feet seem to go under the skin of a white man, and torment him out of every notion of slumber. The negro, however, sleeps so soundly, that the roar of a cannon could scarce arouse him.

Mr. Wyndham owned a most accomplished coachman, if he could only have contrived to keep him awake, which was next to impossible in the summer time. One night he attempted to get into his carriage, having spent a sociable evening with one of his neighbors. The footman opened the door; but the coachman sat on the box, so fast asleep that no pushing or calling could arouse him. As it was only ten o'clock, and a bright moonlight night, Mr. Wyndham thought he would experiment on Jehu's somniferous powers; so he quietly mounted the box alongside of his sleeping coachman, and, slipping the reins out of his hand, drove around the turnpike road for three miles without awaking him; and finally drove home, and had him lifted from the box, before he knew where he was. Another time Mr. Wyndham wished to make a journey to Savannah, some thirty or forty miles off, in his carriage; and as the weather was very warm, and he wished to avoid the noonday sun, he told Jehu, the night before, to have the whole cavalcade ready by three o'clock, A. M. So the next morning, just before he was about to start, he called at the door for the carriage, but no Jehu answered. He then went to the servants' hall, and there lay his man, fast asleep. He pushed, he screamed aloud to him; but he found that the Lacedæmonians were right when they placed the image of Somnus near to that of Death. Finally, Jehu was lifted straight up on his feet, and artistically moved, hither and yon, until his eyes opened, and his master let him know that everything was in readiness for him to mount the box. "Sleep is Death's younger brother, and so like him, that I never dare trust him without my prayers."

On all well-regulated plantations there is a large house built expressly to receive all the infants, and their young nurses, when their mothers go out to work. An old, black, medical crone is at the head of this establishment, and she is required to keep up large fires, to feed, watch over, and report any sickness or accident to her young charges, while their mothers are absent in the fields. The little girls on the plantation, between the ages of nine and fifteen, run about with and amuse their mother's infants, or those of other relatives. Every baby has thus its own nurse, and all under the care, in the daytime, of the above-named old doctress, who, like Argus, has a hundred eyes, only two of which were asleep at any one time — for accidents rarely, if they ever, happen in a plantation-nursery; though no doubt this self-abnegating presider over the rising Ethiopian generation feels like the old woman that lived in a shoe, who had so many children she did not know what to do.

The greatest possible care being thus taken of the young negroes, so that they may attain to perfect health and physical development, such a thing as a deformity is seldom if ever seen on a plantation of slaves. Indeed, neither the girls or boys are put to work in the fields until they are fourteen, fifteen, or sixteen years of age; and even *then*, the master does not allow the overseer to give them more to do, at first, than one-third of the task that the *law* apportions for a matured field-hand, so that their young limbs may by degrees get habituated to the tense exercise of planting and hoeing rice and cotton.

"This rice, two-thirds of which is raised in South Carolina that is used in the United States, besides being provision for man and beast, has, in a commercial point of view, been more beneficial to South Carolina than mines of silver and gold; though when first introduced it was only the experiment of a small bag of it, presented to Landgrave Smith by the captain of a brigantine from Madagascar, touching at Sullivan's Island on her way to Britain. With the introduction of rice-planting into the country, and the fixing upon it as its staple commodity, the necessity of employing

Africans, for the purpose of cultivating it, was doubled. So laborious is the task of raising, beating, and cleaning this article, that though it had been possible to obtain European servants in numbers sufficient for attacking the thick forests, and clearing grounds for the purpose, thousands and tens of thousands must have perished in the arduous attempt.* The utter

---

* Mr. J. R. Creecy remarks about Louisiana, that "for many years the annual influx of the lowest order of *Irish* into New Orleans has been immense, and the numbers who are buried in the "Swamp," subjects of "Yellow Jack" and cholera, are astonishing; and yet their places are instantly filled up, as are the ranks of well-disciplined troops in destructive battle. Eight out of ten who are attacked by those diseases become victims, and perhaps at least one-third of every importation have one or the other, or both of those dreadful diseases. Nine-tenths of all the poor, diseased emigrants, who find shelter and attention in the hospitals, are foreigners, by far the greatest number of whom are Irish, of the lowest and worst character—reckless, abandoned, drunken, lying, dirty, ignorant wretches, who are more at home in the police-office than any where else; and, as the fun-loving John Duggan would say, "'Dthey ar' niver at pace 'dthey ar' in a fight intirely! Thousands of them leave every summer for the upper country, where they do not fare much better than in New Orleans. They are never employed except from necessity. The negroes have decidedly the preference, and readily obtain higher wages. The Irish females are as disorderly and dissipated as the males, and 'tis sickening to see what numbers are every morning taken to the Recorder's office, for crimes and misdemeanors the preceding night."

A far-seeing politician at the North makes the following remarks in 1860:—

"Without a miracle, I see not but that slaves will yet be called for in New England, and by New England men—slaves having the attributes if not the name of slaves, and possibly to worse condition than we now complain of in reference to the

inaptitude of Europeans for the labor requisite in such a climate and soil, is obvious to every one possessed of the smallest degree of knowledge respecting the country. White servants would have exhausted their strength in clearing a spot of land for digging their own graves; and every rice plantation would have served no other purpose than a burying-ground to its European cultivators. The low-lands of Carolina, which are unquestionably the richest grounds in the country, must have remained a wilderness, had not Africans, whose natural constitutions were fitted to the clime and work, been employed in cultivating this useful article of food and commerce."

The little negro boys, from nine to fifteen, are generally employed in attending to the cows, and waggoning the crops out of the fields. These little scamps can run a horse when they are seven years old. They are the noisiest, sleekest looking, mischievous little fellows, on this earth, when they are put into the rice and corn-

---

South. Why not, if our present government should last another eighty years? For Yankees will not perform the menial work of life. They are above it now. The imported free-servants of Ireland and other countries will soon be infected with Yankee independence, and have the means of living, above servile labor, on their freeholds! Then who will be our servants? Shall we have coolies or Africans to hew our wood and draw our water? And what form of government shall be over them, but that which is adapted to their comparative rudeness and imbecility, and conservative of the general system? The children and grandchildren of our present abolitionists may yet be the first to introduce a harder serfdom than has yet been known, unless, indeed, they should themselves be compelled to sell themselves for bread, and suffer the proper chastisement of their fathers' sins for their rebellion against the government of God."

fields to scare away the crows. Their exuberantly cultivated capacity to run and scream, and shout at the said crows, and other covetous motherly birds, when in full blast, sounds almost like an Indian war-whoop. The little rascals are, however, such 'cute eye-servants, that they make traps, and pick blackberries, and roast potatoes and groundnuts in the rice and corn patches, leaving the birds full swing to eat what they please of the growing grain; until they see mausser or old daddy Mingo, coming into the fields, and then they give a signal to each other that the enemy approaches, and with a roguish laugh, and piercing scream, they scamper among the previously appropriating crows, who have already, perhaps, devoured a lion's share of the rice, corn, and peas. It is of no earthly use to switch them, for their devil-may-care spirits are too abandon, and their nerves too obtuse, to remember an hour afterwards that they have been punished.

There is also an accomplished butcher on every plantation, who attends to the killing of all the hogs, beeves, sheep, calves, and lambs. When a great bullock is killed for the negroes, they make some twenty gallons of soup out of the head, heart, liver, and kidneys, and divide it around.

The negroes receive every week their allowance of food, that is determined in quantity, either by law, or universal experience. It is usually corn, rice, peas, and sweet potatoes; together with molasses, and fresh beef, or bacon.

Every black man on a coast plantation, owns a canoe, that they themselves construct, by burning the inside, and then scraping out, a great oaken log, some ten or twelve feet long, that they obtain in their masters' forests. They are the most lucky and expert fishermen, and at moonlight or on holidays, will entrap in their nets, the whole family of fish; together with prawn, shrimps, crabs, oysters, terrapins, clams, conch, and turtle. These they either eat themselves, sell to their masters, or the surrounding neighbors, or present to their wives on the different plantations, for the negroes are, as in Africa, all polygamists.

The sentimental Abolitionist weeps over the separation of husbands and wives when they are sold; but if a woman or a man has a half-dozen husbands or wives, which one of the six is to be selected as the orthodox lover? "Yet the cases of violent separation of husband and wife (says Dr. Nehemiah Adams, of Boston), are not so many, as the voluntary and criminal separations by the parties themselves. For conjugal love among the slaves (or any masses of people on earth), is not invariably the poetical thing which amateurs of slaves sometimes picture it; for there are probably no more happy conjugal unions among the slaves, than among the whites, though the negroes always marry for love." At the Spring term this year (1854), of the Court in one New England State, there were eighty-three applications for divorce. In Kansas, in 1860, the newspapers tell us, there were one hundred and fifty divorces granted in forty days.

"The forms of law are as inconsiderate of our feelings, as though they were acts of barbarians. A sheriff's sale of house furniture in the dwelling of a white man who has fallen from opulence into insolvency, is like the wheel of torture, that breaks every bone and joint one by one. The auctioneer, with precious household treasures, keepsakes, memorials of our dear departed friends, in one hand, and a crumpled newspaper for a hammer in the other, seems the most unfeeling man; but he is not so; it is the law, of which he is the exponent, that is so terrible. His wife, his children, are perhaps entirely innocent of the crime, or the want of discretion, that thus put him in the hands of the law."

"Probably in no slave State are there more voluntary separations of husbands and wives among the slaves, than in some of the New England States that could be specified for the same period," says Dr. Adams. "The only difference is, the slave does not go to court for his divorce." "He absents himself from his cabin, or procures another master;" (almost any planter in the South will let his slave choose a master, and sell him, if he is discontented; for nobody wants a servant *there* who is unwilling to live with him;) "or, belonging to the same master with his wife, and being unwilling to live within possible hearing of her, he flees to the North." . . . "If he has a good degree of address, he can rouse up the deep philanthropy of freemen like a ground-swell of the sea, in overwhelming pity and compassion for him; while the only unhappiness, after all, was, in his particular case, that he could not have laws to countenance and defend him in putting away his wife who had committed no crime, and marrying another." . . . "The people of those communities whose laws of divorce are of questionable morality, will not of course throw the first stone at the South for that looseness in the domestic relations of slaves which allows so many voluntary separations."

"Knowing," says Dr. Adams, "as ministers in cities are apt to do, the statistics of crime, it would be gratifying if we could assert that our (Northern) cities are examples to the South in all goodness." . . . "After reading all that has ever been written respecting the sale and purchase of 'yellow girls,' and the extent to which the sin alluded to prevails at the South, you may obtain from an experienced policeman in our (Northern) cities disclosures which will give exercise to virtuous abhorrence and indignation as great as the statistics of sin and misery elsewhere can excite, unless, indeed, wickedness at home fails to exert the enchantment which belongs to other men's sins. What if there were some way in which this iniquity in the free States proclaimed itself as it does through complexion at the South?" . . . "Some men's sins are open beforehand, going before to judgment; and some men they follow after." . . . . "The negro slaves never commit the crime of infanticide, as many, very many, white adulteresses and free blacks do in every country."

As to infants being sold away from their mothers, it is not believed by the author that such a monstrosity ever has occurred in South Carolina, as a mistress *there* universally takes more care of her little negro property, than a black mother ever does of her children. Whenever negroes are to be sold, the remark may be heard invariably—"that as such or such a woman has a great many small children, who of course cannot be separated from her, she will command only a small price." No orphans on earth are more petted than those of the slaves.

"It seems to be taken for granted that to be sold is

inevitably to pass from a good to an inferior condition. This is as much a mistake as it would be to assert the same of changes on the part of domestic servants in the free States. There are as good masters as those whose death makes it necessary to scatter the slaves of an estate." So that when negroes are sold they are bought by masters whose interest is just as much involved to take the best care of them as their former owner did.

"We must remember that slaves are not the only inhabitants, nor slave families the only families in the land, that are scattered by the death of others." . . . "Sometimes the demand seems to be that slaves should be kept together at all events, and separations never permitted." . . . "This is absurd upon the least reflection. No one ought to demand or expect for them an experience better or worse than the common lot of men. Let the slaves share with us in the common blessings and calamities of Divine Providence. What would become of our families of five or ten children should their parents die? Can we keep our children about us always? Do none but black children go to the ends of the Union and become settled there? How many white people there are that do this who — deplorable truth!—can neither read or write, and seldom, if ever, hear from their relatives from whom they are separated."

Besides all this, what right have we of the nineteenth century to profess to be more sensitive about God's creatures than their infinitely loving Creator is? God ordered His own chosen people to take their slaves from the heathen nations around them, and He knew all the consequences of this command.

Nothing is sin, except disobedience to God. Dare any one affirm that it was a sin, *per se*, to pluck an apple growing luxuriously in the garden, where God had placed Adam and Eve, as sole proprietors? And yet our original mother, doing this simple action, brought death and destruction upon all her children. Why? Because it was God's command that she should not do it. It was the appointed test to determine her obedience to her Creator. "Whosoever offendeth in one point is guilty of all." Because one act of direct insubordination betrays the reigning spirit of rebellion. Eve listened to the Devil, when he softly whispered a "higher law." Yes, this accursed, fascinating higher law turned the most resplendent archangel out of heaven. The Devil believed in equality, and aimed at a levelling system, just like some proud progressionists of the present day; and he, pretending to wisdom above his Creator, was thrust down to hell; and from thence he succeeded in destroying the image of God in man by tempting Eve to the same disloyalty that ruined himself.

The Abolitionists assert, that the South may obey God in all things, except his remarkable order, so repeatedly urged to his chosen people, to "take their bondsmen from among the heathen nations around them." The latter-day saints have made a God to worship, who is a progressionist, like themselves. He is not the same yesterday, to-day, and for evermore. Oh, no! He changes his mind, as the politicians do about the availability of their candidate. At one time they think God made laws that he intended to denounce, as the sum of all villanies, at another time.

Could any thing be more audaciously conceited, than to affirm (without a solitary Scripture-proof, either in the Old or New Testament, that God ever intends to abrogate slavery, while there are any heathen nations in the world,) that holding bondsmen is a sin. Has there been a new revelation of the mind of God, from Joe Smith, or Brigham Young, that many now think more elevated and civilizing than the Bible — than the inspired Word, illustrated by the life of Jesus Christ?

The negroes in South Carolina are allowed, to raise horses, hogs, and poultry of all kinds; and their master permits each head of a family the use of an acre of ground, where he can plant whatever he pleases; and during harvest they sell these provisions, &c., to the neighbors, or carry them in boats to the towns of Beaufort and Savannah.* Some planters *buy* all the eggs and chickens they use from their own servants; for, strange as it may appear, their fowls, like themselves, are much more prolific from being relieved of too much civilization.

The Abolitionists report, that "a negro can own

* The author's father frequently started out in his twelve-oared boat to make a visit to Savannah, fifty miles off; and the negroes would load the boat almost up to the gunnels with their own merchandise.

The Wetumpka (Ala.) Enquirer says that last week thirteen slaves belonging to Governor Fitzpatrick, accompanied by Mr. Gunn, the overseer, brought their cotton to market, and sold it for a sum amounting in the aggregate to nine hundred and ninety-four dollars and ninety-two cents.

Said Governor Fitzpatrick is now, and has been for a number of years, a Senator of the United States.

no property"; but the fact is, were a master to take his negro's horses, hogs, poultry, grain, or any thing he has, without giving him the full market-price for it, he would be despised by all his neighbors as a dastardly dishonest wretch, and would be visited with more indignation than if he cheated a white man. Public opinion in South Carolina so scorns a master that is unjust or cruel to those that God has placed entirely in his power, that such a monster would not be tolerated for a moment. Indeed his neighbors would publicly prosecute him, if he overworked or was cruel to his slaves.

But all experience in the South proves that you cannot overwork a negro. He will do his task, and no human power can make him do any more; for he is so stubbornly obtuse to all enterprise, that no punishment will have any effect — whereas a white man, with motive sufficient, will work till he faints with exhaustion. For instance, the task laid down for an able-bodied negro-man is, to split a hundred rails per day; whereas a white laborer has often been known to split three hundred.

As to the mental suffering of the African race under the galling yoke of slavery, it is a mere fallacy, a joke, a hoax, gotten up by politicians, or a romance eliminated from the brain of our nervously constituted female writers of the present day — for there is not that living man who, on his oath, could assert he ever heard such a sentiment from a slave in the South. No, their only plausible delusion is, that if they can escape to the North they will not have to work. All history proves that idleness and vice is the only liberty the

African aspires to, either in his own country or as a slave in Christian lands.

"Of all the situations in which human beings can be placed, favorable to the salvation of the soul, under faithful efforts on the part of teachers, it is difficult to conceive of one better suited to this end, and, in fact, more successful than the relation of these slaves to their Christian masters." "Suppose a family of them bound to their master by affection and respect. Whatever he can make apparent to their understandings and consciences to be right, he has as much power to enforce upon them as ever falls within the range of moral suasion. So it is, indeed, with pious military and naval commanders and their soldiers and sailors; subordination, attended with respect and love, opens the widest door for persuasion; and if the numbers of pious slaves are an indication, it must be confessed that slave-owners, as a body, have performed their Christian duties to their slaves to a degree which the masters of free apprentices, and the employers of free laborers, have as yet hardly equalled." "Their acquaintance (of these negroes) with the Word of God is, to a great extent, through oral instruction; yet in all that constitutes (says Dr. Adams) Christian excellence and that knowledge of God, which comes directly from him, they have no superiors. A man who has spent a whole life in literary pursuits, and in studying and preaching God's word, listens to these slaves with their comparatively limited acquaintance with the Bible, and feels humble to think that faith and goodness in himself should bear no proportion to his knowledge."

"Judging of them as you meet them in the streets,

see them at work, or at church, or in their prayer-meetings or singing-meetings, or walking on the Sabbath, or holidays, one must see that they are a happy people, their physical condition superior to those of many (Northern) operatives, far superior to the common Irish people in our cities, and immeasurably above thousands in Great Britain."

"As responsibility, anxiety about the present and future, are the chief enemies to cheerfulness, and, among mental causes to health, it is obvious that if one can have all his present wants supplied, with no care about short crops, the markets, notes payable, bills due, be relieved from the necessity of planning and contriving, all the hard thinking being done by another, while useful and honorable employment fills his thoughts and hands, he is so far in a situation favorable to great comfort, which will show itself in his whole outer man. Some will say, 'this is the lowest kind of happiness,' yet it is all that the largest portion of the race seek for; and few, except the slaves, obtain it."

"God has suffered evil to exist in this world; yet we do not conclude that hell reigns upon earth. We reflect, that perhaps through this very antagonism may lie the path of progress; or, at least, we weigh the good against the evil, and believe in the beneficence of the Creator." *

---

* "NEGROES EXPELLED FROM A CANADIAN TOWNSHIP. — The Detroit (Mich.) Free Press (1860) states, that all the negroes have been summarily expelled from the township of Anderdon, Essex county, in Canada. This township was as thickly populated with negroes as any in Canada, but they have lately become so bold in their depredations and crimes that their pre-

"The subordination of an inferior race of men, receiving food, clothing, shelter, religious instruction, government and protection, for moderate labor, is not only philanthropic, but philosophically necessary and practically indispensable, as supplying the raw material for food, clothing, and commerce necessary to the white laborer, who would desire to be, even in a measure, exempt from servitude to capital, through the irresistible demands of hunger, and as securing capital from the danger of 'blood and bread riots,' which a dense population would certainly ensure, where there is no costly and dangerous standing army to arrest *mob-action* till the more peaceable expression of the will of a faction, under the lead of demagogues, shall, through the ballot-box, *deciding the polls by the votes of a few or by club-law*, burden it beyond endurance.

"The mission of the planter is to establish these principles practically, as the *great truth* of this age, by which the 'irrepressible conflict' between the *classes* of older countries, so productive of bloodshed and misery, is to be put down as the first step towards the time in which the church, exercising liberty of conscience and diffusing Bible principles, shall bring all the kingdoms of the earth to be kingdoms of our Lord."

---

sence was no longer endurable. Accordingly, the authorities of the township petitioned the grand jury last fall to take action relative to them; and the jury, in consequence, presented them as a nuisance. Their outrages culminated a few weeks since in an attack upon a number of peaceable and defenceless citizens, and now the day of retribution has overtaken them. The whole lot have been summarily driven out of the township. They had been given homes, but they so abused the kindness extended them, that the authorities were obliged to drive them out as they would so many wild beasts."

Everything conspired for many years to establish the most rational happiness in young Wyndham's household; mother, father, wife, children, hosts of friends; loyal affectionate servants; health, and wealth; Christian trust in the loving providence of God, as a *reconciled* father, and hearts elevated every day by benevolence to all the poor and afflicted around them. "For his bounty, there was no winter in it; an autumn 'twas, that grew the more by reaping."

But as is usual with every consummation of human felicity apparently arrived at, in this mutable world, a skulking foe was prying his sanguinary eyes into this abode of peace and love.

> "Death! to the happy thou art terrible,
> But how the wretched love to think of thee!
> O! thou true comforter, the friend of all
> Who have no friend beside."

Death was a most unpopular tyrant at this particular era of industry, contentment, and virtue, in the United States, though he is now so often courted by the suicidal hand.

Nobody *then* ever embraced the grim monster, who was not bereft of his reason, and indeed very few of these unfortunates, these insane people, could be found in our law-abiding, common-sense population — for the higher law first fulminated by the Devil, through which he made our mother Eve contemn the wholesome laws eliminated by God himself for her wise governance; had not been preached from the pulpit, from the press, and from the political rostrum; tearing down, in its abandon march, every enclosure of civil and divine legislation; and leaving the human mind drifting about on the broad unsounded ocean of life, without compass or rudder, seated on broken fragments of our formerly renowned great ship of state, at the mercy of every gust of passion, and of the God of this world, who is the Devil. Eternal damnation will be the destiny of that man, who strides into power over the ruin of his country. "Oh, mischief! thou art swift to enter into the thoughts of desperate men!" . . . "He that may hinder mischief, and yet permits it, is an accomplice."

> "Treason and murder ever crept together,
> As two yoke devils sworn to either's purpose."

We are already lost, as a nation, if we have become so wise as to give up the Bible as our chart. Jesus Christ, the great Son of God, came on earth as a man, that by this humility, he might daguerreotype to our finite minds, the will of Jehovah for thirty-three years, before he was crucified to reclaim us to the image of God. He, the divine infallible teacher, always obeyed the civil laws of the land wherein he sojourned; and even worked a miracle to pay the Roman tribute where slavery was rampant. Neither the Bible, nor the Apostles, nor Jesus Christ, ever condemned the institution of slavery as a sin.

Death, however, as was before remarked, being no respecter of persons, stalked into Mr. Wyndham's family circle; and without one moment's parley, struck down with his sharp scythe, his venerated mother. She who was regarded a mother in Israel, in that old Euhaw Church, where the never to be forgotten Whitfield preached (during his visit to North America, with the great founder of Methodism, John Wesley). She, in whose heart nestled every affection that makes woman a ministering angel, whose spirit was so gentle, so self-denying, so forbearing, that her husband and friends declared, they had never seen her angry in all her life. She, whose heavenly educated voice, had for twenty years led the praises of God, in the great congregation of this woodland church; where every Sabbath, with all her servants, she repaired, seven miles from her home, to hear the preached word; and *they* to join the hymn of thanksgiving with her (the negroes, numbering some fifteen hundred communicants, occupied two-thirds of this capacious but humble Euhaw Church, the oldest perhaps in Carolina, of the Baptist denomination). Yes, even she had for a moment succumbed to the embrace of that insatiate monster.

> "Lay her in the earth;
> And from her fair and unpolluted flesh,
> May violets spring!"

For,

> "Here lurks no treason; here no envy swells; here grow no damned grudges; here are no storms, no noise, but silence and eternal sleep."

The pastor of the Euhaw Church (Dr. Halcombe) was sent for, and the neighbors for twenty miles around this hospitable mansion were invited to the funeral. Every negro on that plantation surrounded the house in wailing grief; for she had been a guardian angel among them, not only teaching them all the common arts of civilization, and faithfully sympathizing in their sorrows of sickness and bereavements; but also preparing their minds, by gospel instruction, to hail the day when Ethiopia shall stretch forth her hands to God.

"The soul on earth is an immortal guest,
Compell'd to starve at an unreal feast:
A spark, which upward tends by Nature's force;
A stream diverted from its parent source;
A drop dissever'd from the boundless sea;
A moment parted from eternity;
A pilgrim panting for the rest to come;
An exile, anxious for his native home."

HANNAH MORE.

CHAPTER IV.

"Upon whom doth not the sunlight arise?"—*Job* xxv.

"The morning itself, few people, inhabitants of cities, know anything about. Among all our good people, not one in a thousand sees the sun rise once in a year. They know nothing of the morning. Their idea of it is that it is that part of the day which comes along after a cup of coffee and a beef-steak, or a piece of toast. With them, morning is not a new issuing of light, a new bursting forth of the sun, a new waking up of all that has life from a sort of temporary death, to behold again the works of God, the heavens and the earth; it is only a part of the domestic day, belonging to reading newspapers, answering notes, sending the children to school, and giving orders for dinner. The first streak of light, the earliest purpling of the east which the lark springs up to greet, and the deeper coloring into orange and red, till at length the 'glorious sun is seen, regent of the day,'—this they never enjoy, for they never see it. I never thought that Adam had much the advantage of us from having seen the world while it was new. The manifestations of the power of God, like his mercies, are 'new every morning,' and 'fresh every moment.' We see as fine risings of the sun as Adam ever saw; and its risings are as much a miracle now as they were in his day—and, I think, a good deal more; because it is now a part of the miracle, that for thousands and thousands of years he has come to his appointed time, without the variation of a millionth part of a second. Adam could not tell how this might be. I know the morning—I am acquainted with it, and I love it. I love it fresh and sweet as it is—a daily new creation, breaking forth and calling all that have life and breath and being to new adoration, new enjoyments, and new gratitude."

DANIEL WEBSTER.

About one year after the multiflora, and violet, and evergreen nondescript had been blooming over the rural grave of Mr. Wyndham's sainted mother, we find him surrounded by his nine lovely children, and a wife that has been before described; who, now arriving at woman's mellowed age of thirty-six, was so established in the graces that belong to her peculiarly thoughtful, pensive, and intellectual mind, and moral singleness of purpose, that "her husband is known in the gates, when he sitteth among the elders of the land." "Her children rise up and call her blessed; her husband also, and he praiseth her." The whole household were up at sunrise, and lively with noble-hearted enterprise; for there was to be a Baptist Association held at the old Euhaw Church, and Mr. Wyndham was expected to throw open his doors to receive the brethren, who came from all parts of the State to attend this yearly meeting. These Baptist ministers assembled for the purpose of taking minutes of the statistics, etc., of this denomination, and also for the purpose of calling sinners to repentance by consecutive preaching for a whole week, and professing Christians to renewed consecration of themselves to God.

Mrs. Wyndham, though brought up an Episcopalian, was a Christian entirely too elevated to let sectarian feelings prevent her appreciation of the piety of any religionist who believed that the atonement of Jesus Christ was adequate for the pardon of the sins of the whole world, and that the Holy Spirit's abode in the heart is the only means of sanctification. Her husband having joined the Euhaw Church, identified *her* with its interests; and she deeply respected his pastor, the

Rev. James Halcombe. She therefore, in her hospitalities, found room for the very poorest Christians, as well as those who owned broad acres and palatial residences ; fulfilling literally the Scripture injunction of St. James : "If there come into your assembly a man with a gold ring, in goodly apparel, and there come in also a poor man in vile raiment; and ye have respect unto him that weareth the gay clothing, and say unto him, Sit thou here in a good place; and say to the poor, Stand thou there, or sit here under my footstool, are ye not then partial in yourselves, and are become judges of evil thoughts?" "Hearken, my beloved brethren, hath not God chosen the poor of this world, rich in faith, and heirs of the kingdom he hath prepared for them?"

"Blest be that spot, where cheerful guests retire
To pause from toil, and trim their evening fire;
Blest that abode, where want and pain repair,
And every stranger finds a ready chair;
Blest be those feasts with simple plenty crown'd,
Where all the ruddy family around
Laugh at the jest or pranks, that never fail,
Or sigh with pity at some mournful tale,
Or press the bashful stranger to his food,
And learn the luxury of doing good."

Mr. Wyndham joked merrily about how he was obliged, every association-time, to entertain some fifty or sixty guests, arriving in boat-loads from along the coast, and from the towns of Beaufort and Charleston; or travellers in land conveyances, from the upper country and mountainous parts of the State; how he stowed away the brethren at night in the large cotton-house, by spreading counterpanes on our great harvested crop of unique vegetable wool, warmer and more luxurious to sleep on than a spring mattress.

This cotton-house (built to store away the cotton when it is first picked from the fields) was fifty feet long, and forty feet wide, and forty feet high. A capacious receiver, it appropriates all the cotton before machinery touches it at all; and a thrifty planter can estimate by the bulk what number of bags he may calculate on after it is prepared for the market (a bag contains four hundred pounds of this staple). The cotton-house always has a capacious arbor attached to it, boarded with rough planks, but no covering overhead, as it is designed to dry the cotton in the sun. It is astonishing how the negroes will balance on their heads some seventy pounds of cotton, and bring it out of the fields, in baskets, without raising their hands to steady the load, except occasionally, as they trudge along home together, singing in chorus. They certainly have no bump of reverence on the top of the cranium, or they could not perform this remarkable feat. A medical student in Charleston, who, as is usual with these hard-hearted fellows, went out one night to resurrectionize a corpse, that chanced to be a negro, for the dissecting-room; and returning at midnight from the grave-yard, he displayed his specimen, who had died three days previously, to the professors; declaring that his cranium proved so thick that it required all the power of their surgical instruments to get it open for dissection—for even the Esculapian gods are powerless against stupidity. He did not mention, however, the quality or quantity of the brain enclosed therein:

which the faculty might easily have done; for the celebrated craniologist, Dr. Morton, of Philadelphia, ascertained how much mind the North American Indian possessed, by measuring his skull with small shot, to see how much room the brain occupied.

Certain it is, that all the calumnies about the planters knocking their slaves senseless to the earth is the purest fiction; for their skulls are so thick that it is doubtful whether any white man's strength could consummate such a feat, even if he was indiscreet enough to make the attempt; for certainly he would bruise or break his own fists — not their ossified cranium.

Mr. Wyndham's brethren slept so soundly in their delightful spring-beds of cotton, that they could not be aroused from the arms of Morpheus and Somnus even by the wild, shrill horn of the driver, waking the negroes on all parts of the plantation, to cook their breakfasts and go to work.

The children of Mr. Wyndham delighted to play in the cotton-house. Little Selina, thrilling with merriment, would plunge deep into the ocean of cotton, to hide from her brothers and sisters, who could not see her at these moments; and when, in despair, they gave up hunting her, she would jump up from this vasty deep, screaming with laughter, and then shove one of them in, shouting at their cowardice.

The ginning house, at Mr. Wyndham's, was of the same dimensions as the before-described cotton house; but it contained a capacious loft, where the cotton was carried to be packed, after all the yellow portions had been moted out, and all the seed had been removed by the ginning apparatus. A large circular hole, in the middle of the loft, composed a gallows, from which the bag, perhaps four yards long, was suspended, and tightly fastened into the aperture by an iron clasping ring; a stout fellow then jumps into the bag (which is made of the very strongest flax cloth or bagging, and sewed up with twine,) and, with a tremendous iron pestle, he pounds in the cotton, that a dozen surrounding hands, giving it the fourth and last inspection, dash into the bag as fast as it needs feeding.

Among the ministers who came to attend this reunion of the Baptists, was a Mr. John Brown Cheever, of Massachusetts, a Mr. Joab Beecher, of Pennsylvania, a Mr. Cabal Ting, of New Hampshire, and a Mr. Arnold Parker, of Connecticut. They were delighted to see Mr. Wyndham's overflowing barns and cellars, of thousands of bushels of provisions for his family, his negroes, his cows, sheep, horses, hogs, and poultry.*

* "South Carolina produces potatoes of six or seven sorts, and all of them very good; Indian corn, three sorts; Indian peas, of five or six sorts; Indian beans, several sorts; horse pumpkins (so large that a man can scarcely lift one of them,) small sweet table pumpkin also; squashes, pomelons, gourds, cabbage, cauliflower, beets, carrots, tania, indigo, cucumbers, muskmelons, several kinds of watermelon, tobacco, arrow-root, ground-nuts, rice of three sorts, oats, rye, barley, and a little wheat. Sugar-cane can also be successfully raised, but the planters are so much taken up with the staple production of rice and cotton, that they pay no attention to the making of sugar or the planting of wheat, except for table use occasionally. The negroes are not fed on wheat, or on the Irish potato, of which they are not fond, so that thousands of bushels of the sweet potato are raised on every plantation; the Irish potato is generally obtained from the North. South Carolina also naturally produces black mulberries, walnuts, chestnuts, pecan nuts,

On Sunday morning, the whole family of vehicles, foreign and domestic, were brought to the door (for a planter owns any number of horses, and a field negro can be either coachman or footman behind the cavalcade at a moment's notice, for all are expert horsemen), and the company started off to go to church. The Northern ministers were charmed to see hundreds of negroes wending their way to the house of God, seven miles distant, on foot; for the negro is so gregarious, that he loves to go a long distance to church, to hear the news and meet his friends, so that, although the planters engaged ministers, and built churches on their plantations, they found the negro would not attend the service at his door, and, of course, no one but a primitive Puritan would dream of switching people into religion, which these descendants of the cavaliers never did and never will do.

Mr. Beecher thought he never, in all his life, had seen such respectable, well-behaved poor, as these negroes, who, comfortably clad, bowed kindly to every human being that passed them, white or black. They stopped in the bushes, just before they arrived at the church, to take off their coarse shoes and stockings,

---

acorns, of five or six sorts, which the Indians, like the primitive races of mankind, made use of for food, wild potatoes, and several other eatable roots, wild plums, variety of grapes, medlars, huckleberries, strawberries, bennay, hazel-nuts, myrtle berries, of which wax is made, cedar berries, shumac, sassafras, china root, great and small snakeroot, with a variety of other physical roots and herbs, and all sorts of English herbs transplanted there; apples, pears, of different kinds, olives, quinces, crab-apple, *bitter-sweet*, and sour and sweet oranges, pomegranates, blue, yellow, and brown figs, and peaches."

and replace them with the finer Sunday-go-to-meeting overalls and shoddings.

"Oh, my dear brother Wyndham," said Mr. Parker, "God moves in a mysterious way, His wonders to perform; He plants His footsteps on the sea, and rides upon the storm. But for the slave-trade, that sentimentalists are so justly horrified at, these now happy, civilized, Jesus-loving Ethiopians, would be at this moment in heathen Africa, where, for four thousand years, the negro has been a barbarian and savage monster—a slave, whose master would *eat* him * in

---

* "The Interior of Africa.—The Geographical Society held a meeting last week (1860), at which the interior of Africa was the subject of consideration. A letter from Rev. Dr. Livingstone was read, and also a paper by the scientific traveller, who has in this city a collection of most interesting articles from Africa, Mr. Du Chaillu. He has spent four years in Africa, part of the time among cannibals. The trade of these savages, he said, seemed to be confined to an exchange of dead bodies on which to feed. Human bones were found in large quantities everywhere around their villages. He was never in danger among them, inasmuch as he was regarded as a magician, and they were afraid of him. The tribes of negroes in Central Africa, other than the cannibals, were numerous. He had visited thirty-five of them, but found notwithstanding that the country was very sparsely populated. Owing to polygamy, the slave-trade, and a general belief in witchcraft, many of the tribes were disappearing. When a king died, fifty or sixty people would be accused of witchcraft, in causing his demise, and themselves put to death. The foreign slave-trade was calculated on as a principal source of revenue, and slaves were regularly provided as a marketable commodity.

"The Gorilla—that terrible monster, which bears such an unpleasant likeness to man—formed, perhaps, the most interesting topic of Mr. Du Chaillu's lecture. Its existence was

times of scarcity, who, in his own country, stands in the same category with ivory, dates, and other tropical productions; while *now*, transferred to a Christian land, being purchased from idleness, heathen idolatry, superstition, and crime, by a white foreigner, who has the strongest bond, that of undying self-interest, to take the best care of him as long as he lives, we see him basking in the generous sunshine of civilization, a blessing to himself and the whole mercantile world."

"But, my noble-minded brother," replied Mr. Beecher, "are not the laws in South Carolina inexorably severe against the negro?"

"They may be, and probably are," said Mr. Wyndham, "though I have never read them; because, in framing laws to control an idolatrous, barbarous people, necessity compels that they should be stern enough to force down their untamed, fiendish propensities. But these angular laws become a dead letter as soon as Christian teaching, industry, and methodical modes of life, render the negro tractable to the milder government of civilization and kindness."

To produce moral reformation even in England, the

---

long doubted by naturalists, and to America belongs the honor of discovery, or rather re-discovering it. The lecturer exhibited the skull of one of these animals, and gave a description of their habits, size, strength, &c., in terms with which, from their frequent publication, readers are sufficiently familiar, but which were listened to on this occasion with new interest, from the fact that the speaker had seen and shot them in their native haunts. Their tremendous roar, he said, could be heard four miles off, and the beating of their hands upon their chest, a mode of expressing their anger, is audible at a distance of one mile."

most severe laws were imposed. In the days of Queen Elizabeth, and even down to a very modern period, if a man purloined the value of twelve pounds he was fined and imprisoned, but if he stole *ten* shillings *more* than this sum (which constituted the crime of grand larceny), he was hanged. And if you will look back to the laws of Moses, that were framed for the Israelites, to produce both legal and moral reformation in that gross and stubborn race, you will find no laws so arbitrarily severe, known to history or tradition. The death-penalty visited disobedience to parents and Sabbath-breaking; and, in the taking of Jericho, when Achan stole that goodly Babylonish garment and wedge of gold, the commander-in-chief, Joshua, "sent messengers, and they ran into Achan's tent, where, finding these hidden articles, they brought them out before all the congregation of Israel, who took Achan, and the silver, and the garment, and the wedge of gold, and his sons and his daughters, and his oxen, and his asses, and his sheep, and his tent, and all that he had, and they brought them to the valley of Achor. And Joshua said, Why hast thou troubled us? The Lord shall trouble thee this day. And all Israel stoned him with stones, and burned them with fire, after they had stoned them with stones."—(Joshua vii.)

"I have always thought," continued Mr. Wyndham, "that switching a child, or a negro who committed thefts, etc., was a much more edifying and merciful punishment than imprisonment; for the blacks do not feel revenge* about chastisement from their

* "The Malays," says Barrow, in his History of Southern Africa, "are the most active and docile, but the most dangerous

own master, any more than the child does; and a celebrated physician,* who is a man of great talent and observation, says, 'The negro, or even the mulatto, is a very different person, in his mental and physical conformation, from that one who may be presumed to have been held in view in our legislation, the white Anglo-Saxon, Celt, or German. His ancestry, and the prototype of his race, are calculated for the torrid zone; and even the mixed progeny suffer severely and mortally from our cold.† Cheerful, merry, lounging, and careless, the Ethiopian American deeply enjoys the sun and light, delights in the open air, and is, as a general rule, constitutionally free from that deep, thoughtful anxiety for the future, so conspicuous in his paler neighbors.'

---

slaves. They are faithful, honest, and industrious; but so impatient of injury, and so capricious, that the slightest provocation will sometimes drive them to fits of phrenzy, during the continuance of which it would be unsafe to come within their reach." The Southern plantation negro, in North America, on the contrary, never seems to feel any more vindictiveness about his master's punishment than if he was his child.

* Dr. Benjamin Coates, of Philadelphia.

† The Free Negro Question.—"The free negroes who have recently left Arkansas to avoid being sold into slavery have published an appeal to the Christian world to protect them. They say Indiana shuts her doors upon them, Illinois denies prairie homes to them, Oregon will not receive them, and Minnesota is debating whether or not she shall admit them. They complain of being forced into a cold climate suddenly from a warm one, and present a sad picture of the distress that they suffer from a hasty legislation.

"Philanthropists must look this question fairly in the face. While expending sympathy unmeasured on the *slavery* question,

"Dr. Coates also makes the most practical remarks on the dreadful effects of prison discipline, and solitary confinement, for any length of time, on the negro.

---

comparatively little concern is manifested for the moral and physical condition of those negroes who are free. Worse than this, the Northern States, with boundless tracts of lands that wait for tillers to come up and possess them, are shutting their gates against these poor people, who are more to be pitied that now they have literally no home.

"A few weeks ago, Mr. Doolittle, of Wisconsin, a Senator of the United States, and a leading member of the Republican party, said, in a public address in this city, that the free negro question must be discussed and settled before you can determine what to do with the slavery question. There is great good sense in the suggestion, and our thinking men ought to be turning their attention to the subject, to reach, if possible, some solution of the problem. Africa invites her children back. And it is not improbable that the new impetus given to interior explorations of that continent, and the quickened interest which the civilized world is taking in its regeneration, may be providential preparations for the exodus thither of the free and comparatively enlightened negroes of North America."

The New York *Evening Post* has the following very timely and pertinent suggestions:

"In view of the late action of the legislatures of several Southern States, excluding free colored persons from their territories, and the constantly recurring question, 'What shall be done with them?' the following extracts from a letter to the Philadelphia *North American* would seem to be pertinent and well-timed. If it were necessary to urge any other location for such colonization, we should speak in favor of some Central American tract being purchased and used for the purpose; for soon, perhaps, this matter may present itself in a more commanding form, and assume an importance which we should be prepared to meet. The letter says:

"'The action of nearly all the Southern legislatures in regard to the free blacks, and their proscription from all honorable and

'The face of heaven,' says he, 'seems to him, necessary to his existence; and though long confinement is in his case, less productive of gloomy remorse, it is far more depressing to his vitality.' . . . 'The morbid effects of this, are unhappily visible in the production of scrofula, and pulmonary consumption; more than eighty per cent. of the deaths being from chronic affections of the lungs, and from the first named disorder.' . . . 'The moral consequences are, in an equivalent degree, depressing to the mind.'

---

profitable employments at the North, and the fact that large numbers of the colored residents of this and other States are preparing to exchange America for Africa, should prompt and impel the States and Federal governments to aid, by their power and patronage, the vast extent of good which the system of African colonization must confer upon every condition of the African race.

"'The American people of color, with a sagacity for which they have scarcely had credit, foresee the impossibility of their ever being at home in the United States, and are casting about for a resting-place. Many are looking Liberiaward. They are generally becoming more anxious to exchange political slavery and moral degradation for independence and honor. Very few have the pecuniary means to emigrate. Let help be tendered and afforded them on their return to their own soil; shelter them in their new relation, and surround them with the institutions of freedom and religion, and, at the same time, powerfully tend to crush out the odious slave-trade. Every consideration of justice, humanity, and expediency should induce the State and National governments to to make an annual appropriation for this purpose. Let the Legislature of Pennsylvania, by a liberal grant, unite with the wise, patriotic, and benevolent, in the only efficient way of really benefiting the colored race, by securing for it in Africa the rights of settlement and citizenship, and let all give to the exalted enterprise of African colonization their cordial support and co-operation.'"

"'It is not by remorse and anguish, that he is affected so much, as by intellectual and moral weakness and decay; and gloomy confinement becomes thus to him, mentally, as well as physically, a nearer approach to the punishment of death.'

"'The effect of solitary confinement has not been, as has been erroneously charged against it, to produce insanity, although humane and strict analysis has shown many to have been affected both with insanity and imbecility, at the time when they committed the offences for which they are sentenced.'

"'The effect upon the poor colored prisoners, though scarcely perceptible upon the whites, has been to produce not mania, but weakness of mind; dementia, instead of deranged excitement.'"

"The book revealing the mind of God," said Mr. Parker, "has nothing in its commands, that are so nervously sensitive about the moral alterative of a medicinal whipping, that the exquisites of the present day pretend to, as if they were more merciful than God Almighty himself. In Deuteronomy, 25th chapter, *Moses* commanded 'That if the wicked man be worthy to be beaten, that the judge shall cause him to lie down, and to be beaten before his face, according to the fault, by a certain number.' . . . 'Forty stripes he may give him, and not exceed; lest if he should exceed, and beat him above these with many stripes, then thy brother should seem vile unto thee.'"

The Bible says, "A whip for the horse, a bridle for the ass, and a rod for the fool's *back*." . . . "For if thou beatest him with the rod, he shall not die." . . . "Thou shalt beat him with the rod, and deliver his soul from hell." . . . "Foolishness is bound in the heart of a child, but the *rod* of correction shall drive it far from him." . . . "A servant will not be corrected by *words*, for though he understand, he will not answer." . . . "He that spareth the *rod*, hateth his son."

Every mother knows, by experience, that when her child has done wickedly, and is perfectly stubborn in his guilt, that locking him up, produces no moral effect; but a switching is an argument much more convincing to his sensibilities, than all the scolding or imprisonment. And, again, if a child is stupid, and not sensitive to approbation, or disgrace, and you lecture him, and lock him up for crime, he will lie down and sleep soundly until you wake him up; but a switching is a tangible rebuke.

In Carolina, such a thing is scarcely ever heard of, as imprisoning a negro for any crime except that of murder or rape, and for both of these devilish acts he is burned or hanged.

Having every necessary of life, and being constantly employed, the plantation negro rarely steals from his master; but if it should happen that he purloins anything from a neighboring plantation, the owner immediately reports the fact to his master, who sends for the driver, and has him given perhaps twenty or thirty lashes. This is all the punishment; and even this a generous neighbor does not require, being satisfied with giving the scamp a tremendous fright by reporting him. But if the planter who is stolen from is the enemy of the master of the thief, then he prosecutes him publicly, and the negro, by the laws of the State, receives the "forty, save one," of the Levitical law—still in force in Carolina — administered by a public officer, who, having no personal vengeance, performs this duty as leniently and reluctantly as the merciful jailor who accompanies a condemned culprit up to the gallows when he is to be hung.

But a prosecution of this public kind between friendly neighbors never occurs; and is regarded as the meanest and most cowardly act an enemy can be guilty of. It is an outrage that is never forgiven; and no gentleman there resents an injury done to his child sooner than an injury done to his servant. One planter dare not impinge in any way upon the slaves of another, for he knows a never-ending feud would be the consequence.

This law of applying the rod to the fool's back, be he your child or your servant, is surely more wholesome to both body and mind, than imprisonment in a noisome jail a whole year, or perhaps two, where in the Northern States this solitary confinement produces on the negro, according to the experience of Esculapians, *dementia*.

As to all the *lies* told to Abolitionists by *runaway* negroes (who are always the most good-for-nothing, quarrelsome rowdies on the plantation, and flee off to the North merely to escape work and moral discipline), they are pure inventions of their own wicked deceits; or what is far worse, the ravings of bigoted, malignant sentimentalists, or mischief-making politicians; who, to save their lives, could not give even a guess what the profit would be of killing a negro with inhuman labor, above the gain to the master of treating his slave property with kindness.

The slave has much the advantage of the free operatives in the factories of England and the United States;

for, being *property*, his master's interests are all concerned to preserve his health and his life, and the master's character among all his neighbors is a target for calumny if his slaves are not comfortable and happy.

But with hired free laborers there is no such conventional requirements from masters, as the following extract about England plainly shows —

Facts for the Abolitionists.—White slavery in England. —Barbarous treatment of children in the English factories.

We give below a debate in the British House of Commons, upon a bill to prevent the employment of children under fourteen years of age in the bleaching and dyeing works, and to prohibit their being worked over ten hours a day. The debate shows that a system of slavery exists in England quite as barbarous as anything yet discovered in this country by Mrs. Stowe or her assistants. We commend the debate without further remarks to the attention of the white slaves of New England.

"MR. ROEBUCK—I am about to speak on this question under somewhat peculiar circumstances. Very early in my Parliamentary career, Lord Ashley, now the Earl of Shaftesbury, introduced a bill of this description. I being an ardent political economist, as I am now, opposed the measure, and drew a distinction, which I draw now, between women and children and men. Women and children I hold not to be *sui juris;* they are not masters of themselves, but are under the control of other people. I would not interfere between men and those with whom they make contracts for employment, but I would certainly interfere between women and children and their employers. However, I opposed Lord Ashley at that time, and was very much influenced in my opposition by what the gentlemen of Lancashire said. They declared then it was the last half hour of the work performed by their operatives which made all their profits, and that if we took away that last half hour we should ruin the manufacturers of England. I listened to that statement, and trembled for the manufacturers of England—but Lord Ashley persevered. Parliament passed the bill which he brought in. From that time down to the present, the factories of this country have been under State control, and I appeal to this House whether the manufacturers of England have suffered by this legislation? [Cheers.] But the honorable member for Manchester still, I find, makes the same objection. He gets up and prophesies all sorts of evil if we interfere now; but he has kept out of view the evils for the prevention of which we are now about to interfere. [Hear, hear.] He has not told us what was laid before the committee, and what Mr. Tremenheere describes in the course of his investigation. But I will read some facts from Mr. Tremenheere's report, and will then appeal to the House of Commons, to the fathers and brothers of English women and children, if they will not interfere to put down this tremendous evil. [Hear.] There are some sentences in the book now in my hand which make my blood creep, and when the honorable member gets up and tells me that the Manchester manufacturers are likely to suffer, I say, let them suffer. [Hear, hear.]

"I, at least, will not be a party to the perpetration of any such atrocities as I find recorded, and I do hope that the gentlemen of England will not be parties to them either. [Hear, hear.] Says the honorable member, 'the bleachers are servants to the public; the demand for work comes upon them at uncertain times, and there is no analogy between the case of factories and of bleaching and dyeing works.' Now, I don't care a straw whether or not there is any analogy in this respect, but I am sure there is an analogy in the suffering, [cheers;] and, if so, the interference of the House is as necessary now as it was then, whether the bleachers are servants of the public or their own masters. They inflict misery upon the people they employ. [Hear.] That is the question; and having prevented this misery in the one case, let us interfere to prevent it in the other. [Hear.] I will now quote a few passages from Mr. Tremenheere's report. Here is the statement of John Hamer, finisher:—

"'I have been fourteen years in the bleaching trade. I was

employed at Messrs. Hollins, Toolebridge, Bolton. * * One morning we went to work at five o'clock, and worked till six the morning after (twenty-five hours). All the sets were working the same hours (the young with the adults). * * I have been so tired, though I am a strong and healthy man, that I have often to sit at my bedside when I get up of a morning, and my fingers are so stiff and sore that I cannot dress myself. If I feel thus tired, what must the young girls and boys feel?' [Hear, hear.]

"Let honorable gentlemen remember that this is an inquiry made only a year and a half ago. [Hear, hear.] Here is the statement of Ann Simpson, fourteen years old, Elizabeth Hilton, fifteen, and Sarah Higson, sixteen: —

"'We came to work last Friday morning at half-past six (at Mr. Ridgway Bridson's bleach-works, Bolton). We worked all Friday night till half-past five on Saturday morning (twenty-three hours). We did not sleep any time in the night, except on Saturday morning at half-past five we laid down to sleep on the hooking-box, and slept till a little after seven (less than two hours' sleep, and with the clothes still on, after twenty-three hours' work); then we went to breakfast for half an hour, and then came and worked till ten minutes past eleven.'

"We complain bitterly of the hours of this House, and if we come at four, with liberty to go away and dine at seven, and then don't get home till two in the morning, we say, 'What a terrible night's work we have had!' [A laugh.] Well, then, think of the poor child between thirteen and fourteen, or between ten and eleven, not able to go away and get a good dinner, not sitting while at work upon these soft cushions, but standing upon her poor, tired little legs for hours and hours together. [Hear, hear.] Think of her, and compare her work with ours. [Hear.] We complain of the labors which we undergo, but as compared to our life, hers is the life of the damned. [Hear, hear.] Phithian Monk says: —

"'I am foreman of the dyeing and making-up room. I worked last Friday till Saturday morning with those three girls, and what they have said is correct.'

"William Crompton — 'I am seventeen; I have been four

years and a half (that is, since he was twelve and a half years old) in the dressing-shop; we go on till different hours, sometimes early, sometimes late. I worked once three days and three nights; and not long since I began work on Friday morning at four, and worked till five on Saturday night (thirty-seven hours). I mostly slept at meal times, and only stopped one hour for meals; the rest I ate while I was working.'" [Hear, hear.] Now, I ask you, the gentlemen of England, if you will bear this? [Cheers.] I hear great talk of humanity—lip humanity!—[hear, hear] about the American slave. No man can view with more indignation than I do the horrible condition of the black in America; but I cannot help regarding with at least equal indignation the condition of the white slave in England [hear, hear]. I recollect hearing a story, which to me appeared a touching one, and fraught with a pregnant lesson. Mr. Oastler was walking with the late Sir Robert Peel up his splendid picture-gallery. Mr. Oastler, as we know, strongly advocated the shortening of the hours of labor in factories. Sir Robert Peel, on the other hand, as we also know, was a great political economist, and was arguing with his companion upon the impolicy of State interference. In passing along the gallery they came to a beautiful picture, I think by Landseer, which most of us probably have seen — a portrait of one of the daughters of Sir Robert Peel—and Mr. Oastler, stopping suddenly, said: 'My God, Sir Robert! and she might have been a factory girl!' Yes, any one of our daughters might have been a factory girl; and is there a man present, with any feeling for his child, who could think of her working almost without cessation for thirty-seven hours? [Hear, hear.] Think of her tender years—think of her delicate little hands! I have it in this book that children's hands are often blistered, and the skin torn off their feet, and yet they are thus obliged to work — the persons who overlook them being sometimes forced to keep them awake by beating on the table with large boards. [Hear.] For God's sake, then, I say, don't let us listen to the honorable gentleman. I don't want to weary the House; but I appeal to you as men—I appeal to you as fathers — I appeal to you as brothers — and I ask you, for God's sake, not to be participants in this horrible cruelty. [Cheers.] The honorable member says he is sure you will not go into committee on this bill. I, on the contrary, feel certain that, if I know anything of my countrymen, we shall go into committee; that the measure will be carried by a triumphant majority; and that we shall not lay our heads upon our pillows to-night, saying, 'We have deserted those whom God has placed under our charge — the weak, the helpless, the distressed; we think only of ourselves, of the wealthy, and of the great.' [Cheers.] The weak and the miserable appeal to you now for compassion and for aid; and I, their humble advocate, also appeal to you, in perfect confidence that you will listen to their prayer, and will pass this measure for their relief. [Cheers.]

"Mr. Cobbett reminded the House of the history of this question. In 1853, he moved for a committee to inquire into the condition of the bleachers and dyers; but he was met by a proposal for the appointment of a commission, which was issued accordingly, and which made its report in 1855. The report was decidedly in favor of a bill to limit the hours of labor in the case of women and children employed in bleaching and dyeing works. When, however, upon the strength of that report, the House was asked to pass a bill, the opponents of interference moved for a committee. A committee was accordingly appointed, and the inquiry of 1856 was the result. From various causes, however, owing to the necessary absence of some of its members, this committee virtually resolved itself into a Bleachers' and Manufacturers' Committee. He had drawn up a report, but the first resolution of the committee was that the chairman's report should not be considered [a laugh], and the report which was considered was that of the honorable member for Manchester and Mr. Kirk.

"In 1857, the honorable member from Bolton [Mr. Crook] brought in a bill, but the report of the committee that legislation on the subject was unadvisable, had its weight. The committee, nevertheless, recommended that certain alterations in the mode of work should, if possible, be effected between the manufacturers and their operatives. No such changes had taken place, however, in the hours of labor, and the necessity

7*

of this bill was therefore completely justified. [Hear, hear.] The honorable member for Manchester complained of inspection, but had very recently gone up to the Home Secretary as one of the deputation from the manufacturing districts, asking that more factory inspectors should be appointed on account of the immense benefit which had accrued to the factory population from legislative interference. [Hear.] Then it was urged that the bleachers and dyers stood in a different position from that of the cotton manufacturers, because they received goods which they were told must be completed — say for shipment — by a certain day. But in Scotland he had been told by master-bleachers: 'We want the bleachers' bill as much as the operatives do. We shall gladly welcome some legislative restriction which shall put us all on the same footing, and furnish us with a valid plea for resisting the pressure of our customers without giving them offence,' [hear, hear]; and a document, signed by a large number of Scotch bleachers and dyers, admitted that the present hours of labor were too long, and declared their readiness to work sixty hours a week only, if the rest of the trade would consent. He had no doubt that a large portion, at all events, of the Scotch bleachers and dyers were in favor of the bill, because it would compel the merchants to give them fair time for the completion of orders.

"With regard to the loss which it was said would accrue if certain processes in these establishments were interrupted, he had been assured by the foreman of Mr. Heywood's work at Salford, that there was nothing to prevent them from breaking off at any time, and beginning again next day, in any of the processes which he had inspected. [Hear, hear.] But then it was asserted that there were now no long hours of labor in these establishments. Now, he had that morning received from Scotland a statement of the time worked at certain mills by young women and young persons for the fortnight ending March 16, 1860, from which it appears that on Monday, the 5th of March, the number of hours' work performed was 17½; on Tuesday, 16½; on Wednesday, Thursday, and Friday, 15½; on Saturday, 7 hours; on Monday, 12th, 17½; on Tuesday, 15½; on Wednesday, 14; on Thursday and Friday, 15½; on Saturday, 7½.

From the whole tenor of this statement, as well as from letters which he had from time to time received, he believed there had been no diminution whatever in the overwork to which the women and children were subjected.

"The honorable member [Mr. Turner] said that, on the whole year, the average number of hours worked in these establishments was only ten and a half. The same plea was put forward by a merchant before the committee, who said: 'You should spread the work over the whole year.' But if you worked a horse some twenty hours a day for one week, allowing him to rest the next, and repeating the operation until he died of exhaustion, neither the magistrates, nor the Society for the Prevention of Cruelty to Animals, would attach much importance to your plea that you had only worked him on an average ten hours a day. [Hear, hear.] Under these circumstances, he prayed the House to pass the second reading of this bill, and not suffer such enormities to continue, or permit women and children to be worked in a way which any man would be ashamed to work his horse. [Hear, hear.]"

Palsied be the tongue that says a negro is not clothed, fed, and taken care of in sickness, in health, and old age, with a sensibility as morally elevating to the planter, as any instinct that the human heart knows. Besides, the very law of self-interest, that governs mankind everywhere on this earth, secures for the slave everything necessary to life or godliness. For if the master does not have him taught to fear God, he is a lazy, unprofitable eye-servant; and if he does not do everything to promote his bodily health, he becomes a consumer, but not a producer, of the wherewithal to support the plantation.

The master who did not give to his old slave the very same amount of clothing, food, and every other attention that he does to the young, would be scorned by his neighbors as a low-lived wretch; and the negroes themselves would become dissatisfied, did they not know that old age and sickness would never find them without every comfort they enjoyed in health.

"Going into the office of a surgeon, at the South, (says Dr. Adams, of Boston,) I accidentally saw the leg of a black man, which had just been amputated for an ulcer. The patient will be a charge upon his owner for life. An action at law may be brought against one who does not provide a comfortable support for his servants. Thus the pauper establishments of the free states, the burden and care of immigrants, are almost entirely obviated at the South by the colored population."

In the North, "laboring for the present and future welfare of immigrants, we are (continues Dr. Adams,) subjected to evils of which we are ashamed to complain, but from which the South is enviably free. To have a neighborhood of a certain description of foreigners about your dwellings; to see a horde of them get possession of a respectable dwelling in a court, and thus force the residents, as they always do, to flee—it being impossible to live in comfort in close connexion with them; to have all the senses assailed from their open doors; to have your Sabbath utterly destroyed, is not so agreeable as the presence of a respectable colored population, every individual of which is under the responsible oversight of a master or mistress, who restrains and governs him, and has a reputation to maintain in his respectable appearance and comfort, and keep him from being a burden on the community."

Every master and mistress in the South would feel as much mortified at their slave begging for any comfort, as they would at hearing that their child begged others for necessaries they were abundantly able to give him themselves. But, indeed, such a thing as a beggar among the slaves never was, and never can be heard of.

"Eleven thousand paupers have been received at Deer Island, in Boston harbor, during the short time that it has been appropriated to that purpose (writes Dr. Adams, in 1854,) and our large state work-houses, which we so patiently build for the dregs of our foreign population."

The *Boston Post* at that time said: "There were yesterday six hundred and fifty-four prisoners in the House of Correction, with the promise of an addition of thirty more before to-morrow. The accommodations are so limited that about one hundred of them are compelled to sleep in one of the workshops. When a call is made upon any of the idle ones to work out of doors, they jump with great alacrity to perform it, being delighted to have an opportunity to breathe the fresh air."

Is it not most astonishing that these Abolition New Yorkers, Bostonians, and Philadelphians, who have moral and benevolent work enough to do in their own cities to occupy every moment of their lives, to regenerate their abject, starving, ignorant, heathen paupers, should let the Devil delude them into running into the far-off Southern States, to weep over those who are so well off, and with whom neither God's law, nor the laws of the land, allow them to interfere? "To his own master he standeth or falleth," saith the Bible. "Who are ye that judgeth another man's servant?"

Was it not the special deceit of the Pharisees to pull the mote out of their brother's eye, and leave the beam in their own, that Jesus Christ levelled his anathemas against? "He that sees ever so accurately, ever so finely into the motives of other people's acting, may possibly be entirely ignorant as to his own; it is by the mental, as by the corporeal eye, the object may be placed too near the sight to be seen truly, as well as so far off; nay, too near to be seen at all." The Bible says the heart is deceitful above all things, and desperately wicked. Therefore, "He that trusteth to his own heart is a fool," says the wise king Solomon.

As to the killing* of slaves reported by tale-bearers, it is too absurd to be argued about; for suppose a vagabond were to assert that all the gentlemen in New York, and Boston, amused themselves every morning by shooting down their noble-looking horses,—would the Southern people be so daft as to believe it? And yet, a negro is worth one or two thousand dollars to his master, in the rice-fields of Carolina, while a horse does not often command more than one or two hundred.

While slave murder has not occurred more than once, perhaps, in fifty or a hundred years, on a *South* Caro-

* The writer has spent her whole life, until within the last ten or twelve years, in Carolina, and never heard of but one negro being killed, and that was not on a plantation, and entirely accidental. A negro in Coosannatchi disobeyed a positive order, and then attacked his master, who was *alone* with him; this gentleman drew a penknife to scare him, and by chance hit him in a vital part. This happened about twenty years ago, and it created such a tremendous excitement in the whole district, that it was reported that the gentleman's remorse was so intolerable, that he blew his brains out.

lina plantation, where the master exercises unlimited authority, the newspapers *North* announce "daily murders among white men perpetrated there; and husbands poisoning wives, and the wives poisoning husbands; and these pretty wives and husbands, running off with coachmen and misses in their teens; and passée matrons, leaving their helpless children to go off sparking to Europe with hobbledehoys." But the Bible says, "Thou shalt not go up and down as a tale-bearer, among thy people." So we of the South, when we read of all these lawless crimes in New York and Boston, believe sensibly that they certainly are (even if the press reports them truly), the *exceptions*, not the general practice, in society there. Not all the running back negroes, or all the Irish servants in the whole North, could persuade *Carolinians*, that there was not a true wife and husband in New York; that there were not thousands of men there incapable of murder, theft, and lies, and cruelty to Irish and Dutch servants; and it is truly wonderful that civilized, educated, Abolitionists, could be so daft as to believe the monstronsities fulminated by lying runaway negroes, against their masters. We in the South would be the public laughing-stock, if we gave vagabonds as our authority, in calumniating our neighbors. As long as negroes are *property*, no master, unless he was a lunatic, would ever hurt them. Shooting or beating a slave to death, would insure the perpetrators being sent to the asylum for the insane; for such an episode, in plantation policy, could not occur, unless the *reason*, and with it, the *self-love* of the master, was dethroned.

It is an undoubted fact, that a *bad* master will take

more care of his slaves in sickness and in health, than he will of his wife; will sit up with him, administer every dose of medicine, and send for the doctor, and the parson, too, if the slave's mind is troubled so as to increase his fever; while his own poor wife may make her exodus to the other world as soon as she pleases, and her place can be easily, and perhaps profitably supplied, by his marrying a young heiress, which these wicked widowers are very fond of compassing, in a few months.

Surely, in this selfish world, it is good policy to make it the *interest* of our friends to love us.

Thus edifying each other with mutual exchanges of opinion, and experiences of life, during this long delightful ride, where the sunshine and the breeze, alike titillated pleasurable emotions, Mr. Wyndham drove up to the Euhaw Church door; the venerable building being embosomed in evergreen forest trees, where hundreds of negroes had been long waiting for the parsons to arrive.

The church was immensely large, capable of seating, perhaps, two thousand *men* (not women, for their powers of crinoline expansion, if not checked, must eventually fashion the architecture of all public buildings). It had no galleries, so that this multitude of Africans appropriated two-thirds of the seats, and the white congregation, that was not one-tenth as large, satisfied themselves with the locality nearest to the pulpit.

Walking in slowly, and respectfully, the negroes took their seats, and at once struck up the following hymn, which the numerous voices loudly echoed, previous to the services commencing from the pulpit.

"Show pity, Lord, O! Lord, forgive;
Let a repenting rebel live,
Are not thy mercies large and free?
May not a sinner trust in thee?"

The ministers were all deeply moved to see Ethiopia thus stretching forth her hands to God, and when they stood up to preach to these redeemed heathen, no doubt they realized the immediate presence of that God who had so wonderfully overruled the cupidity of men, to glorify himself in the salvation of these benighted wanderers of the human race.

The communion was then administered — the six black deacons handing round the elements to all their colored brethren with clerical dignity; and then the service was concluded with the hymn —

"How sweet the name of Jesus sounds."

All of the coachmen who had been in the church now harnessed up their horses for their masters' families to return home, where they found a plentiful Sunday dinner of cold meats and hot vegetables to satisfy their now clamorously empty stomachs; and, as Nature hates a vacuum, a ride of seven miles to church, and seven miles back, would stimulate the carnal desires of even a self-denying clergyman.

The brethren pleading fatigue, retired directly after family prayer, in which several of the field negroes, and all the house servants came into the parlor to unite in, as was always the custom in Mr. Wyndham's household.

The ministers from Boston, New York, Philadelphia, and Connecticut, were all appointed to sleep in one large room; and the Muse of History afterwards reported that they were so excited about the respectable negro Christians they had just communed with, in remembrance of their common Savior, that they sat up nearly half the night, talking over the developments of plantation life in the South.

Mr. Joab Beecher, walking hurriedly about the room, stopped suddenly and cried out, "My God! brother Parker, suppose, after all, Wilberforce was under the delusion of the Devil; who, appearing as an angel of light, stimulated his zeal to put down the slave trade, that, under God, has been the means of expanding the Gospel in the heart of Africa's poor barbarian children, thus mysteriously introduced into Christian and civilized lands?" "Where there is no law," the Bible says, "there is no transgression." . . . "Crime is the opposite of virtue. It is a wrong within itself, made so by the laws of God and man, founded in the highest necessity of society." But in what part of this whole Bible can a word be found against slavery, though it existed in the time of Christ and his Apostles in its harshest forms?

"Has slavery been punished in every age as a crime? Is it denounced," says Mr. Simms, in his speech in Congress, "by the laws of God and man? Is it the enemy of every virtue and the foe of every right? No, sir; it stands justified, authorized, and vindicated by all of these. Slavery in America is the proudest triumph of humanity and philanthropy in the world's history. It stands guarantied by the Constitution, and has been the lever by which five million human beings have been elevated from the degraded and benighted condition of savage life, ignorant of their responsibilities to God and their obligations to man and society, to a knowledge of their responsibilities to God and their relations to society. When the Africans first landed on the American continent, and passed from the free, indolent life of a savage to the condition of a laborious slave, he found for the first time in his history his natural element of development. He came here illy-shaped and half made up in physical form. Savage degradation and mental weakness enveloped in ignorance his intellectual, moral, and social nature. More helpless and dependent than the beasts of the field, he groped his dismal way without even the lights of instinct. But behold him now. He stands to-day regenerated from savage life. He can look through Nature up to Nature's God; can comprehend the laws of his being; understands his relations to society; has a manly and erect mien, and is no longer a drone in the great hive of humanity. You may track him along his whole history for a period of more than five thousand years, and never before did he occupy such a position in the scale of moral, social, and intellectual being. How do they explain all this? What is the philosophy of his regeneration?

"Sir, he owes it to the dispensation of events that bore him from the land of his nativity, where he revelled in sloth, and where every germ of his social, moral, and intellectual nature was smothered and paralyzed by the superstition and inertness of his nature, to this land, where his feeble powers have been cultivated and developed into strength and endurance by the means of toil, association, and control. When, before, was there ever such a triumph, such a success crowning the efforts of humanity and philanthropy? And, sir, who has accomplished this? Has it been done by the fanatical theories and frenzied abstractions of the sentimental philanthropist of the North? No, sir; it has been done by the wiser and more practical philanthropist of the South. It has been the philosophical result of the institution of slavery. For more than a thousand years the world has been filled with missionaries laboring in the cause of humanity. They have crossed the trackless deep, have braved every clime, penetrated every wilderness wherever the foot-prints of poor fallen man have marked the sands of earth. In this cause millions upon millions have been expended, and thousands upon thousands of the noblest hearts that ever throbbed in a human breast have fallen in distant lands, self-exiles from kindred, country, and friends, in the service of a God-sanctified and ennobling philanthropy. Yet, sir, what has been the result? Egyptian darkness still hangs like a pall of death over that land, where the descendants of him who, driven from a father's presence, bearing the penalties of a father's curse, have wandered homeless savages for thousands of years.

"Though the bones of missionaries whiten the sunny plains of Africa, there is not an enduring monument of all their treasures, their labors, their sacrifices, left. There is but one beam of light, one ray of civilization, shining like a star amid the night, in that devoted land; and that has sprung from the institution of American slavery. Is this no achievement in the cause of humanity, no work worthy of a Christian age in the cause of human redemption? Sir, had you power tomorrow to convert into dollars and cents all the property, personal and real — yea, all the wealth of this continent — and were it gathered into one mighty treasury, to be used and expended in the regeneration and disenthralment of the African race in his own native land of the sun, you might exhaust the last dollar without elevating five millions of that race to the same degree of moral, social, physical, and intellectual being, as that now attained by the five million slaves in this country.

"Practical truths confute all sentimental theories; and the triumph of these truths has been philosophically tested by their application to that unfortunate race under our system of instruction and reform. The negro, sir, in his native state, and even in his developed state, differs from the white race. He has powers of physical endurance, but no powers of self-reliance, or great intellectual development. In his long and monotonous pilgrimage upon the earth, he has left no records of his powers of self-government or self-protection. He has never contributed anything to science or art; he has established no monuments of civilization. His achievements in all the mutations of the past, in the progress and elevation of mankind, forms a blank page in the history of the world. He is dependent and helpless, without inventive faculties. He requires direction, control, subordination, and the native element of his civilization and advancement is in a state of vassalage. Upon this continent, in the providence of God, he has found that state best adapted to his nature, his faculties, his wants, his development; his master is his best friend; and he who would disturb the domestic ties that bind him to the civilization of a Christian household, as now exists in the Southern States, is his worst enemy."

Mr. Cheever declared "that statistics would demonstrate that all the foreign missionary enterprise of the whole world, during the last fifty or a hundred years, could not begin to number the five millions of civilized, Christianized black heathen, now living in the Southern States, whose labor has made them a blessing to themselves and the whole mercantile world."

In the *London Quarterly Review*, January 1860, page 45, will be found the following sentence: "The entire failure of the cotton crop," says Mr. Ashmore, "should it ever occur, would utterly destroy, and perhaps forever, all the manufacturing property we possess; or, should the growth in any one year be only one million instead of three million bales, the manufacturing and trading classes would find themselves involved in losses which, in many cases, would amount to irretrievable ruin—millions of our countrymen would become deprived of employment and food — and, as a consequence, the misfortune would involve this country in a series of calamities, politically, socially, and commercially, such as cannot be contemplated without anxiety and dismay.

"These considerations strongly point to the necessity of encouraging the growth of cotton in the British colonies—in India, Australia, and Africa—that we may escape the perils which seem to attach to our relying so exclusively for our supply, as we do at present, upon the products of American slavery."

Mr. Parker, seeing a volume of eastern travels lying on the table, opened it, and his eye rested on some of the orgies of the heathens of Abyssinia (which was supposed to be ancient Ethiopia,) and he read aloud the passage to his two ministerial brothers, which was thus written:

"In 1774 (anno domini), Mr. Bruce gives an account of the Abyssinians. He says, 'These people are not content with devouring raw flesh: their custom is to cut collups from live animals, which they tear to pieces with their teeth while warm and palpitating with vital motion. . . . The flesh of an animal after it is dead they account quite unsavory. The most expert butcher among them, is he who can cut most flesh from a beast before it is deprived of its life: for doing which, the utmost attention is necessary to avoid the great arteries, or those parts, the destruction of which will soon bring on death. . . . A company of Abyssinians at dinner is a horrid spectacle . . . they are seated each with a cake of flour in his hand; live cattle are brought to the door, and the inhuman butcher cuts morsels off them, which are instantly carried in to the company, who lay them upon their cakes, and eat them directly, all bathed in the tepid blood of the miserable animals, whose lowings and groanings, through violence of anguish, serve for a dinner-bell, or music, to the shocking barbarians.'"

Reader! how would you like the descendants of such sanguinary brethren of the human race to form a confederacy of equal rights and privileges, with the morally and physically, and intellectually and religiously elevated Anglo-Saxons of this country? Are you not rejoiced that the "Supreme Court of the United States" have put their veto on the recently sprung idea, that our Revolutionary sires recognized the negro as a citizen in drawing up their splendid "Declaration of Independence," that the white race, for a thousand years, had been preparing to eliminate; — "for," says Carlyle, "a people should change their government only as a snake sheds his skin; the new skin is gradually formed under the old one, and then the snake wriggles out with just a drop of blood here and there, where the old jacket held on rather tightly."

Is not that man a fool who asserts in the face of every-day experience, and the biography of the whole race of mankind, daguerreotyped in the faithful history of nations in the Bible, and in all ethnological treatises on the subject, who asserts that "all men are born free and equal."* Such absurd lies no one in his secret heart believes, for every civilized man feels himself entirely above the beastly devils whose revelries have just been described in Abyssinia, and every Bible Christian, knowing such heathen existed on this beautiful earth, might well rejoice if their transportation to this Christian land would regenerate them as it has

---

* "Take but degree away, untune that string,
And, hark, what discord follows! each thing meets
In mere oppugnancy: The bounded waters
Should lift their bosoms higher than the shores,
And make a sop of all this solid globe:
Strength should be lord of Imbecility."

SHAKSPEARE.

"Equality is one of the most consummate scoundrels that ever crept from the brain of a political juggler—a fellow who thrusts his hand into the pocket of honest industry, or enterprising talent, and squanders their hard-earned profits on profligate idleness or insolent stupidity."—LANGSTAFF.

done the benighted African slaves of the planters in the Southern States of this confederacy.

Mr. Beecher, still striding disturbedly up and down the chamber, finally remarked that the destiny of the inferior races of men is involved in that unfathomable mystery which clothes the acts of the Deity. It has been manifested from the beginning, that the idolatrous and barbarous races have been the servants of the civilized. The earliest histories we have of Asia Minor, of the rise and progress of the Persian Empire, and of Greece and Rome, give ample illustrations of this.

All experience proves that in one respect the state of slavery has been productive of signal benefits. It has been the efficient cause of civilization and refinement among nations. Men do not primarily adopt a life of labor, who can live without it. The first ambition of man was to excel in arms. The successful warrior does not drop his bow and arrow, and cast aside his spear, to take to the plow, willingly. He turns his captives into the fields of agriculture, and compels them to take care of his horses and cattle.

Pasturage is the first natural occupation of men arising from barbarism. The herdsman succeeds the hunter, and the planting of grain is the next step.

It was not the patriarchs alone that illustrated this: the course is a natural one; and menials are introduced as soon as herds and flocks grow large. This made Abraham and Isaac, Jacob and Esau, gentlemen.

Kingly governments existed long before the Israelites petitioned for a king. Hunting and idolatrous kingdoms first arose. There is something in the bold, predatory, idolatrous life, and the practice of polytheism, to lead to this. Men do not like to submit themselves, mind and manners, acts and morals, to one God, who always rewards virtue and punishes vice. It was so, we see, in the savage tribes of this continent, when they began to grow in numbers and means. Peru and Mexico rushed at once into monarchy.

There is another effect that has attended captive slavery among the aborigines of the United States. The fleeing of blacks into the Indian territories, as a place of refuge, has enabled the Red man to overcome his strong repugnance to labor in the corn, rice, and cotton fields. The negro escaping from his master has taken up his tasks for his Indian protector. But for this, we should never have heard of the sovereignty assumed by the Creeks, Cherokees, Choctaws, and Chickasaws. Here it has been Ham teaching Shem the use of the plow. Indeed, without the agency of African slavery, I doubt very much whether the pestilential savannahs and sea-board plains of the Southern States, in the hot season, where deadly malaria kills the white man, would ever have been cultivated. Certain it is, that neither Virginia nor the Carolinas ever flourished till the introduction of slaves.

"In Egypt, it is evident," says Sir J. G. Wilkinson, "that both white and black slaves were employed as servants: they attended on the guests when invited to the house of their master." . . . "Women slaves were also engaged in the service of families, like the Greeks and Circassians, in modern Egypt." . . . "The traffic in slaves was tolerated by the Egyptians; and doubtless many persons were engaged, as at present, in bringing them to Egypt for public sale, independently of those who were sent as part of the tribute; and the Ishmaelites bought Joseph from his brethren, and sold him to Potiphar, on arriving in Egypt." . . . "It was the common custom in those days; the Jews had their bondsmen, bought with their money." . . . "Moses said to the children of Israel, 'both thy bondsmen and thy bondsmaids, which thou shalt have, shall be of the heathen that are round about you; of them shall ye buy bondsmen and bondsmaids.' 'Moreover, of the children of the stranger that do sojourn among you, of them shall ye buy, and of their families that are with you, which they begat in your land; and they shall be your possession.' 'And ye shall take them as an inheritance for your children after you, to inherit them for a possession; they shall be your bondsmen for ever: but over your brethren the children of Israel ye shall not rule over them with rigor.'"—(Leviticus xxv. 44, 45, 46.)

Bondsmen appear to be one of the last conditions of human society that we hear of. In the final winding up of all things, as described in the Bible, we still find bondsmen alluded to. In the Revelations of St. John, he says, "And causeth all, both small and great, rich and poor, *bond* and free, to receive a mark in their right hand, or on their foreheads."—(Rev. xiii. 16.)

"And the kings of the earth, and the rich men, and the chief captains, and the mighty men, and every *bond* man, and every free man, hid themselves in the dens and in the rocks of the mountains;" "and said to the mountains and rocks, Fall on us, and hide us from Him that sitteth on the throne, and from the wrath of the Lamb." "For the great day of his wrath is come, and who shall be able to stand?"—(Rev. vi. 14, 15, 16, 17.)

"I am fast arriving at the conclusion," said Mr. Ting, "that this whole Abolition question is nothing more than an audacious attempt to be wise above what is written in the Bible. Is the mind of God progressive, so that his moral law, delivered with such fearful solemnity to his chosen people, has now, in this sublimely illuminated nineteenth century, become obsolete 'old fogyism?' Does not the philanthropy of the Abolitionist throw into the shade the beneficent teachings of Jesus Christ during the whole thirty-three years of his ministry on this earth? for *He* never once alluded to the sin of slavery, that these new-light, latter-day saints insist is 'the sum of all human villanies.' Perhaps they think that our blessed Savior was too much of a politician to attack this hoary-headed iniquity. Certain it is he never failed to rebuke his most potential adversaries, the Pharisees, with all the indignation that language can convey: 'Ye whited sepulchres;' 'Ye graves that appear not;' 'Ye generation of vipers, how can ye escape the damnation of hell?' 'Ye make clean the outside of the platter, while within ye are full of dead men's bones, and all uncleanness.' Was not the wickedness of these Pharisees precisely that of the progressionists of the present day? Did they not assume a higher righteousness than that taught by the Son of God himself? Our inflated orators of progress not long since denounced Washington as a slave-holding thief and scoundrel; and declared that that poor, blood-thirsty fanatic, whose diseased liver sought the mercurial alterative of planning a midnight assassination of all the inhabitants of Harper's Ferry, who had for a year extended to him their whole-hearted, unsuspecting confidence and hospitality, — this pitiable old sinner was represented by his peers as hanging on a gallows more glorious than the cross of Jesus Christ."

> "O save, ye gods omnipotent and kind,
> From such abhorr'd chimeras save the mind."

"There are habits of misapprehension and misjudging common among all degrees of men: Fretfulness, industrious to seek or even feign and chew upon matter that may nourish it; Captiousness, ingenious in perverting the meaning of words; Partiality, warping everything to its own purpose; Censoriousness, unable to discern a bright part in characters; Self-conceit, averse to discern the real motives of action; Melancholy, auguring always for the worst; besides many more, some of which I am afraid every man may find lurking in his own breast, if he will but look narrowly enough." — TUCKER.

"Do these progressionists," remarked Mr. Beecher, "really imagine, if God commands all his chosen people to take their bondsmen and bondsmaids from the heathen nations around them, that any human power can prevent the institution of slavery? As well may we attempt to alter the stars in their courses. Slavery is God's appointed means for the civilizing and christianizing the heathen world; and I am rejoiced to see the Chinese brought as laborers from their idolatrous land. If God says, 'Cursed be Canaan, a servant of servants shall he be to his brethren;' 'Blessed be the Lord God of Shem, and Canaan shall be his servant;' 'God shall enlarge Japheth, and he shall dwell in the tents of Shem, and Canaan shall be his servant;'—do we poor insects of a day beg to be allowed to differ in opinion from Omnipotent Wisdom, for *we* believe that all men are created free and equal? The ethnologist tells us that Ham is the father of the black race, Shem of the red race, and Japheth of the white race. If so, is not the above prophecy exactly fulfilled? for do not we pale-faces dwell in the tents of Shem on this American continent, and is not Canaan our servant? The South, in her mighty millions, feels secure; and also in her perfect preparation to discuss this question politically, ecclesiastically, morally, metaphysically, or physically, with the extreme North, and she is willing and able to *persuade others to be calm.*"

"In this connexion, I wish to say for the South, to the North and to the world, that we have no fears from our slave-population," says the Rev. F. A. Ross. "There might be a momentary insurrection and bloodshed; but destruction to the black man would be inevitable." . . . "The Greeks and Romans controlled immense masses of white slaves—many of them as intelligent as their lords." . . . "Schoolmasters, fabulists, and poets, were slaves." . . . "Athens, with her thirty thousand freemen, governed half a million of bondmen. Single Roman patricians owned thirty thousand." . . . "If, then, the phalanx and the legion mastered such slaves for ages, when battle was physical force of man to man, how certain it is that infantry, cavalry, and artillery, could hold in bondage millions of Africans for a thousand years."

But this is only speaking after the manner of men. It is God's Bible decree that puts one race above another.

"Repine not nor reply;
View not what Heaven ordains with reason's eye,
Too bright the object is; the distance is too high.
The man who would resolve the work of Fate,
May limit number, and make crooked straight.
Stop the inquiry then, and curb thy sense,
Nor let dust argue with Omnipotence."

Sin is the trangression of the law, and where there is no law, there is no sin. Can any one of our progressionists produce out of the ten commandments, anything short of the direct institution of slave property; for the order is, "Thou shalt not covet thy neighbor's house, nor his wife, nor his man-servant, nor his maid-servant, nor his ox, nor his ass, nor anything that is thy neighbor's."

If these slaves, rebelling against their Creator's will and that of those masters that God has raised up for them, run away to the free States, allegiance to our Constitution, and every sentiment of honor and religion require us to do as St. Paul did, when he sent the runaway slave (Onesimus), back to his master; and as the Bible tells us the angel of the Lord did, to Sarah's runaway maid, Hagar. (Genesis xvi. 6–9.) But Abraham said unto Sarah, "Behold thy maid is in thy hand: do to her as it pleaseth thee." . . . "And when Sarah dealt hardly with her, she fled from her face." . . . "And the angel of the Lord found her by a fountain, in the way to Shur." . . . "And he said, Hagar, Sarah's maid, whence camest thou? and whither wilt thou go?" . . . "And she said, I flee from the face of my mistress Sarah." . . . "And the angel of the Lord said unto her, Return to thy mistress, and submit thyself under her hands."

Jesus Christ, knowing that some Pharisees would arise to pretend that he came to destroy the law and the prophets, said, "I am not come to destroy, but to fulfil." . . . "For verily I say unto you, till heaven and earth pass away, one jot, or one tittle, shall in no wise pass from the law till all be fulfilled." . . . "Whosoever, therefore, shall break one of the least of these commandments, shall be called the least in the kingdom of heaven; but whosoever shall do and teach them, the same shall be called great in the kingdom of heaven." . . . "For I say unto you, that except your righteousness shall exceed the righteousness of the Scribes and Pharisees, ye shall in no case enter into the kingdom of heaven." Can anything be more truly pharisaical, than the excruciating sensibility of the Northern philanthropist about the slaves in the South, with whom they have no business at all;* while their own poor pine at their very doors, destitute alike of physical and spiritual comfort. "Whoremongers, adulterers, blasphemers, drunkards, murderers, and he that loveth and maketh a lie." Satan's master-piece of cunning is, to tempt Christians to strive after impossible human perfection, while they neglect those attainments in righteousness

* "Human nature is so constituted, that all see and judge better in the affairs of others than their own." — TERENCE.

that are practicable every day of their lives.* Why do not these latter-day saints determine to exterminate with their almightiness, all the thieves, liars, and wicked people out of this beautiful world, by a twist and a jerk, as they expect thus to do with the slavery that God himself ordered through his servant Moses, no doubt to civilize and christianize the barbarous nations of the earth.

"God, in making all things, saw that in the relations he would constitute between himself and intelligent creatures, and among themselves, natural Good and Evil would come to pass. In his benevolent wisdom, he then willed *law* to control this natural good and evil. And he thereby made conformity to that *law* to be *right*, and non-conformity to be *wrong*. Why? Simply, because he saw it to be good, and made it to be right; not because he saw it to be right, but because he *made* it to be right. Hence, the ten specific commandments of the one moral law of love are just ten rules, which God made to regulate the natural good and evil which he knew would be in the ten relations that he himself constituted between himself and man, and between man and his neighbor. The Bible settles the question: sin is the transgression of the law, and where there is no law, there is no sin."

---

* "Those things that are not practicable, are not desirable. There is nothing in the world really beneficial, that does not lie within the reach of an informed understanding, and a well-directed pursuit. There is nothing that God has not judged good for us, that He has not given us the means to accomplish, both in the natural and the moral world." — BURKE.

Now, can any one of the disturbers of our country's peace* show a single prohibition of slavery, after God ordered bondsmen to be made of the heathen? "Or perhaps they think," says Mr. Ross, "the Bible was good enough maybe for the Israelites in Egypt and in Canaan — good enough for the Christians in Jerusalem and Antioch and Rome, — but not good enough, even as a horn-book, for them, the men of the nineteenth century — the men of Boston, New York, and Brooklyn! Oh, no!" They need this old-fogy book? Not at all.

"What next? Why, sir, if I need not God to teach me moral truth, I may think I need him not to teach me any thing. What next? The irresistible conclusion is, I may think I can live without God; that Jehovah is a myth — a name. I may bid him stand aside, or die. Oh, sir, I will be the fool to say there is no God!"

"Some anti-slavery men, we all know, have left the light of the Bible, and wandered into the darkness, until they have reached the blackness of the darkness of infidelity?" . . . "Other some are following hard after, and are throwing the Bible into the furnace — are melting it into iron, and forging it, and welding it, and twisting it, and grooving it, into the shape and significance and goodness and gospel of Sharpe's rifles." . . . "Sir, are you not afraid that some of your

---

* "Is there not some chosen curse,
Some hidden thunder in the stores of heaven,
Red with uncommon wrath, to blast the man
Who owes his greatness to his country's ruin?"

once-best men will soon have no better Bible than that?"

"For he was of that stubborn crew
Of errant saints, whom all men grant
To be the true church-militant;
Such as do build their faith upon
The holy text of Pike and Gun;
Decide all controversies by
Infallible artillery;
And prove their doctrine orthodox
By apostolic blows and knocks."

CHAPTER V.

"Hail, Wedded Love! mysterious law, true source
Of human offspring, sole propriety
In Paradise of all things common else.
By thee adult'rous Lust was driven from men
Among the bestial herds to range; by thee
Founded in reason, loyal, just, and pure,
Relations dear, and all the charities
Of father, son, and brethren, first were known."

MILTON.

"We start in life, an unbroken company. Brothers, sisters, friends and lovers, neighbors and comrades, are with us. There is circle within circle, and each one of us is at the charmed centre, where the heart's affections are aglow, and whence they radiate outward on society. Youth is exuberant with joy and hope. The earth looks fair; for it sparkles, with May-dews wet, and no shadow hath fallen upon it. We are all here, and we could live here forever. The home-centre is on the hither side of the river; and why should we strain our eyes to look beyond?

"But this state of things does not continue long. Our circle grows less and less. It is broken and broken, and then closed up again; but every break and close make it narrower and smaller. Perhaps before the sun is at his meridian, the majority are on the other side. The circle there is as large as the one here; and we are drawn contrarywise, and vibrate between the two. A little longer, and almost all have crossed over; the balance settles down on the spiritual side, and the home-centre is removed to the upper sphere. At length you see nothing but an aged pilgrim, standing alone on the river's bank, and looking earnestly toward the country on the other side."

After the adjournment of the religious Union Meeting, that had been kept up a week at the Euhaw Church (and had not only been successful in determining many to think and act seriously about eternal realities, but had also rejuvenated in the minds of old professors, the great felicity and dignity of sympathizing with Jesus Christ in all their walks through life), we find Mr. and Mrs. Wyndham once more free from company, and quietly enjoying each other's communings around the family fireside, surrounded by their nine happy, healthy, *obedient* children (for in those days they were taught self-denial, and veneration for the wisdom of superiors in age and station, and strict loyalty to the Bible and parental authority.)*

Presently two black waiters, neatly dressed in a livery of fine grey woollen cloth, turned up with black

* "Filial obedience is the first and greatest requisite of a State; by this we become good subjects to our emperors, capable of behaving with just subordination to our superiors, and grateful dependants on Heaven; by this we become fonder of marriage, in order to be capable of exacting obedience from others in our turn: by this we become good magistrates; for early submission is the truest lesson to those who would learn to rule. By this the whole State may be said to resemble one family."—GOLDSMITH.

velvet, announced breakfast; for family prayer had been already offered for God's protection and guidance during that day.

The wife had, as usual, risen early in the morning, with her children, to pluck from the courtyard a mammoth bouquet, to be placed in a rich vase in the centre of the table; for her husband never ate a meal, with pleasure, where flowers did not form the refining accompaniment. Fruit-baskets, also, on either side of the table, contained the yellow, brown, and blue fig, the sugar pear, and pomegranate, and luscious oranges, growing to full perfection, and turning a rich yellow, on the *trees* in her own garden (not plucked half-green in the West Indies and merchandised here, where the color is produced from the "sere and yellow leaf" of *decay*, as is always the case in the Northern market where this splendid fruit is brought so unripe as to give no idea of its natural taste where it grows to perfection), a large covered dish of small hominy (for this bolted corn grits is the standard breakfast of South Carolina), piling plates of rice waffles, and johnny cakes, and sweet potato* fritters, and corn flannel cakes, and fried young drum fish, and whiting, and mullet, completed this family breakfast.

---

* Barrow, in his History of Southern Africa, remarks, "that the Hottentots, whose stomachs are not very nice, dislike the taste of the potato, and refuse to eat it." . . . "It is curious enough," says he, "that this poisonous root has been rejected at first by most nations." . . . "Strong prejudices existed against it when first it was introduced into England, where the privation of it *now* would be one of the greatest calamities that could befall the country."

Arriving at the table, the children having respectfully waited until papa and mamma were seated, little James said (a short *) grace—namely, "Make us truly thankful, O God, for our daily bread; and devote us to thy service as long as we live, for the merits of Jesus Christ our Savior. Amen!" Mrs. Wyndham poured rich cream, fresh from the dairy, into her husband's strong coffee,† and a plenty of wholesome milk into the hot water for her children (the cows feeding in the *rice*-fields yielding the purest milk; and butter yellow

---

* John Wesley, the great Methodist Reformer, says, "Long prayers and slow singing is a sure sign of declension in religion."

† "HOW COFFEE CAME TO BE USED.—It is somewhat singular to trace the manner in which arose the use of the common beverage, coffee, without which few persons, in any half or wholly civilized country in the world, would seem hardly able to exist. At the time Columbus discovered America it had never been known or used. It only grew in Arabia and upper Ethiopia. The discovery of its use as a beverage is ascribed to the superior of a monastery in Arabia, who, desirous of preventing the monks from sleeping at their nocturnal services, made them drink the infusion of coffee, upon the report of some shepherds, who observed that their flocks were more lively after browsing on the fruit of that plant. Its reputation spread throughout the adjacent countries, and in about 200 years it reached Paris. A single plant brought there in 1714, became the parent stock of all the French coffee plantations in the West Indies. The extent of the consumption can now hardly be realized. The United States alone annually consume it at the cost of its landing of from fifteen to sixteeen millions of dollars. You may know the Arabia or Mocha, the best coffee, by its small bean of a dark yellow color. The Java and East Indian, the next in quality, are larger and of a paler yellow. The West Indian, and Rio, have a bluish or greenish-grey tint."

as gold, churned every morning), for she never ate anything herself until all of them were abundantly helped. Then conversation, or rather talking, commenced. James announced that the grey mare had just had a beautiful little colt, and would not dearest papa give it to him for his *own* self? Halcombe begged to let him take a ride to Mr. Gluvoer's plantation to see some nice little boys from New York (whose parents were on a visit to that gentleman, who usually spent his summers North.) Edward said he wanted to go out in the canoe with Nigger Sambo, who was to spend the morning catching fish; and William declared he was not at all afraid of a gun, and would not papa let him go out birding with the black man Robert, and bring home for supper, partridges and doves, and wild ducks and marsh-hens, and fat rice-birds; while Theodore implored that he might be allowed (as he could run a horse through the swamps, and could shoot at a mark) to accompany papa in his fox hunting and deer hunting excursions, where he was sure the hue and cry of the numberless dogs, would start all manner of game? Rebecca begged mamma to order a half-dozen little negro girls to help her work in the flower-garden; Portia said old Mom Bella (the hen huzzy) wanted a larger house for the five hundred young turkeys just hatched, to whom she had given a corn of black pepper to keep them from dying (which they do, by scores.) She had boiled several bushels of tiny sweet potatoes, to mix with the cracked corn for the chickens and Guinea fowls; and little Toney was catching minnow fish for the Muscovy and English ducks, and overgrown *geese* (who are the most sensible of conjugal lovers, choosing one wife and never deserting her during the whole mating season.)

Britannia begged mamma to buy her a great plenty of books, with pictures in them; but, in the meantime, she could send over and borrow some for her from old Mrs. Judge Heyward, who had a whole room full,—"for, mamma," says she, "I don't love to play with dolls, and I don't like to work in the garden, or count the chickens, turkeys, and goslings." Selina entreated to let her jump on horseback, and ride through the woods in search of chinquapins, whortleberries, pecans, hickory-nuts, and walnuts, and then return to set her traps for the red bird,* blue jay, mocking-bird, and

---

* "The Red bird (or Red Ibis,) is remarkable for its bright red color; the tips of the wing-quills are black. The young ones, at first covered with a blackish down, become cinerous, and, when ready to fly, whitish; in two years the red makes its appearance, and continues to increase in lustre with age. This species does not migrate, and lives in flocks in marshy spots in the vicinity of estuaries.

"In South Carolina there are also vast numbers of winged fowls, many of which are good for human use and subsistence. Besides eagles, falcons, cormorants, gulls, buzzards, hawks, herons, cranes, marsh-hens, jays, woodpeckers, there are wild turkeys, pigeons, blackbirds, woodcocks, little partridges, plovers, curlews, and turtle-doves, in great numbers; and also incredible numbers of wild geese, ducks, teal, snipes, and rice-birds.

"There has been found here, near rivers, a bird of amazing size, some think it the pelican. Under its beak, which is very long, it is furnished with a bag, which it contracts at pleasure, to answer the necessities or conveniences of life.

"We have three descriptions of eagles. The grey eagle is the largest, of great strength and high flight. He chiefly preys on fawns and other quadrupeds. The bald eagle is likewise

sparrows (for she was always successful in these sports, by attaching a long string to the john-jumper, and holding it while she hid herself behind an ambush, and watched the birds after baiting the trap with rough rice.) The old colored blacksmith would bore innumerable holes in two broad boards, a yard long, with a hot iron poker; and then, by ramming pieces of swamp *cane*, of suitable length, into the holes between the boards, contrive a very roomy, handsome cage, where Selina kept her birds tenderly nursed for a few days, and then the door was opened for them to fly off again to the woods to report their adventures to their mates, who were of course astonished that birds would be so silly as to venture their necks in a trap, when the Southern fields and the woods contained plentifully every temporality necessary to their dainty wants.

Little Musidora only begged to lie down in mamma's and papa's laps, and kiss them all the day; for the loving little creature must have had a presentiment of how soon she was to be a desolate orphan.

---

large, strong, and a very active bird, but an execrable tyrant. He supports his assumed dignity and grandeur by rapine and violence, extorting unreasonable tribute and subsidy from all the feathered nations. These odious instincts made Dr. Franklin opposed to this bird being our national emblem. The third species of eagle is the falcon, or fishing-hawk. This is a large bird, of high and rapid flight. His wings are very long and pointed, and he spreads a vast sail in proportion to the volume of his body. This princely bird subsists entirely on fish, which he takes himself, scorning to live and grow fat on the dear-earned labors of another. He also contributes liberally to the support of the bald eagle."

These reasonable enterprises of the children,* mamma and papa promised to grant as soon as all the lessons were recited, that they committed to memory the night before, around the long supper-table, after the edibles had all been removed.

The driver, old Mingo, now stepped in to let his master know, as was his usual custom, who was sick among the negroes on the plantation. First, Dinah had symptoms of the pleurisy, and Toney was threatened with the typhoid fever, and Jack must go off on horseback immediately for the doctor (as these diseases were too dangerous to be prescribed for by Mr. Wyndham, although all the planters acquire skill enough to manage the sicknesses of the negroes that are not usually fatal.)

"Tenah has also just given birth to three promising infants," continued old Mingo, "and I have sent the best nurse to take care of her and the babies for a month — and old Liddy has been ordered to send her

* "A child is a man in a small letter, yet the best copy of Adam before he tasted of Eve or the apple; and he is happy whose small practice in the world can only write his character. His soul is yet a white paper, unscribbled with observations of the world, wherewith at length it becomes a blurred note-book. He is purely happy, because he knows no evil, nor hath made means by sin to be acquainted with misery. He arrives not at the mischief of being wise, nor endures evils to come by foreseeing them. He kisses and loves all, and, when the smart of the rod is passed, smiles on his beater. The older he grows, he is a stair lower from God. He is the Christian's example, and the old man's relapse; the one imitates his pureness, and the other falls into his simplicity. Could he put off his body with his little coat, he had got eternity without a burden, and exchanged but one heaven for another."—Bishop Earle.

nice dinners every day from Mauser's own kitchen; for the old black accoucheur says, 'she will need constant nourishment with such a drag upon her as these three sucking babies.'" (The baby-clothes Mrs. Wyndham *had* made for Tenah sometime previously, expecting her to have *one* papoos,* must now be increased quickly for *three* unheralded new comers into this naughty world.)

By-the-by, there is no race on earth so prolific as the well-fed plantation negro; for this very same *Tenah* had *had* twins twice before,—indeed, had averaged a child every year for fifteen years;—the first being born when she was fifteen years of age. The planter's wife provides, and has all the baby-clothes, and, indeed, *all* the clothes that the negroes wear, individually and collectively, cut out and made up by trained black seamstresses under her own inspection.

These planters bought the greatest quantity of an *all-wool* cloth, called "*planes*," that was thicker than beaver-cloth, and a yard wide—it was white, or a deep mazarine-blue. *This* was the winter clothing of the whole plantation. The women wore white skirts of it, and blue bodices; and the men, white pants and blue coats, and red woollen caps. The women, also, were furnished with a fiery red kerchief or turban. These Planes then cost, when bought in large quantities, only one dollar a yard, and were particularly strong, and the *negroes* looked very tastefully dressed when they doffed their summer garments to put this warm clothing on. They are never called *slaves* in South Carolina. *That* is a Northern word for the

* Indian name for baby.

much-esteemed respectable servants of the Southern people, that is never applied to them at home.

Although it is reported that the Northern ladies arrogate to themselves all the enterprise and industry as housekeepers in these United States, they never saw a day in all their lives that could comprise all the responsibilities of a Southern planter's wife — as she has not only every principle of self-interest to urge her to be up and doing at sunrise; but from her very nursery she is taught that the meanest creature on God's earth is a master or mistress who neglects those that Providence has made utterly dependent on them. Her conscience, educated to this self-denying nobility of action, would feel as wounded by the neglect of her helpless children as by disregard for her hard working slaves. And this world cannot furnish more healthy unpharisaical sensibility than what God sees (for no one else is there to applaud or criticise), the planter's wife expend in the humble cabin of the sick or afflicted negro, on her plantation, night or day; for no storm prevents personal attention from house to house of a very ill servant, though they invariably have a nurse of their own color.

The author has repeatedly spent the whole night walking around the cabin of a dying, or dangerously ill negro, so as to be able to administer every dose of medicine herself, and report every change in the developments of the disease to the Doctor the next morning. This loss of rest was endured, not because the said negro was her own property, but because she lived in the same house with the owner of the slave, and had, from earliest youth, regarded it the most morally dignified of employments to wait on the poor and afflicted around her, whether they were red, white, or black; whether they were descendants of Shem, Ham, or Japheth; whether they were saints or sinners, bond or free — for the mind feels an elevating complacency in laboring for the destitute poor that the selfish man never dreams of — and the good-book says, "He that giveth to the rich shall surely come to want."

Let a Yankee lady fancy herself surrounded by a family of two hundred persons (as is often the case with a Southern planter's wife), all dependent, more or less, on herself. Every morning the sick-list is reported by the driver, and the responsible old doctress of the manor insures the mistress's having to attend to the weighing or measuring out of a score or two of doses of medicine, and to see the patients take it, and then be well attended to by the colored nurse, even when the illness does not entail sending a man on horseback several miles for the doctor, who invariably charges fifty cents for every mile he travels, besides one dollar a visit; and as Mr. Wyndham's physician lived eight miles off, he had to pay him five dollars for every visit. Then the innumerable accouchements — which, to be sure, are not so formidable as among the pale-faces, whose sufferings are engendered by sentimentality and too much luxury, but are unknown to the Indians or the negroes; for every plantation has a professor of obstetrics, in the person of a smart old crone of the feminine gender, whose age and experience have had a trial of twenty years; she being now, perhaps, fifty.

Then a schooner from Charleston at Mr. Wyndham's

door, bringing some two hundred blankets, groces of large needles, pounds of skeins of flax thread, brass thimbles, fiery red, white, and blue bandannas, or kerchiefs, for the women, who form them into most becoming turbans, by a coquettish tie around their heads, and then a thousand yards of white and blue stout all-wool plains, that is to be cut into coats and pants, skirts and bodices—small, smaller, smallest—to fit the dimensions of all the men, women, and children on the plantation; and all this sempstress work to be cut out (and personally delivered, to insure equal justice) and made under the eye of the mistress, who has trained some half-dozen or more negresses to the trade of cutting, fitting, and sewing.

I would candidly ask my Northern sister, who has so harshly condemned the ladies of the South, is this yearly enterprise of a planter's wife, with all the other daily etceteras, living a life of idleness? 'T is true, before she is a wife, or head of a plantation, the miss in her teens does no work in South Carolina, except in her flower-garden, in reading, or perfecting her education, and doing amateur fine needle-work; for she *always* has a maid of her own to attend to her chamber, to sew, and to dress her, etc.; so that a young lady's life there is one of great personal liberty, and all sorts of recreation. But the moment she becomes a planter's wife, her domestic talents grow by the square-yard every year; for by a quick transformation, she is changed from a laughing, thoughtless flirt, seeking only to make herself beautiful and admired, into a responsible, conscientious "sister of charity" to her husband's numerous dependants.

But to return to Mr. Wyndham's breakfast-table, and the happy children who had been promised by mamma and papa, that all their requests should be granted as soon as they had completed their daily routine of study — which mamma personally attended to when Mr. Wyndham did not have a private tutor.* Mingo, the driver, received all his orders for the day. Mr. Wyndham went to the store-room, (which is never in a planter's house or cellar, but always in a building across the yard,) to give out dinner to the cook — for *there* gentlemen think their wives so beautiful and delicate, that they never tax them with the exposure of hot sun and damp feet in their journey to the said store-room, nor to the gross inductiveness of mind necessary to concoct a recherche *coast* plantation dinner, where the inhabitants of the river † are almost always

* The author's brother, in Carolina, has just engaged a private tutor, and, with a relative and himself, contracts to pay him fifteen hundred dollars a year, allowing him to take a few more scholars than their own children.

† In the mouth of the rivers, and on the coasts, the shark, the guarr, and devil-fishes, are all found, but in no respect rendered useful. However, the sea-coast and rivers furnish a variety of fine fish for human use, both of the salt and fresh-water kinds. The angel fish, so called from their uncommon splendor; the sheep-head, so named from its having teeth like a sheep's; the cavalli, the mullet, the whiting, the plaice, and young bass, are all esteemed delicate food. Besides these, porgy, shad, trout, stingray, drum, cat, and black fish, are all used, and taken in abundance. The fresh-water rivers and ponds furnish stores of fish, all of which are excellent in their season. The sturgeon and rock fish, the fresh-water trout, the pike, the bream, the carp, and roach, are all fine fish. Near the sea-shore, vast quantities of oysters, crabs, shrimps, etc., may be taken, together with terrapin and turtle.

obliged to contribute their share in making an orthodox meal. After which necessary concomitant of each day's comforts, Mr. Wyndham's horse is brought to the door for him to ride to the several fields, to see how the cotton, corn, rice,* and cow-peas are growing; how the negroes carefully hoe the grass away; how the blacksmith has pleased his customers; and how the carpenters are progressing on the numerous improvements and repairs of the plantation; and then, if no company arrives to dine with him — which is not

* The production of rice in South Carolina, which is of such prodigious advantage, was owing to the following incident: "A brigantine from the island of Madagascar, in 1697, happened to put into that colony. They had a little seed-rice left, not exceeding a peck, or a quarter of a bushel, which the captain offered and gave to a gentleman by the name of Woodward. From part of this he had a very good crop, but was very ignorant for some years how to clean it. It was soon dispersed over the province, and, by frequent experiments and observations, they found out ways of producing and manufacturing it to so great perfection, that it is said to exceed any other rice in value. The writer of this hath seen the said Captain in Carolina, where he received a handsome gratuity from the gentlemen of that country in acknowledgment of the service he had done to that province."

"It is likewise reported that Mr. Du Bois, Treasurer of the East India Company, did send to that country a small bag of seed-rice some short time after, from whence it is reasonable enough to suppese there might come those two sorts of that commodity, the one called red rice in contradistinction to the white rice, from the redness of the inner husk or rind of this sort, though they both clear and become alike white. . . . It was generally planted in South Carolina about the year 1710 — the first planting, 1700." — *Historical Collections by B. R. Carroll.*

About two-thirds of the rice used in the United States is raised in South Carolina.

often the case — he takes his eldest sons, and runs his horse into the island forests, to hunt the deer for food —the mink and fox, because they steal poultry, and the wild cat, because it is a most ferocious, destructive enemy to the lambs. Not unfrequently, too, Mr. Wyndham kills an alligator some ten feet long; which feat can only be accomplished by setting the dogs on him, and firing down his throat when he opens his mouth to snap at them, as his body is encased in an armor of scales that a cannon-ball could scarce perforate, and his roar shakes the ground around him.

On this particular day that has been described, some half-dozen friends had dined with them; Mr. and Mrs. Judge Heyward; Dr. and Mrs. North (he was their family physician); and Mr. and Mrs. Halcombe (he was the pastor of the Euhaw Church.)

These guests, with their children, never left until nearly dark, when their carriages and horses conveyed them gaily off (for the horses are as hospitably entertained, together with the coachman and footman, as their masters.)

Retiring early to bed, after thanking God, in their closets, for his innumerable mercies, Mr. and Mrs. Wyndham were startled at midnight, to see a ghastly bare-boned hideous monster stalk up to the trundle-bed where the smallest of their children slept; and fiercely announcing that his name was Death, he struck five of them with his sharp scythe, having poisoned the point with scarlet-fever; and in four weeks, these beautiful little angels unfolded their wings, and flew up to the abode of their father's and mother's God; where their inestimable mother followed them in one year, leaving a husband, whom *she requested*, with unearthly disinterestedness, soon to supply her place, in that busy household, by another Mrs. Wyndham; her two sons, Edward and Halcombe, who were large boys, to be sent to college, at New York, and her two remaining daughters to be adopted by a noble Christian friend, who promised her, on her death-bed, that she would take them home with her, and be their mother as long as she lived; for she had no children of her own. After all these affectionate responsibilities had been arranged, Mrs. Wyndham, with a faith that appropriates the atonement of her Savior, as the key that opens heaven to all who knock at the gates of Paradise, bid her husband good-night, and then the angels hovering around her dying-bed, took her by the hand, and escorted her safely through the dark valley of the shadow of death, and she found herself in the presence of angels and archangels, who were singing hallelujah, the Lord God omnipotent reigneth; and Jesus Christ, sitting at the right hand of God, in a vesture dipped in blood, and welcoming her with extended hands, in which she recognized the print of the nails that fastened him to the cross. And then when the book of remembrance that had been kept by the Holy Spirit, of all her thoughts, words, and actions, during her pilgrimage on earth, was read out, before countless witnesses, she heard the plaudit, "Well done, good and faithful servant, enter thou into the joys of thy Lord; for I was hungry, and you gave me meat; I was thirsty, and you gave me drink; I was a stranger, and you took me in; naked, and you clothed me; sick, and in prison, and you ministered unto me." After this, she was clothed in a robe befitting the society of angels, and a glittering crown of victory, over the world, the flesh, and the Devil, was placed upon her radiant brow; and we now leave her enjoying heavenly beatitude.

"Oh, thou beautiful and unimaginable ether;
And ye multiplying masses of increased
And still-increasing lights; what are ye?
What is this blue wilderness of interminable
Air, where ye roll along, as I have seen
The leaves along the limpid stream of Eden?
Is your course measured for ye? or do ye
Sweep on in your unbounded revelry
Through an aërial universe of endless
Expansion, at which my soul aches to think,
Intoxicated with eternity.
Oh, God! Oh, Gods! or whatsoe'er ye are!
How beautiful ye are! How beautiful
Your works, or accident, or whatsoe'er
They be! Let me die, as atoms die,
(If that they die), or know ye in your might
And knowledge! My thoughts are not in this hour
Unworthy what I see, though my dust is.
Spirit, let me expire, or see them nearer."

BYRON.

CHAPTER VI.

"Oh Love! no habitant of earth thou art—
An unseen seraph, we believe in thee;
A faith whose martyrs are the broken heart;
But never yet hath seen, nor e'er shall see,
The naked eye, thy form as it should be;
The mind hath made thee as it peopled heaven,
Even with its own despairing phantasy,
And to a thought such shape and image given,
As haunts the unquench'd soul—parch'd—
Wearied—wrung—and riven."

BYRON.

IT is a conventional law in South Carolina, that a rich, respectable, refined lady, who becomes a *widow*, must grieve over her bereavement as long as she lives;* and even if she marries again, which would be a want of sentiment rarely exhibited (as her close, woe-begone-looking widow's cap, and black bombazine bonnet, dress, and cloak, and crape veil reaching to her feet, and avoidance of all recreations, are a panoply of woe †

* The author had three friends, who were sisters, and moving in the first society of South Carolina, and their husbands all died. They forthwith shut themselves up in their houses, in a transport of hopeless grief, and for twelve years have refused everything like consolation. Of course they are rich, or they could not afford to indulge in this luxury of grief.

† The most beautiful woman the author ever saw, became a widow at the age of twenty-seven. She was almost deranged

that even that laughing, irreverent, enterprising little rogue, Cupid, respects.) I repeat, even if she marries again, she secretly wears a miniature of her first husband, in a medallion suspended from a golden chain around her neck, so as to have his image nestle near her heart.*

Colonel Creesy says of the Catholic burying-grounds in New Orleans, on All Saints' day, that "the first of November is indeed a memorable day in New Orleans, and on that day, in 1834, I first witnessed a scene, which, for solemnity and pathetic effect on the finer feelings of the human heart, will never be surpassed. I was invited to accompany a family of friends to the Catholic burying-grounds, and was told that I would be deeply interested in the exhibitions and ceremonies of the day, and would see a vast concourse of people, citizens, and strangers, who annually attend to participate in, or look upon, the sacred rites — a custom never forgotten or neglected by the Creole population. I thought but little of my intended visit, or what I was to see or hear, but walked on, thinking and speaking

---

with grief for a considerable time, and afterwards consecrated herself to religion; and, during thirty-four years, she has never taken off her mourning weeds, or indulged in a recreation of any sort, except instructing her negroes.

* Another consecrated wife, there, who became a widow, and continued in this desolate condition some fifteen years, was finally induced to marry a most excellent man, because her pecuniary affairs were in a desperate condition. She frankly told him she could never entertain any feeling, save friendship, for any mortal man, and as he was willing to marry on these terms, she always wore a medallion of her first husband's image near her heart.

of other things, until we arrived at the first gate to the resting-place of the departed, when my astonishment was great indeed. Magnificent and costly tombs, vaults, and the humblest grave-stones, were adorned, dressed, and decorated; some most richly, with costly materials — silks, satins, muslins, and cloths. Beautiful and many-colored lamps were blazing in all directions and forms; lovely flowers in vases, pots, and jars; splendid bouquets and tasteful wreaths were entwined and interspersed in various forms and figures over all the quiet dead. No festive mirth was there — no gay and sprightly laugh was heard — no merry smile was seen — no prattling wit — no mirthful thought — no joyous sound had *place* in all that humbled assemblage. Oh! how heavenly, holy, how dear and sweet the melancholy sensation, to see, to know, that death had not obliterated from the living the memory of friends and kindred, though deeply buried 'low in the ground.' How pensively happy was I to see the silent tear of affection, still living, trickling down the cheeks of the young and old, while bending with clasped hands in pure devotion over the sad remains of long-lost loved ones: the child thus remembering its parents — the parents their children — the brother his sister — the sister her brother—the husband his wife—the wife her husband and partner of her joys, and sorrows, and hopes! And still more and more interesting, perhaps, to see the slaves sobbing and mourning over the graves of their masters and mistresses, many prostrated and overcome with sorrow; and nurses weeping over the children of their owners, who had died in their arms after months and years of attention, and kindness, and love; the memory retaining a warm place in their honest hearts, and calling forth, year after year, prayers and tears of affection and love. I have witnessed numerous instances of this divine feeling in the breasts of female slaves for the children of their masters intrusted to their care; I have seen them grieve when the name of a deceased child was mentioned, long, long after its father had ceased to drop a tear to its memory. That is the pure love from heaven — holy nature's love! Long may it live! We passed through cemetery after cemetery (for there are three ancient ones, on a line in the rear of Rampart street). All were dressed, beautifully adorned with festoons and fringes, and with all the charms of nature and art, in the richest manner, or most simply and neatly, as the means were had for one or the other. The light continued to burn the live-long night, and many of the devotees never left their places of mourning, where slept the mouldering and decayed remains of loved ones long gone, till the dawn of another day reminded them of worldly duties to the living.

"How hallowed, how soft-heartening, how sweet, how heavenly, is this most affecting custom! Until I then witnessed it, I was ignorant of the existence of such an impressive and endearing ceremony in any country. How consoling must be the thought on the bed of death, to know, that once at least each passing year some friend or relative will certainly visit, ornament, and drop a tear of fond and tender recollection on your grave! — remember your virtues; your faults forgiven, forgotten! How sweet, when we must die, to know there lives even *one* kind friend, who will bend in prayer over our earthly remains, and remember us kindly, at least once a year!

"I had a dearly-loved, a gallant son laid 'low in the ground,' in the bright bloom of youthful manhood, some months after my departure, perhaps forever. A year or more had elapsed, my heart still throbbing with grief for his premature exodus, when I received a letter from an angelic girl, who knew him; telling me, in the purity of her soul, that on her return from a summer-trip North, she had visited my poor boy's grave, and dropped a tear, with a wreath of flowers, on it, in the name of friendship for me and mine. This custom is a heartfelt, pure, and heavenly one, that does honor to the Creole population (of the South) of the Crescent city, and might be adopted by all religious denominations, without suspicion of bigotry or sectarianism, as evidence of living charity, love, friendship, and endearing recollection of deceased associates, too often too soon forgotten."

Col. J. R. Creecy says of the Choctaws of Mississippi in 1835:—"Travelling towards evening I saw a low, rude pen of round logs, and what looked something like sheep lying down around it. My curiosity was excited, and I left the trace, trail or road (as the reader may please) to examine into the matter; and when within ten feet of one corner of the pen I ascertained that the lumps, or what I thought sheep, were Indians doubled up on the ground, and covered entirely with their blankets. Within the pen were several little hillocks, or mounds of earth — two of them fresh, the others covered with grass. I spoke kindly and friendly several times, and wondering looked upon them, but could not, and did not, get any reply or notice of any description; when I left them, and continued my journey. I frequently described, and inquired the meaning of, the exhibition; and was only enabled to get for explanation, that within the enclosure or pen were buried those Choctaws who happened to die thereabouts, and that annually certain friends or relatives of the deceased made a pilgrimage to their places of sepulchre, and mourned their loss in that humble, lowly, and silent manner. There was something peculiarly melancholy and touching in the scene. No sound, no motion, was heard or seen for some time (and how long I knew not). All their hearts and souls and feelings were apparently given to the memory of departed friends and to the Great Spirit, the one mighty God of all creation. I have known no more beautiful and heavenly manifestation of affection, and reverence for loved ones departed, than this simple Choctaw devotion."

Mr. Schoolcraft, the Indian historian, says that "the Indian is always glad to die. Death is not a repulsive state to him; for his belief is, that it is a state of rewards, not punishments. He thinks that when released from the toils of this life, he shall immediately join those who have preceded him to the happy 'Hunting Grounds.'" . . . "An Indian once hated his rival (in the affections of a beautiful squaw, now dead), and took him prisoner, but did not kill him; for, said he, death would give his spirit a good chance to marry her when it gets out of this world."

"Why tell you me of moderation?
My grief is fine, full, perfect, that I taste,
And violenteth in a sense as strong
As that which causeth it: how can I moderate it?
If I could temporize with my affection,
Or brew it to a weak and colder palate,
The like allayment could I give my grief;
My love admits no qualifying dross;
No more my grief, in such a precious loss."

When a gentleman in South Carolina, in spite of the before-mentioned surroundings of hopeless funereal grief, and notwithstanding its being regarded as ungenteel in the South ever to recover from an orthodox affliction, still has moral courage enough to court a rich, young, beautiful *widow*, — which is usually done by poetical love-letters at first, not by personal visits, — she is so astounded at his temerity, that she replies by asking "What levity he ever saw in her, to embolden him to intrude thus lawlessly into her voluntary retirement from the world?" That such a Nænia should reply to him at all, is at once construed into encouragement; so he forthwith makes her a visit, carrying a splendid bouquet of flowers, to remind her of the beautiful that God so lavishly paints for our pleasurable enjoyment, and to persuade her that there are many bright episodes of happiness in store for her yet* — that he himself adores her — "that upon the

* "Hope, of all passions, most befriends us here;
Passions of prouder name befriend us less.
Joy has her tears, and transport has her death;
Hope, like a cordial, innocent though strong,
Man's heart at once inspirits and serenes;
Nor makes him pay his wisdom for his joys;

altar of her beauty he sacrifices his tears, his heart," etc., etc. All of which chivalrous sentimentality is of course very refreshing to her forlorn, long-imprisoned affection; for what natural woman on earth does not believe a man, when, on his knees, he swears that he is desperately in love with her?—not at all because she owns a large plantation, or uncounted shoneau;* but because of her deep devotion to the memory of her dear departed husband.

So this beautiful Southern widow determines to accept him, with the distinct understanding that friendship, not love, is the impulse that is to unite them together; for her heart lies buried in the grave of her

---

'Tis all our present state can safely bear;
Health to the frame, and vigor to the mind!
A joy attemper'd! a chastised delight!
Like the fair summer evening, mild and sweet;
'Tis man's full cup—his paradise below!"

YOUNG.

* *Shoneau*, a Chippewa word, which means *money*.

"Gold—oh, thou sweet king-killer, and dear divorce
'Twixt natural son and sire! thou bright defiler
Of Hymen's purest bed! thou valiant Mars!
Thou ever young, fresh, loved, and delicate wooer,
Whose blush doth thaw the consecrated snow
That lies on Dian's lips! thou visible god,
That solder'st close impossibilities,
And mak'st them kiss, and speak'st with every tongue
To every purpose!"

SHAKSPEARE.

"For this the foolish, over-careful fathers,
Have broke their sleep with thoughts, their brain with care,
Their bones with industry."

first love. And as men are seldom jealous of a dead rival, though women are, he assures her that "the attachments of mere mirth are but the shadows of that true friendship of which the sincere affections of the heart are the substance."

Now, then, our successful cavalier insists that if our Creator had *had a Quaker taste*, we should have mourned over a *drab-colored* universe—that even Solomon, in all his glory, was not arrayed so gorgeously as the flowers of the field; and that therefore *she* must doff that melancholy cap, and let her luxuriant chestnut hair resume its natural waving charm.

All his efforts, however, cannot induce her to part with that everlasting black bombazine dress, and black Italian crape collar, until the very day of the wedding; after which, her whole wardrobe is conscientiously selected in accordance with his taste; and the indulgence of elevated friendship makes her a devoted wife.

> "For friendship is no plant of hasty growth.
> Though planted in esteem's deep-fixed soil,
> The gradual culture of kind intercourse
> Must bring it to perfection."

But the *widower* of South Carolina is as far removed, in his developments of respect for the memory of his dead wife, from the lady described above, as the two poles are one from another; for he generally fixes his mind immediately on some romping little miss of sixteen, exactly the opposite of the partner who has just amiably made her exit; and this is particularly the case if she has left half a dozen orphans.

Step-mothers have been abused ever since the history of Job was written; and this is conceded by antiquarians to be the oldest book in the world. That this prejudice* arises from a superstition of remote ages, there can be no doubt, in this era of progress; for every day there are practical illustrations that no woman on earth, except the step-mother, is expected to love her enemies with all her heart, soul, mind, and strength. She is suddenly thrown into constant propinquity with persons who would have entirely preferred to bury their father deep in the ground than see him marry again. If his children are grown up, they insult and wound her sensitive spirit every day; they (behind their father's back) assume the rule of everything in the house; they make the servants traitors to her, and sneer at her among their friends and relatives; they never believe it possible that she can possess a single virtue, though, with angelic delicacy, she never reports their misconduct to their father, because she knows what a storm would be the consequence; for most men try to protect their wives from such Mohawk attacks.

If her husband's children are small, she will have to wait on them from morning till night — sew for them, think for them, nurse them in sickness, and educate them hourly, for time and eternity, with no hope that all her cares will meet appreciation except at the day of judgment; for in this world her every action towards these orphans is reprobated. She dare not treat them

* "Some prejudices are to the mind what the atmosphere is to the body; we cannot feel without the one, nor breathe without the other." — GREEVILLE.

as her own children; she dare not punish them, as she would her own, when they commit crime; she dare not teach them self-denial, without which every character is perfectly hateful; and if there is a furnace hotter than this crucible to a sensitive, high-mettled, and morally elevated woman, experience has not yet found it out. No class of women in the civilized world have more of the mind of Christ in their self-denying life than an educated, refined, Christian step-mother; and as sure as the sermon on the mount, preached by Jesus, is true, so surely will such step-mothers receive the plaudit from God, "Well done, good and faithful servant; enter thou into the joys of thy Lord."

But when a widower marries a dashing, merry little coquette of sixteen, God have mercy on the children of his former wife! for such a teenish step-mother can think only of her own happiness as a bride; and consequently, even if she is not harsh to the little orphans, she utterly neglects them; and their whole childhood is so lonely and sorrowful that no after years of meridian prosperity can blot it out of the memory, till the dying hour reveals that "whom the Lord loveth he chasteneth, and scourgeth every son [or daughter] whom he receiveth into heavenly abodes."

CHAPTER VII.

"When remedies are past, the griefs are ended
By seeing the worst where late our hope depended.
To mourn a mischief that is past and gone,
Is the next way to bring new mischiefs on,
What cannot be preserved, when Fortune takes,
Patience her injury a mockery makes,
The robb'd that smiles, steals something from the thief;
He robs himself, that spends a bootless grief."

SHAKSPEARE.

WE now find Mr. Wyndham, a rich, handsome widower, of thirty-six years of age; with an incumbrance of four children. His two sons, Edward and Halcombe, were large boys, one sixteen, and the other two years younger; and his two daughters numbered five and seven summers. Perhaps we should now describe him; as a widower is very much more plausible in the matrimonial market, than a young gentleman at his first nuptials.

He was six feet two inches in height; straight as a North American Indian; admirably proportioned, with just muscle enough to be neither wiry, lean, or unromantically fat. His joints turned in their sockets with the suppleness of childhood; so that in company, his long legs and arms fell into natural positions. (These extremities of a large body, generally keep unself-possessed beaux on the tenter-hooks of awkwardness; for their legs are so obtrusive, that they cannot contrive what to do with them, when seated in the drawing-room with fashionable ladies.) His head was large, and broad-fronted; with just enough of volume towards the back of it, to assure the phrenologist that *literature* and orthodox business was not his exclusive taste or recreation. His features were large and manly. His eye a hazel grey, sparkling with vivacity and still-abiding hope (though his excellent wife *was* dead.) His hair, and whiskers, and moustache, were scarce restrained from a non-committal curl, though black and glossy as the raven's wing. His countenance, in its habitual expression, was bold and frank (and though capable of intense rage at times), Mr. Wyndham's manners and appearance, were the embodiment of genial, rich humor, and unpharisaical human kindness. His bearing was most decidedly aristocratic, for noble blood flowed in his veins; and he now lived in a free country, won by the valor of his own sires; and was, moreover, lord of all he surveyed, even the blue firmament above him, for the common law entitles a man to the whole atmosphere overhead of his domain. Sir Walter Scott has exactly described him.

"On his bold visage, middle age
Had slightly press'd its signet sage,
Yet had not quench'd the open truth
And fiery vehemence of youth;
Forward and frolic glee was there,
The will to do, the soul to dare,
The sparkling glance, soon blown to fire,
Of hasty love, or headlong ire.
His limbs were cast in manly mould,
For hardy sports or contest bold,
And though in peaceful garb array'd,
And weaponless except his blade,

His stately mien as well implied
A high-born heart, a martial pride,
As if a baron's crest he wore,
And sheathed in armor trod the shore.
His ready speech flow'd fair and free,
In phrase of gentlest courtesy;
Yet seem'd that tone and gesture bland
Less used to sue, than to command."

Mr. Wyndham, as was before remarked, finding himself a deeply bereaved widower, had his measure sent to Charleston for the finest, most costly suit of black broadcloth, that was ever imported into the country; with orders that the coat and vest should be cut and padded after the newest and most approved fashion, to display his ample chest and graceful shoulders, to the greatest perfection (ladies would never have dreamed of padding a frock body, had the men not set the example in their coats and vests).* His *beaver* hat (for silk was not worn then), was to be of the richest material, and covered with the solemn badge of mourning; and his pantaloons were made to fit as if he had grown up in them, to reveal his splendidly formed legs, and ample calves; his foot was shod with the recherche

* We are told that in the days of Henry I., that Anselm, Archbishop of Canterbury, "not only conducted arbitrarily in the affairs of the church, but he troubled himself about the dress of the laity. He preached so furiously, and so successfully against long hair and curls, which he disapproved of, that the ladies cut off their locks in the church.

"He was not so successful in the attacks he made on the fashionable shoes of the gentlemen; for, notwithstanding his threatenings and exhortations, they continued to wear them so exorbitantly long, that they were obliged to support them by a chain from the end of the toe, fastened to the knee."

English shoe, and tastily buttoned mourning gaiter; while his magnificently fine linen, starched with white wax to glisten like satin; his diamond studs and sleeve buttons; his inimitably tied cravat, together with a large patent lever watch and ample chain; his black kid gloves, and black banded handkerchief, completed the widower's most becoming consecutive arrangement of dress, to attend the church services, shortly after the demise of his lamented wife. (Widowers always are strict about going to church, and even uniting in the praises of the sanctuary, though as husbands they never had sung a hymn before in the great congregation. This sensible attention to the outer man, that widowers always develop in their mourning habiliments, is eliminated, no doubt, from the deep respect they entertain for the memory of their dead wives, whose ghosts take great delight in seeing them thus clad in the *semblance* of woe.)

Every day the bereaved Mr. Wyndham's saddle horse was brought to the door for him to ride over to see the widow, Mrs. Judge Thomas Heyward. She was the most remarkable woman that ever lived in South Carolina. Her husband had been one of the signers of the Declaration of Independence, and she had been noted, during the Revolutionary war, for her daring and sneering arrogance, wit, and sarcasm to the British officers when they besieged the fort near Charleston; when Gen. William Moultrie,* in his enthusiasm and chivalrous valor, cried out, "Our castle's strength will laugh a siege to scorn; here let those traitor Tories and

* The author's sister married a nephew of this Gen. William Moultrie.

pompous Redcoats lie till famine and the ague eat them up." Fort Moultrie, near Charleston, was named after him. The first attack on Charleston, Gen. Moultrie successfully repulsed and routed the enemy, who, however, afterwards successfully rallied and took the city, but finally evacuated it, to the transporting joy of the jaded but zealous patriots.

"The spirit," says Mrs. Ellet, in her work on the Women of the Revolution, "exhibited by Mrs. Thomas Heyward of Charleston, South Carolina, is worthy of remembrance. A British order having been issued for a general illumination in honor of the victory of Guilford, it was remarked that the house occupied by Mrs. Heyward and her sister showed no light. An officer called to demand the reason of this disrespect to the order. In reply Mrs. Heyward asked how she could be expected to join in celebrating a victory claimed by the British army while her husband was a prisoner in St. Augustine? The answer was a peremptory command to illuminate. 'Not a single light,' said the lady, 'shall, with my consent, be placed in any window in the house.' To the threat that it should be destroyed before midnight, she answered with the same expression of resolute determination.

"When, on the anniversary of the battle of Charleston, another illumination was ordered in testimony of joy for that event, Mrs. Heyward again refused compliance. Her sister was lying in the last stage of a wasting disease. The indignation of the mob was vented in assaults upon the house with brickbats and other missiles; and in the midst of the clamor and shouting the invalid expired. The Town-Major afterwards expressed his regret for the indignities, and requested Mrs. Heyward's permission to repair the damages done to the house. She thanked him, but refused, on the ground that the authorities could not thus cause insults to be forgotten which they should not have permitted to be offered."

Mrs. Ellet says, "An American soldier flying from pursuit, sought the protection of Mrs. Richard Shubrick. The British who followed him, insisted, with threats, that he should be delivered into their hands. While the other ladies in the house were too much frightened to offer remonstrance, this young fragile creature withstood the enemy. With a delicacy of frame that bespoke feeble health, she possessed a spirit strong in the hour of trial; and her pale cheek could flush, and her eyes sparkle with scorn for the oppressor. She placed herself resolutely at the door of the apartment in which the fugitive had taken refuge, declaring her determination to defend it with her life. 'To men of honor,' she said, 'the chamber of a lady should be as sacred as a sanctuary.' The officer, struck with admiration at her intrepidity, immediately ordered his men to retire."

On another occasion, when a party of Tarleton's dragoons was plundering the house of one of her friends, a sergeant followed the overseer into the room where the ladies were assembled. The old negro man refused to tell him where the plate was hidden, and the soldier struck him with a sabre; whereupon Mrs. Shubrick, starting up, threw herself between them, and rebuked the ruffian for his barbarity. She bade him strike *her* if he gave another blow, for she would protect the aged servant. Her interposition saved him from further injury.

Another noble woman, named Rebecca Motte, will strikingly display the patriotism of South Carolina's daughters, who, up to the present day, are peculiar for their chivalric bearing and frankness of character. "Fort Motte, the scene of the occurrence (now to be related), stood on the south side of the Congaree river. The height commanded a beautiful view, several miles in extent, of sloping fields sprinkled with young pine, and green with broom-grass or the corn, or cotton crops; of sheltered valleys and wooded hills, with the dark pine ridge defined against the sky. The steep overlooks the swamp land through which the river flows; and that may be seen at a great distance, winding like a bright thread between the sombre forests. After the abandonment of Camden to the Americans, Lord Rawdon, anxious to maintain his posts, directed his first effort to relieve Fort Motte, at the time invested by Marion and Lee.* This fort, which commanded the river, was the principal dépôt of the convoys from Charleston to Camden and the upper districts. It was occupied by a garrison under the command of Captain M'Pherson, of one hundred and sixty-five men, having been increased by a small detachment of dragoons from Charleston, a few hours before the appearance of the Americans. The large new mansion-house belonging to Mrs. Motte, which had been selected for the establishment of the post, was surrounded by a deep trench,

* Ramsay's History of South Carolina. Moultrie's Memoirs. Lee's Memoirs of the War in the Southern Department, &c.

along the interior margin of which was raised a strong and lofty parapet. Opposite and northward, upon another hill, was an old farm-house, to which Mrs. Motte had removed when dismissed from her mansion. On this height Lieutenant-Colonel Lee had taken position with his force, while Marion occupied the eastern declivity of the ridge on which the fort stood; the valley running between the two hills permitting the Americans to approach it within four hundred yards.

"M'Pherson was unprovided with artillery, but hoped to be relieved by the arrival of Lord Rawdon to dislodge the assailants before they could push their preparations to maturity. He therefore replied to the summons to surrender — which came on the 20th of May, about a year after the victorious British had taken possession of Charleston — that he should hold out to the last moment in his power.

"The besiegers had carried on their approaches rapidly by relays of working parties, and aware of the advance of Rawdon, with all his force, had every motive for perseverence.

"In the night a courier arrived from General Greene to advise them of Rawdon's retreat from Camden, and urge redoubled activity; and General Marion persevered through the hours of darkness in pressing the completion of their works. The following night Lord Rawdon encamped on the highest ground in the country opposite Fort Motte, and the despairing garrison saw with joy the illumination of his fires, while the Americans were convinced that no time was to be lost.

"The large house in the centre of the encircling trench left but a few yards of ground within the British works uncovered; burning the mansion, therefore, must compel the surrender of the garrison. This expedient was reluctantly resolved upon by Marion and Lee, who, unwilling under any circumstances to destroy private property, felt the duty to be much more painful in the present case. It was the summer residence of the owner, whose deceased husband had been a firm friend to his country, and whose daughter (Mrs. Pinckney) was the wife of a gallant officer then a prisoner in the hands of the British.

"General Lee had made Mrs. Motte's dwelling his quarters at her pressing invitation, and with his officers had shared her liberal hospitality. Not satisfied with polite attention to the officers, while they were entertained at her luxurious table, she had attended with active benevolence to the sick and wounded, soothed the infirm with kind sympathy, and animated the desponding to hope. It was thus not without deep regret that the commanders determined on the sacrifice, and the lieutenant-colonel found himself compelled to inform Mrs. Motte of the unavoidable necessity of the destruction of her property.

"The smile with which the communication was received, gave instant relief to the embarrassed officer. Mrs. Motte not only assented, but declared that she was 'gratified with the opportunity of contributing to the good of her country, and should view the approaching scene with delight.' Shortly after, seeing by accident the bow and arrows which had been prepared to carry combustible matter, she sent for Lee, and presenting him with a bow and its apparatus which had been imported from India, requested his substitution of them as better adapted for the object than those provided.

"Everything was now prepared for the concluding scene. The lines were manned, and an additional force stationed at the battery to meet a desperate assault, if such should be made. The American entrenchments being within arrow-shot, M'Pherson was once more summoned, and again more confidently—for help was at hand—asserted his determination to resist to the last.

"The scorching rays of the noonday sun had prepared the shingle roof for the conflagration. The return of the flag was immediately followed by the shooting of the arrows, to which balls of blazing rosin and brimstone were attached. Simms tells us the bow was put into the hands of Nathan Savage, a private in Marion's brigade. The first struck, and set fire; also the second, and third, in different quarters of the roof. M'Pherson immediately ordered men to repair to the loft of the house, and check the flames by knocking off the shingles; but they were soon driven down by the fire of the six pounder, and no other effort to stop the burning being practicable, the commandant hung out the white flag and surrendered the garrison at discretion.

"If ever a situation in real life afforded a fit subject for poetry by filling the mind with a sense of moral grandeur—it was that of Mrs. Motte contemplating the spectacle of her home in flames, and rejoicing in the triumph secured to her countrymen—the benefit to her native land, by her surrender of her own interest to the public service." . . . "I have stood upon the spot and felt that it was indeed classic ground and consecrated by memories which should thrill the heart of every American. But the beauty of such memories would be marred by the least attempt at ornament; and the simple narrative of that memorable occurrence has more effect to stir the feelings, than could a tale artistically framed and glowing with the richest hues of imagination.

"After the captors had taken possession, M'Pherson and his officers accompanied them to Mrs. Motte's dwelling, where they sat down together to a sumptuous dinner. Again, in the softened picture, our heroine is the principal figure. She showed herself prepared, not only to give up her splendid mansion to insure victory to the American arms, but to do her part towards soothing the agitation of the conflict just ended. Her dignified, courteous, and affable deportment adorned the hospitality of her table; she did the honors with that unaffected politeness which wins esteem as well as admiration; and by her conversation, marked with ease, vivacity, and good sense, and the engaging kindness of her manners, endeavored to obliterate the recollection of the loss she had been called on to sustain, and at the same time to remove from the minds of the prisoners the sense of their misfortune."

To the effect of this grace and gentle kindness is doubtless due much of the generosity exercised by the victors towards those, who, according to strict rule, had no right to expect mercy. While at the table "it was whispered in Marion's ear that Colonel Lee's men were even then engaged in hanging certain of the Tory prisoners. Marion instantly hurried from the table, seized his sword, and, running with all haste, reached the place of execution in time to rescue one poor wretch from the gallows. Two were already beyond rescue or recovery. With drawn sword, and a degree of indignation in his countenance that spoke more than words, Marion threatened to kill the first man that made any further attempt in such diabolical proceedings." *

"Other incidents in the life of Mrs. Motte, illustrate the same rare energy and firmness of charactor she evinced on this occasion, with the same disinterested devotion to the American cause. When an attack upon Charleston was apprehended, and every man able to render service was summoned to aid in throwing up entrenchments for the defence of the city, Mrs. Motte, who had lost her husband at an early period of the war, and had no son to perform his duty to his country, despatched a messenger to her plantation, and ordered down to Charleston every male slave capable of work. Providing, at her own expense, with proper implements and a soldier's rations, she placed them at the disposal of the officer in command. The value of this unexpected aid was enhanced by the spirit which prompted the patriotic offer.

"At different times it was her lot to encounter the presence of the enemy. Surprised by the British in one of her country residences, on the Santee, her son-in-law, General Pinckney, who happened to be with her at the time, barely escaped capture by taking refuge in the swamps. It was to avoid such annoyances that she removed to 'Buck Head,' afterwards called Fort Motte, the neighborhood of which, in time, became the scene of active operations.

---

* Simms' Life of Marion.

"When the British took possession of Charleston, the house in which she resided — still one of the finest in the city — was selected as the head-quarters of Colonels Tarleton and Balfour. From this abode she determined not to be driven, and presided daily at the head of her own table, with a company of thirty British officers. The duties forced upon her were discharged with dignity and grace, while she always replied with becoming spirit to the discourteous taunts frequently uttered in her presence against her 'rebel countrymen.' In many scenes of danger and disaster was her fortitude put to the test; yet, through all, this noble-spirited woman regarded not her own advantage, hesitating at no sacrifice of her convenience or interest to promote the general good.

"One portion of her history, illustrating her singular energy, resolution, and strength of principle, should be recorded. During the struggle, her husband had become deeply involved by securities undertaken for his friends. The distracted state of the country—the pursuits of business being for a long time suspended—plunged many in embarrassment; and, after the termination of the war, it was found impossible to satisfy these claims. The widow, however, considered the honor of her deceased husband involved in the responsibilities he had assumed. She determined to devote the remainder of her life to the honorable task of paying the debts. Her friends and connexions, whose acquaintance with her affairs gave weight to their judgment, warned her of the apparent hopelessness of such an effort. But, steadfast in the principles that governed all her conduct, she persevered; induced a friend to purchase for her, on credit, a valuable body of rice land, then an uncleaned swamp, on the Santee, built houses for the negroes, who constituted nearly all her available property — even that being encumbered with claims — and took up her own abode on the new plantation. Living in an humble dwelling, and relinquishing many of her habitual comforts, she devoted herself with such zeal, untiring industry, and indomitable resolution to the attainment of her object, that her success triumphed over every difficulty, and exceeded the expectations of all who had discouraged her. She not only paid her husband's debts to the full, but secured for her children and descendants a handsome unencumbered estate. Such an example of perseverance under adverse circumstances, for the accomplishment of a high and noble purpose, exhibits in yet brighter colors the heroism that shone in her country's days of peril."

Numberless such heroines of South Carolina, during the wars with Great Britain, could be described; but this one has been selected as a daguerreotype of the spirit of those times; and should the occasion of a civil war (now so lowering in the United States) again occur, the daughters of the South will develop the same chivalrous love of justice and nobility of purpose.

We must now return (after this long historical parenthesis) to the bereaved widower Wyndham, whom we left just about mounting his horse to ride over to Mrs. Heyward's, who had been the bosom friend of his departed wife, and therefore extended to the mourner all her sympathies. United with a masculine intellect, daring resolution and enterprise, that gave her the sobriquet of "Queen Elizabeth" in South Carolina, she still possessed sensibilities so acute that she wept passionate tears of sympathy with the children of sorrow at all times. She was perhaps fifteen or twenty years older than Mr. Wyndham; but her blazing eye, her beautiful *abandon* of manner when excited on any subject, her princely generosity, her brilliant wit and scathing sarcasm, and her boundless conversational power, proclaimed it impossible for her spirit ever to grow old. It was whispered around that she had always been an enthusiastic admirer of such a splendid specimen of manhood as Mr. Wyndham was acknowledged by all the ladies to be; but whether her marked receptions every day with the widower now meant any tender sentiment, it was impossible to divine. It can scarcely be supposed that *he*, though entertaining such a happy, wholesome, sensible estimate of his Adonis-like attractions, ever aspired to the hand of this eagle-eyed Juno; for Southern gentlemen never repeat appropriatingly those beautiful lines:

"There are some that love the unchangeable dye
And passionless depths of a calm blue eye;
Who worship a brow that is ever serene,
Like the lifeless sky of a painted scene.
Such eyes are too senseless, too patient, too true,
I like not their sickly inanimate hue;
But give me the eye with the soul in its rays;
The brow that can frown, and the eye that can blaze;
A smile from that brow is ever the lightest,
As a flash from a dark cloud is ever the brightest."

Women who are advancing in life are much easier fascinated with a commanding, dignified, muscular physique in a man, than a young girl, who will become distractedly in love with a pale, sickly, gloomy, intellectual face, that indicates to their romance a hero of moral sublimity; when, perhaps, after she has married him, her indignant, sorrowful, disappointed mother, prays —

"Heaven put in every honest hand a whip,
To lash the scoundrel naked through the world."

The old family servants, who keep up a sleepless vigilance in all the courtships of their owners, often declared, "Dat ole Miss Haywood dead gone in lub wid we dear Mausser Jeems, and him could marry um in one minit. Noma say he too skeary ob dem ober fire-blaze, smate ouman."

A month after the death of his wife, Mr. Wyndham began to prepare his two sons for college; for their high-souled mother, who used to devote much of her time to their moral, religious, and mental training, and their musical powers, and every other refining accomplishment, was no longer there to educate them; and his two little daughters he had already delivered to the friend selected by his dying wife, to rear them as her own children.

So he called up Harriet and Bella, the two most highly educated servants in the sempstresses' art (these sewing-women are taught this useful art for several years, before they are competent to do the finest kind of work), and ordered them to prepare Edward and Halcombe everything necessary to a genteel appearance for a whole year, as he intended taking them immediately to Rugbyanna, near Charleston, where a learned pedagogue from Ireland had established himself to keep an academy for boys.

These two admirable servants had dandled Edward and Halcombe on their knees in infancy, with affectionate kindness, and now that their mother was buried deep in the ground, they felt responsible for the happiness and comfort of the youths (a negro never thinks about his moral well-being); and therefore set about preparing them to leave home, with patronizing anxiety. They not only made dozens of the most beautiful linen shirts, and every other garment necessary to an affluent wardrobe, but they threw into one corner of the trunk, pins, needles, thread and buttons, of all kinds; for said they, "Me leetle mausser will hab to soe dem own shirt button on, when us is no dere fur to do it fur dem." After packing two trunks full of clothes for each of them, they sewed up bags of hempen cloth, to be filled with dried chinquapins, and pecans, and benne, and ground-nuts, and walnuts, for them to take with them, as all children delight in nuts; besides, at school, such temporalities, when distributed, make the scholars friends. "Every one is a friend to him that giveth gifts." They also promised to send them a large fruit-cake, whenever any of the neighbors were going to visit Charleston; and Master Edward, who could write so beautifully, must send them a letter every now and then, to let them know what sort of a schoolmaster they had; whether he was very severe with them, and whether his wife was a cross old gumma, or a kind landlady, whether the boys quarrelled with them, &c. &c. &c. All of which promises these motherless boys kept most faithfully, by writing once a month to their father's kind black housekeepers.

Old Jehu, the accomplished coachman, now drove up with his prancing horses to the door, dressed in the usual grey livery, turned up with black velvet, and a mourning band on his hat, out of respect for his dead mistress (house-servants frequently dress in black, when the master or mistress dies.) His horses had been curried and rubbed with oiled flannel, so that their sleek, well-fed bodies, and spirited bearing, were the pride of the doting Jehu. The trunks and etceteras had been carefully stowed away in a carryall, that was to follow the handsome coach, and four horses were led by an out-rider, to be changed every twenty miles; for Charleston was a hundred miles from Mr. Wyndham's plantation home.

Arriving at their journey's end without let or hindrance, Mr. Wyndham and his boys were ushered into a large one-story building, perfectly enveloped with forest trees and shrubbery; and after a few moments, the proprietor made his appearance. His name was M'Elroy, and he was born in Ireland. He was short and stout, had a very fair complexion and blue eyes, whose predominant expression was passionate frankness; and his hair was as white as snow. He was generous in all his impulses, and, as a Christian, always trying to do good; but his ungovernable temper was a continual stumbling-block to all around him. His wife was a close-fisted, angular, old Scotch woman; and was, moreover, such a scold, that all the children (her own not excepted) regarded her with the respectful awe that they would extend to a Bengal tiger. All the preliminaries being arranged for Mr. Wyndham's two sons to sojourn with this learned pedagogue one year, dinner was announced, and in came the schoolmaster's three daughters, who were overpoweringly beautiful. The eldest, Matilda, was perhaps sixteen, and her innumerable auburn ringlets, her blushing transparent magnificent complexion, her dark hazel eye, her perfect features, and recherche little hand and foot, her fascinating naivete of manners, just budding into womanhood, quivered so many unaccountable emotions in Mr. Wyndham's heart, that the morning's dawn still found him sentimentalizing on the charming little woodland girl.

"Wreathed in its dark brown rings, her hair
Half hid Matilda's forehead fair,
Half hid and half reveal'd to view,
Her full dark eye of hazel hue.
The rose, with faint and feeble streak,
So slightly tinged the maiden's cheek,
That you had said her hue was pale;
But if she faced the summer's gale,
Or spoke, or sung, or quicker moved,
Or heard the praise of those she loved,
Or when of interest was express'd
Aught that waked feeling in her breast,
The mantling blood in ready play
Rivall'd the blush of rising day.
There was a soft, a pensive grace,
A cast of thought upon her face
That suited well the forehead high,
The eyelash dark, and downcast eye.
In hours of sport, that mood gave way
To Fancy's light and frolic play;
And when the dance, or tale, or song,
In harmless mirth sped time along,
Full oft her doting sire would call
His Maud the merriest of them all."

Poor Mr. Wyndham was caught in a cul-de-sac, and it was a bootless task to remember how brief a period had elapsed since his wife had been laid in the grave. He was compelled, the more he examined his heart, to confess that it was convalescing from its grief of the exodus to the other world, of the dignified mother of his children.

"All love may be expell'd by other love,
As poisons are by poisons."

Certain it is, however, that Mr. Wyndham lingered around that neighborhood for four mortal weeks, and as he played most sweetly on the guitar and flute, and little Miss M'Elroy did not know that his wife was not yet cold in her grave, he managed his own handsomeness so adroitly, that, at the end of a month, he had inflicted on her ruby pouting lips any number of the most romantic kisses, and on her hand the diamond engagement-ring — and all this in spite of her having an old bachelor millionaire beau, whose *shoneau* had been the blissful dream, day and night, of her money-adoring papa and mamma.

"The poets judged like the philosophers when they feigned love to be blind; how often do we see in a woman what our judgment and taste approve, and yet feel nothing toward her; how often what they both condemn, and yet feel a great deal!"

Old Mr. M'Elroy remarked to his wife —

"He says he loves my daughter.
I think so too; for never gazed the moon
Upon the water, as he'll stand and read,
As 'twere, my daughter's eyes; and, to be plain,
I think there is not half a kiss to choose
Who loves the other best."

Hume says, in his Essays, "That there is nothing in itself beautiful or deformed, desirable or hateful; but these attributes arise from the peculiar constitution and fabric of human sentiment and affection."

The Countess of Landsfeld remarks, in her Lecture on Beautiful Women, "Canova was obliged to have sixty different women sit for his Venus, and how shall we dare point to any one woman and say she is beautiful? When Zeuxis drew his famous picture of Helen, he modelled his portrait from the separate charms of five different virgins."

"But though there is this difficulty in settling upon a perfect standard of female beauty, there can be no doubt about its power over the customs and institutions of mankind." "The beauty of woman has settled and unsettled the affairs of empires and the fate of republics, when diplomacy and the sword have proved futile." "Certainly," observes Lucian, "more women have obtained honor for their beauty than all other virtues besides;" and Tasso has said, that "beauty and grace are the power and arms of a woman;" while Ariosto declares, that "after every other gift of arms had been exhausted on man, there remained for woman only beauty — the most victorious of the whole."

"There is a great and terrible testimony of the power of female beauty in the history which Homer gives us of Helen: when she shows herself on the ramparts of Troy, even the aged Priam forgets his miseries and the wrongs of his people in rapture at her charms."

"And afterwards when Menelaus came, armed with rage and fury to revenge himself on the lovely but guilty cause of so much bloodshed, his weapon fell in her presence, and his arm grew nerveless."

> "Fair tresses man's imperial race ensnare,
> And beauty draws us by a single hair."

"But where are we to detect this especial source of power? Often, forsooth, in a dimple, sometimes beneath the shade of an eyelid, or perhaps among the tresses of a little fantastic curl!"

> "For what admir'st thou? What transports thee so?
> An outside? Fair, no doubt, and worthy well
> Thy cherishing, thy honoring, and thy love—
> Not thy subjection."

> "But did not Adam the very first man
> The very first woman obey?
> And we'll manage it so that the very last man
> Shall the very last woman obey."

No gentleman, except an old widower, could sympathize in the parting scene between the little teenish beauty and her adorer, who was twenty years her senior.

Old Jehu, the coachman, had so many times harnessed up his horses to return home to Palmetto Grove, and then had the order countermanded, that it was not long before he guessed what was the cause of his master's capriciousness, and felt offended that his blessed old mistress, just laid in her grave, should be so soon forgotten. (All old family negroes feel this very much, and rarely, if ever, become reconciled to a second marriage if there are orphan children. Indeed, in the South nothing is more potent in a child's mind than the prejudice its black nurse instils against a step-mother.)

Business on the plantation, however, had all been neglected for a whole month, or at least the inductive part of it; so now Mr. Wyndham must tear his passionate heart away, saying to himself —

"I leave myself, my friends, and all, for love.
Thou, thou hast metamorphosed me;
Made me neglect my studies, lose my time,
War with good counsel, set the world at nought;
Made wit with musing weak; heart-sick with thought."

Old Mr. and Mrs. M'Elroy were in ecstasies; for they had not been able to force their daughter to marry the ugly, deformed old millionaire that had sued for her hand, some time previous to the meeting with the handsome widower, Wyndham. Besides old Quackenbush (for that was his jaw-breaking name) could not boast of aristocratic blood or societarian refinement of manners, such as Wyndham possessed; so that they felt anxious to marry their daughter to her new, rich, aristocratic lover on the spot, rather than trust the vicissitudes, if not the constancy, of the twain, to be now separated several months by a hundred miles. Respect to the friends of his dead wife compelled a postponement of the marriage at least six months; though her parents could not comprehend the common sense or delicacy of the delay; for, said they —

"The course of true love never did run smooth;
But, either it was different in blood,
Or else misgraffed in respect of years,
Or else it stood upon the choice of friends,

Or, if there was a sympathy in choice,
War, death, or sickness, did lay siege to it:
Making it momentary as a sound,
Swift as a shadow, short as any dream,
Brief as the lightning in the collied night,
That (in a spleen) unfolds both heaven and earth;
And ere a man hath power to say, Behold!
The jaws of darkness do devour it up:
So quick bright things come to confusion."

Old Jehu, the coachman, drove to the door, and the out-riders and the whole cavalcade had been waiting an hour for the last parting word between the lovers; finally, one of the little sisters heard Wyndham say to Matilda:—

"Doubt thou the stars are fire;
Doubt that the sun doth move,
Doubt truth to be a liar;
But never doubt I love."

The disconsolate lover now rushed into the carriage, having provided himself with that excruciating book, "The Sorrows of Werter," to read on his homeward journey; where, arriving safe, if not sound, all the negroes hurried from the fields to greet him, and to wonder at his long stay, which of course he dared not explain.

Old Jehu, the coachman, having the horses rubbed down carefully, and walked around the stable-yard for an hour before giving them food or water, lest they should founder after so long a tramp, now repaired to the servants' hall to communicate his suspicions about his master beginning to "cote dem gal."

"Wudder dat you da' talk bout, Jehu," said old

Liddy; "I sway if me mausser Jeems, wid fou' leetil chillun, is a gwining fur to marry such a good-for-nuttin, poo', nung ting, to mine dis yere plantation; us old missus will cum frum de grabeyad fur to skear dem ebery night. Fur de Laud sake, you no tell me dis yarn fur trute? enty him got ebery ting he want fur, wuffer he no go cotein Miss Heywood, ef he mus hab a wife rite off. Him is a settle oman, berry handsum, berry rich; got tree hundud nigger; lib in awful big house; and den de chamber-maid, and de dining-room sarvants, long time dun tell me dat dere missus dead in lub wid me mausser Jeems. I gwine right into de house fur to ax my own blessed mausser if dis lie you bin da tell me am de trute."

Suiting the action to the thought, old Liddy, who had been the maid of the departed wife, and therefore was very jealous of her memory, walked into the parlor, where Mr. Wyndham was pensively meditating on the absent dimples, and, with motherly confidence, said:

"Mausser Jeems, dat debil ob a Jehu bin da tell me dat you is cotein vun nung chile. Us knowed dis lie cum frum sum ole maid Buckra, dat bin da poke fun at dat tarnal fool ob a coachman."

"Do not fret yourself, my faithful old Liddy," said Mr. Wyndham, "as you know I cannot marry any one for some time to come, though my late thoughtful wife earnestly desired, on her death-bed, that I should not long live single."

"Ki, mausser, enty you know wuffer us poo' missus baig'd you git marry fur? Him tink you monstracious fond ob dem nung gal, an' nomisay you dum blong to me Ba'tise church, de debil gwine tem'tation you 'bout libbin in dis yere big house all by you'self. I watch you all de time, maus' Jeems, fur de chillun mus hab a good mammy, not dem wile crazy gal."

Mrs. Wyndham, 'tis true, had requested her husband to marry soon after her demise; for her mind was naturally so much graver, and her religion so much deeper than his, that her love for him, as she grew older, partook of the anxious care of a mother; and knowing his gaiety of heart and gregariousness, she was well assured that he could neither be happy or comfortable without "wife, children, and friends," always about him.

Most dying requests are held sacred by superstitious or loving friends, but such an angelic evidence of self-abnegation as this last exhortation to marry again, by an expiring wife, was so binding on the conscience of Mr. Wyndham, that he set about preparing the plantation anew, for the in-coming of the beautiful, affianced Matilda.

"Marriage is a desperate thing: the frogs in Æsop were extremely wise;—they had a great mind to some water, but they would not leap into a well because they did not know how to get out again."

CHAPTER VIII.

"A HISTORY of the beginning of the reign of gallantry," says the Countess of Lansfeldt, "would carry us back to the creation of the world; for about the first thing that man began to do after he was created was to make love to woman.

"The Jewish and Christian accounts seem to agree in this matter; and as for the heathen record, the life of Jupiter himself was little else than a history of his gallantry. In the service of the fair sex, he was converted into a satyr, a shepherd, a bull, a swan, and a golden shower; and so entirely devoted to the cause of love was he, that his wife, Juno, mockingly called him Cupid's whirligig.

"Alas! this old heathen divinity has never been wanting for millions of disciples, even among the high and noble of Christian lands. The proudest heroes, and the mightiest kings have been just about as pliant 'whirligigs' to Cupid as was the great thunderer of Olympus; and history teaches that the above observation is confirmed by the lives of some of the gravest philosophers and bravest generals of antiquity. If we look to an Alcibiades, a Demosthenes, a Cæsar, or an Alexander, we find that their gallantries form no inconsiderable portion of their histories.

"Gallantry arose particularly with the institution of chivalry, and formed, we may say, the soul of the most noble and daring exploits of chivalry during its brilliant career. Indeed, the eighth and ninth virtues of chivalry which every knight had to swear to obey, were to 'Uphold the maiden's right,' and 'Not see the widow wronged.'

"There was nò discussion then about 'Woman's Rights,' or 'Woman's Influence'—woman had whatever her soul desired, and her will was the watchword for battle or for peace. Love was as marked a feature in the chivalric character as valor; and he who understood how to break a lance, and did not understand how to win a lady, was held to be but half a man. He fought to gain her smiles—he lived to be worthy of her love. Gower, who wrote in the days of Edward III., has thus summed up the chivalric devotion to woman—

> What thing she bid me do, I do,
> And where she bid me go, I go;
> And when she likes to call, I come,
> I serve, I bow, I look, I loute,
> My eye it followeth her about.'"

This long extract, on the subtleness of chivalry and love, has been introduced to apologize for poor widower Wyndham, who, being a descendant of the lordly cavaliers of England, was, of course, always under subjection to beauty.

As has been before remarked, although the ladies of South Carolina, in their romantic adhesiveness of affection, seem to sympathize with those widows who threw their bodies on the funeral pile with their dead husbands, to be consumed in the same flame, (which is certainly not an unnatural instinct in the *consecrated wife*,) the *gentlemen* are by no means so transcendental, for *they* know not the luxury of grief, and, therefore, scout the idea of remaining single a moment longer than conventional propriety requires from the *widower*, which is, perhaps, twelve months; while this same conventional sentimentality exacts a lifetime of utter isolation of heart from the bereaved *widow* of South Carolina.

Mr. Wyndham was so abstracted, thinking only of those dimples, and those auburn ringlets, and that merry, wild, romping laugh of the wood-nymph, at Rugbyanna, that old Mingo, the driver, did not know what to make of his continued pensiveness; but, believing it was caused by the death of his inimitable wife, he very delicately refrained from telling him any of the bad news about the plantation. So that one day he was surprised by a hurried messenger, calling on him to repair immediately to his master, who said, "Well, Mingo, did you have the boat-house repaired; you remember I told you, before leaving home, that the under-pinning was entirely rotten, and the first storm would blow it down and crush my whole fleet of boats."

"Yes, Mausser Jeems, I 'member; but den I gone forgit, 'till wun heaby gust bin dar cummin up; and him bin so suddant, dat de win' blow de house rite down, and smash up ebery one ob you boat."

"Well really, Mingo, this is such a monstrous disobedience of my most positive orders, that I would punish you on the spot were you not so much older than I am, and did I not know that your love for me from my childhood would induce you sooner to cut off your right arm than willingly do me an injury; but why *don't* you try to remember? this is the only fault I find with you."

"Mausser, I cry all night, when de boat-house fall down, but seberal gentleman roun' de plantation, hab got boat fur to sell, and I beg you to buy dat big one at Mr. Glubbers', name '*Never Lend*.'"

While they were mourning over the destruction of the boats, in rushed Sambo, crying out, "Mausser! one ob you oxen dead, sir; turrer one dead too, sir; us 'fraid to tell you bote at a time, nomissay you couldant bore it."

Old Lucy, the nurse and doctress of the plantation, now walked in to announce that Toney, the carpenter, had died last night, of inflammation of the stomach; and as his good wife, Bina, was born in Africa, and could not speak our language plain, and was very simple-minded, Toney's relations, who knew he was quite rich, were pretending that he had left all his property to them.

"Go instantly, Mingo," said Mr. Wyndham, "and see that Bina is not disturbed by Toney's covetous relations until after the funeral. I will then myself attend to her getting half of her husband's property, as he left no children. After which, order Ben and the other carpenters to make a neat pine coffin, and I will send immediately to Coosahatchie for black cloth to cover it. All the negroes must be allowed to come out of the fields at once, to prepare for the funeral to-night; for you know they always club together to cook a great feast, to be eaten as soon as they have buried their fellow-servant deep in the ground."

The negroes invariably have their burials at night.

As soon as a man or woman dies, their fellow-servants send off couriers to the adjoining plantations, to invite their friends to the funeral. About dark they begin to assemble, and their preacher exhorts, and sings, and prays over the body of the dead man until midnight; when six black fellows take hold of the coffin, and proceed slowly to the negro grave-yard (one of which is on every plantation, and sacredly guarded from outside pressure), accompanied by innumerable torch-bearers.

Arriving at the grave, which has been previously dug, they lower the coffin with ropes, and sing the most mournful dirges while the men with their spades are filling the grave. They then, all in order, form a procession, and return, singing in chorus, to the house of mourning; where a sumptuous hot supper awaits their now hungry stomachs, and where they gorge like turtles for an hour, on the principle that eating a great deal will mollify any grief that flesh is heir to—it certainly is a catholicon for theirs. Indeed, it is perfectly true, that if, instead of blowing out his brains, a hopeless swain will only take to eating fat turkeys and old sugar-cured ham, the newspapers will soon cease their constant details of horrible suicides.

"In the South," the doctors say, "there is not a man or woman who has a sound liver." Anatomists and divines tell us that the affections reside in the heart. But does not experience prove that grief and enthusiastic, romantic love, always bring on the most intense pain in the right side, where the *liver*, not the *heart*, is located?

Toney's proud relatives, not knowing that our most

learned, talented, and great men almost invariably selected a silly, unappreciating wife,* wondered how he, being the smartest black carpenter for fifty miles round, should have married poor little Bina, whom they all despised; for, coming direct from Africa, she had none of the good looks of the American-born negro; and, moreover, had marks in her face that looked as though they had been burnt in by some process unknown in this country. Native Africans often have all their bodies striped with a dyeing material, peculiar to their heathen superstitions, the marks of which they carry to their graves.†

---

* Macaulay tells us that the great giant of English literature, Dr. Samuel Johnson, fell in love with and married a widow [Porter], whose children were as old as himself. "The lady was a short, fat, coarse woman, painted half an inch thick, dressed in gaudy colors, and fond of exhibiting provincial airs and graces of the most affected description. To Johnson, however, whose passions were strong, and whose eyesight was too weak to distinguish ceruse from natural bloom, and who had seldom or never been in the room with a woman of real fashion, his Titty, as he called her, was the most beautiful, graceful, and accomplished of her sex." . . . "That his admiration was unfeigned, cannot be doubted; for she was as poor as himself." "The marriage proved a happy one, and the lover continued to be under the illusions of the wedding-day till the lady died, in her sixty-fourth year. On her monument he placed an inscription extolling the charms of her person and manners; and when, long after her decease, he had occasion to mention her, he exclaimed, with a tenderness half ludicrous, half pathetic, 'Pretty creature!'"

† A stranger, on an intensely hot day, was driving by a plantation in South Carolina, when his attention was attracted to a man busily working with his hoe, who had stripped himself of all clothing save his pants. There was, on his back, a black

The next morning after the funeral Mr. Wyndham again called up old Mingo, to inquire after a splendid colt he was raising — as he had not seen it since he returned home.

"My mausser, forgib you poe ole nigger!" said Mingo, "for turrer night us did'nt member to lock him up in de stable, and storm cum up suddant, and de lightnin strike de colt dead on de spot in de rice-field."

"Begone out of my sight!" said his master. "Your head is just like a sieve: every thing that is put in on *one* side shakes out of the *other*. I only wish those New-England Yankees, that profess to love you so much, had a hundred servants to manage, as stupid and forgetful of orders as mine are — they would beyond a doubt beat their brains out. — Begone!"

"Mausser, please, mausser Jeemes, don't git mad wid you ole nigger. Me's got tree nice leetle colt, an us pick out one ready to gib me mausser, jest like him own, wa gone git kill."

"You know I would not take your colt, if you was to beg me on your knees; so be off, you cunning old fox, and order my saddle horse to the door. I will ride over to see my good friend, Mrs. Heyward."

White Hall, the name of Mrs. Heyward's palatial

mark half an inch wide, that extended the whole length of the spine, and was then crossed in stripes like ribs, covering the whole back. He was so astonished that he stopped his carriage to inquire what it meant; and was told that "his parents had marked him in this way in Africa." The skin must have been punctured, and then some very black substance introduced into the pores.

mansion, was built by Judge Heyward, on an arm of the Broad river. It stood about fifty yards from the water's edge, and commanded a splendid view of the river and its surrounding woodlands and forests of every hue known to the ever-enduring spring of the sunny South. The numerous boats passing and re-passing up and down was pleasantly exciting; for the black oarsmen sing songs merrily to the cadence of the oars, and then all unite in an amen chorus. This wild music on the water at night is enchanting; for the broad dome of the skies seems to reverberate the sound.

The shrubbery in the court-yard leading from the river to the house consisted of flowers of every magnificence of hue; besides trees, including the palmetto, the myrtle, the cedar, the olive, the pomegranate, the several kinds of fig, the cape and yellow jessamines; the mimosa, popynack, orange, lemon, and citron; beside the usual fruit-bearing trees common to a Southern clime. The odor from many of these trees, particularly the cape jessamine, when in bloom, is too strongly aromatic to be wholesome. The whole atmosphere also becomes impregnated with the orange-blossom and the mimosa when in bloom. The entrance to White Hall from the land side was a long avenue of live oaks and a hedge of nondescript evergreen. The house contained twenty-one rooms, each thirty feet square. The imposingly large architecture, set off with wings, gave the building quite the appearance of a palace. It was furnished richly and tastefully, to accommodate friendly visitors from all parts of the country.

Judge Heyward's second wife (Miss Eliza Savage,) was the reigning queen of this American castle. Her husband, who, during the Revolutionary War, was one of those heroes who dared to sign the Declaration of Independence, was, in private life, a learned, quiet, unobtrusive, studious man, and never happier than when shut up in his large library, enjoying companionship with the mighty dead embalmed in history.*

Not one of the heroes of the Revolution, who signed that instrument, deserved greater praise than he, for his loyalty to his country; for he had inherited from his father great wealth, had received a refined classical education, and was on the high road to success in the profession he had chosen. During his imprisonment by the British at St. Augustine, they had taken one hundred and fifty slaves, and other valuable property, from his plantation, which his heirs have never applied to the Government to reimburse.†

When some of these rich, aristocratic gentlemen, who had everything to lose, and a halter to gain, for treason against King George, if they failed in their adventure of independence of the crown of Great Britain, remarked to Dr. Franklin, "We must all hang together;" "Assuredly," he wittily replied, "for if we

---

* Tacitus says: "This I hold to be the chief office of history, to rescue virtuous actions from the oblivion to which a want of records would consign them, and that men should feel a dread of being considered infamous in the opinions of posterity, from their depraved expressions and base actions."

† The author's brother married this Judge Heyward's granddaughter.

do not hang together, it is very certain we will separately."

Judge Heyward, when a widower of thirty-eight years of age, married Miss Eliza Savage, who was fifteen: — the antipodes are not further apart than the tastes of this refined, modest, Revolutionary hero, and his dashing, self-willed, enterprising, brilliant, whole-souled, fearless, adhesive, learned, sarcastic, and witty young bride. She revolutionized the stately mansion of her husband immediately, to suit her erratic, girlish fancies, extravagant tastes, costly open-house hospitalities, and aristocratic display. She sent thousands of dollars to England, to have forwarded to White Hall services of plate, and services of the richest cut glass, (which her descendants have now inherited.)

Everything that wealth, intellect, refined taste (foreign as well as domestic), and generous, whole-souled, Southern hospitality could germinate, was enjoyed at White Hall for many years after the war of the Revolution ended, by Judge Heyward and his girl-wife. They had recherche company from abroad, and guests from all parts of the United States. Their dinner-parties and wines were unexcelled; and the guests, driving up that long avenue of centennial oaks, could well have fancied themselves about to be admitted into the palace of a prince. The negro houses, all in a straight line too, and prone to every beholder, beautifully white-washed, with green windows, and surrounding evergreen trees, gave evidence of the owner's wealth. No doubt the negro houses on the coasts of Carolina, being always built prominently on a line with the great homestead of the master, is a species of display of wealth; for as almost every family has a house to themselves, the number of negro families, owned by Judge Heyward, could easily have been ascertained by the long row of cabins that the planter is so ambitious to have kept in the neatest order.

Death, however, finally knocked tyrannically at the door of this lordly mansion too, and Judge Heyward was summoned to that Paradise that no doubt was prepared for all the pure-minded heroes of our Revolutionary War — whose unbending virtues have never been excelled in these United States, or in the world, and who are now reaping all the rewards of their noble self-denial for their country's good.

"Among the distinguished men that fell victims during the war of the American Revolution, was Colonel Isaac Hayne, of South Carolina; a man, who, by amiability of character and high sentiments of honor and uprightness, had secured the good-will and affection of all who knew him. He had a wife and six small children, the eldest a boy thirteen years of age. His wife, to whom he was tenderly attached, fell a victim to disease; an event hastened probably by the inconveniences and sufferings incident to a state of war, in which the whole family largely participated. Colonel Hayne himself was taken prisoner by the British forces, and in a short time was executed on the gallows, under circumstances calculated to excite the deepest commiseration. A great number of persons, both English and American, interceded for his life. The ladies of Charleston signed a petition in his behalf· his motherless children were presented on their bended knees as suitors for their beloved father; but all in vain.

"During the imprisonment of the father, the eldest son was permitted to stay with him in prison. Beholding his only surviving parent, for whom he felt the deepest affection, loaded with irons and condemned to die, he was overwhelmed with consternation and sorrow. The wretched father endeavored to console him by reminding him that the unavailing grief of the son tended only to increase his own misery; that we came into this world merely to die, and he could even rejoice that his troubles were so near at an end. 'To-morrow,' said he, 'I set out for immortality. You will accompany me to the place of execution; and when I am dead, take my body and bury it by the side of your mother.' The youth fell here on his father's neck, crying: 'Oh, my father! my father! I will die with you!' Colonel Hayne, as he was loaded with chains, could not return the embrace of his son, and merely said to him in reply: 'Live, my son — live to honor God by a good life, live to serve your country, live to take care of your brother and sisters.' The next morning Colonel Hayne was conducted to the place of execution.

"His son accompanied him. Soon as they came in sight of the gallows the father strengthened himself and said: 'Now, my boy, show yourself a man! That tree is the boundary of my life, and all my life's sorrows. Beyond that the wicked cease from troubling and the weary are at rest. Don't lay too much at heart our separation; it will be but short. To-day I die, and you, my son, though but young, must shortly follow me.' 'Yes, my father,' replied the broken-hearted youth, 'I shall shortly follow you. For, indeed, I feel that I can't live long.' And his melancholy anticipation was fulfilled in a manner more dreadful than is implied in the mere extinction of life. On seeing his father in the hands of the executioner, and then struggling in the halter, he stood like one transfixed and motionless with horror. Till then he had wept incessantly; but soon as he saw that sight, the fountain of his tears was stanched, and he never wept more. He died insane; and in his last moments often called upon his father in terms that brought tears from the hardest heart."

Two-thirds of a century after these heroes were gathered to their fathers, we, in 1860, make the following eloquent extract from a late speech of Senator Hunter, of Virginia. In speaking of the possibility of the efforts of the Republicans to overthrow the government proving successful, he said: —

"Sir, in that event, the accusing voice of human history will ring through all the ages to impeach them at the bar of posterity for having destroyed the noblest scheme of constitutional liberty which the wisdom of man has ever devised; and upon that fearful issue each of the succeeding generations of men will record its verdict of guilty against them. Their own descendants will heap reproaches upon the names of those who disappointed them of the destiny which would have been the richest inheritance that one generation could bequeath another. But when it is asked upon what view of the constitution, upon what consideration of religion or philanthropy; upon what calculation of interest, general or sectional, the fatal deed was done, where will the satisfactory answer be found, and who shall arise in that day to defend their name from the foul reproach?

"Mr. President, when I think of what it is that may be destroyed by this narrow spirit of sectional hate and bigotry, I turn away from the contemplation with a feeling of almost indignant despair. But I will not, as yet, despair of my country. I will yet hope that the great army of Northern Democrats and conservatives will arise in the might of a noble cause, and expel the intruders from the seat of power. I will trust in the influence of truth, whose empire is felt in every human heart when once it has touched it. I will put my faith higher yet — in Providence, for it cannot be that God will permit such a scheme of government as this, freighted, as it might have been, with the highest hopes of humanity, to be wrecked in the wild orgies of madmen and fanatics."

As soon as Judge Heyward died, and was buried in the venerated grave-yard of his ancestors, his wife, in disgust of the world and all its vanities, retired to the third story of her palatial mansion, where she remained excluded from all society save a few intimate friends, until she died, some twenty or thirty years afterwards. These few friends * and relatives whom she allowed to

* Mrs. Heyward was the bosom friend of the author's mother, who died not a great many years after the second war with Great Britain. She was so adhesive in her friendships, that where she loved the parent, she would love the children to the second and third generation. She therefore encouraged the orphans of this friend to visit her, and confide all their troubles to her; and her generosity to them was constantly frustrated by their knowledge that they must not accept presents from a

visit her in her private boudoir, were made to understand that she expected them, as a point of etiquette, to leave in one hour, which was all the time she devoted each day to receiving company. She lived entirely alone in this ghostly big house, and dismissed her numerous retinue of black servants every night. There was, however, a deep-sounding bell at the head of her bed, that communicated with the servant-hall, which is usually, in the country in South Carolina, some twenty feet from the master's house. Her only amusement, or rather recreation, was knitting for her grandchildren and gentlemen friends—an art that she carried to the most beautiful perfection; and a bookseller in Charleston had orders to send to White Hall every new work in the market, for her affluent library.* She

---

person who was so heedless of gifts as to cause her children "to rejoice that her head was fastened indissolubly to her shoulders, or she would give away that too, with its great wealth of brain." The author, in all her life, was never so happy as when allowed reverentially to listen to the sparkling conversational powers, and noble natural sentiments of this brilliant, imposing friend of her dead mother.

* "God be thanked for books. They are the voices of the distant past ages. Books are the true levellers. They give to all, who faithfully use them, the society, the spiritual presence of the best and greatest of our race. No matter how poor I am. No matter though the prosperous of my own time will not enter my obscure dwelling. If the sacred writers will enter and take up their abode under my roof, if Milton will cross my threshold to sing to me of Paradise, and Shakspeare to open to me the worlds of imagination and the workings of the human heart, and Franklin to enrich me with his practical wisdom, I shall not pine for want of intellectual companionship, and I may become a cultivated man, though excluded from what is called the best society in the place where I live."—CHANNING.

rode through her fields occasionally, and would ride eight miles to spend the day with her only daughter, Mrs. Parker; but this, too, she finally gave up.

It was too tantalizing to her admirers, who frequently took advantage of the etiquette to visit her one hour in her impregnable castle (where, high up towards the dome, she held her unique levees), to see by her expressive eagle eye that they must leave; for her great conversational powers, and deeply interesting, speaking countenance, her captivating wit, her withering sarcasm, and her erratic independence of thought and action, made her new every morning, and fresh every moment, to the appreciators of female genius and noble sentimentality. She particularly liked Mr. Wyndham, though he was not a genius; for who ever heard of a genius who was happy or rich, or contented or prosperous in the world? Indeed, if poets were not always in ecstasies of grief, joy, or despair, from some imaginary cause that their sickly sentimentalism, or largely developed nervous system is so fruitful in producing, their effusions would be too flat to find a market in the literary world.

Oh, how entranced with delight would Mr. Wyndham's children have been, had he succeeded in obtaining the hand of this far-famed Juno; but, no, he had become earnestly in love with the innocent, unimposing, little woodland nymph of Rugbyanna; and galloped round to Mrs. Heyward's every morning, to communicate his plans for his nuptials with his beautiful Matilda. In Mr. Wyndham's case, it was no mere figment of the imagination to be in love — for he was profoundly, furiously, almost ridiculously in earnest, about the charms of his ideal; and every day that the conventionality of mourning for his dead wife, kept him disunited from the living Hebe, appeared an interminable age. Twelve months, however, now elapsing since he became a widower, and every temporality being arranged for his wedding, he was about starting for Rugbyanna to claim his bride, when the driver, old Mingo, came running up to the carriage to let him know that one of the negro men, in cutting down a piece of timbered land, had had a tree to fall on his legs, and though he was alive, they could not extricate him from his perilous confinement.

Mr. Wyndham sprang into the saddle of one of his out-riders, and running the horse to the spot where his faithful servant lay pinioned down in excruciating torture, he forgot everything else, except the desire to release him, and therefore throwing all his herculean strength, with his servants, against the fallen tree, succeeded, to their astonishment, in rolling it away, and extricating the poor sufferer; but from that hour, to the day of his death, he never recovered entirely from the wrenching strain of the back, that this adventure cost him. Indeed, he lay six months in bed from spinal disease; and must have died, but for the unwearied devotion of his servants, who never left him night or day. Old Liddy, his dead wife's maid, watched over him with the tenderness of a mother; and as soon as he was able to write, he forwarded to Miss M'Elroy, at Rugbyanna, a release from her engagement to him, as *now* there was every prospect of his being a cripple for life, even should he ever rise from his present bed of anguish.

But old Mr. and Mrs. M'Elroy were too fond of money and position, and their young daughter too much in love, to give Mr. Wyndham up as a son-in-law. So they wrote, that Matilda would start out forthwith for Palmetto Grove, where the marriage ceremony could be performed in Mr. Wyndham's house. This was joyful news, indeed, to the despairing lover, who now engaged a minister to be in readiness the moment Miss M'Elroy arrived, to unite them.

"Across the threshold led,
And every tear kiss'd off as soon as shed,
His house she enters, there to be a light
Shining within, when all without is night;
A guardian angel o'er his life presiding,
Doubling his pleasure, and his cares dividing."

CHAPTER IX.

"All day, like some sweet bird, content to sing
In its small cage, she moveth to and fro—
And ever and anon will upward spring
To her sweet lips, fresh from the font below,
The murmur'd melody of pleasant thought:
Light household duties evermore in-wrought
With pleasant fancies of one trusting heart,
That lives but in her smile, and ever turns
To be refreshed where one pure altar burns;
Shut out from hence the mockery of life,
Thus liveth she content, the meek, fond, trusting wife."

MRS. E. O. SMITH.

HOPE, and the love and companionship of a beautiful merry girl-wife, will cure a chivalrous cavalier of any diseases that flesh is heir to, Mr. Wyndham declared; so that in a few months after his marriage, we find him springing up into new life and activity, heart happiness having exorcised all his bodily pains. He sent down to Charleston, and ordered a splendid phaeton and curricle; he bought blooded horses to drive tandem with his charmer; he filled his cellars with the choicest wines; he gave recherche dinner-parties, and carried his wife to all public places, magnificently dressed, to display her beauty; he indulged frequently in fox-hunting, and deer-hunting, and yachting, with his gentlemen friends; he seemed to have his cup of earthly pleasure running over. He forgot the holy example of his dignified Christian wife, whose prayers of faith, and whose chastened conversation, had always kept his wild abandoned spirits within the consistent enclosure of his profession of religion. Tremble, Mr. Wyndham! for your sainted mother, and former saintly wife, by their prayers during their sojourn on earth, entered into covenant with God, for your soul's salvation, and He heard their supplications, and therefore must punish your present worldliness. "Whom the Lord loveth he chasteneth, and scourgeth every son whom He receiveth."

> "The good are better made by ill —
> As odors crush'd are sweeter still."

"Whosoever shall look heedfully upon those who are eminent for their riches, will not think their condition such, as that he should hazard his quiet, and much less his virtue, to obtain it; for all that great wealth generally gives above a moderate fortune, is more room for the freaks of caprice, and more privilege for ignorance and vice, a quicker succession of flatteries and a larger circle of voluptuousness."

A year of constant jubilee left but one affectionate want to Mr. Wyndham's heart, and that was children— for how could a man who had been surrounded with nine prattling cherubs, not feel the present dearth of those boisterous, laughter-loving, musical children, who used at sunrise to wake him —

> "Gathering round his bed, they climb to share
> His kisses, and with gentle violence there,
> Break in upon a dream not half so fair."

Mr. Wyndham now determined to bring his daughters home. The first Mrs. Wyndham, having had for some months previous to her death, a presentiment that she was not long for this world, though only thirty-seven years of age, determined to pray to God night and day for direction, as to whom she should entrust her two little daughters when she should be taken from them. She had many friends of high mental culture and position in society; but she desired her children to be educated for eternity, as well as time, and therefore selected a clergyman and his wife who had no children of their own, and were the most remarkable persons in Carolina for their philanthropy. They were rich, aristocratic in descent, highly polished in mind and manners, consecrated to the service of God, and particularly devoted to children, having already adopted two orphans. These pious persons had always deeply respected the splendid moral elevation and sanctified religious sensibility of the gifted Mrs. Wyndham, and, therefore, when she went to them and announced her certainty that she would not live to rear those two infant daughters whose future lay so heavily on her heart, these noble friends made her a solemn vow, that in the event of her death, they would take the little girls to their home and their hearts, and educate them to be an honor to her memory, and useful in their day and generation. Mrs. Wyndham then called her husband and induced him too to vow in the presence of these friends, to give up the charge of these children to them if she was called away, which he did only to pacify her mind, for he had no idea of her dying. A month afterwards, however, the measles broke out on the plantation, among the negroes, and her unceasing care to see that all the nurses did their duty to the sick, brought the disease home to herself in so violent a form that she died from the effects of it; but with her last expiring breath she whispered to those two friends, who stood weeping at her bedside — "Remember, remember my two little girls I leave to you."

Such a solemn scene, such a dying sensibility for the welfare of her children, should have prevented Mr. Wyndham from wresting her orphan daughters from such noble Christian friends, to place them under a girl step-mother who had no religion—no experience—no self-knowledge, no fixed character. Poor children, their whole happiness in life was wrecked by this fatal mistake.

> "Alas, what stay is there in human state,
> Or who can shun inevitable fate?
> The doom was written, the decree was past,
> Ere the foundations of the world were cast."

The little girls, under the indignant protest of their dead mother's chosen friends, were brought back to their father's house. Their youthful step-mother, though well-educated, was a woman without fixity of purpose in anything; but was led hither and yon, in her opinions and pursuits, by the last person thrown into companionship with her. She was entirely divested of that chivalry of sentiment, so remarkable among South Carolina ladies, from the times of the 'Revolution,' up to the present day. Though not at all obstinate, she had a fiery temper (but who cares about passionate temper in a beautiful, pouting, ruby-lipped, inconsistent, powerless woman?) Her manners were never coquettish, sprightly, pert, or even self-possessed; and her voice in company was as soft as a zephyr. She was radiantly lovely in face, but a skulking bend in the neck * destroyed the imposingness of her person, though her feet and hands were lily-white and aristocratically small. This unobtrusiveness of figure and hesitancy of carriage is usually regarded in society as a mark of humility of mind, and therefore was of great service to Mrs. Wyndham, as it proved a non-conductor to the envy and detraction her beauty would have stimulated among her lady friends.

The greatest admirers of female beauty among men have decided that enterprise, learning, or any kind of serious or anxious thought, destroys the fascination of a dimpled, lovely face. Mr. Wyndham had not married this belle as a housekeeper, or a blue-stocking, or a philosopher, or a busy bee; for his former wife had been the highest type of an intellectual and morally-elevated, useful woman, who had kept his house, and all his temporalities, under the rules of orthodox order, and he had rather respected than loved her dignified character. His present girl-wife, however, he idolized with romantic, chivalrous, protecting admiration—she had not a spark of philosophy, or enterprise, or angularity, or thriftiness, or indeed any responsibilities at all, except to increase her beauty by every art, and to keep on the right side of his opinion, that "she was faultlessly an angel."

* A skulking bend in the neck is a sure indication of cowardice, fox-like cunning, and a stereotyped purpose of deception and hypocrisy. Never trust the possessor of it.

"Her lily hand her rosy cheek lies under,
Cozening the pillow of a lawful kiss:
Without the bed her other fair hand was,
On the green coverlet: whose perfect white
Show'd like an April daisy on the grass,
With pearly sweat, resembling dew of night.
Her eyes like marigolds, had sheathed their light;
And canopied in darkness, sweetly lay
'Till they might open to adorn the day."

Socrates called beauty "a short-lived tyranny;" Plato, "a privilege of Nature;" Theophrastes, "a silent cheat;" Theocritus, "a delightful prejudice;" Carneades, "a solitary kingdom;" Domitian said that "nothing was more grateful;" Aristotle affirmed that beauty was "better than all the letters of recommendation in the world;" Homer, that "'twas a glorious gift of Nature;" and Ovid, alluding to him, calls it a "favor bestowed by the gods."

Though Mr. W. was twenty years her senior, he waited on her with the Quixotism of a young lover, and would not allow the winds of heaven to touch her alabaster cheek too rudely. His trained servants attended to his housekeeping, and his petted Matilda was so cunning that she could dupe him into prejudices against his best friends that she capriciously disliked; and as soon as his two sons came home from the Academy, she took such a dislike to the eldest one (Edward), that his father forthwith despatched him to college at New York, where his dying mother had requested that her sons should be educated.

Becoming a mother herself shortly after her step-daughters came home, she so much neglected these little girls that their father was compelled to send them off fifty miles to school, and to board with their step-mother's parents, who had by this time removed to Savannah, Georgia, where they opened a large academy. These little travellers from the home-circle, one five, and the other seven years of age, were provided by their father with an affectionate black nurse, who was competent to sew and wash for them, and take motherly care of their health and playful exercises during their school-days in Savannah; and having abundant wealth, Mr. Wyndham left an ample purse with old Mrs. M'Elroy when he placed his little daughters under her charge, so that they might have no ungratified wants during their absence from him.

No sooner, however, did he turn his back on Savannah, to return home to Carolina, than this angular, utilitarian old scold determined to take the children's accomplished nurse and laundress to wash for her whole establishment; so that, although Bella was devoted to the little orphans of her dead mistress, and loyal in her deepest heart to the charges about them, so often reiterated by her master before he left, she found very little time to attend to them, and they suffered from neglect as only a mother can appreciate. Mrs. M'Elroy switched them for every accident or mistake common to very impulsive, uninstructed children. She made them clean the brasses, and rub the mahogany furniture,* and do all the drudge work in her

* Mahogany furniture was never varnished in the South, forty years ago, but kept splendidly polished by daily rubbing it with cloths, moistened with a mixture of beeswax and turpentine, melted together. The fenders and irons, shovel, tongs,

own and their chamber, and sent them running hither and yon with messages they could not remember, and indeed kept them so constantly under the influence of that mortal dread of her unsparing temper, that the desolate little creatures were entirely wretched; and their only comfort at night was to pour their sorrows into the ear of their sympathizing nurse, after her day's work for Mrs. M'Elroy was done. They were made to go to bed precisely at sunset, previous to which a slice of perfectly hard, stale, baker's bread, and a table-spoonful of molasses apiece, were handed to them on a plate for their supper. They were never allowed a light or a fire at any time in their chamber; and, as little Musidora was a superstitious child, and her nurse had told her innumerable ghost stories, she was always on the look-out for spirits appearing at her bedside, in a great white sheet.

One night Mrs. M'Elroy's youngest daughter came into the room after the two little girls were in bed. She was a mischievous miss, in her teens, whose name was Julianna; and knowing Musidora's weakness, she determined to amuse herself by frightening the child. So, drawing a chair alongside of the little trundle-bed, all in the dark, she told a long story about the devil, whose special enterprise was to slide in, through the key-hole, to fight an old gentleman up-stairs, who was

---

and handles to the drawers of the bureau, and everything else in this line, were all of fine brass, so that the house-servant's work was treble what it is now—for he daily had to rub the mahogany, and clean brass furniture. The floors, too, of the country houses, in the summer, were scoured three times a week, to keep them cool and neat, for they did not use matting.

in the habit of studying the Bible before he went to sleep, and then putting it under his pillow, after saying his prayers. And she declared that one evening his Satanic majesty spirited himself earlier than usual into this pious man's room, and found him singing the last two lines of the hymn,

> "Satan trembles when he sees
> The weakest saint upon his knees."

Whereupon, hearing a sneering laugh near him, the old gentleman looked up; and seeing his intimate accusing enemy, he threw his ink-stand at his head, though, unfortunately, he did not hurt him half as much as if he had simply continued his hymn, and thereby foiled him with silent contempt.

"Now, Musidora," continued the teasing Julianna, "you are a bad little girl, and I have brought a Bible to put under your pillow, so that Old Nick may carry you off, too, before morning."

The credulous, superstitious little creature, believed every word of it, and yet hoped that, by rolling up her whole body tightly in the bedclothes, she might be able to hide from old Timothy Brimstone, and let him carry off the Bible as soon as he chose to do so. The poor child's nervous system was kept on the tenter-hooks of terror, so that she never closed her eyes to sleep, and was nearly smothered in the blankets. Every creaking of the sash almost threw her into a spasm, so sure was she that it was Satan squeezing through the keyhole; and as her nurse had told her that hell was a big fire, she expected to be burnt up alive.

The next morning, Musidora could not rise from her

couch. A scorching fever, accompanied with convulsions, confined the little sufferer to her room for weeks; but neither the doctor nor old Mrs. M'Elroy knew the cause of her illness; and her little sister was afraid to tell, lest she should make an enemy of the young lady who had perpetrated the mischief.

> "I would not enter on my list of friends,
> (Though graced with polish'd manners and fine sense,
> Yet wanting sensibility), the man
> Who needlessly sets foot upon a worm."

As Mr. M'Elroy kept a school for boys only, Musidora and her sister were sent to a Miss Merriam, not far off; and there, too, the little orphans endured every mortification that sensitive children can be made to feel. Old Mr. M'Elroy bought all their clothes, and he knew about as much as an elephant how to do it; so that every old-fashioned remnant was palmed off on him by the merchants; and of course the children were made to wear whatever was bought for them.

One morning he took them to a milliner's, to buy bonnets; and she, seeing instantly how easily he could be imposed upon, handed him two bottle-green silk hats, which had remained in her shop from the last season. These he forthwith purchased, though they were large enough for grown-up young ladies; and as there was to be an exhibition at Miss Merriam's establishment that day, Musidora and her sister put on the old-fashioned, long, scooped bonnets, and wended their way to the school-room; where a roar of laughter from every one of the scholars greeted their elaborate bottle-

16 *

green head-gear;* and the proud daughters of Mr. Wyndham were so mortified and depressed all day, that they felt in no spirit to recite their lessons creditably before the examiners of the school.†

Old Mrs. M'Elroy never gave these little girls a single cent (out of the purse their father left for them), to buy a doll, or a plaything of any description;‡ indeed, they never had a moment to play after they came out of school, for the old utilitarian always had towels and sheets for them to hem, or some other work; and then, though she had a large yard, beautifully shaded with immense locust trees, she kept a malignant dog, who, like herself, was as fierce as a tiger, and the children never entered the premises without expecting to be torn to pieces.

---

* "Processions, cavalcades, and all that fund of gay frippery," says Goldsmith, "furnished out by tailors, barbers, and tire-women, mechanically influence the mind into veneration: an emperor in his night-cap would not meet with half the respect of an emperor with a crown."

† "Small miseries, like small debts, hit us in so many places, and meet us at so many turns and corners, that what they want in weight they make up in number; and render it less hazardous to stand the fire of one cannon-ball than a volley composed of such a shower of bullets."

‡ Sidney Smith, speaking of Utilitarians, says, "Yes, he is of the Utilitarian school. That man is so hard, you might drive a broad-wheeled wagon over him, and it would produce no impression; if you were to bore holes in him with a gimlet, I am convinced saw-dust would come out of him. That school treat mankind as if they were mere machines; the feelings or affections never enter into their calculations. If everything is to be sacrificed to utility, why do you bury your grandmother at all? Why don't you cut her into small pieces at once, and make portable soup of her?"

Mr. Wyndham's friends often visited Savannah on business, and never failed to call on the little Musidora and her sister; and on leaving would slip two or three dollars in their hands, to buy a great wax doll apiece. The children had none of that concealment or cunning (which is always foreign to a noble nature), and so they invariably ran to Mrs. M'Elroy with their presents, and she as invariably assured them, "that it was wicked and foolish to buy dolls with their money;" and then advised them "to go to Mr. Fair's store, where they could get beautiful book-muslin for one dollar a yard, (which was the price of this article then), and put it up carefully till they grew to be young ladies, and then embroider collars, and sleeves, and tippets, out of it."

"To-morrow didst thou say?
Methought I heard Horàtio say, to-morrow!
Go to, I will not hear of it. To-morrow!
'Tis a sharper who stakes his penury
Against thy plenty. Who takes thy ready cash,
And pays thee nought but wishes, hopes, and promises,
The currency of idiots. Injurious bankrupt,
That gulls the easy creditor. To-morrow!
It is a period nowhere to be found
In all the hoary register of Time,
Unless perchance in the fool's calendar.
Wisdom disclaims the word, nor holds society
With those that own it. No, my Horatio,
'Tis Fancy's child, and folly is its father;
Wrought on such stuff as dreams are; and baseless
As the fantastic visions of the evening."

When Musidora's school dresses got torn, or were worn out on the elbows, Mrs. M'Elroy would take down her scrap-bag, and without the least reference to similarity of color or pattern, select a patch large enough for the hole, and make her sew it on; so that, as the gay *new* piece was prone to every beholder, the scholars used to ask her sneeringly, "Where she got Joseph's coat of many colors?"

Mrs. M'Elroy determined that children's shoes should last a specified, orthodox time; and as Musidora was a very active, romping child, her shoes never held together as long as her sedate sister's; and she was, therefore, compelled to go to school with her little rebellious toes sticking out, to the derision of the motherly cared for little girls who attended Miss Merriam's school.

During this whole season of penurious restriction to the proud little orphans, Mr. Wyndham's young wife was sending constant orders to Savannah, for the most costly garments for herself, and the richest thread laces, and embroidered cloaks, &c. &c. &c., for her own infant. One item of value for this incomparable papoos, was a chinchilla cap, that at that time cost some sixteen or twenty dollars.

While Mr. Wyndham's daughters were crushed with mortification every day about their outlandish clothes, and unseemly bonnets and torn shoes (for who but a philosopher can bear to be the target of ridicule), their whole-souled, generous, loving father, was revelling in wealth, and congratulating himself that his dear little girls had so pleasant a home with his wife's pious, experienced parents, who would treat them with so much more forbearing affection, than if he had placed them at a stranger's boarding-school.

No persons on earth make their household more

miserable, than violent-tempered,* unsanctified puritans, like old Mr. and Mrs. M'Elroy, who expected everybody, except themselves, to keep to the letter, as well as the spirit, of the ten commandments.

The children could not write, and indeed would not, under any circumstances, have been guilty of the folly, or mischief-making, consequent on complaining of their step-mother's parents, to their father. Oh, could their *own* noble, highly-educated, wise, and Christian mother, have been privileged by destiny to rear them herself, there is not the smallest doubt that they would have proved an honor to every society they moved in; for they inherited all their proud mother's self-respect, talent, enterprise, adhesiveness, and beautiful conscientiousness.†

The very year that these orphans suffered so many privations and mortifications among their fashionably dressed schoolmates, their father, Mr. Wyndham, had made one hundred bales of the fine, long staple sea-island cotton, that forty years ago sold for seventy-five to ninety cents a pound. Each bale contained four hundred pounds; so that his income from this silky species of cotton alone, was perhaps thirty thousand dollars. But his most impracticable, teenish wife,

* "Discord, a sleepless hag, who never dies,
With snipe-like nose, and ferret-glowing eyes,
Lean, sallow cheeks, long chin, with beard supplied,
Poor cracking joints, and wither'd parchment hide,
As if old drums, worn out with martial din,
Had clubb'd their yellow heads to form her skin."

† "As the soil, however rich it may be, cannot be productive without culture, so the mind, without cultivation, can never produce good fruit." — SENECA.

whose beauty gave her the *entrée* to his purse at all times, wasted his money in presents to her relations, without ever being able to show how she spent it; for had she even bought services of silver, and splendid cut-glass, that many of her rich neighbors sent to England for at this time, these articles would have remained as heirlooms in the family, or helped him out of the pecuniary embarrassments which finally brought his grey hairs in sorrow to the grave. But so far from possessing any such common sense, she allowed the splendid silver urns, and other enduring household luxuries, which the first Mrs. Wyndham had formerly accumulated, to be stolen out of her husband's house without even acquainting him with the theft until too late to recover them.

But these tender-eyed, characterless, useless, pretty dolls, are the only women who walk through life on velvet carpets. Everybody waits on them, patronizing their good-for-nothingness, because they are too weak to elicit envy or opposition. Their husbands bow to their caprices morning, noon, and night; and really love them because their laziness and want of enterprise make them utterly dependent. They never know an affliction greater than not being able to obtain a humming-bird's wing for breakfast, and finally "die of a rose in aromatic pain." Where they make their exodus to, is a mystery; for they are not intelligently wicked enough to be prepared to live forever with fiends in the other world, and yet have not passed through that tribulation on earth necessary to refine them for the beatitudes of heaven.

The unfortunate, neglected little Musidora, and her

sister Britannia, found at last *one* most admiring, sympathizing friend, and that was the dry-goods merchant, Mr. Fair, who was always entertained by their artlessness, and who laughed outright when these little customers, in obedience to Mrs. M'Elroy, invariably called "for a yard of book-muslin." He often followed them out of his store to a confectioner's, where he purchased pounds of sugar-plums and candy for them to take home; and bought beautiful dolls, and even visited them at old Mr. M'Elroy's Academy occasionally. The little Musidora would climb into his lap, part and curl his waving chestnut locks, for he was very handsome, pinch his cheeks, and kiss him a dozen times in succession. Her little heart always overflowing with affection, she was in ecstasies to find somebody to love, for she had been separated from the only two beings who never scolded her; and those were her father and Mom Phillis, who had nursed her at her own breast from the moment of her birth,—it being a custom in Carolina to obtain a wet-nurse from the healthiest and most faithful negroes on the plantation, when the master's wife is too sickly to perform this delightful duty herself.

"I miss thee, my mother, when young health has fled,
And I sink in the languor of pain;
Where, where is the arm that once pillow'd my head,
And the ear that once heard me complain?
I miss thee, my mother! thy image is still
The deepest impress'd on my heart,
And the tablet so faithful in death must be chill
Ere a line of that image depart——"

Musidora's sister Britannia had never been a child, but was a stereotyped woman at the very time that little girls usually enjoy play exquisitely; she loved nothing but books, had no spirit for romps, or for any thing gay or mischievous, and therefore was always giving didactic lectures to the erratic, high-mettled, fun-loving, enterprising Musidora, who, consequently, regarded her as a stern Mentor, not a gentle sympathizing playmate; and, indeed, knowing her to be so superior, that she never felt much tenderness for her, except when she got into trouble with old Mrs. M'Elroy, who sometimes found occasion to switch even the stable-minded, discreet Britannia.

As Musidora was only as yet learning her A B C's, there were only three scholars in her class, whose names were Telfair, Bullock, and Habersham. Miss Merriam had a small silver medal, attached to a gay blue ribbon, that she hung around the neck of the child who was at the head of this class; so that the little creature's heart was almost broke when the ribbon was given to the rival that had dispossessed her of her place in the van of learning. Musidora frequently obtained the coveted prize, but when her antagonist was going home, she would run after her and throw the blue ribbon round her neck, remarking, "Take it, dear, till to-morrow, for you have a mamma who will be grieved to see you come home without it; while Musidora has nobody to care whether she is at the head, the middle, or foot of the class."

One day Mr. M'Elroy told the little Wyndhams that he would take them to market with him at sunrise the next morning, and on the way back would stop and buy them each a pair of red morocco bootees. This was charming news, for what tiny girls are not delighted with such gay understandings. So, without fail, they were ready, and without fail the red shining shoes were bought; "and now," said the old gentleman, "go home; for I have other business up town."

He was scarcely out of sight before the two children forgot the streets that would lead them home, and therefore one took to the right and the other to the left; and both were completely bewildered and began to cry aloud at their foolishness and obstinacy in separating from each other. They stopped people frequently on the street, to know if some of them had not seen a little girl with red morocco bootees on. In perfect misery they wandered up and down looking for each other until eleven o'clock, when they both met unexpectedly at the great iron gate of the academy — that they had stumbled upon by accident — and they were so overjoyed that they rushed into each other's arms.

Old Mrs. M'Elroy was so enraged at their stupidity in getting lost, that she would have switched them on the spot, had the postman not handed her at the moment, a hurried letter from Mr. Wyndham, saying, that his carriage would be in waiting at Screven's ferry, to bring her immediately to Carolina, for her daughter (Mrs. Wyndham) was at the point of death. The old lady hurried off immediately from Savannah, leaving her house in charge of the before-mentioned mischievous Miss Julianna M'Elroy. Britannia and her little sister were in ecstasies that the old lady was gone, who had kept them in constant terror; but the very next day Musidora had a slight fever, and Miss M'Elroy forced her to take a dose of medicine that was very nauseating. Whether this lawless girl really thought so, or merely tried to frighten the child for her amusement, is not known; but she suddenly declared that she had made a mistake and had given Musidora poison. The poor little orphan always associated the idea of death with being delivered over to Satan, who (her nurse told her) would throw bad children into the fire and burn them up; and as everybody but Mr. Fair scolded her, she was never divested of the belief that she was a hopeless little sinner, and was, moreover, the Devil's child; so that when she heard she had swallowed poison, she screamed and shrieked as if her heart would break, and though her tormentor now tried to assure her that she was only joking, she could not pacify the wild excitement of the child until the doctor had to be sent for, and he convinced the credulous little sufferer "that there was no danger of her dying at all."

A few days after this, a friend of Mr. Wyndham's came from Carolina, and, before leaving, gave Musidora and her sister several dollars to buy a beautiful baby-house, all furnished. Miss M'Elroy, whose parents allowed her very little pin-money, said, "Girls, send a half-dollar of your money out for some nice little tarts and iced-cakes." This they were only too glad to do — but the young lady nearly devoured them all herself. Musidora, finding they could buy what they pleased, got into such wild spirits that the rest of the money was not to be spent in laying up for futurity book-muslin, but that they would at once have a baby-house and give a tea-party in it, that she jumped and pranced around the room and was wild with delight; and, indeed, for two days saved up for the feast all the fruit, and bits of watermelon and pie that Miss M'Elroy gave them at dinner. The end of the week being holiday, the children's grand supper-party was to come off in the precious baby-house which Miss M'Elroy promised to buy, with the assistance of Mr. Fair, and have it brought to their room very early on Saturday morning. But a sad disappointment awaited all these childish hopes, for Britannia accidentally broke the large looking-glass on the bureau, and the poor girls, trembling lest old Mr. M'Elroy should find it out, ran to Mr. Fair with all their baby-house money, and got him to replace the mirror that same day.

From the first moment that Mr. Wyndham sacrilegiously broke his vow to his dying wife, and took his daughters away from their dead mother's selected guardians for them, the children seemed doomed to misery and neglect—and though the calm temper of Britannia made her bear her fate with stoical fortitude, severity and disappointment almost deranged Musidora's excitable disposition, and, indeed, saddened her whole life afterwards.

"Mankind," says Sidney Smith, "are always happier for having been happy; so that if you make them happy now, you make them happy twenty years hence by the memory of it. A childhood passed with a due mixture of rational indulgence, under fond and wise parents, diffuses over the whole of life a feeling of calm pleasure, and in extreme old age is the very last remembrance which time can erase from the mind. It is probably the recollection of their past pleasures which contributes to render old men so inattentive to the scenes before them, and carries them back to a world that is past."

How little do the guardians of youth realize all the trifles that lead to the formation of character! "I hardly know," says Greville, "so melancholy a reflection as that parents are necessarily the sole directors of the management of their children, whether they have or have not judgment, penetration, or taste, to perform the task." "Discipline, like the bridle in the hand of a good rider, should exercise its influence without appearing to do so; should be ever active, both as a support and as a restraint, yet seem to lie easily in the hand. It must always be ready to check or to pull up, as occasion may require, and only when the horse is a runaway should the action of the curb be perceptible."

Never were children so unappreciated and, consequently, utterly mismanaged. "A child," says Bishop Earle, "is man in a small letter, yet the best copy of Adam before he tasted of Eve, or the apple; and he is happy whose small practice in the world can only write his character. His soul is yet a white paper unscribbled with observations of the world, wherewith, at length, it becomes a blurred note-book. He is purely happy, because he knows no evil, nor hath made means by sin to be acquainted with misery. He arrives not at the mischief of being wise, nor endures evils to come by foreseeing them. He kisses and loves all, and when the smart of the rod is past smiles on the beater. The older he grows, he is a stair lower from God. He is the Christian's example, and the old man's relapse; the one imitates his pureness, and the other falls into his simplicity. Could he put off his body with his little coat, he had got to eternity without a burden and exchanged one heaven for another."

Can any one, with the least experience of the pliability of childhood, believe that Byron would have proved such a miserable, useless being, had he been reared by a dignified Christian mother? He possessed not only sparkling genius, but a most affectionate, sympathizing, emulating heart; and had these blessed traits of character been healthfully directed, he might, with his miraculous gift of poetry, have proved a blessing to society, by clothing his vigorous thoughts in the language of pure and elevating affection. Let us drop a tear of pity, that a nature so impulsively frank that he gave utterance to every wrong emotion that prudent dunces conceal, has been handed down to posterity so odious as never to be forgiven by those, who, without even his genius or excitability of temperament, might, with such a virago-mother as he was cursed with, have proved as hopelessly and morally undeserving.

One evening Miss Julianna M'Elroy, who always amused herself with the eccentricities of Musidora, came into the room with a Scotch snuff-box in her hand, and said, "Children, everybody should clean their teeth with snuff, to keep them from rotting;" and she insisted that they should dip their fingers in the box, and rub their teeth. Britannia would not; but Musidora, who often had the toothache, at once commenced to put this horrid stuff into her mouth, and in a short time got so deadly sick, that her nurse had to sit up with her all night; for the nerves of the child were dangerously and violently excited, and she would start and scream at every noise; and indeed did not for a whole week recover from the effect of this poisonous narcotic.

After a month's absence Mrs. M'Elroy returned from Carolina leaving her daughter convalescing, with another fine baby. But the yellow fever now broke out in Savannah with fearful havoc; and old Mr. M'Elroy, who believed that tar-water could exorcise any plague, rose up at daylight every morning, and compelled every human being in his house to drink a large glass of it; and, strange to tell, though the dead-carts with six corpses in them sometimes passed his door, victims of this all-conquering disease, not a person in the academy took it; though there were thirty boys, who boarded with, and went to school to, this old pedagogue.

This tar-water he concocted by burying several immense stone-jars in the ground, then pouring into them three or four quarts of pure tar, and adding six or eight gallons of hot water; and after three days, having closely covered it with tight-fitting tops to the jars, to prevent the aroma from escaping, he dipped it out, and himself handed it to every individual that belonged to his household; and this singular practice he kept up twenty years, and his family were always healthy.

The moment Mr. Wyndham heard the fearful accounts of the pestilence, he manned his twelve-oared boat, and despatched a most faithful female servant to bring his daughters home. If these little creatures ever revelled in ecstatic delight, it was to pack up bag and baggage, and obey the order to leave Savannah instantly. And Mr. Wyndham, learning previously how kind Mr. Fair had been to his children, invited him to flee from the fever with them in his boat, which this gentleman gladly did.

Horrór of horrors! the dreaded disease was however already lurking in good Mr. Fair's blood; and in less than a week it broke out on him with such violence, that, though Mr. Wyndham employed three physicians and waited on this isolated Englishman night and day, he died after three or four weeks of intense suffering, and was buried in the family grave-yard.

This was a severe trial to Musidora, who, in spite of all the watchings to keep the children from his room, had managed every now and then to slide in, and tell her dying friend how dearly she still loved him. Never did she forget the look of despair that this desolate stranger would cast on her, as he bade her "run away, for it would be her death to come near him."

Mrs. Wyndham, having no faith in God, had all her life been kept in bondage to the fear of death. As soon, therefore, as the wretched man appeared to be dying, she ran out of the house, carrying the two nurses, with her babes, and her step-daughters, to a distant neighbor's, where she remained till the funeral was over, and every article, bed, pillows, and all, belonging to the fatal chamber of Mr. Fair, were burnt up; and her husband had all the place fumigated with burning tar, and then painted and whitewashed.

None of the family, or any of the negroes, caught the pestilence, except Mr. Wyndham's son, Halcombe, who had been unwearied in his attention to the interesting stranger; sitting up with him at night with the affectionate anxiety of a brother. He, however, soon recovered, and Musidora, childlike, got so enchanted with her step-mother's babies, that she became reconciled, after shedding many tears, to the loss of her kind friend. Indeed, she never had been happier, than in loving with all her heart, these little brothers; and every day would go without dessert, and steal off with her plate to bribe the nurses, to let her hold them in her own lap, so that she could kiss them to her heart's content.

> "Look how he laughs and stretches out his arms;
> And opens wide his blue eyes upon thine,
> To hail his father; while his little form
> Flutters as wing'd with joy. Talk not of pain!
> The childless cherubs well might envy thee
> The pleasures of a parent. Bless him!
> As yet he hath no words to thank thee; but
> His heart will, and thine too."
>
> BYRON.

CHAPTER X.

"Say, ye who scan the Sanscrit, teach the Greek,
Pray tell me how the African should speak?"

"CRICETY crio, Sambo, wudder this comicle yawl boat bin, dah sail down to we landin' fur."

"Ki, Toney, you too fool; enty you yeddy us mausser, las week, bin dah tell pauper Mingo, dat Mr. John Seabrook, ges dun gib him one swanger boat; and dis tis de laud's trute, am him."

"Sambo," said Mr. Wyndham, "run to the new ground cotton-field, and tell the driver that the yacht, Mr. Seabrook gave me, has just arrived; and I would like to take a sail down the river this morning, to try her speed. He must bring along eight of the hands with him to row the boat, and they must put on their red dandy caps and jackets, and look very smart; for I may stop at Pinkney Castle, on the island, to see the daughters of General Charles Coatsworth Pinkney; he must also be in a great hurry, for the tide is half way up now, and I wish to start exactly at the ebb, so as to sail down with it."

"Run, *run*, RUN, pauper *Mingo*, mausser (said the boys), hab jes git de beautifulest skuner you ebber bin seed in all you life, and he sen me fur to tell you to come quick, wid eight ob dem mens, fur to row him down to de Broad ribber dis berry ob a maunin."

Old Mingo, the black driver, had been Mr. Wyndham's body servant from his earliest boyhood; for being the only child of rich parents, his mother perfectly idolized him, and had selected from the numerous slaves on the plantation, the most trustworthy man to follow the restless little fellow wherever his youthful pranks led him, through his father's grounds, that were miles in extent; and consequently the said Mingo loved the affectionate boy as if he was his own child; and was his most faithful friend after he arrived at manhood; and in consequence of his great experience, and affectionate oneness in all his young master's interests, Mr. Wyndham had now promoted him to the responsible post of driver, to manage the whole plantation of two hundred slaves. He knew his master delighted in all kinds of hardy sports; and was, therefore, never better pleased than when opportunities occurred for gratifying them; so with affectionate haste, he let the workmen in the field know what a grand frolic mausser was going to have, and that eight of the best oarsmen (prudently naming them), must throw down their hoes, and run home, put on their swangar boat-clothes, and be ready in a "giffee" with their oars.

With a loud, prolonged shout of laughter, the men selected scampered off; and in less time than the reader has taken to peruse the order, the stalwart black oarsmen were at the landing, grinning from ear to ear, ready to take their master in their arms, and carry him through the mud into the boat. But old Mingo shook his head the moment he examined the yacht, and found out how very disproportioned she was; being much too wide and deep for her length. So, with almost parental confidence, for he never was known in all his life to be insolent, he warned his master not to trust that comical boat; and being decidedly angry with Mr. Seabrook for making such a dangerous present, he said:

"My own chile, my Mausser Jeems, we'll nebber 'gree to us trussin' you life on de ribber in dat diccunce ob a raf. We nigger what's lib on de coas, knows eberyting 'bout de right shape ob dem safety boat; an as fur Mingo, him bin der manage dem craf, long 'fore you bawn from you murrah. Now, Mausser Jeems, you dun tell we dat you is agwine fur to sail down clean to Pinkney Island; and jes so sho as us git to dat squally place, Debbil Elbow, dis yere harum-skarum, bowl-shape huzzy, gwine to tun rite strate ober wid we, mausser."

Mr. Wyndham, deeply appreciating the fatherly care of this old negro, and relying on his mellowed experience in many things, still felt so inspirited by the sight of the beautiful yacht (a souvenir of a most genial friend), determined to take a sail, if it was only to the adjoining plantation; so he kindly bade old Mingo to come aboard with him, only for a trial.

The good old driver was Sir Oracle among all his master's family and servants, about everything that endangered their interests. No sooner, therefore, did Mr. Wyndham's young wife, yet in her teens, learn Mingo's adverse opinion of the yacht, than she rushed to the landing, and clung to her husband's neck, weeping and imploring him, as long as he lived, *never* to try an excursion in that horrid crazy yawl. Laughing at her childish fears, and kissing the tears from her transparent cheek, he bade her run back into the house, for the hot sun was browning her beautiful skin. She would not leave, however, until he promised to let the men row the yacht four or five hundred yards from the shore, and then return to take him in. Mr. Wyndham's little daughter Musidora stood near by, almost wild with fright, and therefore would not follow her stepmother into the house; and *her* father, seeing the negroes sail off so splendidly, with wind and tide both in their favor, sprung into a little canoe, and paddled after them. Quickly overtaking, he thoughtlessly reached out his hands to cling on to the taffrail, when, losing his footing, he fell overboard, and sunk to the bottom of the river unobserved. The agonising shrieks of little Musidora, who plunged into the water herself to perish with her father, apprised the crew of what had happened. Quick as lightning four of them leaped out, and rescued their master from his perilous condition, which in a few moments more would have compassed his death; for though he had always been an expert at swimming, the accident to his back, that had confined him to his bed six months, had obliged him to use a stout cane in walking, as a precautionary prop to the nervous system. Musidora's nurse, Phillis, had fortunately caught hold of her impulsive little charge before she got into deep water; but her fright about her dear papa caused the child to continue screaming hysterically for a whole hour afterwards, while her frail stepmother was carried, by old Mingo, swooning into the house. When dry clothes and cordials had restored the lord of the manor to his usual kind joviality, and his beautiful wife, pale, but smiling through her tears, had kissed him over and over again, with the stereotyped matrimonial expression, "*I warned you not to do it*,"—Mr. Wyndham called for his impetuous little Musidora, and taking her fondly in his lap, said, "My dear little daughter, why did you scream so long after papa was all safe? Indeed, my child, I had no idea you loved me so much."

Little did he dream that he had deeply wounded that morbid young creature's heart; for she had no mother, and her only sister, two years older than herself, had been the idolized pet, and every day caused her much painful jealousy (for what child acknowledges the *justice* of her sister being more admired and loved than herself by their parents?), so that Musidora's large and handsome father, and her dear old black nurse Phillis, were the only two beings in the household who entirely commanded her confidence and love. Phillis had nursed this child with her own infant, from her breast; and the acutest observer would have failed to ascertain which of the two babies this affectionate slave loved the best. Musidora's own mother had been in such delicate health, that she had not nursed either of these, her last-born daughters, by the advice of her physician.

It is very customary in South Carolina for the most healthy matured slaves to nurse their master's infants, as well as their own; for the wide world does not contain a more affectionate, unselfish foster-mother, than the black family-servant; indeed, the author has often seen more violent grief over the death of their white foster-child than she ever witnessed over the corpse of one of their own; and children are regarded as more healthy and vigorous in their constitutions ever afterwards, who have been nursed by the good, kind, Christian negro, on the patriarchal plantation. The affection thus germinated between the nurse and the child never becomes obliterated while life lasts; and in all the South, not a man could be found who would neglect or ill-use his slave foster-mother when she is advanced in years.

The people of the North sneer at the "chivalry of the South;" but it is nevertheless true, that every child in the Southern States is taught from the nursery that to insult or abuse those human beings whom the providence of God has placed in their power, argues the greatest possible meanness and cowardice; and no race of people on earth could be brought up from earliest youth in the atmosphere of such a high-souled public opinion on this subject as the slave-holders' children all are, without growing up into manhood with a noble, patronizing kindness towards their dependants. Effect must follow cause; and the Bible says, "train up a child in the way he should go, and when he is old he will not depart from it."

Dr. Rush, the celebrated physician and philosopher, remarks, that the body and the mind are so mysteriously united, that the great King Solomon might have said with perfect truth, "Train up a child in the way he should go, and when he is old he *cannot* depart from it;" for the physical, mental, and moral nature of the child, growing up together in rectitude from his earliest powers of thought, would render a disunion of this threefold cord *impossible* in maturer years.

The Northern moralist fancies that the slave-holding Christian in the South lives in the conviction that "he is outraging his conscience by selfishly holding his black brother in bondage;" whereas, the contrary is just the fact; for the most practically pious persons there regard the training and evangelizing of the African heathen in their midst as a great work of God, who will eternally reward their self-denying and yet successful missionary enterprise among the slaves; for what mission to Africa, since the discovery of the New World, has numbered three, or four, or five millions of converted civilized heathen, like the slaves of the Southern States.* Their very physique is altered; for, in the place of the great blubber-lip, and flat nose, and idiotic countenance, we find every new generation of them improving; so that some of the race, like Fred Douglas, only a few generations ago besotted heathen, can even go to England now, and edify the nobility there, by abusing that institution which has done more than anything else to open a door for the future regeneration of Africa.

Many pious persons, who do not, and never expect to, own a slave, doubt very much the religious policy of abolishing the slave-trade, that has been over-ruled by God, they believe, to send his gospel into the hearts

* Malcolm, the celebrated Baptist preacher, who spent several years in travelling over India, found that all the missionaries together had not made a single convert among the people *proper* of that unhappy land since England invaded it. The missionaries have made a few converts among the Kareens and other wild tribes inhabiting the mountains and the borders of the various provinces,—occupying a somewhat similar relation to India that the gipsies do to England,—but in no instance, says he, has a single Hindoo proper been converted to Christianity.

of so many millions of savage Africans. All this sensitiveness about children being torn from their parents in Africa by the slave-trade, has no religion in it; for of what use can parents be who will sell their children to a trader for a string of beads, or a glass of whiskey, as many of these wretches in the interior of Africa have done? As to their sufferings on board ship, that has been caused by laws making the trade piracy; for otherwise the very self-interest of the merchant would necessarily induce him to provide every comfort for these emigrants that any other travellers command at sea. No one in his senses, however, would wish such brutes thrust into our midst, except as slaves; for their physical as well as mental indolence, their untamed animal vices, their inherent hatred of work, their erratic night revelry, and their stolid indifference to to-morrow, would make such food-consuming, useless drones, a curse and incubus upon the most flourishing country on the earth. Whereas, the *compulsory* industry of this hardy race of laborers, in the produce of indigo, corn, cotton, rice, and sugar, in the South, has made slave labor a civilizing benefit to the negro and all the rest of mankind. Could greater vandalism be practised against the march of progress in this nineteenth century, throughout the world, than the blotting out of cotton, rice, tobacco, and sugar as articles of commerce?

"When Columbus discovered the New World, the fact became disclosed that there existed a vast intertropical region, extending from twenty to thirty degrees on each side of the equator, which contained the richest and most prolific soil to be found on the face of the globe, but the immense resources of which, without the employment of African labor, could not be developed. Africa was populous, teeming with millions of the darkest skinned and wildest tribes, whose prisoners captured in war were continually destroyed. When a field was opened in the hot latitudes of America,—the only climate suitable for their employment,—their captives, instead of being killed, were purchased and sent hither, where their services have been attended with the most important results.

"The negro races of Africa are estimated as comprising about 30,000,000. Since the commencement of the slave-trade, only about 5,000,000 have been imported into the New World; which amounts to but a small per centage of the number slain in their savage warfare. And the exportation of the 5,000,000 was, to a great extent, a mere question of death or deportation. Of the whole number of Africans introduced into the New World, 1,700,000 were landed in the British West India possessions, 375,000 (up to 1808) in the United States, and the remainder were sent to other European possessions in the New World. African labor in the tropical regions of the West has done more to advance and extend commerce and the arts of civilization over the world than any other cause that we know of; and to-day civilization is from one to two centuries ahead of what it would have been without it; because white labor could not have accomplished what it has performed.

"There exist at the present time in the New World, including the United States, Brazil, Cuba and Porto Rico, about 7,000,000 of African slaves, the results of whose labor exceed those of any similar number of persons, white or black, bond or free, to be found anywhere else on the face of the earth. Without descending into particulars, we may state that the annual value of products raised by African slave labor, amounts to not less than $400,000,000, nearly $240,000,000 of which is supplied by the United States. In this estimate we include cotton, coffee, sugar, tobacco, rice, naval stores and indigo. The consumption of these articles by the white races of the temperate latitudes has become an immense necessity. Of the general aggregate, the cotton crop of the United States for 1859–60, estimated at 4,200,000 bales, may be put down at $200,000,000. The transportation of these immense supplies, their transformation by manufacturing processes, and their redistribution, in changed forms, give employment to millions of tons of shipping, and afford support to millions upon millions of free white laborers all over the civilized world. By the increase and expansion of commerce, civilization has been spread to the remotest corners of the globe, while steam-ships have been multiplied, railroads extended, and communications of all kinds increased to an extent they would not have reached in a century without the development of the agricultural resources of the tropics in the west by African labor.

"And yet we find the monstrous doctrine taught that African labor is inimical to the free labor of the North."

England, in her sickly sentimentality, abolished slavery in her West India colonies, and now see the result in the appended editorial, just forwarded (in 1860) to the United States from England:—

British Confessions in regard to the West India Freed Negroes.

The publicity given in England to the Harper's Ferry affair, and to the debates in Congress relating to the anti-slavery agitation, have reawakened the discussion of the whole subject of the emancipation of the African race among the best-informed journals of that country. The philosophic temper, the judicial impartiality, the exact and comprehensive knowledge, and the manly superiority to prejudice and fanaticism, which distinguished some of the articles of both the London and the Edinburgh press on these questions, put to shame the ignorance and bigotry and animosity of our Northern republican journals. Here, for instance, is a frank and full confession of the London Times of the Working of the West India free negroes:—

"There is no blinking the truth. Years of bitter experience, years of hope deferred, of self-devotion unrequited, of poverty, of humiliation, of prayers unanswered, of sufferings derided, of insults unresented, of contumely patiently endured, have convinced us of the truth. It must be spoken out loudly and energetically, despite the wild mockings of 'howling cant.' The freed West India slave will not till the soil for wages; the free son of the ex-slave is as obstinate as his sire. He will not cultivate lands which he has not bought for his own. Yams, mangoes, and plantains — these satisfy his wants; he cares not for yours. Cotton, sugar, and coffee, and tobacco — he cares but little for them. And what matters it to him that the Englishman has sunk his thousands and tens of thousands on mills, machinery, and plants, which now totter on the languishing estate that for years has only returned beggary and debt. He eats his yams, and sniggers at 'Buckra.'

"We know not why this should be, but it is so. The negro has been bought with a price — the price of English taxation and English toil. He has been redeemed from bondage by the sweat and travail of millions of hard-working Englishmen. Twenty millions of pounds sterling — one hundred millions of dollars — have been distilled from the brains and muscles of the free English laborer of every degree, to fashion the West India negro into a 'free and independent laborer.' 'Free and independent' enough he has become, God knows! but laborer he is not; and, so far as we can see, never will be. He will sing hymns and quote texts; but honest, steady industry he not only detests, but despises. We wish to Heaven that some people in England — neither government people nor parsons nor clergymen, but some just-minded, honest-hearted, and clear-sighted men — would go out to some of the islands — (say Jamaica, Dominica, or Antigua) — not for a month or three months, but for a year — would watch the precious *protégé* of English philanthropy, the freed negro, in his daily habits; would watch him as he lazily plants his little squatting; would see him as he proudly rejects agricultural or domestic services, or accepts it only at wages ludicrously disproportionate to the value of his work. We wish, too, they would watch him while, with a hide thicker than that of a hippopotamus, and a body to which fervid heat is a comfort rather than an annoyance, he droningly lounges over the prescribed task on which the intrepid Englishman, uninured to the burning sun, consumes his impatient energy and too often sacrifices his life. We wish they would go out and view the negro in all the blazonry of his idleness, his pride, his ingratitude, contemptuously sneering at the industry of that race which made him free, and then come home and teach the memorable lesson of their experience to the fanatics who have perverted him into what he is." — LONDON TIMES.

From the observations of *Hanno*, (the naval commander sent by the Carthaginians on a voyage of colonization and discovery along the Atlantic coast of Africa, *five hundred and seventy years before Christ*,) the African is shown to have been then the same barbarous, idle, non-progressive being that he is now in the interior of his own country: averse to labor, unknowing of arts, and prone to sensuality and midnight revelry. Hanno says, in some of the places where he landed "he could see nothing in the daytime, except trees; but in the *night* the people crept from their dens, and he saw many fires burning, and heard the sound of pipes, cymbals, drums, and confused shouts." . . "We were terribly afraid, and our diviners ordered us to abandon the island." . . . "Though we pursued the men, whose bodies were covered with hair, we could not seize any of them; but all fled from us, escaping over the precipices, and defending themselves with stones." . . . "Three of these savage, naked women however were taken; but they attacked their conductors with their teeth and hands, and could not be prevailed upon to accompany us." . . . "Having killed them (in the scuffle), we flayed them, and brought their skins to Carthage" (no doubt as ethnological curiosities).

Reader, "all men," say the Abolitionists, "were born free and equal," and therefore when the "higher law," that you must bear in mind was first whispered in the ear of our original mother, Eve, by his majesty, old Timothy Brimstone, in the garden of Eden, when this irrepressible conflict party comes into power in 1861 they will force their refined, beautiful Anglo-Saxon daughters to marry the descendants of the above-described Booliobooligahs; and with the assistance of the votes of our millions of slaves, the Quixotic new-light Abolitionists will some day elect to the Presidency of these United States one of the purest African-blooded gentlemen, named Mumbo Jumbo. Hurrah! hurrah! hurrah, to our progressive age! For after this black consummation, so devoutly to be wished by the equality-of-races preachers, we, the (white) Washingtonian ladies, will have fine times, with our negro gallants escorting us to the levees at the White House, to dance attendance on the Ethiopian "powers that be," whose chief employment will consist in Bacchanalian orgies, and in dancing jigs the live-long night to the music of the fiddle and the banjo, between the alteratives of gluttony, drunkenness, obscenity, and brawling; while the day will be devoted to sleeping in the streets, where old Phœbus can unceremoniously dart his hottest rays through the pores of their sun-attracting black skins; for it is the negro's hereditary delight to go naked, and to sleep throughout the day, always selecting the spot in the fields where the meridian sun can blaze in his face. Good God! what a doom for the morally, mentally, physically, and religiously elevated Anglo-Saxon race!

A far-seeing philosophical writer remarks—"As the subordinate place in society, called slavery, is normal to him, he is the gainer, and not the loser, by denying him that political liberty which, from time immemorial, he has always abused, and will continue to abuse until his organization of body and mind is changed by the Power that made him. The natural distinctions in society on which our model republic rests as a basis is the true secret of its strength, wealth, prosperity, and durability. To none is this secret better known than to the political leaders of America's enemies across the water. Hence they have expended more time, means, and resorted to more Machiavel expedients, to induce our people to drop the natural distinctions in society on which our new system of civilization is founded, and adopt the European system of *artificial distinctions*, than have ever been expended to gain any other object in the whole history of nation struggling against nation for supremacy. It is a struggle of the artificially-created nobility, that rule in Europe, against Nature's noblemen, that rule in America. Three times as long as the siege of Troy lasted have the rulers of Great Britain been thundering at the adamantine walls that Nature has interposed between Ethiopian and Caucasian equality. In this they are warring against a stronger power than Russia—Nature herself. The fiat of the Imperial Parliament declaring the West India negroes equal to their white masters did not make them so. They have shown their inferiority and unfitness for freedom since the emancipation act more than they did before. Yet, in view of this fact, British abolition schemes continue to be urged upon us with increasing pertinacity through every channel, at home and abroad, and by every possible artifice.

"Negro abolitionism in Leadenhall street, among the East India stockholders, means a transfer of the culture of cotton, sugar, rice, and tobacco from America to their own possessions in India. In Exeter Hall abolitionism means a war of extermination against the republican institutions of America. In our Northern States abolitionism means a sort of craziness that has become epidemic among the pious Puritans, inducing them to profane their churches by setting up a black idol, in the form and likeness of a runaway negro, to worship. The loss of India to England would arrest the progress of the epidemic frenzy, so destructive to the interests of our religion and our country's peace, by removing its causes—the poison and corruption that Leadenhall street and Exeter Hall have caused to be poured into the whole current of English literature. For many long years no book or paper has been patronized unless it contained a few or more hard hits at negro slavery in America. But if I. land comes out of the war with Russia with the loss of her Indian possessions, and Mrs. Stowe should revisit the Sutherlands, she will find that they and other holders of East India stocks have lost all interest in Uncle Tom; for, in that case, Tom's freedom would add to the poverty and shame of England, by making her manufacturers dependent upon Russia for cotton."*

* "If the Devil ever laughs, it must be at hypocrites: they are the greatest dupes he has; they serve him better than any others, and receive no wages; nay, what is still more extraordinary, they submit to greater mortifications to go to hell, than the sincerest Christian to go to heaven."—COLTON.

The aforesaid newly-elected President of the United States, Mr. Mumbo Jumbo, will no doubt select his cabinet from among the Hottentots, after the abolitionists have abolished the "Constitution" framed by the prayerful wisdom of our revolutionary fathers, and substituted the higher law of Satan, that ruined our primitive parents. The proclamation "that all men are born free and equal" will be so unique a revelation (for neither the Bible, inspired saints, Jesus Christ's teachings, or the every-day experience of any human being, ever verified such an absurdity, since the fall of man from the image of his Creator)—I say the proclamation of this transcendental theory, will drive from this country every truly cultivated noble mind, and their places will be supplied with hordes of bestial Africans—Hottentots, Kaffirs, Ghonacuas, Boesjesmans, and indeed the whole family of Booliobooligahs; so that in the end the United States will return to a worse barbarism than Columbus found at the discovery of America.

As we are likely to have all these barbarians emigrating here under the new regime of negro equality with the white man, perhaps it will be edifying to quote the opinions of historians in their travels among the most civilized of the races. Barrow says of these Hottentots, or, as they call themselves, "Quaiquæ" (for the word Hottentot has no place or meaning in their language, and they take to themselves the name, under the idea of its being a Dutch word),—Barrow says: "It is true there is nothing prepossessing in the appearance of a Hottentot, but they have been much abused by ridiculous representations. A Hottentot would share his last morsel with his companions. They have little of that kind of art or cunning that savages generally possess. If accused of crimes of which they have been guilty, they generally divulge the truth!!! They seldom quarrel among themselves, or make use of provoking language (like the members of Congress, in the august House of Representatives, in the United States — even the Hottentots are too genteel to be guilty of such a want of civilization and dignity.) Though naturally of a fearful and cowardly disposition, they will run (like the genuine negro) into the face of danger if led on by their superiors, and they suffer pain with great patience." . . . "They are by no means divested of talent, but they possess little exertion to call it into action; the want of this was the principal cause of their ruin." . . . "The indolence of a Hottentot is a real disease, whose only remedy seems terror." . . . "Hunger is insufficient to cure." . . . "Rather than have the trouble of procuring food by the chase, or of digging the ground for roots, they will willingly fast the whole day, provided they may be allowed to sleep." . . . "Instances frequently occurred in the course of our journeys when our Hottentots have passed the day without a morsel of food, in preference of having the trouble to walk half a mile for a sheep." . . . "Yet, though they are so patient of hunger, they are at the same time the greatest gluttons upon the face of the earth." . . . "Ten of our Hottentots ate a middling sized ox, all but the two hind legs, in three days." . . . "With them the word is either to sleep, or to eat." . . . "When they cannot indulge in the gratification of the one, they generally find immediate relief in flying to the other." . . . "They cut their ox in long strings and lay them on the ashes, and when they are just warmed through, they grasp it in both hands, and applying one end of the string of meat to the mouth, they soon get through a yard of flesh, covered over with ashes, as a substitute for salt. As soon as a string of meat has passed through their hands they are cleaned by rubbing over different parts of the body. Grease thus applied from time to time, and accumulating perhaps a whole year, sometimes melting by the side of a large fire, and catching up dust and dirt, covers at length the whole surface of the body with a thick black coating, that entirely conceals the natural color of the skin."

They are, of course, naked all summer, and "the Hottentot women, fond of finery, like those of most nations, by their immoderate rage for dress accelerated the ruin of their husbands, which they themselves had brought on by as strong a rage for ardent spirits and tobacco." The principal covering of the women is a gauzy sort of an apron, reaching half-way to the thigh, that cannot conceal their persons, and yet they attract all eyes to the said apron by the gewgaws of large metal buttons, shells of the cypraca genus, with the apertures outwards, or anything that makes a great show. Others, who cannot afford this apron, wear one of the skin of an animal cut into threads, etc., etc.

These are the instincts of the masses among the negroes, even to this day in the United States. The generality of our Africans hate civilization, and are never happier or more healthy than when allowed to live in the abandon, nakedness, and filth, their instincts crave. In winter, every planter buys them shoes (made by the late "*strikers*" in Massachusetts, where, it is understood, there are 40,000 shoemakers that would starve to death but for the custom of the Southern planters), but it is next to impossible to get the field-negroes to wear them, and the soles of their feet become as hard as an alligator's scaly hide. And yet there are abstractionist fools that tell us, in the face of ethnology, and history, and common sense, that "all men are born free and equal." God intends the civilized, Christian nation, to rule over barbarians. Moses, the great lawgiver of Israel, tells us so. "Equality is one of the most consummate scoundrels that ever leaped from the brain of a political juggler." "It is an easy and a vulgar thing to please the mob, and not a very arduous task to astonish them; but essentially to benefit and to improve them, is a work fraught with difficulty and teeming with danger."

"It is now conceded," says a great statesman, "by all who have examined this subject with any impartiality, that the abolition or emancipation of slaves, in the West India Islands, has proved most disastrous in its effect upon the commercial preponderance of the British Empire. In fact, England is now dependent mainly on the slave labor of other nations for her supply of all those tropical productions which she had before, almost without competition, furnished to the various markets of the world." This much it has done for England. Now let us see what abolition will do for the slaves emancipated, by showing what it has done.

The following is an extract from the Colonial Magazine, in the "Gazetteer of the World"—a description of the people of Hayti, under the black Emperor:

"So jealous are the swarthy inhabitants of those rights which they have acquired, that every white man is viewed with suspicion; and, to prevent his gaining any degree of superiority, he is placed under a variety of disabilities. White men may reside on the island, but they are expressly forbidden to purchase land, or even to inherit any such permanent property, in what manner soever it might have been acquired. A white merchant may import cargoes and ship them off to other islands; but the produce of the country is placed under an interdiction, and secured from his unhallowed touch. He may procure a livelihood by his labor; but the merchandise which he is permitted to import, he dares not sell as a retailer. He is viewed as a being who is degraded from his forfeited rank in society; and the descendants of his father's slaves exact from him that homage which his progenitors once extorted from their ancestors. Among the lower orders the intercourse between the sexes is almost promiscuous; not one, scarcely, out of a hundred knows anything about marriage. For a man to have as many women as he can procure, is tolerated by law and sanctioned by established custom. Among these domestic hordes quarrels frequently happen; and when they occur, the man takes his departure with indifference, leaving the women and children to load his memory with reproaches, and to provide for their own support. No provision is made by law for the maintenance of the poor; and this furnishes a reason why legislative authority has never interposed in these departments of domestic life. Residing in a climate which seems congenial to demi-nakedness, they view clothing as an article of subordinate consideration; and while they can procure plantains and a little fish, they feel but little solicitude for other food. In this state of indolent tranquillity and moral depravity, bearing a striking resemblance to that of the aboriginal inhabitants, many thousands spend their days with but very few anticipations either of time or eternity. Among the higher orders, vice has not resigned her dominion;

polygamy is not considered as dishonorable, and other modes of life are scarcely branded with the name of sensuality."

"I will ask leave also to submit information which I have procured from those having charge of the commercial relations of the country as to the condition of Jamaica, showing the condition of the free negroes there, as follows:

"It appears that the colored people are not satisfied with a bare equality of civil and political rights, but aspire to their exclusive enjoyment. Not content with acquiring lands by free sale and purchase, and by squatting on tracts which, twenty years ago, were valuable plantations, though now abandoned to the first comer, they wish to force the proprietors of the estates still under cultivation to dispose of the remains of their property exclusively in favor of the 'colored sons of the soil;' menacing the colony, in the event of continued recusancy, with the fate of Hayti.

"For many years the negroes have enjoyed all those advantages over the whites which are the unavoidable result of their numerical superiority in a country governed under a very liberal representative constitution. Negroes and mulattoes fill a majority of public offices; and if there are still some of the most important places held by whites, it is, in some cases, because the incumbents date from a period antecedent to the emancipation; and in others, because individuals of the fashionable color, with anything like the indispensable qualifications of a mental character, are not readily found. Whenever they do possess some education and ability, they obtain a preference. I do not say that this is the deliberate policy of the British Government and its representatives here. It may well be the natural consequence of the predominance of the colored people at the hustings and in the legislature—the colonial government being what is here called 'parliamentary.'

"The little influence and respectability retained by the whites being derived from their superior wealth and intelligence, the leading spirits among the 'colored party' have always endeavored to effect the overthrow of the former at the expense of the agricultural and commercial interests of the island; and, with that view, have either legislated against property, or refused to legislate when protection was required, and as magistrates have used all their authority in favor of vagrancy and crime, all in the hope of driving away the remaining whites. In the fulfilment of this scheme their progress has been wonderful, yet too gradual to comport with their impatience. Its originators are growing old, and some of them, like Moses, have died before entering the promised land. A number of whites still cling to their professions here, as drowning wretches catch at straws. Hence the wrath of the colored politicians, which occasionally swells too high to be restrained by prudential considerations."

. . . .

"I wish it were in my power in a few words, without dwelling too long on a most unpleasant subject, to convey to you an adequate idea of the poverty, misery, and degradation which the emancipation of the slaves has brought upon a country which the anti-slavery papers in the United States basely represent as an example for emulation. I cannot think of these shameless falsehoods without feeling an indignation which it would ill become me to express in adequate language. . . . I am induced to bring the subject before the department by observing, in the colonial newspapers, extracts from some anti-slavery publication respecting Jamaica, which have recently appeared in the United States.

"Nothing can be more untrue than the supposition that the idle, dissolute, and criminal population of Kingston presents an unfavorable contrast to that of the country.

"In the interior, where the whites are thinly scattered, the police insufficient, where example for good is wanting, where the means of subsistence for man in his savage state is abundantly provided by the liberal hand of nature, the negroes give themselves up to African idleness, obscenity, and vice without the shadow of restraint which exists in towns; and disease, the consequence of their crimes and carelessness, is gradually felling their numbers."

"I have just returned from a visit in the parish of Metcalfe, one of the most fertile, and once one of the most flourishing agricultural districts of the Island. I spent some days on what was once a coffee plantation, producing from seventy to one hundred hogsheads of coffee. It is now overgrown with wood and almost impenetrable jungle, the exuberant production of a fertile soil abandoned to the culture of nature." . . . .

"From the property referred to may be seen coffee plantations, or rather the ruined mansions of five abandoned coffee plantations, which once gave an income to their respective owners of from two to five thousand pounds a year. Not a coffee-tree is now cultivated in the district; the proprietors have gone; some of them are in great poverty in England; some have died beggars; and others have left the country, or sunk into obscurity somewhere—no one knows what has become of them.

"Their successors, the negroes, with abundance of the finest possible soil around them, which they can cultivate for their own profit, live in squalid idleness, preferring to sleep in the sun and satisfy the cravings of hunger with wild fruits, to the easy labor required for the cultivation of garden vegetables—articles now in great demand, at high prices, in the towns. Such is the dearth there, of every article requiring the most trifling exertion of forethought and industry, that I was compelled to bring from Kingston a horse loaded with American corn, intended for the food of the animal on which I rode, as well as his own consumption." . . . . . .

"This island, like Trinidad and British Guiana, is about to set on foot a plan of immigration from India, and perhaps China, in order to supply the deficiency of labor suffered by agriculturists. There could not be a better proof of the worthlessness of the negro as a free laborer. No such deficiency existed prior to the emancipation, although twice the number of estates now worked were then in full cultivation, and although the present agricultural and other industrial products of the island are but a third of what they then were. You will understand the cause of the deficiency of labor now unquestionably existing, when informed that the laborers of the plantation have not *yet* turned out for work since the first of the month, having been all this time engaged in celebrating the anniversary holidays of their emancipation, and that, after last Christmas, no work was done on the plantations until the middle of February. By the last-mentioned holidays, the planters, it is estimated, lost a fourth of their crops, owing to the diminution of saccharine matter in the canes and the ravages of the cane rats.

"The traveller who lands in any of the seaport towns of Jamaica, finds a collection of ruins whose extent alone indicates the seat of former prosperity.

"The traces of civilization are gradually disappearing in a jungle composed of the *cactus opuntia*, the gigantic *cactus tuna*, called by the Spaniards *Higuero del de monio*, or 'fighter of the Devil,' and the equally formidable *acacia tortuosa*. Fortunately, we have no beast of prey in the island, and these jungles harbor nothing worse than flocks of vultures and the legion of unclean spirits generated by malaria. Amidst this desolation swarms a populace of negroes whose filthy looks and habits, idleness, open vice, noisy and demonstrative obscenity, beggar description, and cannot even be conceived by those who have not visited Jamaica. The authorities punish thefts and violent crimes when these are brought to light; but with these exceptions there is no restraint on the brutal propensities of the lower classes. White females living here must accustom themselves to sights and language which, in America, men would scarcely tolerate.

"The main edible resource of our idle population is the fruit of the mango — *mangifera indica* — which grows wild now in every part of the island, not above an altitude of two thousand feet, although its first introduction here is within the memory of many old persons.

"In the mango season, the lands belonging to the Duke of Buckingham, at Hope, which twenty years ago were a magnificent sugar estate, supply the means of sustaining an indolent, yet miserable, destitute existence. The owner of a large estate near Kingston, some years ago, destroyed all the mango-trees on his lands in the hope that, deprived of this mainstay of idleness, his tenantry would be compelled by necessity to earn a little money.

"The mango season is followed by that of the sweet-sap — *annona squamosa* — which, also, most unhappily, affords the means of indulgence in the idleness which the negro seems to cherish above every other sensual enjoyment.

"Such are the free citizens: or rather, I should say, this is a feeble attempt to convey to you an idea of the degraded state of the inhabitants of this island. It is wonderful to what an extent the public mind in England and in America is deceived with respect to the result of negro emancipation, notwithstanding the notorious decadence of this colony, in an economic point of view." . . . . . . "The ruin of colonial agriculture and trade is denied whenever the class addressed is sufficiently ignorant to swallow the falsehood; or, when a part of the truth is already known, artfully imputed to the whites.

"No candid person, even the most inveterate generalizer, who scorns to consider the question from an economical point of view, could remain attached to the anti-slavery party after a visit to Jamaica. He would learn from beholding the result of British interference in the affairs of this country, the prudence of leaving to those communities which suffer, or suppose they suffer, under bad institutions, the exclusive care of providing a remedy in accordance with their experience.

"Now, by way of accumulation of evidence against the wisdom and humanity of the anti-slavery party in their efforts, I beg leave also to read a portion of a communication from Tunis, dated June 26, 1859: —

"Perhaps there is no country besides this wherein so much misery exists:—at least one-half of the population (one million) are miserably fed and clothed, yet the poor are taxed the same as the rich, to pay which often a hundred-fold is taken; or when no property, the bastinado and prison starvation must be their lot. Yet the philanthropist has traversed this land, shut his eyes to the miseries of his own color, and, having taken the negro to his special keeping, prevailed upon the Bey to abolish slavery, and at one dash thousands of human beings have been cast into a state of wretchedness and want who were unacquainted with it before; and thousands, too, added to the already naked, hungry, and houseless millions. Having accomplished this much, the philanthropist took his flight, perhaps to America, where, in his fanaticism, he may make more wretched the condition of the negro.

"Thus, thrice have we seen the foul fiend appear. In contempt of human experience, and in mockery of Divine authority, it comes with words of angelic grace upon its lips, and the flaming fires of hell in its hands. Wheresoever it touches the earth, blight and desolation mark its train. Bright promises always herald its advent; but the echo of its departing footsteps ever mingles with the rising wail of human woe. When will vain man be taught by experience? or impious ignorance bow to the wisdom of God's decrees?"

God uncompromisingly asserts in His word, that "If thine eye be single, thy whole body shall be full of light." That there are Christians North and South, whose every prayer and sympathy is that God's "will may be done upon earth as it is done in heaven," there can be no doubt; why, then, is it that consecrated saints of God cannot arrive at the same conclusions about this high moral question of African slavery, that has already made us quarrel and fight as if the wrath of man worketh out the righteousness of God, or as if we had been given up to strong delusion to believe a lie, preparatory to our land becoming a hissing and a by-word to all the other nations of the earth? When the orthodox Christian reads the sermons of eminently talented men at the North, breaking down with their irresponsible eloquence, all the fences that have enclosed the human mind, they are filled with terror, for assuredly this reckless ranting about a "higher law" than the laws of the land in which we live, must, and has, already introduced endless confusion and strife, and bloodshed. The marriage tie even has been loosened by this lawless preaching — for every newspaper *now* details the most heartless, cruel abscondings of wives from their respected husbands and helpless children, with some worthless vagabond or coachman.

Murders, of the most fiendish character, are everyday occurrences since freedom of speech and free thinking, and contempt of the powers that be, whom God has ordained, has been proclaimed from the pulpit in these United States. Mormonism, free-loveism, higher-law-ism, and the whole family of mischievous isms, has gained a foothold in our once virtuous, single-minded, law-abiding, and practically religious people. It is appalling that Satan should manifest himself as an angel of light to the mind and heart of these disorganizing preachers,* and many patriots fall on their knees and pray to God to strike them dumb until they learn that "Christ crucified" is the only theme that can exorcise the selfishness of the human heart, and thus cause us to fulfil the splendid law of loving our neighbor as ourselves, and God with all our heart, mind, and strength. St. Paul said, "The weapons of our warfare are not carnal (like Sharpe's rifles), but spiritual, mighty through God to the pulling down of strong-holds."

The exemption from *manual* labor, which slaves have furnished to the sons and daughters of Carolina, forms one of the chief characteristics of Southern life—a characteristic which is at the foundation of a class of elevation and refinement, which could not, under any other system, have been created. It was, in fact, the stimulus of these incentives to plantation life, that

---

* "He could raise scruples dark and nice,
And after solve 'em in a trice;
As if divinity had catch'd
The itch, on purpose to be scratch'd."

Butler's Hudibras.

served to fill up this, and other Southern colonies, with gentlemen of aristocratic taste and refinement.

Slave labor is, indeed, due to that anomalous condition of African life, which has marked that portion of the globe from the earliest historical dates. While the Moorish, Libyan, and Numidian tribes of the shores of Africa, bordering on the Mediterranean, were well known, and entered into relations of commerce, treaties and war, during the whole period of the Roman Empire, the interior tribes of that vast continent remained like the sources of the Nile, and the Niger that flow from it, unknown and unexplored — and all that the civilized world knew of them was that they were barbarians cut up into a thousand petty tribes, always at war with each other, who sold their captives as slaves. As commerçe approached its Atlantic shores, and ships anchored on its coasts, it was not alone its gold dust that attracted mariners — but these wretched captives, doomed to death, were also freely bartered. In this slave traffic, the Portuguese and Spanish, and the bold commercial States of Holland, early engaged. England was slow to share in this traffic; it had *there* been an early sentiment of the people that no slave could touch its shores without being free. But in spite of this plausible sentimentality, her colonies, all the world over, were considered, as the peculiar theatre for her merchants to operate in. England had herself risen to affluence and power by commercial enterprise and energy. She had indeed imitated and excelled her nearest neighbor, Holland; and her merchants never approached the throne without being sustained and encouraged. Elizabeth was too great a Queen not to acknowledge these principles of national prosperity, so that when the bold and successful voyager and hero, Sir John Hawkins, returned to England laden with the wealth of the Indies, and commended to her this traffic in slaves, she turned a favorable ear.

The first introduction into England of a traffic in the human species, called Negroes, was in 1562. "William Hawkins, an expert English seaman, having made several voyages to the coast of Guinea, and from thence to Brazil and the West Indies, had acquired considerable knowledge of these countries. At his death he left his journals with his son, John Hawkins, in which he described the lands of America and the West Indies to be exceeding rich and fertile, but utterly neglected for want of hands to improve them." . . . "He represented the natives of Europe as unequal to the task in such a scorching climate, but those of Africa as well adapted to undergo the labors requisite." . . . "Upon which John Hawkins immediately formed a design of transporting Africans into the Western world; and having drawn a plan for the execution of it, laid it before some of his opulent neighbors for encouragement and approbation." . . . "To them it appeared promising and advantageous. A subscription was opened, and speedily filled up by Sir Lionel Ducket, Sir Thomas Lodge, Sir William Winter, and others, who plainly perceived the vast profits that would result from such a trade. Accordingly their ships were fitted out and manned by a hundred select sailors, whom Hawkins encouraged to go with him by promises of good treatment and good pay." . . . "In 1562, he set sail for Africa, and in a few weeks arrived at the country now called Sierra Leone, where he began his commerce with the negroes. While he trafficked with them, he found some means of giving them a charming description of the country to which he was bound. The unsuspicious Africans listened to him with apparent joy and satisfaction, and seemed remarkably fond of his European trinkets, food, and clothes. He pointed out to them the barrenness of the country, and their naked and wretched condition, and promised, if any of them were weary of their miserable circumstances and would go along with him, he would carry them to a plentiful land, where they should live happy and receive recompense for their labors." . . . "He told them that the country was inhabited by such men as himself and his jovial companions, and assured them of kind usage and great friendship." . . . "In short, the negroes were overcome by his flattering promises, and three hundred stout fellows accepted his offer and consented to embark along with him." . . . "Everything being settled on the most amicable terms between them, Hawkins made preparations for his voyage. But in the night before his departure his negroes were attacked by a large body of Africans from a different quarter. Hawkins being alarmed with the shrieks and cries of dying persons, ordered his men to the assistance of his slaves, and having surrounded the assailants, carried a number of them on board as prisoners of war." . . . "The next day he set sail for Hispaniola with his cargo of human creatures; but during the passage treated the prisoners of war in a different manner from his volunteers." . . . "Upon his arrival he disposed of his cargo to great advantage, and endeavored to inculcate on the Spaniards who bought the negroes, the same distinction he observed; but they, having purchased all at the same rate, considered them as slaves of the same condition, and consequently treated all alike."

"When Hawkins returned to England with pearls, hides, sugar, and ginger, which he had received in exchange for his slaves, multitudes flocked after him to inquire into the nature, and learned the success of the new and extraordinary branch of trade." . . . "At first the nation was shocked at the unnatural trade of dealing in human flesh, and bartering the commodities and trinkets of Europe, for the negro races of Africa. The Queen (Elizabeth), though a patroness of commerce, was doubtful of the justice and humanity of this new branch, it appearing to her equally barbarous as uncommon, and therefore sent for Hawkins to inquire into his method of conducting it." . . . "Hawkins told her that he considered it as an act of humanity to carry men from a worse condition to a better,—from a state of wild barbarism to another, where they might share the blessings of civil society and Christianity; from poverty, nakedness, and want, to plenty and felicity." . . . "He assured her that, in no expedition where he had command, should any Africans be carried away without their own free will and consent, except such captives as were taken in war, and doomed to death; that he had no scruple about the justice of bringing human creatures from that barren wilderness, to a condition where they might be both happy themselves, and beneficial to the world." . . . "Queen Elizabeth seemed satisfied with his account, and dismissed him by declaring that while he and his owners acted with humanity and justice, they should have her countenance and support." . . . "She offered him a ship-of-war for his assistance and protection, but he declined her offer, by telling her majesty 'that the profits of the trade would answer for all the risk and expense attending it.'" . . . "Afterward, however, he fell in with the Minion,—man-of-war,—which accompanied him to the coast of Africa. After his arrival, he began as formerly to traffic with the negroes, endeavoring by persuasion and the prospects of reward, to induce them to go along with him. But now they were more reserved and jealous of his designs, and as none of their neighbors had returned, they were apprehensive that he had killed and eaten them." . . . "The Anglo-Americans have been fully exculpated from being leaders in this traffic. More than half a century before America was discovered, the slave trade was extensively carried on by the Venetians; and if the system can be at all supported, by its antiquity and general prevalence, we certainly have abundant authority in the practices of nations, from the creation of the world, to the present time." — *Collections of South Carolina History.*

The first negroes introduced into Carolina, were brought from the Island of Barbadoes by Sir John Yeamans and his followers. There were no laborers but Europeans, for the purposes of culture, as the Indians would rather die of starvation, than make their bread by the sweat of the brow; and no doubt the unconquerable stubbornness of the red man, against labor of all sorts, was the primary necessitating cause of the resort to African slavery, in a climate so fatal to the white man, when much exposed to the scorching, blistering heat of the lower part of South Carolina.

But we must not forget the family circle of Mr. Wyndham, whom we left making merry over the constantly idle alarms of his little pet wife; who, by the by, had good reason to feel concerned, for the Southern planter is the most daring, adventurous, fearless, self-reliant of men. The boy children, almost before they can walk, are straddled on a horse, papa holding them on, and they grow up in the practice of all sorts of daring, manly sports, so that their very education from the nursery makes them "leap *first*, and look out for a landing afterwards, like the grasshopper." They scorn concealment, as if it were cowardice; are as generous as the sun-light; and in all the author's life in South Carolina, she never heard the sentiment uttered, "Of paying attentions to people, because you intended to make use of them." If any calculator entertained such niggardly ideas of the pleasures of social intercourse, public opinion compelled him to hide it in the depths of his nutshell heart.* But when she came to live in the great political omnium gatherum — the metropolis of these United States, she found that not to seek self in every bow, every smile, every hospitality extended to strangers, was an evidence that you had no inductive powers of mind, and were not far removed from the simplicity of Abrahamic manners.

Mrs. Wyndham spent a sleepless night, from a pre-

* "Self-pride is the common friend of humanity, and like the bell of our church, is resorted to on all occasions; it ministers alike to our festivals or our fasts; our merriment or our mourning; our weal or our woe."

sentiment of trouble; for her husband, having been bedridden so long from the accident before alluded to, was not, she feared, in robust health enough to bear harmlessly that most sudden immersion in cold water. Her fears proved only too prophetic; for in a short time he developed unmistakable symptoms of pleurisy, a disease very common on the coast-settlements of South Carolina, and sometimes very fatal.

Old Liddy, who had been the accomplished maid-servant of Mr. Wyndham's first wife, as soon as she heard of his illness, rushed into the house from the kitchen (for she was now the family cook), to know what was the matter "wid her own belubbed Mausser Jeems." Finding his hands hot and dry, and his eyes bright with fever, she turned in fright, with tears rolling down her cheeks, to her master's girl-wife, and said:

"Now, missus, yu'se nuttin but a chile; you nebber hab no speriunce ob sick people; derefore I sway to de Laud, I wunt lef my mausser's bedside, till he git hattie as ebber. So you mase well jes sen to de driber, ole Mingo, fur wun ob de fiel-niggas to cum to de kitchen, an tek me place."

The negroes are born cooks; so that a planter's wife, when her scientific culinary professor reports himself or herself sick, need only send to the driver for help. Dozens of the slaves working in the cotton or rice fields are fully competent, at a moment's notice, to drop the hoe and repair to the kitchen, where, in an incredibly short time, they will cook a luscious family dinner; and the blacks are proverbially cleaner in scouring the cooking-pots, and securing fresh water from the spring to put into them to boil, than any *white* French cook, of much greater pretension.

Mr. Wyndham's old physician, Dr. North, was immediately sent for, and arrived as soon as practicable, for he lived eight miles off. He felt the patient's pulse, examined his tongue, etc., and ordered a large blister put on his side, bled him profusely, and then weighed out twelve or fifteen grains of calomel, which mineral abomination is a catholicon for all diseases that flesh is heir to in the South. The afflicted family, servants and all, followed the doctor to the bedside of the patient, to watch his countenance, for he rarely expressed his opinions when there was a case of serious illness. Old Liddy guessed in a moment, by his looks, that there was great cause for alarm; so she slid into the closet near by, and shutting the door, indulged noiselessly her heartfelt grief. The doctor, knowing Mrs. Wyndham's inexperience, carefully wrote down when, and what medicines, were to be administered; for all the planters living far from Charleston, buy every year quantities of physic of every kind necessary for the whole family, negroes, horses, and all, in that fever-and-pleurisy-begetting climate of the South Carolina coasts. Indeed, the master finds it necessary to acquire much precision of knowledge in the management of the common diseases of his negroes himself; for the physicians sometimes live far off. Moreover, the slave thinks that his master knows more than all the Esculapians in the world; and when the doctor is sent for, he regards his entrance into their cabins as the sure presage of death, and will not voluntarily take his physic. As the black nurse is always leagued in with the patient in this superstition, the master is forced to see him take every dose with his own eyes.

After Dr. North left, old Lydia in the plenitude of her affectionately assumed power, allowed the young wife to sit at the bedside and measure out the drops of the fever-cooling nitre, and then hand them to her husband; but she considered all the nursing (outside of pouring hateful drugs down his throat) as her own peculiar department. As soon as the blister, therefore, had drawn perhaps six hours, so as to insure the fact that it had effectually performed its office, in the violent distress of pleurisy, she called her master's wife and said: "Now, my chile, i'se a gwinin to larn you how fur to dress sick people blister — fur you see us ole finger, dun git so stiff, dat him can't cut dis blister, nomisay I gone hut, we darlin Mausser Jeems. Now den, clip saftly, ebery wun ob dem leetle bladders—so —dats him. Now take dis fine linen rag, and hole on wid you finger to dis side, and dat side, and den lay um on top de blister, fur to dry off de yaller water — den take dis nice waum corn-flour, and lard-poultses, and put him on quick. But stop — I member dat de Doctor put on dis blister fur de pleurisy, derefore him must be keep sore nuff long time — so spread sum ob dat wax and ile ting and put him on de raw place *fus*, fur de poultses will heal um too fast. Now den gib me dat bandage, an us will tie um, or pin um, so dat de double fole ob de rag wunt scratch or bruise de blister, and us mus be caful, too, to fix de place where de pin is stick, handy to git de plaster off dis ebening, nomisay us gone 'sturb Mausser by pushin me han under he back to loosen dem bandage."

Mr. Wyndham was very, *very* sick, and his disease now took the form of typhoid fever, with its attendant greater or less degree of atony or exhaustion, smothered burning fire, and, at times, alarmingly weak pulse. With a mother's tenderness old Liddy bathed his feet, and hands, and head, with spirits, whenever he was most weak from fever and with cold water when it was at its height. She fixed a comfortable cot close up to his bedside *every morning*, and arranged the pillows on it, and then sent for two men-servants to softly lift up both ends of the sheet on which her prostrate master laid, and slid him on the cot, so that he would enjoy the change of position, while she thoroughly beat up and put on fresh linen sheets, and aired his bed (which alterative to a person with nervous or typhoid fever, is a luxury above all price.) She then did not hurry him back to the bedstead, but waited until he desired to return. (Nothing is so tormenting to a sick nervous person as hurried movements and whispering communications.) This affectionate creature seemed proud never to have any one sit up with him at night, or watch over him in the day—beside herself —for it was her husband (the before alluded to old Mingo) who had been his body-servant from childhood. After a month of suffering, Mr. Wyndham began to convalesce—to the abounding joy of his despairing wife, and sensitive little daughter Musidora, whom nobody (not even the despotic old Liddy) had been able to force out of her father's chamber during all his long illness—and who would not lie down at night, but sat before the fire with her trembling young step-mother, who seemed to believe in spirits, and was terrified at every noise in that ghostly mansion after midnight — where five or six generations of the Wyndhams had died, and were buried not far off. So that *that* timid woman lived in nameless fear and superstitious consciousness that her husband's *first* wife had an ubiquitous eye upon all her movements — perhaps angry at his choice, or envying the superlative beauty, youth, innocence, and fascinating helplessness that had so soon filled the void in her late husband's heart — or, watching her conduct towards the little orphan daughters she had left behind. (The Southern gentleman widower, never mind how old he is, or how many children he has got, has no ideas of marrying a sensible, experienced, managing, thrifty old maid, to take care of his household — not a bit of it; he instantly falls madly in love with some romping, unstereotyped, dashing, smart-spoken, coquettish little miss in her teens—who does not know how to work, or keep house, or to do a single practical thing—who has no knowledge of human nature, or even pondered much about philosophy; but who is instinctively appreciative of his (her husband's) perfections — who never argues a point with him, but has her *own way* invariably, by jumping into his lap, kissing him twenty-five times, and declaring, truthfully, that he is the handsomest fellow in the whole world. Such a gem of a wife leaps on a horse with the agility of a squirrel—races with him all over the woods and the fields, has very beautiful little hands and feet, springs with him into a tiny canoe and paddles round to see how the cotton is growing on his adjoining islands; echoes all his opinions about his neighbors; and if he should be (which is not at all probable) the veriest of Mormons, *she* never can be made to condescend to believe it—but lives and dies in the conviction that he never *did* love anybody but herself (no, not even his *first* wife.) As she has never heard the "*higher* law" doctrines now preached at the North, or any of the isms about "free-love," et-cetera, so rife among the strong-minded women there, she never dreams of allowing her affections or romances to wander, even in thought, from her own husband—for there is no "Divorce Law" in *South Carolina*, and a *wife* would be utterly scorned for her negrofied vulgarity, if she entertained, or was suspected, even of a penchant for her husband's young white overseer. A South Carolina lady marries her husband "for richer, for poorer, for better, for worse, until death do them part."

Hearing of Mr. Wyndham's convalescence, all his negroes repaired to the house, and one by one came in to to tell him how "dey hab pray to de Laud fur him git well, fur nuffer we bin dah' gwinin to do widdout us own mausser." The little negro boys (whose official engagements were to scream at the top of their lungs, and scamper hither and yon to scare the blackbirds out of the corn and rice fields) hid from the driver long enough to carry a present of partridges, caught in their traps, and some marsh hen and terrapin eggs, to tempt the feeble appetite of their master. But old grandma Amey (who had been brought from Africa when she was seven years of age, and had lived in the Wyndham family one hundred and ten years) declared "that mausser could nebber git him strent back rite good tell old Liddy mek dem rich turtle-soup and shrimp, and crab pie, an roas de fat saddle ob venison fur him dinna." (A negro can never be made to comprehend the benefit of fasting, religiously or physically, and one special reason why the master has to administer every dose of medicine to his sick slaves, and personally watch over them, is, that the black nurse will be sure to coax the almost dying patient to eat the strongest food—believing, perhaps, that the grim monster, Death, cannot quiver his fatal dart so long as the stomach is full.)

Happy was the day for every person on that large patriarchal plantation, when Mr. Wyndham ordered his favorite sorrel mare to the door, for him to ride out once more to his fields. When the negroes at work, gaily hoeing the cotton, caught a glimpse of his genial face, they all set up a shout of joy, that he was to be among them every day—for the planters are in their fields morning and evening, directing, and talking to, and laughing at the men, who so often let their wives beat them at their tasks. Frequently, women finish their own allotted portion, and then help their husbands, though the task of all grown-up healthy negroes, men and women, is the same, and regulated in quantity by law.*

* The author never daguerreotypes from memory her father's kind manners and yet potent affectionate rule over his slaves, without coming to the conviction, (after travelling, as a moral observer, over most of the United States and Canada,) that so whole-hearted a confidence and friendship coúld not by any possibility exist, between different races, as is germinated in the South, by the patronage on the one hand, and dependence on the other, of the *master as his property*. *There* the negro never assumes equality, and therefore you are never afraid he will take liberties from kindnesses bestowed. He seems as

The merest allusion to anthropology denotes the inferiority of the African mind. The negro, as far back as we historically know him, never has developed one single trait of the Anglo-Saxon race in reference to enterprise, or discovery, or art, or science, or independence; and the only incentive the abolitionist spy on a Southern plantation, can give him to run away from his master, is to assure him that at the North he will not be obliged to work.

Let us now, for a moment, glance at the early history of the Britons, and their subsequent greatness, and compare them with the non-progressive African race, who, for four thousand years, have remained stationary in barbarism in the interior of their country. History tells us "that the original inhabitants of England, Ireland, and Scotland, were almost barbarians.

"Settlements are supposed to have been made several hundred years before the Christian era in Ireland, by the Phœnicians; and these old Britons seem to have been of the same Celtic stock that peopled France and Spain, though they were divided into numerous tribes,

---

satisfied that God never made him the equal of the white man, as he is that a horse was made larger than a mouse. The author could not help laughing most heartily over the brilliantly imaginative tale of "Uncle Tom's Cabin;" for the progressionist continually puts sentiments of lordly ambition and constant friction of the mind against their social inequality, into the mouths of the slaves, when she could take a solemn oath before any legal court, that in all her life in South Carolina, talking with hundreds of negroes, with unrestrained familiarity every day for twenty-five years, she never heard one single expression from them that could be tortured into a hint of such elevated sentimentality.

some of whom were more savage than others. A few among the southern tribes practised agriculture in a rude fashion, and wore artificial clothes for dress, and were acquainted with some of the arts of civilized life. To the north, the people were mere savages, living in holes in the winter, using the undressed hides of cattle for clothing, pinning them on with a thorn, and tattooing their skins for ornament. They had no books, and could not read or write. The women, like those of our present savages, were practised in basket-making, the material being the twigs of the willows. They also sewed together the skins of animals for dress, their thread being made of vegetable fibre or leather, and their needles of bone. Such was the condition of the people when Julius Cæsar, having completed the subjugation of Gaul, now called France, began to think of adding the island of Britain to his conquests."

But to us this history of England is the history of our father-land — the history of our ancestors and of most of the institutions that belong to society in the United States. And at the present day, the United Kingdom of Great Britain and Ireland exhibits the most extraordinary spectacle of national glory which the world has ever witnessed. Rome, in her brightest days, could not compare with it in point of wealth, power, and civilization. Can the quixotical romance of even such revilers as the new-light abolition saints, germinate the idea that the barbarian negro race will ever, this side of the millennium, reach or even aspire to the elevation that has been attained by the barbarian Briton? So far from it, that the African can be perfectly happy if he has the privilege of living like a wild beast, without work, and without any of the restraints of civilization or religion.

When reading the hideous fate of good "Uncle Tom" being whipped to death because his religion made him so much more valuable as property, and that, too, by the master himself, who was the party most benefited by the virtues of his slave; the philosophical question arises, What kind of a heart can that novelist have, whose sanguinary imagination concocted such atrocities, and such violation of all the laws that universally govern the human heart? Does a man kill his horse, because it is perfectly trained to remarkable usefulness? Great God! did Satan himself inspire that fiendish imagination of a Southern master, who in fact would as soon whip his own father to death, as a faithful, pious old slave, who is as much respected in the South as one of our noblest old Revolutionary pensioners. But perhaps Mrs. Stowe read the following account of a white man in the North, published in the Ohio newspapers:

"UNNATURAL CRUELTY.—A man named Jos. Shubart, said to be in comfortable circumstances, resides near Springfield, Ohio. He has three or four brothers living. A few days ago he turned his mother, aged eighty years, out of doors, and sent her to Springfield, to die in the street or to be supported by the county. She wandered about till the keeper of the poor-house found her, when she was taken care of by the authorities. Some of her clothing had not been washed for four months."

CHAPTER XI.

"It is a common thing to hear sentimental wonderings about the unfairness of the distribution of things in this world. The unprincipled get on in life; the saints are kept back. The riches and rewards of life fall to the lot of the undeserving. But if you look into it, the balance is adjusted even here. God has made his world much better than you or I could make it. Everything reaps its own harvest; and before you covet the enjoyment which another possesses, you must first calculate the cost at which it was procured. The religious tradesman complains that his honesty is a hindrance to his success; that the tide of custom pours into the doors of his less scrupulous neighbors. My brother, do you think that God is going to reward honor, integrity, high-mindedness, with this world's coin? Do you fancy that he will pay *spiritual* excellence with plenty of custom? Now consider the price your unscrupulous neighbor has paid for his success. Perhaps mental degradation and dishonor. His advertisements are all deceptive; his treatment of his workmen tyrannical; his cheap prices made possible by inferior articles. Sow that man's seed, and you will reap that man's harvest. Cheat, lie, advertise, be unscrupulous in your assertions — custom will come to you. But, if the price is too dear, let him have his harvest and take yours. Yours is a clear conscience, a pure mind, rectitude within and without. Will you part with *that*, for his? Then why do you complain? He has paid his price—*you* do not choose to pay it."

"It is not an uncommon thing to see a man rise from insignificance to sudden wealth by speculation. In this case, as in spiritual things, the law seems to hold, 'He that hath, to him shall be given.' Tens of thousands soon increase and multiply to hundreds of thousands. His doors are besieged by the rich and the great. Royalty banquets at his table, and nobles court his alliance. Whereupon some simple Christian is inclined to complain: 'How strange that so much prosperity should be the lot of mere cleverness!' Well, are these really God's chief blessings? Is it for such as these that you serve Him? And would these indeed satisfy your soul? Would you have God reward his saintliest with these gew-gaws,—all this trash, and wealth, and equipages, and plate, and courtship from the needy great? Call you *that* the heaven of the holy? Compute, now, what was paid for that. The price that merchant-prince paid, perhaps, with the blood of his own soul, was shame and guilt. The price he is paying now is perpetual dread of detection; or, worse still, the hardness that can laugh at detection; or, one deep lower yet, the low and grovelling soul which can be satisfied with these things as a paradise, and ask no higher. He has reaped enjoyment,—yes, and he has sown, too, the seed of infamy. It is all fair. Count the cost. 'He that saveth his life shall lose it.' Save your life, if you like; but do not complain if you lose your nobler life,—yourself. Win the whole world; but remember you do it by losing your own soul. Every sin must be paid for; every sensual indulgence is a harvest, the price for which is so much ruin to the soul. 'God is not mocked.'"

Mr. Wyndham now, for the first time in his life, began to know the meaning of disappointment and real trouble; for tidings poured in from New York, that his most talented, brilliant son, Edward, whose letters had been such splendid pieces of composition, that Mr. Wyndham's literary friends had borrowed them to read at public meetings, — this highly educated, gifted son, had become one of the most reckless, dissipated young men in the whole college.

Edward Wyndham not only possessed great mental powers, but a magnificent physique; and now at the age of seventeen, was more than six feet high, well proportioned, self-reliant, and daring as Lucifer. He fell in love with every pretty girl he met.

> "Ah! woman, fond and gay deceiver,
> How prompt are striplings to believe her!"

Addison says, "Ridicule perhaps is a better expedient against love, than sober advice; and I am of opinion that Hudibras, and Don Quixote, may be as effectual to cure the extravagancies of this passion, as any of the old philosophers."

But Edward was so infatuated with pleasure, that to gratify these silly Venuses who beset his path everywhere, he branched out into every species of extravagance, in horses, sleighs, and carriages, to take them to all places of amusement, theatres, operas, balls, etc. Indeed, his chivalry towards the sex was so great, that when he first went to New York, and saw a handsome white girl walking into the parlor with a heavy armful of wood, or coal, to make up the fire, he would instinctively rush to relieve her of the load, to the great amusement of the Northern dandies; for he had never seen any but black men performing this labor in Carolina. He also ordered rich wines every day for his dinner; and invited friends to private suppers, dinners, and breakfasts, all on the most recherche scale, knowing his father's great wealth could furnish these luxuries. He was thoroughly dissipated, which in New York, or any large city, means, walking straight in the road to perdition. He would write to his father for a thousand dollars at a time, feeling confident that that generous, unsuspecting parent, was so proud of his genius, that he would withhold no gratification of his tastes, and that he never dreamed those tastes were corrupt. Oh, how this infatuated young man needed the counsel and discipline of that wise mother, who was buried deep in the ground.

"The mother in her office holds the key
Of the soul; and she it is who stamps the coin
Of character, and makes the being who would be a savage
But for her gentle cares, a Christian man.
Then crown her queen of the world."

Why, oh, why is it, the moralist asks, that such a multitude of children are born to the most mentally and morally irresponsible, inefficient, and ungovernably passionate, of the whole family of women (who will be almost certain to live to rear them a curse to society), while the very few women who have great moral stamina and intellect, if they ever have any children at all, so often die before they have had an opportunity to impress the image of their nobility of heart and mind on their offspring, who so invariably inherit their talents? The greatest men that history has ever known, have acknowledged that their wise mothers shaped their destiny, and so far from common sense mourning over the exit, through death, of silly, unprincipled mothers, society has the best reason to rejoice that such a stumbling-block to the prosperity of the morals of the country, has been removed from the sphere of her vicious influence over the rising generation, who at least will have a chance to grow up self-made men, uninfluenced by improper maternal influences.

Mr. Wyndham's friends finally persuaded him to stop the wild young man's allowances; and Edward, who was deeply in debt, wrote to his father that if he did not send him five thousand dollars to liquidate his responsibilities, he would blow his brains out. There was a striking difference, however, between this infatuated young man, and the generality of roués and spendthrifts; for he scorned ever to tell a lie, or to write hypocritical letters to his father, or to contract any debts that he did not intend to pay. His noble mother had lived long enough to impress on his heart, scorn and hatred of dishonesty and lies.

"The affairs of this world," says Colton, "are kept together by what little truth and integrity still remains amongst us; and yet I question whether the absolute domain of truth would be compatible with the existence of any society *now* existing upon the face of the earth. Pure truth, like pure gold, has been found unfit for circulation, because men have discovered that it is more convenient to adulterate the truth, than to refine themselves. They will not advance themselves to the standard, therefore they lower the standard to their minds." Obsequiousness begets friends; truth, hatred.

If a young man, however, has the ground-work of truth and honesty deeply implanted in his heart, *these* moral beauties will bring forth eventually the wheat that will crush out the tares of youthful excesses; and parents are unwise who despair of a son whose *truth* and *honesty* are not yet wrecked by dissipation.

This same Edward Wyndham, that so bowed his father's spirit in the dust, lest he should become a confirmed sot, and whom the trustees of the college regarded as so reckless in his dissipation that they expelled him fron the institution, this same gifted but misguided young man, had a *mother*, who entered into covenant with God for his salvation long before she died; therefore he was kept (though unknown to himself or others) within that charmed circle of God's providences, that he could not break through; and ere the meridian of manhood, he became such a consecrated saint that all his acquaintances declared that "there was such a halo of holy light and joy encircling his brow at all times, that they never met him without involuntarily thinking of God." But it may be edifying to detail his youthful career, and therefore we proceed with our story.

He was almost driven to madness, now, by the want of money; for Dr. Franklin says, "Think—think what you do when you run in debt: you give to another power over your liberty. If you cannot pay at the time, you will be ashamed to see your creditor; you will be in fear when you speak to him; you will make poor, pitiful excuses, and by degrees come to lose your veracity, and sink into base, downright lying; for the second vice is lying, the first is running in debt, as Poor Richard says; and again, to the same purpose, lying rides upon debt's back; whereas, a free-born American ought not to be ashamed or afraid to see or to speak to any man living. But poverty often deprives a man of all spirit and virtue. It is hard for an empty bag to stand upright."

How many of the most brilliant geniuses have marred the scintillation of their great mental gifts by contracting debts they could not pay! Poor Savage advertised himself as "An Author to Let," and, in the greatest misery, died in jail. Otway perished of starvation in a garret; and Goldsmith was such a child in managing his pecuniary temporalities, that the admirers of "The Vicar of Wakefield" and "The Deserted Village" recall with a sense of humiliation the innumerable subterfuges he resorted to in order to hoodwink his creditors.

Poor Edward Wyndham was in a hornet's nest, indeed, among his numerous creditors; but a tailor, of whom he had purchased many splendid suits, was so insulting and unceasing in dunning him at every corner, that he determined to punish him the moment he had the means of paying him the large bill he owed him.

Still no money came from South Carolina, and Edward was becoming more and more desperate. At last he was so crushed with anguish, that he elicited the compassion of the white waiter who attended his room in the hotel where he had put up after being expelled from college.

This kind-hearted son of Erin came into his chamber with a cup of coffee; and while, in the deepest gloom, Edward was sipping it, the waiter, in the simplicity of his philanthropy, offered him *his* place in the hotel, as dining-room servant, till he could get remittances from his father.

In one instant Edward flew at him, and, clutching his throat with the fury of a lion, screamed out, "Dare you to think *I* would be a servant?"

But the meek looks of the astounded Patrick recalled him to a sense of his folly, and he apologized to the mistaken Irishman for his ungrateful rage. He then gave orders not to be intruded on again until he rang his bell; determining he would neither eat, drink, nor leave his chamber, till he heard from his father, whom he had always loved with the deepest sensibility of his heart; for what child could have found it possible not to love Mr. Wyndham?—a father who always treated them with appreciating respect, always gratified their tastes, thought no expense too great to educate them in every accomplishment, and loved them with a woman's tenderness. When he told them their faults, he talked so kindly that they rushed into his arms, exclaiming, "Papa, I know it was all wrong, and I never will do it again." The child's mind, heart, and conscience were all convinced, and had no dernier resort from conviction, which children usually have who are scolded until they are too enraged to listen to the still small voice within.

Wherever Mr. Wyndham lived, young men flocked to his house. He sang delightfully, he played scientifically on the flute and guitar, and his tiny daughters were taught to sing little songs and dance for the amusement of his guests. In the summer, when the planters spend all the time from sundown till near midnight on their piazzas, Mr. Wyndham's verandahs were always crowded with young men and young ladies. His horses were ever at the command of the young folks. male or female, who wanted to take a ride, but owned none of those valuable quadrupeds themselves. His boats and his servants could at any time be had by the young people for a pleasurable fishing excursion; and, indeed, his handsome, genial, benevolent face and manners seemed so contagious, that he could heal every dissension among his neighbors with the unobtrusive simplicity of a child. His religion was love, gentleness, goodness; and commended itself to all except those malignant Pharisees who pray at the corners of the streets. He was strictly truthful; and so honest, that society would have profited by the daguerreotype if his heart had been as transparent as glass. He loved God with the fervor of a natural, confiding child, who receives every gratification that parental love imparts as long as it is beneficial; and he felt that his *reconciled* Father gave him all things richly to enjoy. He made larger crops than any of his neighbors, because his servants loved to be employed in his service. He was an Abrahamic patriarch on his plantation, and his negroes were often heard to say they loved the ground he walked on.

Not a solitary, bilious, green-eyed abolitionist, like those that partook of all the hospitalities of the generous, confiding Virginians, while they were skulking around "Harper's Ferry," to induce the negroes to suspect, to hate, to fly from, and to murder the master who had reared them up from infancy—who had given them everything necessary to life or godliness — who had protected them from every foe, even the foes of their own lazy and evil nature—who had watched over them in sickness, supported them in old age, and tried to educate them, through religion, for happiness beyond the tomb; even such a treacherous, double-faced, savage abolitionist, could not, perhaps, have visited Mr. Wyndham's plantation without being forced, *nolens volens*, to the conviction that slavery, in the mild, humanizing form in which it now exists in the South, is a paradise of civilization and Christianity, compared with the misery of the runaway and free negroes at the North, and the abject, white pauper population of the cities there, whose name is legion.

A Philadelphia gentleman says that, "not a half mile from that city, he understood there were three or four houses, in which three hundred of the most degraded class of negroes lived. Their food, when they had any, was bread and grog; and, in 1846, the ship-fever got in among them, and they died like dogs. Finally, the city authorities had to interfere, and break up these pestilential abodes." *

* An Enterprising Southerner.—The Detroit Free Press says that an enterprising Southerner, named C. J. Brown, has opened an office in Detroit, with a view of rendering material assistance to such negroes as are disposed to return to their masters at the South. Mr. Brown states (the Press says) that "he has made such investigations in Canada, especially at Chatham, and other places where Africans most congregate, as satisfy him that large numbers of them are anxious and ready

In a pamphlet of the statistics of the *black* population, published in Philadelphia, may be found this sentence from one of the committee:—"During the fall and winter of 1845–46, I observed much misery and distress among the colored population of the city and suburbs of Philadelphia, which was greatly increased in the fall and winter of 1846–47. During the period from September, 1847, to April, 1848, it increased to such an extent as made it necessary to ask the intervention of the Board of Health and Guardians of the Poor." . . . "In that time, there came under my notice 76 cases, colored male and female (mostly within six blocks of the district of Moyamensing), whose deaths, after a full and thorough investigation of each case, were attributable to intemperance, exposure, want of nourishment, etc.; of this number, 18 were from 18 to 30 years of age, 46 from 30 to 50 years, and 12 from 50 to 90 years; besides some chil-

---

to return to their masters at the South, if they only had the means;" and he proposes to furnish them with transportation tickets, and to send them in company with an agent, looking to their owners for remuneration for his benevolence.

The Charleston Mercury thinks there are in New York at least 10,000 poor people who would be happy to exchange places with Southern slaves. All they want in the world is plenty to eat, decent clothes, and a reasonable amount of labor, and that any kind Southern master would insure them. During one week, 6000 persons applied to the Almshouse-office for pittances of money and coal. Most of them would work if they could, but they cannot get anything to do, or are too sick to do it. The only "liberty" that such poor creatures have any practical knowledge of, is the liberty to freeze and starve, and the only slavery, a slavery to pinching want.

dren who also died from exposure, want of nourishment, and care." . . . "Many were found dead in cold and exposed rooms and garrets, board shanties, five and six feet high and as many feet square, erected and rented for lodging purposes, mostly without any comforts, save the bare floor, with the cold wind penetrating between the boards, and through the holes and crevices on all sides; some in cold, wet, damp cellars, with naked walls, and in many instances without floors, and others found dead lying in back-yards, in alleys, and other exposed situations."

Gracious God! can any hallucination equal in cruelty this master-piece of the devil: deluding the pharasaical abolitionist to entice away the well-fed, well-clothed, well-housed, religiously cared-for, respectable negro of the Southern plantation, to a doom like this that awaits them in the cold North? No such degradation could exist while they had a master interested in their welfare, and every generation of these starving Moyamensing brutes must sink lower and lower in the scale of humanity.

A Mr. Gorsuch, an old, white-haired, Christian planter, was brutally murdered near Philadelphia, some ten years ago, who went there for several of his fugitive slaves, who had stolen all his wheat in Maryland, and fled into Pennsylvania. No doubt these poor, foolish, runaway negroes are now to be found starving at Moyamensing, if they have not died of want already. It is understood, too, that the destitution of the colored population of New York city is even more hopeless than it is in Philadelphia.

The enslaving of African heathen, that brings them

into a Christian land, seems the only school opened by Providence to educate them for time and eternity—and woe be to that man or woman who, pharasaically and insolently, assumes to be *wise* above what is written in the word of God.* "If any man shall add unto these things, God shall add unto him the plagues that are written in this book; and if any man shall take away from the words of this book, God shall take away *his* part in the book of life, and out of the holy city." —(Rev. xxii.)

The people of the United States are now obliged to

---

* "THE FLY IN THE CATHEDRAL.

"A fly, while walking on the dome
Of great St. Peter's Church at Rome,
Exclaim'd: 'To me this lofty pile
Of stones seems built in wretched style;
I scarce find one smooth place o'er all
The surface of this crooked wall;
Go where I will, I still detect
Some excrescence or some defect.'
A spider, from his web o'erhead,
Had heard the critic speak, and said:
''Tis not for you, poor puny flies,
To judge of things of such a size;
This structure was not raised for you,
But creatures in whose larger view
The workmanship you censure so
No sign of ruggedness may show;
While they see what you never can,
The beauty of the building's plan.'

Thus often narrow-minded men
Will judge of things beyond their ken;
They spy slight faults that cannot mar,
But see not where high beauties are."

decide whether God is to be the judge of what is sin, or themselves. God ordered slavery. "Thou shalt take thy bondsmen from among the heathen nations around you." We say: No, sir. We of the 19th century are too wise to be governed by a Bible that was, perhaps, good enough for the Israelite in Egypt and in Canaan — good enough for the Christian in Jerusalem, and Antioch, and Rome — but not beginning to be progressive enough for the abolitionists of this 19th century.

"But these two theories of Right and Wrong—these two ideas of human liberty — the right in the nature of things, or the right as made by God — the liberty of the individual, of Atheism, of Red Republicanism, of the devil,—or the liberty of man, in the family, in the State — the liberty from God: these two theories now make the conflict of the world. This anti-slavery battle is only a part of the great struggle; God will be victorious, and we (Southerners) in his might." For slavery of the heathen is His ordinance, and we are greatly honored in being employed to civilize and Christianize many millions of brutal idolators.

God is *not* progressive, and when *he ordered* his chosen people, through Moses, to take their bondmen and bondmaids from the heathen nations around them, and keep them as a heritage forever, does any fanatical Pharisee dare to assert that the Almighty ordered the Israelites to *sin* in so doing? or that *He* did not in love intend the master and the slave both to be benefited? Not all the corrupt self-adoring politicians who scatter fire-brands, arrows, and death, and then say, Am I not in sport? Not all the malignant, narrow-minded, bilious fanatics in Christendom can reverse *God's* decree about the inequality of races, or convince Bible Christians that *they* are more loving to their black (not red) brother than the God of love is to all his creatures.

No one but an idiot or a lunatic believes that "all men are born equal." (Even Robinson Crusoe's wild man Friday found out this every-day fact.)

We left young Edward Wyndham shut up in his chamber, with the gloom of rash despair fastening upon his spirit; he knew his young step-mother hated him more intensely than she did any of the family, and he had had experience enough of her power, for it had hurried him out of his father's house the moment almost that she took possession of it; he knew, too, that most husbands would suspect, and therefore defend their children from a woman of stamina of character and great religious consciousness, but at the same time would be led by the nose by a capricious girl-wife, who, having no inductive powers of mind, could not, he thought, plot any designed mischief. This is the greatest possible mistake, for no woman on this earth is more cunning and more full of petty design than that same timid-looking, hypocritical, soft-voiced inanity, whose weakness is her infallible strength, and who has her own way throughout life, just because nobody considers her of sufficient consequence to oppose her selfishnesses and littlenesses.

Edward Wyndham knew, too, that there were other influences behind the throne; that old Mr. and Mrs. M'Elroy, his step-mother's parents, would oppose, through their daughter, his father's *first* children receiving any benefit from his wide-mouthed purse.

Then the poor wretched young man recalled the image of his sainted mother, and her prayers of faith, that he would become in early youth the friend of God, and that all his talents would be enlisted in the cause of righteousness, and then he repeated to himself—

"'Nay, mother,
Where is your ancient courage? You were used
To say extremity was the trier of our spirits;
That common chances common men could bear;
That when the sea was calm all boats alike
Show'd mastership in floating. Fortune's blows,
When most struck home, being gently wounded, crave
A noble calmness. You were used to load me
With precepts that would make invincible
The heart that conn'd them.'

"But how is it with me now? 'I have sinned and am no more worthy to be called thy son.' . . . 'The way of the transgressor *is* hard.' . . . 'Wherewithal shall a young man cleanse his way?' . . . 'By taking heed thereto according to thy word.' Yes, this *last* Scripture was dwelt upon in all my wise mother's teachings, and her pure life ever magnified the meaning of the Scriptures, and this holy mother was mine—

'She was my friend—I had but her—no more,
No other upon earth—and as for heaven,
I am as they that seek a sign, to whom
No sign is given. My mother! Oh! my mother!'"

He was startled by a loud rap at his door, and the post-man handed him a letter from Carolina. He tore it open and found a check for five thousand dollars that his kind father had sent him to pay all his debts and immediately return home. Tears of gratitude streamed down his face, and he determined not to lose a moment in obeying to the letter his gentle father's instructions. So with rejuvenated spirits he ran to the bank, had his draft cashed, and went to the livery stables and paid his debts for horses and carriages; went to the restaurants and paid for his numerous recherche dinners, suppers, and breakfasts, and costly wines; went to the jewellers and landlords, and friends' houses who had advanced him money, and cancelled every cent that he had so foolishly involved his credit in.

He then purchased a substantial cowskin and returned to the hotel, packed up all his trunks, and books, and presents for the family at home; sent all his baggage down to the ship where he had engaged his passage to Charleston, and finally he forwarded a note to the tailor who had so often insulted him, demanding his presence immediately *with his bill.*

The knight of the goose and shears, perfectly delighted at the prospect of recovering a debt he had regarded so hopeless, hurried to the hotel, and then up the stairs to No. 17. He was received arrogantly by the proud young Southerner, who paid him every cent his bill called for, and stepping to the door he locked it on the inside, and, drawing out his cowskin, he inflicted on the wondering tailor a chastisement that proved, no doubt, a life-long alterative to his bilious system. Feeling very satisfied with giving the man of stitches a practical illustration of righteous retribution, he said: "Now, sir, remember never again to insult a gentleman's son, in a land of strangers, as you have done me; remember that *Southern* gentlemen *honestly* pay their debts." Edward then locked his door and put the key in his pocket, leaving his prisoner inside; and now rushing to the ship, we hear no more of him till he lands at his father's door in Carolina.

The poor afflicted father, who had shed so many tears over his son's expulsion from college, and his dissipated habits, forgot all his griefs in the joy of beholding him once more; and now engaged one of the first lawyers to take him into his office to study law, who declared that his talents were so commanding, that he could with application become one of the most prominent men in the whole State. It is hard, however, suddenly to reform a young man who has quaffed so deeply the cup of pleasure. In a few months, Edward fell desperately in love with a beautiful girl who seemed to admire him greatly; but when he addressed her, she declared, with tears in her eyes, that she was already engaged to be married. He immediately sought her lover, and challenged him to fight a duel with small-swords, to determine who should carry off the coveted prize. Whether the fight *did* actually take place, tradition does not inform us; certain it is, however, that Edward Wyndham married the lady.

A few months after his marriage, his fond father determined to buy him a plantation, and settle him down to the cares of domestic life, as a means of saving him from further dissipation. So hearing that a planter near Coosahatchie or Pocotalago, had a very valuable place for sale, he forthwith bought it, with the negroes, for a hundred and fifty thousand dollars.

Old Mr. and Mrs. M'Elroy, Edward's step-mother's

parents, were enraged to the last degree when they heard of the purchase; and forthwith visited their daughter, to know how *she* was so daft, as to sit still and let her husband act with such generous fool-hardiness towards his dissipated son? And, indeed, these crafty old people persuaded Mr. Wyndham, that if he did not pay for the place for *two* years, Edward's wife's father would liquidate at least half of the debt. He listened to this counsel, and was ruined; for afterwards he made no crops; negroes, who at one time commanded a thousand dollars apiece, were not now worth three hundred. Edward's wife died in giving birth to a still-born daughter, and then her father died, without a will, and all his immense property was claimed by his brothers; and the poor, distracted Mr. Wyndham could not sell the land he had bought, and the sheriff was sent down to seize his property, and he was utterly hopeless. But at this particular moment, a stern, rich old millionaire, who belonged to the same church with him, stepped forward and paid the debt, giving Mr. Wyndham his *own* time to repay it.

And now commenced a system of economy that had never before intruded into Mr. Wyndham's affluent mansion, for he was determined to pay his friend for the kind loan, even if he had to go to the plow himself. Wine was the first luxury driven from a table, that in all his life had never been set without it; then every article of food, that the plantation did not yield, was excluded from his larder. His cellars, filled with the choicest wines, were yielded to his rich neighbors. His superior old Holland gin, and Jamaica rum, shared the same fate; together with all the great hogsheads of whiskey and tobacco, that had been purchased for his negroes. His West India candied fruits, and every such fanciful luxury, were all discarded; and his *first* children, Edward, Halcombe, Britannia, and Musidora, who had property independent of their father, through their dead mother, nobly refused to appropriate a cent of their private income, but gave it all up to the payment of the debt, and even allowed their father to sell a part of their principal.

Mr. Wyndham's beautiful doll-wife now wilted down into a mere imbecile; and spent all her time reviling Edward as the sole cause of his father's ruin; indeed, she so influenced Musidora, that the child would indignantly spurn every offer of kindness from her own brother Edward, declaring how she hated him for making her papa cry so much; and then the irritable, despairing young man, would slap her little face, and this created such an enmity in that child's breast, that she never entirely recovered from it. Her sister, Britannia, on the contrary, was always in Edward's lap, soothing the torments of his conscience; for although he could not blame himself that his father chose to buy him a plantation, and was ruined by the speculation, still his follies had helped to break down the genial heart of that incomparably loved parent, and he could not forgive himself.

He gave his sister Britannia his dead wife's costly casket of jewels, and all her expensive wardrobe, while poor little Musidora did not receive a single present; and he was always telling her how very much smarter, handsomer, and better-behaved her sister Britannia was than herself. Everybody but the humbled child's father reiterated the fact; so that Musidora was driven out of the house by her sensitiveness to these odious comparisons; and as her step-mother, who had now three sons of her own, never troubled herself as to Musidora's whereabouts, she would take the little negroes, and wander through the woods all day, collecting whortleberries, chinquapins, walnuts, and hickory nuts. At other times she would go to the grave-yard, and kneel down on the ground where her own mother had been buried, and talk to her as if she were visibly present; and, indeed, throughout life she never was divested of the impression that her mother's spirit always held communion with her own, for those loving eyes were daguerreotyped on her heart.*

Sometimes she would jump on her beautiful saddle-horse, and ride for hours through the deep forests surrounding her father's extensive domain; and then again she would spring into a tiny canoe, and paddle round to the islands belonging to Mr. Wyndham's peninsular home, where the rattlesnake,† alligator, eagle, and

---

* "Mark her majestic fabric; she's a temple
Sacred by birth, and built by hand divine:
Her soul's the deity that lodges there;
Nor is the pile unworthy of the god."

† "There is no reptile merits more particular notice than the rattlesnake, which is one of the most formidable living creatures in the universe. Providence has kindly furnished him with a tail which makes a rattling noise, and no doubt was intended to warn every creature of the danger of approaching nigh him. He indeed possesses that noble fortitude which is harmless, except when provoked or molested. He is never the aggressor, and seems averse from making use of the weapons of destruction. He flies from man; but when pursued, and he cannot escape, he instantly gathers into a coil, and prepares for

beautifully plumaged birds and flowers, revelled in undisturbed possession; fearing nothing under heaven so much as the everlasting fault-finding and detraction that she had to bear morning, noon, and night in the family, who seemed never to appreciate character, and only approved of women who could spend a life-time sitting down, like her step-mother, before the fire, and executing occasionally amateur sewing-work; or, like her sister Britannia, who could lie in bed all day, and read novels. The moment that little Musidora would come in from the excursions she undertook in order to make her young life endurable, they would all, in chorus, declare she was the wildest and the worst child that ever lived; so that, as she had not been taught to understand the Bible, she grew up with the idea that wearing out your shoes, tearing your dresses accidentally, and roving about among the birds and flowers, constituted the deepest crimes that a child can be guilty of. "Woe be to them that call evil good, and good evil."

---

self-defence. He has a sharp and sparkling eye, and quickly spies any person approaching towards him. The greatest danger is when we inadvertently tread on him. On either side of his jaw he has two fangs, which are hollow, through which he injects the wound they make. When he penetrates a vein or nerve, certain death ensues, unless some effectual remedy be instantly applied. The Indians cured themselves by the strongest decoctions of snake-root, that grows wild all over the country; and having sucked the poison out of the wound, they chewed the snake-root, and applied it *externally*." The rattlesnake's whole back is cross-barred with the most brilliant colors, like calico; and might indeed, if he could speak, with those bright eyes have charmed our original childish mother, Eve.

Sometimes Musidora would take the little negroes, and put her father's flower-garden in beautiful order. Indeed, she regarded it as her special vocation, now that the family had no money to spend, to rear the young turkeys and goslings, and the whole family of poultry, for the use of the table; for her step-mother never stirred out of the house to attend to a single thing, and Musidora prided herself in waiting on and patronizing this frail being, who seemed utterly dependent on everybody around her.

Musidora taught herself to sew, and would hem and stitch any little piece of needlework that the old negroes could not see to do for themselves; and these grateful creatures would give her dozens of eggs, that she was so proud to store away until her step-mother wanted them. Everything she obtained she gave to this unappreciating woman; and when she would sink down into hypochondriacal fears of dead people, at night, Musidora would sit up and talk to her until after midnight, so that her dear depressed papa might not be disturbed out of his rest.

Mr. Wyndham's two daughters were now large enough to engage earnestly in study; but how could he afford to send them to Beaufort or Charleston, to Savannah or Columbia, to be educated?

His daughter Britannia had been named after a rich literary lady of Charleston, who, at her birth, was her (now dead) mother's bosom friend. This lady, as soon as she heard of Mr. Wyndham's reverses of fortune, came for Britannia to give her a superior education with her own daughters. After four or five years, this noble friend died, too, and Britannia returned home an accomplished woman, to tower over the morbidly sensitive Musidora, who had to listen now to the praises of this learned sister, everywhere, in antagonism to her own supposed inferiority. All the money that Mr. Wyndham could allow to dress these girls, their step-mother insisted must be spent for Britannia; as *she* had a rich beau, and it was necessary to secure him by every extraneous attraction. Musidora knit her own stockings and gloves, and worked embroideries for herself, as she was compelled to wear her sister's old dresses. About this time Mr. M'Elroy also failed in Savannah, and therefore came to live with his daughter, Mrs. Wyndham, hoping to set up a school in Beaufort District. Mr. Wyndham, kind as he had always been to his wife's relations, could not tolerate the idea of living always in the same house with persons so puritanically antagonistic to *his* views of religion and society — whose stern angularities would drive him to madness, now that his health was sinking under accumulated misfortunes. He therefore sent his negroes into the forests to saw out all the lumber necessary for the building of a house near his own, for the old M'Elroys. In the meantime his neighbors sent their children to be taught by old Mr. M'Elroy, and little Musidora and her eldest half-brother, were also among his scholars—which was the greatest possible affliction —for he punished her severely in school for everything he saw her do in her father's house that displeased himself or her step-mother. Here, again, was Musidora mortified continually by the meanness of her wardrobe, for all her rich schoolmates had mothers who delighted to make them look well; while she, poor child, was utterly neglected in her person, her manners, and her school lessons—for nobody at home taught her *how* to commit them to memory or understand their meaning. As she had a natural genius for arithmetic, old Mr. M'Elroy would sometimes give her a sum in the rule of three, though she did not understand long or short division—and then switch her severely as a lazy dunce. One day, after he had punished her more than usual, she carried her slate home, and begged her gentle father to explain the rules in her cyphering-book; and he did it so patiently that in a few hours she gained the information that she never afterwards forgot.

One day one of the little girls picked up a piece of childish poetry (ridiculing this impulsive, passionate, pedagogue) and carried it to him. The moment he saw the scrawl, he rose up in great wrath and ordered Musidora to walk up to his desk and say her prayers, for it was such a wicked piece that he knew *she* wrote it. Musidora protested that she did not and could not write the poetry, and would not pray in the school;—whereupon the old tyrant took a switch and whipped her all over her arms and hands, and said he would continue to punish her until she confessed, and kneeled down to pray the words he would dictate to her.

This poor orphan girl had relied on herself so long, that she had acquired perfect mental independence of those around her, and she determined that no power on earth, short of her father's, should induce her to kneel down and pray as a punishment in that public place. Mr. M'Elroy threatened and abused the child as a vile, obstinate little huzzy, who had been so spoilt by her father that she would come to ruin. He switched her over and over again, but he might as well have vented his wrath on a North American Indian as have moved Musidora's pride to stir one inch after her mind was made up to endure to the bitter end. The teacher could not bear to be foiled before the whole school, and therefore ordered all the little girls to fall on their knees and pray for that bad girl. The terrified children ran up to his desk and fell down on their knees to pray—after which devilish sacrilege he turned to Musidora and said, "You vile little wretch, now that you have had the example of all your schoolmates, drop instantly on your knees." But the child held up her resolved little head without moving an inch. Mr. M'Elroy finally began to feel afraid to switch her any more, and after school was out he walked home with her, and made so many concessions that Musidora forgave him and never told her father about it.

Her step-mother could not bear the children to have nuts, or figs, or oranges, or sweet potatoes, lest they should litter her room; but the moment Mr. Wyndham went to the store-house, Musidora would rush after him, and he gave her everything she wanted, and she would steal off slyly to the servants' hall and crack and eat her nuts and delicious sweetened potatoes; and she used to think how charming it would be when she became a young lady, to make everybody respect her, as they did Britannia, and get as many lumps of sugar as her sweet-tooth craved.

Mrs. Wyndham had no sternness in her character, and never treated Musidora harshly—she simply neglected her; and never felt the least responsibility about her, either for time or eternity, being wrapped up in her own three children, whom Musidora loved with an enthusiasm that none but a morbidly sensitive child could have felt who had nothing else to love. She would get so angry when old Mr. M'Elroy switched them, that she was often punished for this impudence, as he termed it.

One evening, Mr. Wyndham saw that a thunder storm—an autumnal gale, was coming up; which on the coast plantations of South Carolina is a fearfully grand phenomenon, especially at night. "The frequent balls of fire bursting from cloud to cloud—the forked flashes darting from the clouds to the earth, and from the earth to the clouds, alternately illuminating the whole surrounding atmosphere—the continual mysterious muttering noise of thunder at a distance—the dreadful explosion on the right hand, the repercussive roar on the left, while the solid foundations of the earth shake, and the goodly frame of nature seems ready to dissolve. The beasts of the field retire from the thicket and show evident symptoms of silent awe and astonishment during the storm; and man's ultimate source of confidence is in the divine protection." Mr. Wyndham's negoes all rushed to their master's big house, for these childish creatures believed that *he* could protect them from the fury of the elements as well as from every other harm. The rain began to pour in such overwhelming torrents, that it seemed as if a new deluge was about to drown the world a second time. Every soul in Mr. Wyndham's house sat up in terror the whole night—the great centenarian oak-trees were wrenched up by the roots, and the pines, one, two, and three hundred feet high, were blasted by the lightning, so as frequently to produce the dread lest they would fall on the house and crush it asunder. Prayer to the great God of the universe would at such a time of awe and suspense force its naturalness even into the mind of an infidel. Mr. Wyndham called on several of his dignified old servants during this night of horror, to pray to God, who was the only hope — and sometimes the negroes would sing above the howling of the storm, that hymn beginning with

"This awful God is ours,"

Little Musidora, every now and then, would slip off from her father, and run to the windows to look at the magnificent lightning, and see the great trees fall with a tremendous crash. She fearlessly enjoyed the sublimity of the scene that almost demented her stepmother with alarm, and this superstitious woman would rush between feather beds, believing *them* to be a non-conductor to the lightning.

The next morning the clouds cleared off, and the sun shone out as brightly as if nature had had no convulsion at all; but in every quarter you could meet with the blasted trees of the forest which wither and decay at the lightning's stroke.

No earthquakes, such as are commonly known in the West India Islands, are felt here; but the whirlwinds sometimes make avenues through the forests, by levelling the loftiest trees, or sweeping them before them like chaff.

These terrible blasts are generally confined to a narrow tract, and run in an oblique and crooked direction. Hurricanes have often visited the country, and through such low and flat lands have spread their desolation far and wide.

A few days after this frightful storm, Mr. Wyndham's millionaire friend, who had paid his debt for him, died, leaving all his property to two young nephews. So that now Mr. Wyndham's debt to that estate must be paid immediately.

Had that Christian man made his will to forgive the debt, or to allow ten years to pay it to his said nephews, he would have been a noble benefactor to a large family of refined, worthy, useful persons; whereas this property proved the utter moral ruin of his two nephews, and they died in the early meridian of life, drunken sots.

"Now gaudy Pride corrupts the lavish age,
And the streets flame with glaring equipage;
The tricking gamester insolently rides,
With loves and graces on his chariot sides;
In saucy state the griping broker sits,
And laughs at Honesty and trudging wits."

This blow to all the hopes poor Mr. Wyndham had had, of *time* to pay what he owed, now was blasted, and the sheriff came and seized many of his negroes, that had been in his family from generation to generation. This broke his heart; and when he looked at that helpless, frail wife and her children, he gave himself up to despair—the "iron, indeed, entered into his soul." With his last expiring energy, he went among his rich friends to get them to buy his negroes that were seized for the debt, and he had the satisfaction of knowing that they had all obtained masters whose interest, and whose kindness, and conscientiousness would secure for them all the comforts they had had when he owned them.

As soon as Mr. M'Elroy's house was finished, and himself and wife comfortably settled in it, the now penitent old man, with some presentiment of death, would rise at three o'clock in the morning, plunge into a cold bath, rub himself thoroughly dry with friction towels, and, after putting on his clothes, would repair to the garden, and dash himself prone to the ground, and there pray for hours against that ungovernable temper that had caused his good to be evil spoken of during his life-long profession of religion. "Bodily exercise profiteth little," says St. Paul; and if this mourning believer could have known the secret of those that fear and love God, namely, *faith in Jesus Christ*, as our purifier from sin, he would have proved in his actions a living epistle known and read of all men. He took cold from this fanatical exposure in the chill morning air, and died of pneumonia, rejoicing that the load on his conscience was at last removed.

Mr. Wyndham's despair of mind so overwhelmed him at times, that he was perfectly unmanned; and when he would look at his uneducated, strong-willed, impulsive Musidora, and ponder over the destiny that awaited her chronic sensitiveness and fearful adhesiveness; when he glanced at his lovely, helpless young wife, soon to be a mother again, and then at her three interesting, beautiful boys, he would fall down in a swoon, and lay insensible, till his dutiful son, Halcombe, would carry him to his bed and administer restoratives.

His splendid hair had become as white as snow, and

he, at the age of only forty-eight, was an emaciated old man; for the spinal disease that had been caused by lifting a tree fallen on one of his negroes, now returned on him, and no doubt was the cause of his utter hopelessness of mind; for who has yet fathomed the sympathy between body and soul?

One of his rich friends, who lived in a flourishing village, some ten miles off, invited him and all his family to spend a month with them, hoping thus to rejuvenate his prostrated strength, and finally gave an evening party, at which they induced Mr. Wyndham to play on his long-neglected flute, and sing a sweet accompaniment to his guitar About nine o'clock, without saying a word, he walked out of the piazza, (that encircled the house,) and proceeded to his chamber, where his younger children slept, and laid himself down beside them. In five minutes, little Musidora, seeing that her father did not return to the piazza, went in search of him, and, horror of horrors, there he lay, dead on the bed, surrounded by his three sleeping little sons. Musidora uttered a piercing scream, and all the company rushed into the room — some rubbing him, others trying to bleed him, others vainly urging restoratives; but that loving, suffering spirit had fled to its mansion in the skies. He died of disease of the heart. "Blessed are the dead who die in the Lord."

In the midst of the uproarious grief of the startled children, and servants, and friends, nobody noticed the overwhelmed wife, who, escaping from the room, ran out toward the woods frantic. Musidora, however, did not forget her step-mother, but ran after, and held on to her arms, till her cries brought assistance. She was then taken into a carriage, and hurried to her mother's house, where, in an hour afterwards, she gave birth to a daughter, while she herself was almost in a dying state. But she had a very skilful physician with her all night, and the child's life was saved.

Three of the waiters were dispatched by friends to run their horses ten miles, to Mr. Wyndham's plantation, to carry the heart-rending news to Edward and Halcombe, who had remained there to attend to their father's business. They sprang into a curricle, and, at the top of their horses' speed, reached the place where their adored father had made his exit from this vain world: and when Halcombe looked at that face, heavenly in death, he wailed over the body for two hours, with groanings so heart-rending that he was heard throughout the neighborhood; and when kind friends tried to force him away, he fell down into convulsions so fearful, that his life was only saved by cutting off his coat and bleeding him profusely.

Edward stirred not all night from that adored father's dead body; but his self-condemning bitterness of anguish was surely working that "repentance that need not be repented of." In his deepest heart he cried to God for pardon of his innumerable offences against light and knowledge. Let no one in this Christian land dare to doubt that the heart can become *new* through the application of the atonement of Christ, by that faith that crucifies our sins to His cross; and thus regenerates our ambition, making its aspirations more holy, and making all our natural passions the willing servants of righteousness.

Edward Wyndham afterwards became a true Christian; and *then* all his enterprise was directed to the salvation of those young men who, like himself, had been intoxicated with the pleasures of sin. Indeed, in a few months he left Carolina, and entered a Theological Seminary, a perfect example to the students there, of self-abnegation, and consequent Christian sanctification.

"Philosophy is a goddess, whose head indeed is in heaven, but whose feet are upon the earth; she attempts more than she accomplishes, and promises more than she performs; she can teach us to *hear* of the calamities of others with magnanimity; but it is religion only that can teach us to bear our own with resignation."

"Place not thy amendment *only* in increasing thy devotion, but in bettering thy life. This is the damning hypocrisy of this age, that it slights all good morality, and spends its zeal in matters of ceremony, and forms of godliness, without the power of it."

"Men will wrangle for religion, write for it, fight for it, die for it, anything but live for it."

CHAPTER XII.

PERSONS who live in a great populous town, can form very little idea of the solemnities of a funeral in the country, where every individual has a fixed identity in the minds of his neighbors; and where a *good* man (without any of the fashionable poetical licenses of expression) is regarded as a public loss, and his family command the sincerest sympathy in their bereavement.

In Washington, the Metropolis of the Union, where employees of the Government form the principal part of the male population, almost every man regards his neighbor as standing more or less in his sunlight; and it is deplorable to see how the selfishness of the human heart stares out like a bare-boned frightful skeleton, making them facetiously jest about their prospects of advancement, when grim Death strikes his dart into the vitals of their rival. "Our virtues disappear when put in competition with our interests, as rivers lose themselves in the ocean."

"There are some tempers—how shall I describe them —formed either of such impenetrable matter, or wrought up by habitual selfishness to such an utter insensibility of what becomes of the fortunes of their fellow-creatures, as if they were not partakers of the same nature, or had no lot or connexion at all with the species."

"God in mercy saves all beings but himself,
That hideous sight, a naked human heart."

But in this humble country village of Iodilla, at Mr. Wyndham's funeral, every eye was moistened with sensibility, for every person present remembered some kind action with which that noble, generous man's life had been perpetually associated; and his genial manners and conversation diffusing itself healthfully as the sunshine, was missed as a personal, irreparable loss, to his numerous acquaintances. It was deeply affecting, and remarkable too, to see all the young men and maidens put on the sombre badges of mourning to attend his funeral; the funeral indeed of their best friend.

> "And all clung round his bier weeping bitterly,
> Weeping the more because they wept in vain."

Would that the new-light saints, whose poetical lamentations resound through our land that God has been so partial to his creatures as to condemn the descendants of Ham, to the degrading influences of slavery, could have attended Mr. Wyndham's funeral, where his whole plantation of negroes assembled to mourn over the dead patriarch, with a refinement of tender affectionate grief, that would have elevated the *morale* of even the most civilized abolitionist. They formed a long wailing procession of the truest mourners that ever followed a coffin to the grave.

A "Reverend" Chattel.—O. P. Baldwin, Esq., of the Richmond *Dispatch*, writing from Augusta, Ga., under date of April 6th, says: "Speaking of churches, there is an African Baptist Church here which owns its minister. What do you think of that? They bought him of his former owner, and he is held in their behalf by a gentleman of this city. They give their spiritual servant a thousand dollars a year, which is a good deal more than some white preachers receive. The Methodist Church is said to be one of the largest in number, in Georgia. It has its full proportion of the wealth and refinement of the State."

In South Carolina, in the country, the females of the family of the deceased never attend the funeral, for a wife shudders at the exposure of her grief to a promiscuous throng; and would be horrified at the idea of cutting and fitting mourning dresses, when her bereaved heart only seeks retirement with that God who has promised to be a father to the fatherless, and a husband to the widow.

"The strife is o'er! The loved of years,
To whom our yearning hearts had grown,
Hath left us, with life's gathering fears,
To struggle darkly, and alone.

"Green be the turf above thee,
Friend of my better days;
None knew thee but to love thee,
Nor named thee but to praise."

The widow of Mr. Wyndham, whose years had perhaps only numbered some twenty-five summers, remained many weeks at her mother's house; but when it was arranged for her to return to her bereaved home, her noble step-children vied with each other to soothe her grief, with every delicate and affectionate attention. Their father's love to her, was the bond that sacredly cemented their hearts in her interest. Musidora had followed her step-mother to old Mrs. M'Elroy's, and indeed never left her room for a month, and would sleep on the floor at her bedside at night, to devote herself exclusively to her little new-born fatherless sister, who was named Gulielma. Mrs. Wyndham at last began to appreciate what a noble, sympathising, elevated heart throbbed in the breast of that faithful Musidora, who had been so misunderstood, so unappreciated, by the family; and she really seemed now to love and respect her.

The ministers for twenty miles around visited Mrs. Wyndham, to soothe her grief with Bible consolations; but Musidora ran out of the room when they began to talk, for she could not bear to hear any one insist that we should not grieve for our loved ones. Surely, when God afflicts, he means us to feel his rod, and to feel it *deeply;* and entire resignation under the loss of a tender husband, or father, or mother, must argue an ossified heart; for religion itself says, "Blessed are they that mourn, for they shall be comforted."

It is surprising how much patronizing sympathy the world expends on a weak woman like Mrs. Wyndham, who is incapable of that sorrow that bruises and blisters the heart, while it withholds it from a sensitive, adhesive nature like Musidora's, whose grief consumes like a canker-worm. "The spirit of a man may sustain his infirmity, but a *wounded* spirit, who *can* bear?" Musidora never recovered from this stunning blow, and her heart was doubly orphaned throughout life — for her father had been her last remaining hope on earth. Nobody, however, noticed *her* affliction, for all thought Mrs. Wyndham the most to be pitied; though she had four children to rejuvenate daily her interests and pleasures in the world.

'Tis true she retired from society, as conventional

sentimentality in South Carolina requires from a widow, but she allowed her four children to grow up with no knowledge whatsoever of their noble father's beautiful character, which no wife could possibly have done, had she returned the romantic love her husband had so lavished on her during their whole union. No; Mr. Wyndham's beautiful Matilda had no elevation of sentiment to appreciate her loss of his manly, consecrated heart, and indeed had no affection at all, except the natural *instincts* that every animal feels for its young. She loved her children with the weak, passionate fondness that Byron's mother at times expended on him—and, with just as much judgment, would switch them when they did not deserve it, and kiss them when they should have been sternly rebuked.

Halcombe, who was nearly the same age as his step-mother, now had all the responsibilities of managing his father's estate thrown entirely upon his inexperienced shoulders; for Edward had left Carolina, to settle himself, for many years, at a Theological Seminary in New York.

His first thought was that Musidora must no longer be overlooked; for she was budding into womanhood, without education, and without any training at all, mentally, morally, or physically—and consequently, from utter neglect and non-appreciation, had become so self-reliant, that she spurned control, except through her affections, *now* that she had neither father nor mother to command obedience. The family had ever treated her as if she was the only black sheep in their fold; and, as human nature prompts us to aim to be what our friends think we are, she rather gloried in her own wild independence of their opinions, and whenever they commenced their stereotyped expression of rebuke, that she was "the worst child that ever lived," she darted out of the house, and spent most of the day in the woods, gathering the magnificent wild flowers that, in the barren pine swamps of South Carolina, are brilliant and varied beyond description.

"In travelling along the coast, partly by water and partly by land, the traveller has an excellent view of the natural beauties and rural inhabitants of the forest. At a distance, the marshes and savannahs appear like level meadows, with branches or creeks of the sea running through them. On one hand, the evergreen pines appear, and engross almost the whole higher lands of the country; on the other, the branching oaks and stately hickories stand covered with mossy robes: now he passes a grove covered with cypress; then the towering laurels, the bays, the palmettoes, the beech, or mulberry trees surround him — all growing as the hand of Nature hath wildly scattered them. In the spring, the dogwood trees, with their innumerable white blossoms, and the wild-cherry trees, and many others, perfume the air; while the luxuriant, satin-leafed vines climb over the loftiest trees, and bushes or shrubs of humbler growth fill up the thickets." Indeed, the yellow jessamine climbs from tree to tree, and then hangs down from the topmost branches, bearing millions of sweet-scented flowers, that entice innumerable gay-plumaged birds to sip of this nectar of the woods Nothing can be more beautiful. "Consider the lilies of the field, how they grow: they toil not, neither do they spin; and yet Solomon, in all his glory, was not arrayed like one of these."

Musidora knew every wild flower, without ever having looked into a book on botany—and had an intimate acquaintance with every bird and snake of the forest.

"Beyond doubt, Carolina teems with animals, both of the useful and hurtful kind. The alligator, probably a species of the crocodile, is found here near the rivers and ponds, and is very destructive to young creatures about a plantation. He is perhaps the largest animal, except the crocodile in Africa, of the ovarious kind. The bear is a fierce animal, but, in many respects, had been a rich prize to the Indian hunter. The beaver is also a native of Carolina, and his fur was a precious article of American commerce." . . . "The racooon and opossum are also natives of the country, and are scarcely found in other parts of the world. The wolf, the fox, the rabbit, and the wild and pole-cats, are all found here, and, in the last century, the leopard and the panther, on whom the hunter poured his vengeance. Squirrels of various kinds and different hues are innumerable;" and their graceful activities, as they sprang from tree to tree, would charm Musidora by the hour, and she often caught the little flying-squirrel in her traps, or the negroes gave them to her for a pet. It is called the "flying-squirrel," not from its having wings like a bird, but from its being furnished with a fine, loose skin, between its fore and hind legs, which it contracts or expands at pleasure, and which buoys it up, and enables it to spring from branch to branch, at considerable distances, with amazing nimbleness.

It is so small that a little girl can keep it in her tiny pocket or work-basket, but its teeth are very sharp, and the bite severe, though not dangerous.

Musidora had been outlawed by the family on account of her eccentricities, and therefore sought to soothe her griefs by amusements in these woods, where she never realized a feeling of fear even at the roar of the alligator, or the hiss of the snakes in the grass. One day she climbed up a picket fence to gather the high-bush-blackberries that grew up against it, and after securing a calabash full began to descend on the other side; but on looking down to the ground, all covered as it was with briars, she espied a monstrous rattle-snake coiled up just on the spot she was about placing her foot: quick as thought, she sprang back and jumped safely over into the enclosure. Another time she carried her little maid with her into the woods to pick wild grapes or bullaces that grew on vines lying flat on the ground; immediately after arriving at a large patch of them, she heard a hissing sound, and looking around saw that the little negro had placed her foot exactly on the head of a snake: she seized the girl's arm and threw her off some distance, and the snake glided away; indeed, in all her experiences, Musidora had never been chased by any of these reptiles, save a black-snake, that is so nimble that it is scarcely possible to get out of its way.

One morning the family had said something that deeply wounded her feelings, and she wandered off as usual to indulge in the bitterest tears; she had on a very long dress and sun-bonnet, and was musing despondingly on her hard fate, deprived of both a father's and mother's love, and having a sister who was so much more admired and respected than herself, that she assumed entire superiority over her — when suddenly her meditations were arrested by receiving a hard blow that knocked her down, and she discovered that one of the wild cows in the woods was trampling upon her prostrate body. Instead of remaining flat on the ground, which was her only chance of safety, the idea of those cold horns being insinuated into her side, caused her several times to spring up, but the long dress entangled her feet and threw her down again. The cow, more enraged at this attempt to get out of her way, would, no doubt, have killed her on the spot, had not her brother, Halcombe, accidentally hunting in that part of the woods, rode up at the instant and rescued her from her perilous situation.

He at once determined to send this erratic orphan sister to that admirable academy for young ladies kept by Dr. Marks, at Columbia; and when he told Musidora of his plans, she could scarce contain herself with joy at the prospect of getting away from a home that had not a single association in her mind except that of sorrow. Her brother went to Coosahatchie and purchased the necessary clothing, and the now hopeful girl sat up half the night, and got up at dawn to sew, in order to complete her wardrobe at the earliest possible moment. But a heart-rending disappointment awaited her again; for as soon as her trunks were all ready, her brother walked into her room, and told her he had changed his mind, for the *estate* could not afford several hundred dollars a year to keep *her* at Dr. Marks's.

Musidora actually screamed with disappointment, but she had no power to reverse this cruel decree, and therefore shut herself up in her room for three days, so sunk in despair that the thought flashed through her mind several times to run into the river and drown herself; but the mystic consciousness that her dead mother's spirit was always around her, eventually soothed her troubled spirit, and she would say to herself, surely I shall not *always* be so miserable, so hopeless, and so unnoticed.

About a week after this final determination of Halcombe's, that he was not prepared to make any sacrifices to educate this heart-broken orphan sister, Mrs. Wyndham came to her chamber, where she found her still sobbing with disappointment, and remarked, "Now, Musidora, as you are not going to Columbia, you will not need so many clothes."

She then opened the afflicted child's trunks, and took out whatever she fancied for herself and Britannia. Musidora had had no especial wardrobe since her father's reverses of fortune, but had been supplied from her step-mother's and Britannia's old dresses, altered to fit her; so that she was very proud when everything had been bought *new* for her to go to Columbia. She protested passionately, therefore, against having her wardrobe, which she had worked so hard to make up, portioned off in this heartless manner. But all the family roared with laughter at what they called her high-mettled spirit and covetous stinginess; and they again asserted that she was the very worst-tempered child in the world.

Halcombe Wyndham was a man without genius, but

he possessed great business tact. He was therefore enabled to settle up all his father's debts, and yet secure a competence for his family. His devotion to the memory of his father now took the eccentric form of giving his whole affection to his step-mother and her children, regardless of the interests of his own orphan sisters, Britannia and Musidora. So he sent for the appraisers of the deceased Mr. Wyndham's remaining estate (for he left no will), and after the property had been divided according to law among all the children and the widow, he said to Musidora and her sister, "We have property besides this of our father's; therefore it would be kind and generous to give our share of the estate back to our step-mother."

Childlike, Musidora and her sister never reflected on the value of this property, and therefore freely consented to give it up; and Mrs. Wyndham actually got some gentleman to draw up a paper renouncing their claims, and brought it to her step-daughters to sign; which they cheerfully did, though they were infants in the eye of the law, and could not legally give away property, being under age.

This fanaticism of Halcombe's was the more singular, from the fact that he had given to his step-mother, previous to the appraisement of the estate, all the property that descended to her from her father, Mr. M'Elroy; though, having had no settlement at her marriage with Mr. Wyndham, she had, of course, no exclusive right to anything that came into her possession after she became his wife; and therefore, in accordance with the laws of South Carolina, it should not have been separated from her husband's estate after his death.

After all these temporalities had been arranged according to Halcombe's notions of generosity and justice, he ascertained, by reference to the public records, that his paternal grandfather had deeded the venerable homestead of the deceased Mr. Wyndham to Edward and himself, in the event of their father's death; so he at once took possession, and, with the property he already owned, he became comparatively rich. These two brothers had also taken other property of their own dead sisters. Britannia and Musidora, on the contrary, having given up all share in their father's estate, were merely enabled, with the greatest economy, to make all ends meet in their expenses.

Halcombe now bought a piece of land in the village named Iodilla, where his father had died, and building a comfortable house upon it, gave it to his step-mother free of rent as long as she should live; and he required his own orphan sisters to pay her for their board, which consumed nearly every cent of their income; so that all their ingenuity was taxed in order to sustain their necessities.

About this time an Episcopal minister came into the neighborhood; and, not having a large salary, he determined to take a class of young ladies, to be taught at the parsonage. All of Musidora's companions went to this morally elevating school; still, Halcombe was so absorbed in his step-mother and *her* children, that he again refused to give the uneducated Musidora this plausible advantage. He had but one idea in his head, which was constantly stimulated by the applause that the world extends to great disinterested philanthropists; so that, like others of this shade of character, often neglected his own sensitive, talented orphan sister, under the delusion that it was more magnanimous to expend all his enterprise for his father's *second* wife, and her family.

Mrs. Wyndham, after the death of her husband, had united herself to the church; and as her step-son never allowed her to be crossed in anything, she soon took up the idea that herself and children were the special favorites of Heaven, and any person who disagreed with her notions on any subject, committed a crime against God Almighty, who would certainly punish them here and hereafter. She would, with orthodox fervor, confess that she was a sinner, according to the Bible declaration; but then she was a sinner in the gross, never in the details, and considered herself outraged if every action of her whole life was not applauded as an evidence of angelic perfection. She took Britannia to occupy the same chamber with her, her own children sleeping in an adjoining dressing-room; and Musidora was assigned to an apartment all by herself, in the other end of the building, where there was no fire-place, and no comforts, except those which her own thriftiness soon accumulated. She was not at all fearful, however; but as she was too unhappy to sleep, the nights would have been intolerably long, had her mind not acquired the ghostly relief of communion with the spirit of her idolized dead mother. Indeed, she was so depressed from a feeling of loneliness in a family that cared nothing about her, that often the thought crossed her mind whether it was not better to end her existence, than struggle on with a destiny seemingly so hopeless.

Her step-mother's caprices were a constant irritation, too, just like the incessant buzzing of a fly, though she never regarded her character as strong enough to elicit her hatred, or even her ill-will; and she shared with her brother Halcombe in the romantic sentimentality, that a woman who had commanded their noble father's affections, should be sacred as a goddess in their esteem. This woman, who had been petted and indulged all her life, had many fancies that rendered her a daily and hourly annoyance to her loyal step-daughters; but her dependence made such constant appeals to their generosity, and veneration for their father's memory, that they lovingly bore all her tempers and unreasonable restrictions, feeling proud of their self-abnegation. Mrs. Wyndham was so cunning* that she took advantage of this nobility of sentiment, and deprived poor Musidora of many little things that would have been a great comfort to that unhappy child. Under pretence of economy, she only allowed Musidora a piece of candle long enough to go immediately to bed with; and as the poor girl delighted in reading, and then writing out her melancholy thoughts, the want of a light at night was a great deprivation.

Mrs. Wyndham, too, never allowed a fire in any part

* "The common contrivances of cunning put me in mind of the preservative instinct I have sometimes observed in beasts, which lay a plot that is extremely artful and well-concealed in many parts, but at the same time left so open in some one that it is perfectly easy for superior intelligence to see and understand the whole complication of the contrivance."

of her house, except her own chamber; so that the family had to go *there*, or else remain in the cold. There was no fire made in the parlor at all, except when company visited them; and as Mrs. Wyndham often wished to be alone herself, she would put on the look of a martyr at their intrusions, and they would of course retire early to bed—Halcombe himself, when he happened to be there, leading the van in obedience to her eccentricities.

It would have been amusing to a philosopher to have canvassed the power of this weak woman over grown-up step-children of the greatest decision of character, and commanding intellect. Her very impotence, however, was her strength; for had she been a strong-minded woman, she would have been held up, perhaps, to consistency in the management of her household, that would at least have shown her her selfishness. At the very time she pretended to such great economy towards Musidora, in not allowing her a light to read by, she never restrained her own children in the enjoyment of every privilege her means could command; and doubtless they would have grown up as all spoiled children do, had not Musidora and her sister taught them what was right, every day, with an affectionate enthusiasm for their well-being that was truly beautiful, and commended itself to all who knew these elevated step-daughters.

Musidora was now about fifteen years of age, and yet was as fully grown as a woman of twenty. She was constantly invited into ladies' society, and, for the first time in her life, began to lose confidence in herself; for she found that all her companions distanced her in education and accomplishments, and she never returned from a party without recalling some blunder that she feared had subjected her to ridicule, and her pride would be so stung that it added to her hopelessness of the future. Still she had considerable nimbleness of conversational ability, and her inherent frankness rendered her interesting to all, from the unaffected enthusiasm with which she expressed her feelings and opinions on all subjects. She had sparkling large dark eyes, small, but regular features, and all that natural grace of person that belongs to children who have not received a stereotyped training from fashionable mothers and school-mistresses, so that her father's old gentlemen friends declared she was the most interesting of his children, and often compared her to Walter Scott's "Lady of the Lake."

"And ne'er did Grecian chisel trace
A Nymph, a Naiad, or a Grace,
With finer form or lovelier face!
What though the sun, with ardent frown,
Had slightly tinged her cheek with brown;
The sportive toil, which, short and light,
Had dyed her glowing hue so bright,
Served but in hastier swell to show
Short glimpses of a breast of snow;
What though no rule of courtly grace
To measured mood had train'd her pace—
A foot more light, a step more true,
Ne'er from the heath-flower dash'd the dew;
E'en the slight harebell raised its head,
Elastic from her airy tread:
And seldom was a snood amid
Such wild luxuriant ringlets hid,
Whose glossy black to shame might bring
The plumage of the raven's wing;

Her kindness and her worth to spy
You need but gaze in Dora's eye;
Not Katrine in her mirror blue
Gives back the shaggy banks more true,
Than every free-born glance confess'd
The guileless movements of her breast."

It is a custom in South Carolina, in the country villages, to make hundreds of bonfires (on either side of the public roads running through them,) on the fourth of July; and as these fires are built up of great knots of pine wood, they last or are kept blazing till midnight, and the ladies and gentlemen promenade up and down this turnpike till a late hour.

The State troops everywhere parade on this venerated day, and the young orators deliver addresses. Indeed, a military spirit has always been kept up by the Governors of the State holding encampments in various districts, where the militia are drilled and reviewed, and where the gentlemen have much sport in sham fights, and the cavalry charge upon a square of infantry whose fixed bayonets receive the frantic rushing onset of the shouting cavaliers, and whose prancing steeds appear to feel quite as much pride of military glory as the mad warriors who spur them on to the conflict. Indeed, those Southern horsemen bestride their martial chargers so gallantly, that it is not wonderful that, soon after the discovery of America, in the battle of Otumba, the poor ignorant Aztecs who had never seen a cow, a sheep, a hog, a horse, or a white man, imagined that Cortez's powerful war-steeds were a part of the bodies of the pale-faces who bestrode them, and were amazed, indeed, when killing one of the horses they found his rider separated from him and yet alive. Cortez, with less than a hundred cavalry, put twenty thousand of these superstitious Aztecs to flight; and, indeed, to this day, nothing is so terrible to the Indians as cavalry and long-sword warfare. The Algonquins call the Americans "*Chi-mo-cho-mun*," or long-knives.

Halcombe Wyndham was an accomplished military officer, and rode a horse so gallantly, and looked so martial in his splendid uniform and commanding stature, that all the ladies romantically claimed him as their knight of chivalry.

Every fourth of July, prominent officers spent the night with Halcombe; and one of these imposing looking fellows took a great fancy to Musidora, and offered her his arm to promenade in company with all the grown-up ladies. During this walk, he told the child, just entering her teenish life, that she was as beautiful and graceful as Venus or Hebe; that her eyes were in mourning for the murders they had committed among the officers that very day; and that she was the golden pivot upon which all his future hopes of felicity must turn. He also drew his sword from his belt, and snatched off one of the luxuriant curls that waved so truantly and freely over her neck and rounded, dimpled shoulders; and when he bade her good-night, he kissed her most gallantly, and said she must not forget him. And, indeed, the innocent Musidora, who had never been flattered before, thought her knight the most sensible person she had ever known, and was so proud of his admiration, that the next morning, when the whole family were assembled at breakfast, she could not resist the vanity of detailing every word and action of her lover, as a triumphant evidence that Britannia was *not*, in reality, superior to herself in personal attractions.

The perfect shout of laughter that followed this exposé of her first flirtation, convinced Musidora in an instant of the ridicule she had brought down upon herself from her want of knowledge of the world, and tears of mortification streamed down her face, until at last her step-mother's very learned, witty brother, who happened to be there on a visit, pitying her wounded pride, came to her relief and defended her from the unbounded ridicule of the family, and declared that he was himself charmed with her frankness. Indeed, Musidora's soul was so ingenuous, her heart so sincere, so right-minded, so at variance with everything that could seem to disagree with its natural elevation, that she had no thought of guile in allowing her admirer to kiss her childish cheek, or grasp her hand, or steal one of her countless curling locks of hair, and realized more a feeling of gratitude in being at last appreciated, than in any passionate complacency at making a conquest of a lover; so that when Britannia took her into the room to upbraid her imprudence for a whole mortal hour, Musidora felt as guiltless as an angel. Indeed, throughout life her mind was too pure to be contaminated with the sinuosities of fashionable, heartless flirtation, and to all her lovers, after this her first experience of courtship, she maintained unequivocal frankness and naturalness of conduct, and never realized the ambition of making conquests for the mere gratification of coquettish vanity.

From this day henceforward, Britannia took upon herself to lecture her for every word she said in company, which, of course, was very irritating to Musidora, as it was done with such a seeming, holier-than-thou-spirit, and from one, too, who had been placed above her all her life by the family; and who, indeed, was the only being she was jealous of in the whole world, for this peace-destroying passion had been germinated in Musidora's heart only through the odious comparisons that were always indulged in by her brothers, Halcombe and Edward, for she was too self-respecting ever to condescend to *envy* the generality of her companions, for her genius was altogether superior to theirs, and she knew it.

The learned Virulan observes, "that diseases arising from emptiness, are generally the most dangerous, and the most hardly cured;" "and amongst the diseases of the mind, envy, grounded upon domestic penury, is certainly of the same nature; especially where a neighboring opulence shows what the remedy is, but not how it may be had; like the thirst of Tantalus, where the desired object was near enough and yet out of reach too." . . . "And in such a case envy will be sure to work and boil up to a more than ordinary height, while the envious person frets, and raves, and swells at the plenties and affluence of his abounding neighbor, and is even ready to burst with another's fulness."

Musidora, now launched into the responsibilities of life, found daily causes of humiliation to her pride, for the extent of her educational acquirements was comprised in the fact that she could read, write, spell, and cipher. She, therefore, determined, on this foundation, to educate herself; but how was she to commence without books? She finally went to her dead mother's learned friend, the before-mentioned Mrs. Heyward, and entreated the use of her library, together with her general instructions as to what books she should read; and this princely old lady generously promised to instruct her, conversationally, one hour whenever she found it convenient to visit her. Musidora borrowed the best grammars and unabridged dictionaries, and geographies, and maps, and histories; and her delight in acquiring knowledge often made her resigned to the narrow-mindedness and malevolence of the judgments of those around her.

Where the mind is fixed on the love of knowledge, the impediments in its way often appear to operate as a stimulant to acquisition. Musidora progressed rapidly in every element she studied. The principles of syntax, definitions, etymology, and pronunciation, were all readily mastered, and she soon became an adept in the higher rules and classical applications of the language, by closely listening to the pronunciations and intonations of the learned clergymen in their pulpits, and the conversations of highly accomplished scholars whom it was her good fortune sometimes to be thrown into juxtaposition with, in her visits to her patronizing learned old friend, the said Mrs. Heyward. Every minister and every orator thus became to her a professor of pronunciation and a teacher of eloquence; and when this foundation in elementary knowledge was laid, geography, history, moral didactics, literature and poetry melted away before the noble art of reading. But of all helps in her vigorous efforts at self-education, her visits and literary hours with Mrs. Heyward were the most efficacious and improving, for she here corrected, enlarged, and consolidated her studies. No woman ever possessed more brilliant powers of conversation than Mrs. Heyward; her sparkling sallies of wit, her biting sarcasm — her absolutely fearless and whole-souled expressions of opinion about men and things, from the time of the Revolution up to the present day—made a visit to White Hall a faithful daguerrotype on the memory of the young of their country's history. This lady had accumulated one of the largest English libraries in the State of South Carolina. Her reading was of the most extensive and appreciative character, and there was no subject that this library did not furnish ample means of investigating. She was particularly versed in English and American history, having herself lived through the vital era of the American Revolution and Indian warfare, and she would sometimes digress in this direction, giving local anecdotes of that most unequal contest with the fleets and armies of the greatest military power on earth, at a time that our whole population numbered only three million souls.

Musidora drank in these draughts of knowledge from the lives of the mighty dead, whose works live after them, with delight; and she finally became the standard in Beaufort District in all questions relating to book-knowledge. Mrs. Heyward's majestic intellect rose superior to all envy and jealousy of her sex, and she delighted to tell of the heroism of the ladies of all ranks of society during the Revolutionary War;

for she regarded the women of South Carolina as the most chivalrous, frank, patriotic, adhesive in their sentiments and attachments, refined in their manners, and courageous in the expression of their opinions, of any women in the world; though they never dispute about women's rights, nor aspire to any more power in the country than the highest civilization, religion, and chivalry has and always will secure to them. Many of the ladies moving in the highest circles in Charleston, South Carolina, possess the whole-souled piety of a Lady Huntington or Mrs. Fletcher; for their religion is eliminated from the Bible, and not from any of the isms that intoxicate the strong-minded women of the Northern cities. Consequently, they go about doing good, as opportunity offers, to the people around their *own* doors; believing that if they take the beam out of their own eye *first*, they will then be enabled to see more clearly how to remove the mote from the eye of their brothers and sisters in the Northern States.

In South Carolina there are no noisy philanthropists or self-adoring progressionists — indeed, there is so little of the fashionable enterprise of the present times there, that not one couple, it is believed, since the first settlement of the State, has ever been divorced there by law. A sensitive lady would abhor even the idea of having two living husbands, or eloping with a coachman or pretty young overseer. But perhaps this old-fashioned, orthodox refinement and non-progressiveness has been adhered to through their never having heard of a higher law than that which they pledged themselves to abide by when they took the matrimonial vow. And surely the Bible sustains them; for Jesus said to his disciples, "Whosoever shall put away his wife, except it be for fornication, and shall marry another, committeth adultery; and whosoever marrieth her which is put away doth commit adultery."

The reason why so few ladies direct their attention to authorship, is not because they lack the genius necessary to eliminate books, but because the *gentlemen* are so unadmiring of blue-stockings in South Carolina, that a spinster has only to get the odious reputation of pedantry, and the beaux shun her as they would the plague.

Mrs. Heywood described to Musidora many dashing, daring replies made by the ladies of Charleston to the British officers, during their occupation of that city, in the first war.

"Anne Elliott," she said, "the wife of Lewis Morris, was born at Accabee. While the city was occupied by the British, she wore a bonnet decorated with thirteen plumes, as a token of her attachment to republican principles, and, for her patriotic spirit, was called 'the beautiful rebel.' Kosciusko was her admirer and correspondent; and an English officer, the second son of a noble family, who was billeted upon her mother, became so enamoured of her, that he sought the good offices of one of her female friends to intercede in his behalf, and even offered, if she would favor him, to join the Americans. Miss Elliott bade her friend say to him in reply, that, 'to her former want of esteem was added scorn for a man capable of betraying his sovereign for selfish interest.' She had before declined the gift of a splendid side-saddle and English horse, of which he wished her acceptance. She would not attend church as she had been accustomed in Charleston, while prayers were offered *there* for the success of the British arms — preferring to join in the service read at her mother's house, where petitions were put up for the downfall of the invaders.

"At one time, while Colonel Morris, to whom she was engaged, was on a visit to her at Accabee, the attention of the family was drawn to the windows by an unusual noise, and they perceived that the house was surrounded by the Black Dragoons in search of the young officer, who had no time to escape. Anne went to one of the windows, opened it, and, presenting herself to the view of the dragoons, demanded to know what they wanted. 'We want the —— rebel!' was the reply. 'Go and look for him in the American army!' answered the girl; 'how dare you disturb a family under the protection of both armies?' Her firmness and resolution conquered, and the enemy departed without further molestation." *

Mrs. Heyward also interested Musidora in the Indian character, by detailing anecdotes of their fidelity to their white friends. It was a common thing, when South Carolina was first settled, for the traders who resided among the savages, "to single out a particular warrior of influence and authority among them, and to court his favor with presents and constant civility. Among the Yamasees, one named Sanute was the friend of a trader named Fraser, but who, previous to the great Yamasee massacre, went with his fellow-warriors to Florida, to share the insidious liberality of

* Mrs. Ellet's *Women of the Revolution*.

the Spaniards. During his absence, Fraser married a fine woman; and Sanute, who had a great regard for him, after his return home, went to his house, and brought with him some sweet herbs, to show the lady a mark of respect, agreeable to the customs of the Indian nations. As soon as he entered the habitation of his friend, he called for a basin of water in which he bruised the herbs, and first washed Mrs. Fraser's face and hands,* and then, clapping his own hands to his breast, told her he would communicate to her all he knew in his heart. She, in return, thanked him, and made him some present. Accordingly, about nine days before hostilities commenced, Sanute came to Mrs. Fraser's house, and told her that the English were all wicked heretics, and would go to hell, and that the Yamasees would also follow them if they suffered them to live in their country; that the Governor of St. Augustine was their king, and that there would be a terrible war with the English, and they only waited for the bloody stick to be returned from the Creeks before they began it. He told them that the Yamasees, the Creeks, the Cherokees, and many other nations, together with the Spaniards, were all to engage in it; and advised them to fly to Charleston, with all they had, in the greatest haste, and if their petiauger was not large enough to carry them, he would lend them his canoe. Fraser, not a little astonished at the news, asked how the Spaniards could go to war with the Carolinians, while at peace with Great Britain? To which Sanute replied that the Spanish Governor told

* This was the Indian's mode of professing friendship.

him there would soon be a war again with the English, and that while they attacked the Carolinians by land, he would send to Spain for a fleet of ships to block up the harbor, so that not a single man, woman, or child among them should escape. Fraser asked him how long it might be since they had formed this horrid design? Sanute answered: 'Do you not remember, about twelve months ago, that Ishiagaska, one of our chief warriors, with four more Indians, went to the Creeks?' Fraser said he remembered it well. '*Then* it was,' said Sanute, 'he carried with him a Spanish talk for destroying all the English inhabitants of the province;' and, laying his hand upon his heart, declared he had told them all he knew, and repeated his advice to them to fly with all expedition; but if they were determined to stay at all hazards, he concluded by assuring them that, to prevent torture, he would claim the privilege of performing the last friendly office to them, which was to kill them with his own hands. Fraser still entertained some doubts, but his wife being terrified, he resolved at all events to get out of the way, and accordingly put his wife, his child, and most valuable effects into his boat, and made his escape to Charleston.

A few days after this, about the break of day, being the 13th of April, 1715, all the colonists were alarmed with the cries of war. The leaders were severally out under arms calling upon their followers, and proclaiming vengeance. The young men, burning with fury and passion, flew to their arms, and, in a few hours, massacred above ninety persons in Pocotaligo town and the neighboring plantations,* and many more must have fallen a sacrifice on Port Royal Island, had they not providentially been warned of their danger. Mr. Burrows, a captain of the militia, after receiving two wounds, by swimming one mile, and running ten, escaped to Port Royal, and alarmed the town. A vessel happening fortunately to be in the harbor, the inhabitants repaired on board in great haste, and sailed for Charleston. It was computed that the southern division of the enemy consisted of above six thousand bowmen, and the northern of between six hundred to a thousand.† Governor Craven, of Charleston, after a desperate fight, conquered these savages.

"On the suppression of the Indian ravages, the inhabitants of Port Royal parish returned to their plantations. They were encouraged to do so the sooner because Port Royal Island had a very capacious and safe harbor, and was likely to become a place of great trade, as being a commodious station for shipping, and the country around furnishing plenty of provisions. There were computed to be about seventy families, who obtained a considerable sum of money from the government, and worthy gentlemen added contributions; and in 1724, built a small neat brick church, the adornments of cedar. There was pressing occasion for this church, as the inhabitants of the parish live at great

* "Captain Nairn, who was among the number massacred, was buried at the Episcopal Church in St. Andrew's parish, where a monument is erected to his memory, giving an exact account of his death."

† Historical collections of South Carolina, by Carroll.

distances from each other, and none nearer than forty miles from any other parish."

"In 1712, Mr. Gilbert Jones became the minister of Christ Church parish: he persuaded the masters and mistresses to assist in teaching their negroes the Christian faith. He wrote thus concerning the matter: 'Though laboring in vain be very discouraging, yet, by the help of God, I will not cease my labors; and if I shall gain but one proselyte, shall not think much of my pains.' Out of regard to the poverty of his parishioners occasioned by the Indian war, he declined taking any contributions from them, lest some unsettled persons might think religion too dear, and therefore forsake it. Ill health, from arduous labor, finally forced him to return to England."

"The earliest teachings recorded in history of the negroes of Carolina, was under the first royal Governor, Sir Nathaniel Johnson, at Goosecreek, near Charleston, by an English clergyman named Thomas, whose parish was twenty miles in length, and eight in breadth; and who discharged his duties with very good success, having thirty-two communicants. He took much pains in instructing the negroes, and learned twenty of them to read. This worthy missionary died in 1706, after having laid a good foundation for his successor to carry on the self-denying work he had commenced."

"His successor, Dr. Le Jeau, says, 'Parents and masters were endued with much good-will, and a ready disposition, to have their children and *servants* taught.' He says 'he instructed and baptized many negroes and Indian slaves.' After Dr. Le Jeau died, he was succeeded by a missionary named Ludham. There were in his parish a large number of negroes, natives of the place, who understood English well. He took pains to instruct them in the principles of the Christian religion, and afterwards admitted them to baptism. He told their masters 'that if they concurred heartily in the work, all those born in the country would, without much difficulty, be instructed and received into the church.' He died in 1728, leaving his property in trust for the erection of a school for the poor of that parish, that amounted, after his debts were all paid, to two thousand pounds."*

History bears ample evidence, that from the earliest settlement of South Carolina, the negroes have been instructed in useful arts, and in religion, both by their masters, and the clergymen of the several parishes; though our Abolitionist brethren believe, that because we bring the black heathen into bondage, as Moses commanded, therefore the Southern slave-holder is incapable of any principle, save that of irresponsible selfishness. To our own Master, however, we stand or fall; and the Abolitionists, of whatever religion, may be comforted in the assurance that they will never be held responsible for any of the sins of their far-off Southern neighbors, if they exert their utmost ability and Christian zeal in perfecting the morals of those poor, degraded pale-faces, that surround the doors of their own State; and surely, if the following resolutions of the Massachusetts white laboring freemen be not exaggerated, all the philanthropic abstractionists of Boston have a life-time of work to do in advancing

* History of South Carolina, by Mr. Hewat.

their own operatives to the comforts always enjoyed by the South Carolina Slave.

White Slavery at the Massachusetts Pemberton Mills a year ago (1859).

A correspondent sends the New York Herald the following resolutions, adopted by a portion of the operatives of the Pemberton Mills, while on a strike about a year ago, and for sympathising with which strike the correspondent was discharged from a situation in the mills.

"1. *Resolved*, That we, the spinners of the frame or ring spinning on the Pemberton Mill Corporation, have long enough endured the low prices for our hard labor — wages which are too low to live by, as we cannot meet our bills for the necessities of life with such a contemptible compensation for our labor as has been paid us for the past year.

"2. *Resolved*, That we respectfully solicit a public investigation of the facts of the case, and a public exposure of the oppression and tyranny, abuse and obscenity, which has been perpetrated upon the female department of the Pemberton spinning-room, from time to time, by cringing tools of a monopolist corporation.

"3. *Resolved*, That such language, and such obscene behaviour, such malicious abuse, as we have endured from time to time, perpetrated upon us by the menials and slave-drivers in high and low places, placed over us to drive and hunt us down in our labor, from early morning until late at night, is more appropriate to the barbarous or dark ages than the enlightened age of the nineteenth century; yes, more appropriate to the slave-drivers of the negroes of the South, than to the tyrannical monopolists of an enlightened community, who seek to make the condition of the white laborers at the North worse than that of the slaves of the South.

"4. *Resolved*, It is our firm belief, that if our condition and grievances could be fully exposed, and the tools of tyrants fully unmasked before the eye of a generous public, a furious indignation would spontaneously burst from every candid and unprejudiced mind.

"5. *Resolved*, That such abuses, such violent and oppressive means, as have been resorted to, to still persist in crushing our every right and just demand into a perfect annihilation, are too much for a brute creation to withstand, and much more for a white and intelligent community.

"6. *Resolved*, That it is these wrongs, and this vile tyrannical oppression, combined with incompetency of government, and wages so low that negro slavery is far preferable, and death sweet rather than continued durance vile.

"7. *Resolved*, That we believe a generous and just public will sympathize with and investigate our affairs and our condition; and also that, after such investigation, every candid and unprejudiced individual, black—yes, even the despised negroes of an abolition community—as well as the white Anglo-Saxon, both high and low, will render the verdict, viz., that such abuse, and such oppression and wrongs, such mean, contemptible tyranny over us, in the shape of sneaking, cringing tools to the meanest tyrannical dynasty that exists in the manufacturing world at large, have driven us to this revolt, or strike, for our rights and for justice at this inclement season of the year.

"8. *Resolved*, That, unless a different state of affairs exists in the future, both in regard to wages and in the mode of government over us, that we will die on our strike rather than submit to such heinous and outrageous injustice from the Pemberton tyrants.

"9. *Resolved*, That, in the language of a noted anti-slavery agitator, in regard to the perpetuation of the Federal Union, that we also say, that under these circumstances that now exist and have existed between us and our employers, let the former union and the present slide for ever, before they shall any longer enslave and abuse us.

"10. *Resolved*, That we hereby tender our heartfelt thanks and sincere gratitude to the members of the Niagara Engine Company, for their generous disposition to aid us by opening their hall for our benefit.

"11. *Resolved*, That the above resolutions are the unanimous sentiments of the Pemberton Frame Spinning operatives; also, that the same are authorized by us to be printed in one or more of the public presses in this city.

"LAWRENCE, Feb. 14, 1859."

The correspondent says, "The poor white slaves were not successful in their strike. They were told that if they would not submit to their present wages and situation, the owners would stop the whole mill, as they could not afford to pay any more for their labor. By this threat, the most of the operatives were driven to submit; but a few of the most useful never returned to work, and still remain alive as witnesses of the tyranny and abuse of the masters placed over them. I now see it stated in the papers that this Pemberton corporation has been doing a very successful business the past year (which includes the time the poor operatives struck for living wages), having made $150,000 for the owners."

CHAPTER XIII.

"There are three modes," says Colton, "of bearing the ills of life: by Indifference, which is the most common; by Philosophy, which is the most ostentatious; and by Religion, which is the most effectual."

"Know, without star or angel for their guide,
Who worship God shall find Him. Humble Love,
And not proud Reason, keeps the door of Heaven;
Love finds admission, where proud Science fails."

MUSIDORA and Britannia boarded with their step-mother at the village of Iodilla, where Halcombe had built her a dwelling-house; for in his judgment she needed these helps to make all ends meet in her housekeeping. He did not pay her any board himself, but gave her all the surplus temporalities of his own Bachelor's Hall; so that this step-mother enjoyed every necessary comfort. Musidora had daily, hourly vexations in that house, where Halcombe insisted that Mrs. Wyndham's will, or rather her caprices (for she had no fixed character), should reign supreme. Like many very cunning *antinomian* professors of religion, Mrs. Wyndham would irritate her step-daughters about the most petty things in her household arrangements, and then put on the face of an innocent Abigail and roll up her eyes to heaven to testify to her angelic perfection of motives; and Halcombe, though he knew she inherited all her Irish father's temper, and her Scotch mother's envy of the rich, and petty stinginesses in her household, still was deceived by her. She entertained such jealousy of her step-daughters' intellect, and the little property they had inherited through their dead mother, that she could not bear them to take a lump of sugar from her lock-up without almost the formality of an official letter announcing what necessity there existed for such eccentric wants; and after all the diplomacy to get said lump of sugar was gone through with, she would pout and frown, or sigh like a martyr, that for *peace* sake she had to give up everything in the world. Philosophy may sometimes rise above such flippant annoyances in the stern battle of life, that Musidora had had marked out for her to enlist in, by Providence; still, Socrates himself would have been irritated out of his equanimity had a thousand sand-flies, almost too small to be seen, constantly buzzed around his ears, and bit him with their infinitesimal little mouths; so that although Musidora never dignified her childish step-mother with her serious resentment, still she was incessantly irritated that Halcombe sustained and encouraged a capricious tyranny in an unmeaning baby-minded woman, that made his two orphan sisters perpetually uncomfortable, in reference to this "much ado about nothing."

Mrs. Wyndham, however, never dared to annoy Halcombe *himself* with her tempests in a teapot—far from it. She was cunning enough to know that all her power depended upon *his* patronage; and therefore when *he* wanted anything in her house, she flew to get it; and when *he* had a finger-ache, it was laughable how she ran hither and yon for the whole family of pain-killers in her medicine-chest; and how she winked to her children to forestall Musidora and Britannia in waiting on their brother Halcombe, who was thus entirely weaned from his own fatherless and motherless sisters. Indeed, this woman acquired such power over him with her soft voice, pretty face, and hypocritical assumptions of saintliness, that all his affections and all his enterprises were directed to the one absorbing romance of advancing her, and her children.

This designing, weak, and superstitious woman, finally became so conceited that she believed all the fixed stars of the universe would be turned topsy turvy, just to meet her imaginary ideas of a superintending Providence. If a whirlwind blew down a neighbor's house, it was because the owner had slighted her and her children. If Musidora asked for a bit of candle to read by: Satan, from all eternity, in the person of Musidora, had been ordained to tempt her thus.

"Many persons make their own God, and he is much what the French may mean when they talk of *Le bon Dieu*—very indulgent when weak, near at hand when we want anything, but far away out of sight when we have a mind to do wrong. Such a God is as much an idol as if he were an image of stone."

"It is with nations, as individuals, that those who know the least of others, think the highest of themselves; for the whole family of Pride and Ignorance are incestuous, and mutually beget each other."

Mrs. Wyndham was so suspicious that, although her noble step-daughters had given up every cent of their father's property to her, and in their deepest heart tried to advance her interest from romantic veneration to their father's memory (who had sanctified her with his love, in their esteem), she was always imagining they meant to cheat her, sooner or later; and brought up her four children ignorant of all the sacrifices *for them*, that the noble girls had made; and perverted the moral effect of the elevated teachings of these elder sisters, by secretly encouraging mean suspicions of their motives. Judging others by herself, she could not comprehend how Musidora and Britannia could feel disinterestedness and anxiety for the well-being of a step-mother's children; so she brought them up to develop all her own cunning, suspicion, and narrow-mindedness.

Musidora, in all her trials and hopelessness of the future, had never once imagined that *religion* could be a solace to a desolate heart; her piety consisted in idolizing the memory of her dead mother, and invoking her spiritual sympathy; indeed, Musidora had never been taught anything about the Bible, and never had attended a Sabbath-school in all her life. When she was a little child, she had heard the minister read out of the Bible about the thirty naughty children that ran after the prophet Elijah, mocking him and saying, "Go up, thou baldhead;" and how God had sent three bears out of the woods to eat them up. This story made such an impression on her mind, that it induced her, during all her childhood, reverently to call every old gentleman *uncle* who had a bald head; and she never saw any one halt, or blind, or deformed, that she did not humbly salute them with sincere expressions of pity.

Who can tell the thousand nameless influences that assist in forming human character? — for during all

Musidora's life afterwards, this little story, expressive of God's indignation against mockery of his prophets, made her remarkable for her sympathy with unfortunates, and veneration for the hoary head. Her childish notions of religion were, that as her father was a Baptist, and she believed him to be the holiest human being that lived on the earth, therefore none but the Baptist denomination could be Christians *indeed;* and when a learned clergymen took charge of the Episcopal church in the village, she would not listen to the prayers because they were read out of a book, instead of coming red hot from the heart — and she even thought that as the twelve apostles were ignorant fishermen, the success of the ministry ought to be independent of education. Mrs. Heyward, however, told her, that so far from this being true, God had worked a miracle to impart the knowledge of tongues to the above-named apostles.

"For mystic learning wondrous able
In magic talisman and cabal,
Whose primitive tradition reaches
As far as Adam's first green breeches."

Butler's Hudibras.

About this time three Episcopal clergymen came to the village to hold a convocation. Musidora and Britannia, who were chiefly prejudiced against *that* church, determined, nevertheless, to attend this unique three days' meeting, as two out of the three ministers were bachelors — one of whom was so spiritually handsome that he could have captivated any female heart. His forehead was high and broad, and white as polished marble; his eye was a deep blue, and sparkling with genius and religious enthusiasm; his hair was jet black, and luxuraintly waving in its silky fineness; his features chiselled; and his whole face partook of that fascinating refinement and pensive ghostly purity of expression so irresistible to a romantic girl's imagination; while his cheek had that hectic flush of excitement, whenever he was animated, that betokened incipient consumption. His name was Melancthon.

"Would I describe a preacher such as Paul
Were he on earth, would hear, approve, and own,
Paul should himself direct me. I would trace
His master strokes, and draw from his design.
I would express him simple, grave, sincere;
In doctrine uncorrupt; in language plain,
And plain in manner; decent, solemn, chaste,
And natural in gesture; much impress'd
Himself, as conscious of his awful charge,
And anxious mainly that the flock he feeds
May feel it too. Affectionate in look,
And tender in address, as well becomes
A messenger of grace to guilty men.
Behold the picture! Is it like? Like whom?
The things that mount the rostrum with a skip,
And then skip down again; pronounce a text,
Cry, hem; and reading what they never wrote,
Just fifteen minutes huddle up their work,
And with a well-bred whisper close the scene!
In man or woman, but by far in man,
And most of all in man that ministers
And serves the altar; in my inmost soul I loathe
All affectation. 'Tis my perfect scorn!
Object of my implacable disgust.
What! will a man play tricks, will he indulge
A silly fond conceit of his fair form,
And just proportions, fashionable mien,

And pretty face, in presence of his God?
Or will he seek to dazzle me with tropes
As with the diamond, on his lily hand,
And play his brilliant parts before my eyes,
When I am hungry for the bread of life?
He mocks his Maker, prostitutes and shames
His noble office, and instead of truth
Displaying his own beauty, starves his flock."

Musidora and Britannia were astonished when they heard the prayers read by Mr. Melancthon, as if he was assured that God was at his right hand listening to his earnest petitions; and the litany seemed to them, for the *first* time, the lifting up of the heart in natural expressions of penitence, supplication, and holy hope; so that the next day, when this interesting stranger preached about the Savior's advent, and mysterious sorrows upon earth, Musidora felt that his "more than human solemnity made her blood run cold, and her whole frame shiver." . . . "He then drew a picture of the sufferings of the Son of God, his trial before Pilate, his ascent up to Calvary, his crucifixion and death." Never, until then, had Musidora heard the circumstances so fearfully daguerreotyped, so selected, so arranged, so colored. It was all new; and she seemed to have heard it for the first time in her life. "His enunciation was so startling, that his voice trembled on every syllable, and every heart in the assembly trembled in unison." . . . "His peculiar phrases had that force of description, that the original scene appeared to be at that moment acting before the eyes of the congregation." . . . "They saw the very faces of the Jews; the staring, frightful distortions of malice and rage. They saw him scourged, spit upon, and finally mocked, when he was in his dying agonies. Every listener's soul kindled with a flame of indignation, and hands were involuntarily and convulsively clenched against his murderers." . . . "But when he came to touch on the patience, the forgiving meekness of the Savior, when he drew to the life his blessed eyes streaming in tears to heaven, his voice breathing to God a soft and gentle pardon on his enemies, 'Father, forgive them, for they know not what they do;' the voice of the preacher, which had all along faltered, grew fainter and fainter, until his utterance being entirely obstructed by the force of his feelings, he raised his handkerchief to his eyes, and burst into a loud and irrepressible flood of grief." . . . "The effect is inconceivable. The whole house resounded with the mingled groans and sobs of the congregation," and fifty persons were truly converted from the love of *sin*, by that heart-convincing exposition of its cruelty to the only Savior ever found for the redemption of man into the image of God, since the fall of Adam and Eve from their primeval estate.

The next evening, Musidora and her sister, who had been deeply impressed, visited Mr. Melancthon, to converse with him on the subject of religion. The Apostle Paul could not have explained the simplicity of the gospel more convincingly; and he then told these two young girls to kneel down, and try to follow him, with their hearts, in the prayers and confessions of the litany. Musidora, for the first time in her life, prayed in earnest to be received into the family of God on earth; and when she went home, a peace passing all understanding, imparted such happiness to her long-troubled spirit, that she remained nearly all night on

27 *

her knees, asking herself if it was possible that *this* was the love of God that was now beginning to shine so gloriously in her heart, as to clear away all its hopelessness and gloom. She had never known mental peace or happiness before. She had never known how faith can bring an orphan child into such nearness of communion with Jesus Christ, as to fill the aching void in the heart. The next morning, at nine o'clock, Mr. Melancthon called, and with the characteristic truthful simplicity that had always distinguished her, Musidora described to him her feelings, and he astonished her by at once asserting that she was now a Christian, and must unite herself to the church; and indeed insisted that she should be baptized that very day, for she certainly had the witness in herself, that she was born of God.

Many persons are astonished that Christians have internal evidences of religion, or love to God; but in fact we do not love or hate any human being, that we have not the witness in our hearts, the internal evidence of the truth of our emotions, that regulate our outward actions. Faith, and love to God, is just as demonstrable to a Christian, from the witness within himself, as rage, fear, love, or hatred, towards a human being. If we love God's commands, we know it as surely as when we love to please our friends.

"The expulsive power of a new affection, is constantly illustrated in change of personal habits and characters, in love, in business, and religion; attachments, seemingly invincible to certain views, are at once and wholly destroyed by the entrance of a new master passion." . . . "Whosoever believeth that Jesus is *the* Christ," the accepted atonement for his every sin, is born into a world of power over his sin, by that simple act of humble faith; and if he keeps up undying watchfulness, he cannot again fall from this godlike power, over Satan; for he runs every moment into the covert of Omnipotence and is safe. "I can do all things through Christ strengthening me," saith St. Paul.

"When a man is told that the whole of religion and morality is summed up in the two commandments, to love God, and to love our neighbor, he is ready to cry, like Charoba in Gebir, at the first sight of the sea. 'Is this the mighty ocean? Is this all?' Yes, all: but how small a part of it do your eyes survey. Only trust yourself to it, launch out upon it, sail abroad over it, you will find it has no end; it will carry you round the world." . . . "All things are possible to him that believeth."

Musidora's brother Halcombe, and sister Britannia, were violently opposed to her committing herself to religious responsibilities that they did not believe her prepared to assume; and her step-mother seemed so heartlessly indifferent, that she was almost discouraged. But she had long since learned to think and decide for herself; so she ordered the carriage and repaired to the church, and Mr. Melancthon baptized her, and she partook of the sacrament; and thus commenced a new life, that governed her destiny ever afterwards.

She now diligently searched the Scriptures that she had never read before, and was amazed at the revelation *there*, that "*pride* is the abominable thing that God hates"—that inordinate self-love is the stimulating cause of all sin, and that it is utterly impossible to be holy, except through the crucifixion of that selfishness that sits enthroned in such high places in the soul that it cannot descend to the humiliation of seeking righteousness in another's merit—even in that of the Lamb of God, slain to redeem us from sin. The very idea of the moral perfection of the man Christ Jesus, during the thirty-three years that he sojourned upon earth, encompassed with a fleshy body just like ours, and, consequently, "tempted in all points like as we are, yet without sin," was transporting to the now heavenly ambition of Musidora; for she saw in the whole spirit of the New Testament, that the Christian was privileged, through the mysterious agency of faith, to attain to that blood-bought righteousness exemplified by Christ. She began to feel that her heart was no longer orphaned, for God was the father of the fatherless; and the promises in the Bible sounded as distinctly in her mental ear as a voice from heaven proclaiming that all her errors and transgressions against the laws of God were forgiven, and she was allowed to start in the race of life under a new dispensation of grace.

"Grace, 'tis a charming sound,
Harmonious to the ear;
Heaven with the echo shall resound,
And all the earth shall hear.

"Grace first contrived a way
To save rebellious man;
And all the steps that grace display
That drew the wondrous plan."

Though Musidora realised no fear of hell, she revelled in the mystery of obtaining sympathy in all her aims with Jesus Christ, who, during all his sojourn upon earth went about doing good.

Every enthusiasm of her nature was aroused to attain the heights of moral perfection held up to the Christian in the Word of God. "Eye hath not seen, ear hath not heard, nor hath it entered into the heart of man to conceive what God hath prepared for those who love Him" (even in this world). The extatic, the blissful heart of Musidora, no longer wondered at the martyrs of olden times rejoicing in the flames, and the tortures of the rack; for she realized *herself* that the spirit could become so wrapped in holy joy as to rise superior to bodily pain. She no longer worshipped God as a far-off Jehovah, but as brought near, even into her heart's love, by His endearing manifestations in the advent of Christ, and all night she talked aloud in her lonely chamber to the Great Spirit of the universe, who seemed ever present. She studied the mystic love of the Saviour breathed in the diary of Madame Guyon, Lady Maxwell, Thomas à Kempis, the Countess of Huntington, Mrs. Rowe, and Mrs. Fletcher. She read the sermons of the celebrated divines, John Howe, Robert South, Massalon, Toplady, Barrow, Calvin, Whitefield, Wesley, Fletcher, and Law, until her mind became so absolutely absorbed on the subject of religion, that her very dreams at night were continuations of her meditations on the Savior's love, in so dignifying fallen man as to enable him by mere faith in the completeness of the atonement, to recover the moral perfection he had lost in Adam — and she cried out in holy rapture at times, "I love thee, O Lamb of God, that takest away the sins of the world; and O thou that knowest all things, read the characters that love has drawn on my heart. What excellence but thine, in heaven or earth, could raise such aspirations of soul, such sublime and fervent affections as those I feel? What could fix my spirit but boundless perfection? What is there else for whose sake I could despise all created glory? Why am I not at rest here among sensible enjoyments? Whence arise these importunate longings, these infinite desires? Why does not the complete creation satisfy, or at least delude me with a dream of happiness? Why do not the objects of sense awake more ardent sentiments than things distant and invisible? Why should I, who say to corruption, Thou art my Father, aspire after union with the immense Divinity?

"Ye angels of God, who behold his face, explain to me the sacred mystery. Tell me how this heavenly flame began; unriddle its wondrous generation. Who hath animated this mortal flame with celestial fire, and given a clod of earth this divine ambition? What could kindle it but the breath of God which kindled up my soul? and to Thee, its amiable original, it ascends; it breaks through all created perfection, and keeps on its restless course to the first pattern of beauty.

'A worm! a God! I tremble at myself,
And in myself am lost.'"

Musidora determined that her every enterprise should now be directed to acquainting her young companions with the fact, that felicity in this world or the next could only be obtained through loving that mysterious Savior who had left a throne in high heaven, where he had been surrounded with adoring angels and archangels, to come down to this earth, where enemies the most malignant would spit in his face and mock him, and finally murder him most cruelly.

But her gay young companions declared she was demented, and shunned her as an infatuated Methodist. She then canvassed the enterprise of going as a missionary to China, to Jerusalem, to Africa, or any heathen land where *this* splendid Gospel was not known. Thorough examination, however, soon convinced her "that the heart is deceitful," and that the human mind ever aspires pharisaically to do some *great* impracticable thing, while it overlooks imperative duties entirely within its grasp—and she said to herself, "Why should I go off twenty thousand miles to work for the conversion of foreign heathens, when my own State, nay, my own District, teems with the poor; and African slaves have been brought from a heathen land to our doors expressly by the Providence of God, that they might be regenerated to the righteousness and civilization that accompanies Christian faith."

Musidora now formed a Sunday-school in the village of Iodilla, and the negroes, old, young, middle-aged, and children, all flocked to attend. She also induced her brother, Halcombe, to vest some of her property in a one-horse carriage, by which she was enabled to visit and *instruct* the poor *white* people for ten miles around where she lived. She determined, also, that there should be no paupers in her district, and therefore sought out all who were in the habit of begging for a living, and offered them work.

She was much encouraged by reading in the "*New*

York Observer" the following letter from one of her countrywomen now living in London.

"*The London Poor, and Woman's ways to help them. Letter from an American Lady.*

"LONDON, Jan. 28.

"*Messrs. Editors*:—As I sat a few days since in my quiet home across the wintry seas, reading your account of the 'Happy New Year' in New York, my heart was completely touched by its concluding paragraphs: —

"The fashionable parts of our city were never more crowded with elegant equipages and well-dressed gentlemen. It seemed a perfect carnival of social life and delightful festive enjoyment.

"But there were drawbacks to it all. The hungry, half-clad children were there, their limbs exposed and their hands and faces livid with the bitter cold, articulating with chattering teeth and almost inarticulate speech, a 'Happy New Year,' to the crowd of passers-by, to secure a penny. *They were freezing in the midst of houses warm almost as tropical heat. They were starving while surrounded by an abundance equal to anything which covered Dives' table.*

"What a sad commentary on sin, and the fruits it produces! Much of this wretchedness and want could be traced to vice in some form, in parent if not in the child, and their sad results thus manifest themselves publicly, when self-respect is all gone.

"*These contrasts on New Year's day suggest the urgent necessity of more efficient means to relieve the wretchedness of the poor in our large cities.* It is easy to say that the poor are also vicious, but they are miserable, and ought to be cared for by those who have abundance.

"This gave rise to a train of thought which determined me upon telling you what is being done here for these poor outcasts. It is easy (alas! how easy) to say that 'the poor are also vicious, *but they are miserable also.* They are our brethren. They are those for whom Christ died, and however blotted from their hearts and from their faces the image of the Heavenly, we know that through patience and hope, with God's added blessing, they may be created anew in Christ Jesus.

"No one more fully appreciates the noble charities of my lovely countrywomen than I do. No one can watch with more eager eye their care for those who have been cast out as the 'offscouring' of the old world, and thrown as a plague-spot upon the new. I desire to help them, and as the ever-aggressive policy of Christian love in England has lately opened a new door to the thronging thousands who have hitherto remained unreached, you will perhaps allow me, as briefly as possible, to call their attention to the plan through your widely circulated columns.

"Since I have been in England, I have heard despairing philanthropists say that it was too late; that the evil had struck its roots too deep, and the masses infected by sloth and ignorance, drunkenness and filth, were too formidable to be raised. And so it would almost seem. Always busy as are 'English hearts and English hands,' ever on the '*qui vive*' to feed the hungry and clothe the naked, and to bring the cast-out under influences for good, there yet remained thousands who could not be reached, whom no devoted city missionary, or godly colporteur, or Scripture reader, nor yet the most self-denying lady could ever search out, or home for the homeless embrace.

"But thanks be to God that though the children of this world are wiser in their generation than the children of light, yet the children of light have at last been guided to an agency which promises such successes amongst the most debased class in this country, as no other has ever held out. While I try briefly to explain the plan, I feel sure that my sisters in New York will recognize it as the 'Missing Link' in the chain which must raise the fallen, and bring to the light, that their deeds may be reproved, those who will otherwise become a plague-spot and a curse to our young and beautiful country.

"There are certain localities in London, where vice, and crime, and wretchedness, and despair congregate and fester, each year growing worse, and spreading the poisonous influence wider and deeper. It is not necessary to my present purpose to give statistics of the criminal classes here. It is enough to point to such localities as St. Giles, Clerkenwell, the Potteries, &c., &c., to show that in the heart of the most Christian country in the world, there is a plague which no human means has yet availed to wipe out. It is in these awful places that this new agency has been employed—this new evangel has been proclaimed—an evangel first of the Book and then of the scrubbing-brush—the broom—of cleanly habits and cheering hope; something humanising, civilising, and Christianizing. The principle is so simple, that one wonders that it has not been set at work before. It is simply proving the great truth 'The entrance of Thy word giveth light; it giveth understanding unto the simple.'

"An organization of City Missions and Scripture readers has long been at work in these desolate places, but after all it has been the lot of a poor, uneducated woman to find the key which has unlocked the gates of this Castle of the Giant Despair, and let so many captives escape into the glorious liberty of the children of God.

"There was a poor woman (Marian by name) whose heart God had touched. She was born in one of these awful spots, and grew up there. Losing her mother at a tender age, she was thrown with a little sister upon the cold charities of that awful world. She never knew a home till at the age of eighteen, she married a man as poor as herself, and commenced a new sort of battle with the powers of darkness around her. By what means she was led to Christ I cannot spare room to tell. But it was through the perusal of the Word of God, which is quick and powerful, which having received into her heart, she yearned to go among her poor and down-trodden sisters, and pour out upon them the balm which had brought healing to her own wounded heart.

"So means were found through a kind-hearted lady, who procured for her a bag of Bibles from the Bible Society, and giving her a small weekly compensation for her time (which of course she could not afford to *give*) sent her forth on her mission of mercy. Marian was not to *give* the Book to any one, but selling it at the lowest possible price, she was to collect a penny or two at a time, till it was paid for. Meantime, calling often for the payment, she was to drop a word in season, to help the distressed, aid the sick, and with true woman's tact show the poorest and the most helpless *how they could help themselves.*

"As soon as the plan began partially to succeed, a room was rented in the neighborhood; and here, at times which did not interfere with her agency for the Bible Society, she invited the poor women to tea. While they sat in a clean room, by a cheerful fire, and took, probably for the first time, a *decent* meal, she read to them from the 'Book,' and encouraged them to try to help themselves. Knowing their habits of gin-drinking, she taught them to make a cheap soup, which she persuaded them would be more nourishing to their families than the beer and bread which was the ordinary meal. She helped them to mend their tattered garments, to use soap and water, and brush and comb, and patiently led them on till the desire for a clean, humble house like hers, began to dawn in their hearts. Encouraged and aided by the 'Lady Superintendent,' Marian opened her room as a depot for calico, flannel, and prints of a cheap sort, and by degrees assembled these forlorn women, a few at a time, to teach them to cut and make garments for themselves and their families, retaining each garment till paid for, a penny or sixpence at a time. At each of these meetings there were readings of a portion of the 'Book,' and prayer to Him who hears even the cry of the ravens. After a time came another addition. In many of these gloomy abodes were many men and women, who not only possessed no article of furniture beyond a basket and a broken chair, but who had never known what it was to sleep on a bed, be it ever so humble. Beds at six shillings sterling were placed at her disposal, so that soon one and another provided the means to possess the coveted luxury, paying for the same before removal to their humble homes. Other simple furniture was from time to time added, till step by step these poor outcasts began to see that *they too* might be comfortable by husbanding those means which hitherto had all gone to the gin-shop.

"I might please you by telling you how wonderful were the results of 'taking of the people to mend themselves,' but I refer you to some soul-stirring books on this subject, where you may read for yourself, and wonder at the good which so humble an instrumentality has accomplished. I refer to 'The Missionary Link,' 'Ragged Homes, and How to Mend Them,' and a periodical, 'The Book and its Mission,' for facts which will show even the most thoughtless how much better it is to help the poor to help themselves than to give alms on never so liberal a scale.

"I cannot drop my pen without giving you a few 'results' of this humble work, from its first beginning in St. Giles by the patient and loving 'Marian' and her 'Lady Superintendent,'— to whom the Bible Society made a grant of £5 in 1857. There are now about forty 'Bible women' employed in this metropolis. Already between 5000 and 6000 copies of the Scriptures have reached a class which no other agency could have reached.

"A report which I have before me states the receipts of these missions to have been upwards of £2000, nearly £650 of which have been paid in for beds and clothing by the poor people themselves — money saved to *their* comfort, and rescued from the clutch of the gin-palace keeper. All these articles have been furnished at the very lowest cost, and to the honor of these poor be it said, scarcely any loss has accrued to the missions from non-payment.

"The report goes on to say: 'In the east of London, some of our women are familiar even with scenes of murder and violence which might shake the strongest nerves, yet no evil has been permitted to happen to any one of them, and their presence has been permitted when that of the police is defied.' The influence which the 'Bible women' have gained is wonderful,— from being mobbed by wicked men and boys, they have come to be 'waited and watched for' by those poor hopeless ones, for whose souls no one has heretofore cared. The appeal to their better natures, made by 'one of themselves,' has not been in vain, and the invitation of the poor weary one: 'Come again— come often—for no one has ever brought *me* such good news'— is daily repeated. 'Ruffianly men pass her on the stairs, the screams of wives beaten and kicked make her sick at heart, oaths are showered on her which make her shudder,—will she go home, and give up her work? Oh, no! for the feeble, pleading voice of her suffering sister rings in her ear: "Come again, come often."'

"In closing, may I ask my countrywomen, through you, *who* will begin this work in our large cities? To carry it on, a 'Lady Superintendent' is essential. She must judge of the fitness of the 'Bible women'—superintend the meetings for cutting and making garments—visit those cases of illness or other calamity to which her attention is called—make the purchases, and receive the money collected by the women. It is not necessary to wait for large means. The missions are almost self-supporting. They help the poor to help themselves. It begins with the women—the mothers, who have always, and will always, mould those about them. Do we need a wider sphere? We who are mothers know how, with all the appliances of health, and means, and education, our hearts are often wearied in our work; can we wonder that the hearts of our outcast sisters sink and utterly fail them, sunk as they are, with none of these helps? Let those of our sex who *will*, wrangle for a wider sphere, while we, content with the work which God has given us to do, go forth to teach our miserable sisters how to accept the 'glad tidings,' to 'guide the house,' to influence their children, and, at last, how with us to attain to that rest which remains to the children of God!"

Musidora obtained work for the poor by writing a circular, stating their ignorance, drunkenness, hopelessness, and penury, and sent it to all the planters of the district: she pledged herself to rid their neighborhood of paupers and street-beggars, if they would furnish her subscriptions of money, clothing, blankets, wool, cotton, or provisions. These elevated gentlemen of South Carolina gladly entered into her plans for making the poor respectable by giving them work; and the planters requested Musidora always frankly to state what she needed in this home-missionary enterprise.

Musidora bought spinning-wheels, and cotton and

wool cards, and gave them to the poorest women, promising to pay them for every pound they spun of the cotton and wool she furnished for their employment. This work the most inveterate street-beggars joyfully engaged in; and every week came to Musidora with their great balls of thread, which she weighed in their presence, and paid them for in exact accordance with the stipulated price. This thread was then given to other poor women to weave, for which they again were paid; and after the cloth was brought to her, she invited all the ladies of the village to assemble at her house, and cut and make it up for the orphan children among the said poor. Of course Musidora's enterprises were confined to the female sex; but the men became so stimulated with hope in seeing their wives obtaining a respectable livelihood, that they gave up the dram-shop, and tilled their lands, and finally made abundance of provision every year for their families.

In one of her visitations among the poor, she found an old woman named Culclaisur, living in what seemed a deserted poultry-house, with a ground floor. She was nearly seventy years of age, and had broken her arm without having it set, and therefore it was comparatively useless. She was so mercurial in her temper that nobody could live with her, and so she was alone. She declared she could not sleep in those woods at night, from fear of the rattlesnakes crawling up into her bed; and that she had no means of living except the erratic charity of her poor neighbors. Who but God knows the numerous charities of the poor?

Musidora begged her brother for a piece of land, and Halcombe freely gave it. She also begged a friend for lumber, and another for the loan of two carpenters; and then she had a small house built for this desolate old scold, Mrs. Culclaisur. She then went in her carriage to bring her to her new residence; for her worldly effects, with the exception of a bed, could be tied up in a pocket-handkerchief. Musidora had had a pine table, and buffet and bedstead, made by the carpenters, so that she furnished the singular old genius's house very comfortably. Remember there are geniuses among the poor, too. Mrs. C. certainly was one of them, for she could portray her exact meaning in conversation (and her tongue was perpetual motion) with a vast deal more clearness than half of the authors. She ridiculed professors of religion with the sarcastic power of Voltaire or Tom Paine; and she could read and write.

Musidora thought such a bright-minded person, if converted to Christianity, might be very useful in her intercourse with her poor neighbors. So she requested her to find somebody that she could live peaceably with; and Mrs. Culclaisur selected an old maid, which was not very wise, as report says these *passée* females, though very useful, are very angular. Musidora gave each of these women a warm blanket, and some flannel and other clothes. She gave them also a Bible, and a great many tracts; and promised them a peck of corn or rice apiece every week, and some meat. They could raise their own poultry and vegetables in the garden she had fenced in around the house; and she employed their time by giving them cotton to spin, and then to knit socks for sale. But the old woman could not be satisfied with anything; and got angry with Musidora, because the long drought dried up the well one day, and it could not be dug deeper under twelve hours. In the meantime, the old virago stormed with rage; and reminded Musidora of Jonson's effusion on the silent woman:

> "All my house
> But now steam'd like a bath with her thick breath;
> A lawyer could not have been heard, nor scarce
> Another woman; such a hail of words
> She has let fall."

After the water sprang in the well again from being dug deeper, the old crone got pacified; but her next complaint was that the corn and rice given to her every week was not a faithful peck measure, and so Musidora afterwards let her measure it out herself, though her minister was outraged at her thankless impudence. Musidora, however, had the high motive of reclaiming this smart old beldame, hoping then to make her talents useful among her own poor neighbors; so she bore patiently all her infirmities of temper, and want of appreciation, and finally she became a true Christian, and rewarded abundantly all the long-suffering kindness that Musidora had so hopefully extended. "Charity suffereth long, and is kind; it hopeth, believeth, and endureth all things, and never faileth," saith St. Paul.

"A physician," says Seneca, "is not angry at the intemperance of a mad patient, nor does he take it ill to be railed at by a man in a fever. Just so should a wise man treat all mankind as a physician does his patient, and look upon them only as sick or extravagant."

Public charities and benevolent associations for the gratuitous relief of every species of distress, are peculiar to Christianity; no other system of civil or religious policy has *originated* them; they form its highest praise and characteristic feature. Why do we demand such everlasting *gratitude* from the most degraded poor, when we never find this godlike emotion among the rich? Gratitude is the very rarest sensibility of the human heart. None but the noblest natures, like Andrew Jackson's, feel it. He, though elevated to the Presidency of the United States, *never*, in all his pomp of power, forgot to reward and sustain with his iron will the humblest of his lang syne friends; and, therefore, he ruled the hearts of the people.

Musidora established schools among these paupers, by ferreting out educated geniuses who were very needy, and getting the commissioners of the free school fund to employ them. These schools she visited once a week, and herself taught the children the catechism and the prayers of the Episcopal service, besides making them commit to memory many parts of the New Testament.

"Knowledge," says Webster, "does not comprise all that is contained in the large term *education*. The feelings are to be disciplined; the passions are to be restrained; true and worthy motives are to be inspired; a profound religious feeling to be instilled; and pure morals inculcated under all circumstances. All this is comprised in education."

Musidora visited the poor constantly. She taught the women how to sew, and how to cut and fit their garments; she healed their contentions among each other, and taught them manners, and truth, and honesty, so ingeniously, that their pride was never offended at her youthful assumption of superior wisdom. "Men should be taught as though we taught them not."

As labor was her only rest, Musidora also established a sewing-society among the ladies of the village; and as they were thirty miles from any town, these planters' wives sent all their fine pieces of linen, and silk dresses, and embroideries, etc., to this society to be made up; and, as all the young girls joined it too, they soon learned to be accomplished in the most beautiful sempstresscal arts. The money from this enterprise, numbering yearly hundreds of dollars, was sent to the foreign missionary board. The whole community gladly entered into these *practical* modes of advancing human progress; for there was no new-light Don Quixotes among them, raving about "all men being born free and equal," and blasphemously springing up a higher law than the Bible to make them so. The idea is rife among the Northern abolitionists that this wicked world is to be converted to righteousness by a twist and a jerk, and that *they* (not God Almighty,) are to inaugurate this millennial consummation of driving all evil out of the world. They have not yet found out that "old Adam is too strong for young Melanchthon." Oh no! Providence works too slow for their impatient idolatry of negro equality with the white man; *they* "are the men, and wisdom and virtue will die with them; and when their absorbing fanaticism is accomplished, of depriving the poor African of the only friend he has on this American continent, namely, the Southern planter, his master, and have seen this feeble black race skulking about the Northern cities, the most degraded, vicious, lazy, unenterprising, and starving paupers, they, the new-light philanthropists, ought to collect all the Sharpe's rifles and exterminate every thief, and every liar, and every sinner out of the whole world; so that the population, inheriting from our first parents, Adam and Eve, a fallen nature, being all thus silenced in the grave, they, the aforesaid new-light progressionists or latter-day saints, may enjoy a millennial season of a thousand years on this earth, and then be transported into heaven, high up above angels and archangels, and even above Jesus Christ himself—for it is understood that some of the abolitionists believe that the hero of the attempted massacre at Harper's Ferry, hung on a gallows, more morally exalted than the Savior's cross.

"We hold this truth," says a wise man, "to be self-evident to every believer in the proper inspiration of the Bible, that no moral reform is possible on principles that are not supported by the Word of God. In our zeal, and ignorance, and short-sightedness, we are often tempted to believe that a certain course of action is right and desirable, and even necessary, although the principles of the Divine law, and the example of inspired men, and the teachings of the Lord himself, furnish no warrant for the course we have assumed to be right. And the further we go under the impulse of our feelings, the less reverence we are likely to feel for the Bible, as the only rule of faith and practice."

"He who reforms *himself* has done more towards reforming the public than a crowd of noisy patriots."

Musidora, still finding that her enthusiasm to live

only for usefulness among her fellow-creatures, was ever reaching after further employment, determined to offer her services to the sick among all her neighbors, and to sit up with them at night as a nurse—for in the country in the South, nurses cannot be hired, and the slaves have not inductive powers of mind sufficient to administer *wisely*, either medicine or nourishment. And as Musidora's naturally sympathetic nature had been so elevated by religion, that it embraced the whole brotherhood of mankind, she was sent for by every family, high or low, who was afflicted in mind, body, or estate. She rejoiced with those that rejoiced, and she wept with those that wept, and she proved that "it is better to go to the house of mourning than to the house of feasting."

Unfortunately for poor Musidora, she was now called off from her numerous missionary enterprises, to accompany a friend to a watering-place who was sinking under a pulmonary disease. Here she found a great crowd of fashionable people and invalids, and soon her frank, whole-souled manner, good-humored wit, and striking conversational powers, made her to be sought after by every grade of people—for she thought it great folly to put on aristocratic reserve at a place where everybody goes for the express purpose of healthy relaxation and amusement.

Among her serious admirers were ministers and literary men, several of whom, during her stay of three months at Saratoga, offered her their hand in marriage. She finally selected a Dean Swift looking clergyman, whose caustic sarcasm, inimitable wit, gloomy, mystical piety, genius, learning, and lonely misanthropy of feeling, united with the unbending will of a John Knox, commanded her whole-souled and first romantic love.

The affections of such a man, when once fairly enlisted by a woman, are fearfully strong, and now a rival, that she could not control, occupied those thoughts that had formerly been by Musidora altogether fixed on heaven. The wildest enthusiasm of her affections, so long imprisoned from any earthly object, centered in fearful idolatry on the object of her heart's choice; for Mr. Fletcher, now, was never one single moment out of her thoughts. When she knelt in prayer her supplications were for *him*, not the poor paupers she had left in Carolina. When she slept, she dreamed only of him; every plan seemed to embrace this one object of life exclusively; and when she was absent from him, her mind was too abstracted to engage sensibly in any practical employment; she was perfectly infatuated; for all that sympathy that all her life long had been the most ardently coveted blessing, but never enjoyed since the death of her mother and father, was now extended to her in boundless measure by one whose commanding intellect, morally majestic character, poetical fancy, and singleness of affection, might well have flattered any romantic girl in her teens.

"Man," says Irving, "is the creature of interest and ambition. His nature leads him forth into the struggle and bustle of the world. Love is but the establishment of his early life, or a song piped in the interval of the acts. He seeks for fame, for fortune, for space in the world's thought, and dominion over his fellow-men. But a woman's whole life is a history of the affections. The heart is her world: it is there her ambition strives for empire; it is there her avarice seeks for hidden treasures. She sends forth her sympathies on adventure; she embarks her whole soul in the traffic of affection; and if shipwrecked, her case is hopeless — for it is the bankruptcy of the heart."

Tremble, Musidora! your heavenly Father has all your life kept you in the furnace of affliction, because you needed the hottest fire to separate the gold from the dross of your character; and as He is the covenant God of your sainted mother, he cannot allow you to become an idolator; you will again, and again, and yet again, be scourged by the rod that Providence provides for backsliders from holiness; for the Christian must acquire by experience that temperance in all things which should characterize the sensible people of God.

Musidora's lover, Mr. Fletcher, was a man of mystical, gloomy temper, which made him almost constitutionally misanthropical. He was very poor, of course; for poverty is the orthodox condition of great genius; and as he had not yet been called to a church, he still continued his studies at the theological seminary—finding his living cheaper and his surroundings more agreeable than elsewhere; for he had neither father, mother, brother, nor sister, and had been isolated in heart and lonely in sentiment nearly all his life. Indeed, his religion partook of the monomaniacal gloom of the poet Cowper, while he did not possess his gentle spirit.

Musidora was at times alarmed by the wild vehemence of her lover, as, in Byronic strains, he poured out the wildness of his joy in finding one human being at last who understood and appreciated his heart and mind. And he would gaze in her face, and then draw her near him almost frantically, and kiss her "hard, as if he plucked up kisses by the roots, that grew upon her lips."

When he spoke of their temporary separation,—for he had just received a call from a church at Boston, and was compelled to go there to transact some business previously to repairing to South Carolina to claim her as his bride,—when he even alluded to their short separation, he would tremble with some nameless fear that their love was too deep for earth, and, therefore, they would never again meet except in heaven.

Musidora, on the contrary, thought that both of them had suffered so much from an orphaned childhood, that surely their turn, too, for happiness, must be realized sooner or later.

Men often indulge the idea that the passion of love cannot exist in the heart of a spiritually intellectual woman. This is a great mistake; for, although true genius is foreign to grossness, still, the imagination of such a woman is so extravagant in its boundless fertility, that her lover is endowed with the attributes of a god, and her whole soul bows down to the magnificent creation of her romance; and a handsome, arrogant, gifted, gloomy satirist and hopeless misanthrope, like Dean Swift, acquires absolute dominion over her mind and heart.

Musidora, therefore, like another Stella, felt that Fletcher was her whole world; and the very idea of existence without him was too intolerable an anguish even to contemplate without distraction. And yet she had been such a child of disappointment, that her heart constantly trembled with presentiments that even the sparkling wit and brilliant conversational powers of her now happy lover could not at all times exorcise.

Her consumptive, invalid friend, who had been the sole cause of her visit to the far-famed Saratoga, was now improved in health, and prepared to return home. She was a person of wealth and high station, and had paid all Musidora's expenses to this celebrated watering-place, in order to enjoy her elevated sympathies and companionship; and, indeed, she loved her as a sister.

Musidora and her idolized and idolizing lover bade each other a farewell that can only be appreciated by those who understand the depth of sentiment which two persons of such strength of character, and isolation from the world, must have felt in the new-pledged and altogether satisfying sympathy that had so suddenly made life loom up into blissful hope for them. They both possessed natures that were not congenial with the crowd of men and women who seek amusement in shows, and happiness in luxury or wealth; and he said to her, feelingly,

> "From my youth upward,
> My spirit walk'd not with the souls of men,
> Nor look'd upon the earth with human eyes;
> The thirst of their ambition was not mine,
> The aim of their existence was not mine;
> My joys, my griefs, my passions, and my powers,
> Made me a stranger."

Steam-boats and rail-cars soon landed Musidora and her friend in Charleston, South Carolina, where all the wedding-clothes were bought, and Musidora retired to her country home, there to expend all her sempstressical arts in preparing her wardrobe for her bridal.— She remembered every expression of her lover's tastes about her dress, and had purchased every temporality with an eye thereto; and she sat all day to sew, shut up by herself in that once lonely room, that was now illuminated with the daguerreotype of his image, that by some optical delusion, seemed always present, so palpably, that she almost reached out her hand to smooth that romantic lock of brown hair, that truantly curled on his broad, pale brow; and she said:

"It is a fearful thing
To love as I love thee; to feel the world
A blank without thee. Never more to me
Can hope, joy, fear, wear different seeming. Now
I have no hope that does not dream for thee;
I have no joy that is not shared by thee;
I have no fear that does not dread for thee;
All that I once took pleasure in—my lute,
Is only sweet when it repeats thy name;
My flowers I only gather them for thee;
The book drops listless down, I cannot read
Unless it is of thee; my lonely hours
Are spent in shaping forth our future lives,
After my own romantic fantasies.
He is the star round which my thoughts revolve
Like satellites."

Musidora bribed her young black coachman to go to the post-office at sunrise, so as to be the very first messenger to whom the letters were handed, when the mail was opened,—but no letters came; presentiments of evil crowded upon her mind, and made her too sick at heart to take nourishment, or sleep, for two, or three, or four weeks; when one morning, her dream of human felicity ended, in learning that Fletcher was a hopelessly raving maniac, closely confined in a lunatic asylum. She threw herself on her knees, and stared up into the heavens, but she could not utter a prayer. Her fate for this world was sealed. Her idol had been hewn to pieces by the order of a jealous God. "Thou shalt have no other gods before me."

"Oh, that this too solid flesh would melt,
Thaw, and resolve itself into a dew!
Or that the Everlasting had not fix'd
His canon 'gainst self-slaughter! O God! O God!
How weary, stale, flat, and unprofitable,
Seem to me all the uses of this world!
Fie on it! O! fie. 'Tis an unweeded garden
That grows to seed; things rank, and gross in nature,
Possess it merely."

CHAPTER XIV.

"The love of a delicate female," says Irving, "is always shy and silent. Even when fortunate, she scarcely breathes it to herself; but when otherwise, she buries it in the recesses of her bosom, and there lets it cower and brood among the ruins of her peace. She is like some tender tree, the pride and beauty of the grove; graceful in its form, bright in its foliage, but with a worm preying at its heart. We find it suddenly withering, when it should be most fresh and luxuriant. We see it drooping its branches to the earth, and shedding leaf by leaf; until, wasted and perished away, it falls even in the stillness of the forest; and as we muse over the beautiful ruin, we strive in vain to recollect the blast or thunderbolt that could have smitten it with decay."

The shock to Musidora's concentrated hopes, prostrated her at once on a bed of languishing, where nervous fever slowly burnt out all the vitality of her system; and finally, the poverty of her flesh caused constant invention in her nurses, to keep the bones from working out of their natural enclosures; indeed, for weeks she lay in one position, lifeless as a corpse, and often Britannia had to feel if the heart throbbed, or the pulse indicated any signs, that she still lived.

"She look'd on many a face with vacant eye,
On many a token without knowing what;
She saw them watch her without asking why,
And reck'd not who around her pillow sate;

Not speechless, though she spoke not; not a sigh
Relieved her thoughts, dull silence and quick chat
Were tried in vain by those who served; she gave
No sign save breath, of having left the grave."

In the midst of this extreme illness, Britannia was alarmed one day when she approached the bed, to hear Musidora whisper feebly that she saw Fletcher's dead body carried in a coffin, in a great black hearse, near her window; and as she could not be persuaded to the contrary, Halcombe and Britannia soon found out that the poor sufferer had lost her senses. She ceased to remember any of the faces around her, and softly raved all day about her lover, and the numerous characters in history, that had lang syne commanded her wonder and admiration. Seven long months did the heart-broken Musidora remain in a state of dementation; and lunatic lamentations for the presence of *him*, who could never more return, to be the idol of her affections, on this earth.

Halcombe and Britannia were now unwearied in their attentions to this forlorn child of disappointment and misery; and even Musidora's step-mother would sometimes knock at the door, pharisaically to satisfy her conscience, by asking if she could do anything for her? The physicians declared that her mind had only been dethroned by the sympathy of the brain, with the extreme poverty and want of the vitality of the body; and that as soon as appetite and health were again generated, her reason would also assert its empire.

As soon as she could be moved from her bed, Halcombe carried her down to his plantation on the sea-coast, where the salt air produces not only a rampant appetite, but a constant disposition to slumber, in the heat of summer; and consequently it is very beneficial to nervous disorders of body or mind.

> "Sleep, that knits up the ravell'd sleeve of care."

> "Oh! thou best comforter of that sad heart,
> Whom fortune's spite assails; come, gentle sleep,
> The weary mourner soothe! For well the art
> Thou knowest, in soft forgetfulness to steep
> The eyes which sorrow taught to watch and weep;
> Let blissful visions now her spirit cheer,
> Or lull her cares to peace in slumbers deep,
> 'Till from fatigue refresh'd and anxious fear,
> Hope, like the morning-star, once more shall reappear."

> "Thou hast been call'd, O sleep! the friend of woe,
> But 'tis the happy who have call'd thee so."

> "He, like the world, his ready visit pays
> Where fortune smiles; the wretched he forsakes:
> Swift on his downy pinions flies from woe,
> And lights on lids unsullied with a tear."

Halcombe was now advised by the physicians to carry Musidora to all her old childish haunts around the plantation; and consequently old Mingo, the faithful, sympathizing, black driver, would order the large, comfortable boat, manned every day by the most gaily-dressed oarsmen, and brought to the landing, where two kind slaves would form a sedan-chair by clasping their hands into a square seat, and thus they tenderly carried the poor maniac every morning, through the mud, into the boat; and the men would strike up those wild, shrill, boat-songs, to the cadence of the splashing oars, that only a plantation negro can sing loudly, and clearly, and merrily. These accomplished black oarsmen were most deeply interested in the sufferings of their dead mistress's and master's orphan daughter, though they knew not the cause that had produced the wreck of her body and her mind. They, therefore, remembered all her peculiarities, and rowed the boat to all the places where as a child she had roamed; for the doctors thought that her mind would be restored if memories of the past could be rejuvenated. It would have affected any human being to tears to hear the poor thing softly talking to her dead parents, and her worse than dead lover, as if they were all around her couch; indeed, she had not recognised Halcombe, or Britannia, or her step-mother, or any friend, save her old nurse, black Phillis, who never had left her room, except on errands for her comfort, since her illness — and no mother on earth could have been more loving than this sympathizing, adhesive slave.

"Gentle as angel's ministry
The guiding hand of love should be,
Which seeks again those chords to bind
Which human woe hath rent apart—
To heal again the wounded mind,
And bind anew the broken heart."

Halcombe, almost in despair lest Musidora should continue a lunatic for life, suddenly remembered the little canoe that this strange sister, during her girlhood, used so often to spring into alone, and paddle over to the islands, to spend the whole day away from the family. He therefore ordered old Mingo to have a canoe brought to the landing, where, fixing a couch for her to recline on, he jumped in himself, and carried her to the place where the great over-spreading, motherly oak trees, centuries in age, had been her childhood's tent, and associated with her youthful loneliness of soul.

Here her *mind* awoke from its long mental sleep, and no language can describe the torments of a sensitive maniac genius, when reason first begins again to assert her supremacy. Oh! it was indeed a remorseless awaking to the broken heart of Musidora — and she cried piteously night and day to heaven, to be released from the crushing load of existence that was a burden to her too intolerable to be borne.

"Who would bear the whips and scorns of time,
The oppressor's wrong, the proud man's contumely,
The pangs of despised love, the law's delay,
The insolence of office, and the spurns
That patient merit of the unworthy takes,
When he himself might his quietus make
With a bare bodkin? who would fardels bear,
To groan and sweat under a weary life,
But that the dread of something after death,—
The undiscover'd country from whose bourne
No traveller returns — puzzles the will,
And makes us rather bear those ills we have,
Than fly to others that we know not of?
Thus conscience doth make cowards of us all."

Halcombe, as soon as Musidora could bear the fatigues of travel, was advised by her physician to take her to Saratoga or Newport. The generous, noble-minded Mrs. Heyward, offered to pay all her expenses at these places, and also purchased a suitable wardrobe, and overlooked her own seamstresses, while they were making every temporality necessary for her summer sojourn at these far-famed watering-places. But the crowds of gaily-dressed, thoughtless people, she there met, made Musidora feel

"Like one who treads alone
Some banquet-hall deserted:
Whose lights have fled, whose garlands dead,
And all but he departed."

It was all in vain, and Halcombe realized that he might as soon have amused a galvanized corpse, as this thrice-desolated orphaned girl, whose heart was now widowed indeed, though she wore not a strip of the semblance of woe, and had never told her grief, or its cause, out of her own family circle; and therefore society only regarded her melancholy or misanthropic: they never knew the living death she daily, hourly, groaned under — and she often tried as a Christian to feel an interest in those around her, by forgetting the irrevocable past.

"But ever and anon of griefs subdued,
There comes a token like a scorpion's sting,
Scarce seen but with fresh bitterness imbued;
And slight withal may be the things that bring
Back on the heart the weight which it would fling
Aside forever; it may be a sound —
A tone of music — Summer's eve — or Spring;
A flower — the wind — the ocean — which shall wound,
Striking the electric chain wherewith we're darkly bound;
And how, and why, we know not, nor can trace
Home to its cloud this lightning of the mind,
But feel the shock renew'd, nor can efface
The blight and blackening which it leaves behind,
Which out of things familiar, undesign'd
When least we deem of such, calls up to view

The spectres whom no exorcism can bind
The cold — the changed — perchance the dead anew,
The mourn'd, the loved, the lost — too many! yet how few."

After a few months Musidora returned to Iodilla, and determined to commence again her mission among the poor; but how different were her feelings — *now* stern duty, not enthusiastic youthful religious hopefulness, governed her sincere philanthropy; and in those long lonely rides in the woods, where the recipients of her charity lived, tears rained down her cheeks; yes, tears of rebellion against that great Almighty Ruler of the universe who had thus broken her heart on the wheel of despair.

Oh God! how happy are those disciplined, softly natures, that can say with *truth*, "Though he slay me, yet will I trust in him." Musidora, like Job, mourned the day of her birth, and believed there had never been to *her* any pleasures in life that compensated for its pains. She often madly wished she could have filled her niche in creation as part of a granite mountain, rather than have been fenced up with sensibilities so acute as to open a thousand avenues of torture, incomprehensible to those of rougher, hardier natures around her. Strange and inconsistent as it may seem, Musidora, all the while that her heart so foolishly rebelled against the scourging rod of the Almighty, felt that she was God's child; and so *near* to her faith was this relationship, that she talked aloud and said, "Why, oh! why is it, my heavenly Father, that my brothers and sisters in the family of God, have found out a road to Paradise so covered with soft, green grass, that it is altogether refreshing to soul and body to walk on its velveted turf — while I, surrounded with briars and thorns, push my way through interminable swamps and morasses, and venomous reptiles, and wild beasts ready to devour; so that at the end of every day's journey through life, I have to search out a dry spot in the quagmire wherewith to recline for the night, and start out again in the morning unrefreshed with hope, to encounter new adversaries and new fatigues, and renewed unconquered yearning thirst for the clear spring, whose waters will rejuvenate the heart and the mind." But the answer to all this raving against Providence is, "Be still, and know that I am God." "Why, oh! why," she reasoned with her murmuring spirit, "should I wish myself a nonentity when the wisdom of Omnipotence has decreed that every atom of *His* broad creation should exactly fill the space it was made for." There is a harmony and order in this world which should reconcile every human being to his condition; and injustice is done to the inscrutable Jehovah, when we regard any person endued with reason as a *membra disjecta*, or a floating pebble on the earth's surface.

"What if the foot, ordain'd the dust to tread,
Or hand to toil, aspired to be the head?
What if the head, the eye, the ear, repined
To serve mere engines to the ruling mind?
Just as absurd for any part to claim
To be another in this general frame:
Just as absurd to mourn the task or pains
The great directing Mind of all ordains.
All are but parts of one stupendous whole,
Whose body Nature is, and God the soul;
That, changed through all, and yet in all the same,
Great in the earth as in the ethereal frame;

Warms in the sun, refreshes in the breeze,
Glows in the stars, and blossoms in the trees;
Lives through all life, extends through all extent,
Spreads undivided, operates unspent;
Breathes in our soul, informs our mortal part,
As full, as perfect, in a hair, as heart;
As full, as perfect, in vile man that mourns,
As the rapt seraph that adores and burns;
To him no high, no low, no great, no small;
He fills, he bounds, connects and equals all.
Submit—In this, or any other sphere,
Secure to be as bless'd as thou canst bear:
Safe in the hand of one disposing Power,
Or in the natal or the mortal hour.
All nature is but art unknown to thee;
All chance, direction which thou canst not see:
All discord, harmony not understood;
All partial evil, universal good.
And, spite of pride, in erring reason's spite,
One truth is clear, *Whatever is, is right.*"

After five years of heart-consuming grief, Musidora received tidings of her lover's death; his mind had never been relieved of the awful phantom that brooded over it, until a few hours before his departure from a world that had been a wilderness indeed to a nature so lifted above the gross carnalities that occupied and satisfied the minds of the utilitarian materialists around him. He had been (as all true children of genius are) inured to sorrow, but it had in the end worked out the peaceable fruits of righteousness, for he died in full hope of the immortality that awaited his exodus to heaven. His only earthly idolatry had been Musidora, and God by his inscrutable providence had blotted her out of his deepest affections by blotting out his reason. Who can look into the eye of a man of genius who has become a raving madman, without feeling a mysterious awe? for this blazing orb seems to penetrate into the most secret recesses of your soul.*

Musidora, now that all the irritability of hope deferr'd, that maketh the heart sick, was blasted, by the death of her lover, became convinced of her sins of idolatry, and consequent wandering of heart and mind

* The author's step-daughter was engaged to be married to the celebrated poet Charles Fenno Hoffman, who, just one week before his bridal-day became a raving maniac. It was impossible to get him conveyed to an asylum for six or seven days, so Mrs. Schoolcraft determined to have him enticed to her house, as she could not tolerate the idea of his being exposed to the rude curiosity of strangers in a boarding-house, and she believed that his romantic loyalty to woman would restrain him from harming her, even though a maniac. One day she wrote a letter to a friend to come and take him to the asylum; but as the Secretary of State (Mr. John M. Clayton), who had been very friendly to her many years, kindly offered to send a strong man that evening to convey him to Mount Hope Asylum, she concluded not to put her said letter in the post-office at all. So, throwing it aside, she left the study, and in five minutes the madman picked it up and read it. Rushing to the room where she was seated, he said, "Why did you send a letter about me to my brother, Ogden Hoffman, telling him I was crazy?" She replied, "You are mistaken, I have forwarded no letter to New York." Never, as long as she lives, will the author forget the withering look he gave her, for she had never told him what was false, even in jest, in all her life, and he regarded this as a breaking down of her moral character. His blazing eye of genius was so piercing that she at once explained that the letter was written, but never sent; and she came to the conclusion that if human beings were generally gifted with such soul-reading brilliancy of orbs as those of this maniac, it would be impossible to deceive each other with their tongues, for such an eye explores the spirit.

from the great God whom she had so solemnly professed at her baptism to love with all her heart, soul, mind, and strength.

Oh! what suffering might be saved from the excesses of passion and self-will, were children from the nursery taught obedience to the powers that be; that are ordained of God, to prepare the mind for submission to himself. Poor Musidora, having been subjected to no discipline save that of reproachful detraction, had grown up with a will so strong that it could not bow even to Omnipotence itself, when that great Power broke to pieces her earthly idol.

All her murmurings against a Being who was perfect in wisdom, perfect in justice, and perfect in his love to all his creatures, particularly to those of them whose every impulse daguerreotyped his image in their souls, rose up to her contemplation with all their early vividness, and she fell on her knees, to confess her backslidings, and to pray for forgiveness, and power to commence anew her Christian pilgrimage on earth. There is no longing for sanctification so deep as that generated by *proving*, in our own experience, the utter vanity of the world. Musidora literally hungered and thirsted after righteousness, and she attended all the services of the sanctuary; but the ministers, in their sermons, never ventured to go one step beyond what she had already arrived at: namely, the tormenting conviction of sin. So that she went to church famishing for the bread of life, and returned without even a crumb to satisfy her spiritual cravings for holiness.

There are many discourses preached about our being perfected in righteousness on our death-beds. Is not this to make *death* our Savior from sin, and not the atonement of Jesus Christ? Surely all the fruits of *charity*, mentioned in the thirteenth chapter of Corinthians, are graces designed for *this* world; for we will not need them when we are relieved from all contact with sinful creatures. "Charity suffereth long, and is kind." "Charity endureth all things;" "is not easily provoked;" "thinketh no evil," etc.

Can we imagine a necessity for these suffering virtues, when we are surrounded by angels and archangels in heaven? No! *this* Christian perfection of St. Paul's *is* attainable in our earthly existence, where alone forbearance and hope are needed; and *that* minister starves his flock who does not preach that the atonement of Christ has purchased this righteousness for every believer exactly in accordance with his faith; and the church never can put on her beautiful garment of holiness to the Lord until every convert is taught to expect *that* religion so magnificently detailed in St. Paul's exposition of charity, or Christian love. Nothing less, nothing more, is required to make "your light so shine before men that they may see your good works, and glorify your Father which is in heaven." "If thine eye be single, thy whole body shall be full of light."

A kind literary female friend, about to travel in the mountains of the upper part of South Carolina, now invited Musidora to accompany her; and taking their seats in a comfortable carriage, they drove down to the town of Beaufort, where they stepped into a steamboat that landed them at Charleston the next morning, and in a few hours the railroad hurried them from that place to Columbia, the capital of the State. Here they were obliged to take passage in a stage-coach, with nine passengers inside. It was intensely hot, the road was very dusty, and there had been no rain for a month.

"Three days of uninterrupted company in a vehicle will make you better acquainted with another," says Lavater, "than one hour's conversation with him every day for three years. Some men are very entertaining for a first interview; but after that they are exhaused, and run out. On a second meeting, we shall find them very flat and monotonous: like hand-organs, we have heard all their tunes."

But Musidora regarded every individual she met with the interest of one who is intensely analyzing the human heart; and therefore *she* was never wearied, as her friend was, of this everlasting clatter of tongues for three whole days.

"There are braying men in the world, as well as braying asses; for, what's loud and senseless talking and swearing any other than braying?"

This tedious journey was occasionally relieved by an impulse of pity for the four stage-horses, that induced every passenger to spring out of the coach and walk up-hill for a distance of three or four hundred yards. Their first resting-place was Greenville, a village three hundred miles from the sea, surrounded by mountains, and the air so bracingly cold, that even in July and August an oak fire, morning and evening, would be most acceptable.

Musidora here met with her brother Halcombe's particular friend, the Governor of the State, who was sojourning there for the purpose of holding a large military encampment; when seven thousand people assembled on the ground where the tents were struck; the greatest enthusiasm prevailing among all classes of society in South Carolina in regard to these yearly martial exercises — indeed, the very boys are infused with a military spirit. The Governor insisted that Musidora should accompany him to a very large party, given in compliment to himself; and the effect of all this running hither and thither was wholesome, inasmuch as it drew Musidora's mind away from uselessly brooding over past sorrows.

The next morning the two friends continued their journey until they arrived, by invitation, at the residence of the far-famed John C. Calhoun, whose plantation was named Fort Hill, from the ruins of a fort found there, and believed to have been erected by the Cherokee Indians, in their terrible wars with the Iroquois, or Six Nations. The tradition of the South is, that the Shawnees came from the Suwanee river, in Florida, and that the first place they settled was the banks of the Savannah. At this position they became involved in a war with the Cherokees. The latter prevailed, after a long and sanguinary contest, and drove the Shawnees north. They cherish the memory of this event as one of their proudest achievements.

Mr. Calhoun was devotedly loved by all classes of men around his home. "His great mind and soul was given to politics." . . . "In earnestness he was never surpassed by even a religious devotee;" for he was a patriot, whose whole body was full of light, and his integrity of purpose blazed from his eye, and from every action of his whole life. The tricks of politicians never found one single loop-hole to hang by in his magnificent, daring, noble character. You could not converse with him ten minutes without ascertaining that *truth* sat enthroned in his inmost soul; and no living man could ever have approached him with ambiguous proposals. "As a public speaker, Calhoun occupied the foremost rank among the great orators, not of America only, but of the world." . . . "His diction was remarkable for the absence of ornament and metaphor, and for its clear, terse, and logical compactness. Avoiding all discursiveness of the imagination, his speeches are characterized by a salient pressure to the point, and a fiery vehemence of dogmatic argumentation, unbroken in its flow."

Musidora now had a long-coveted opportunity of seeing this intellectual giant around his family fireside. His wife was a quiet woman, not possessing genius, but a fund of every-day sense; and it was surprising to Musidora how much influence she exerted over this godlike genius. Mrs. Calhoun, however, was one of the few wives of great men who appreciated proudly her husband's majesty of mind and character. Indeed, as a husband, father, master, or friend, there is probably no living being who could say aught except in his praise. Musidora felt in his presence that his very simplicity of manner was so imposing, that she trembled with awe. He indeed became so much interested in her frankness and originality, and precision of sentiment on all subjects, that he was her friend ever afterwards.

In the midst of the purest intellectual delight she

had ever experienced from the conversation of any genius since her lover's death, poor Musidora received dispatches to hurry home, as her brother Halcombe was in a dying state. Bidding farewell to South Carolina's most august statesman, and his natural, affectionate, and numerous family, Musidora arrived at Palmetto Grove as soon as it was in the range of possibility to reach there. She found her brother had been accidentally shot by a friend, who was on a visit to him at his plantation. The whole load of shot entered immediately under Halcombe's knee, as the sportsman, standing near him, was about starting on a deer-hunting excursion. The negroes, when they saw their loved master's blood spouting and streaming on the ground, from the great gaping wound, could scarce be restrained from laying violent hands on the perpetrator of the mischief, and mobbing him on the spot. Halcombe himself was in such an agony of pain, that it was some time before he could be moved out of the bed of weltering gore that overspread the grass on which he lay. Finally, his deeply sympathizing servants contrived the least-jolting means of transporting him to the house, where for two years he was imprisoned, with no hope of ever again being able to walk, except on crutches. The faithful slaves were unwearied in their attentions, taking turns at night to sit up with him. Indeed, being up all night, and sleeping in the sun all day, exactly suits the taste of the black man; and whenever he offers to sit up at night with his ill master (which they all most cheerfully do), the housekeeper provides quantities of food for him to eat, during his hours of watching.

A smart black sempstress, named Harriet, dressed his wide-mouthed wound, every day, with a mother's careful tenderness. Musidora now found exercise for all her sensibilities, in making her brother's imprisonment tolerable to him. She was a splendid reader, and therefore entertained him with her great ingenuity in making all authors speak as if they were bodily present; so exquisite was her mimicry of the tones and manner each one was supposed to demonstrate in their conversational powers. Indeed, in reading Shakspeare's plays, she merely introduced the different characters that were to act their parts on the stage; and afterwards her brother knew exactly which one of them was then speaking, by the great versatility of Musidora's voice. She never read a book without making her mind well acquainted with the idiosyncrasies of the author, so as definitely to receive or reject the sentiments or theories he advanced.

Halcombe at last recovered so as to be able to walk, though the wounded leg shrunk up an inch shorter than the other. He, however, finally became as strong and robust as ever; and as Musidora had been so absorbed in his restoration as never to allude to her own blasted hopes, he believed her mind free from all its former sorrows, and he fell back on his old habit of utterly neglecting her.

"O Thou, who driest the mourner's tear,
How dark this world would be,
If, when deceived and wounded here,
We could not fly to Thee!

"The friends who in our sunshine live,
When winter comes are flown;
And he who has but tears to give,
Must weep those tears alone.

"But Christ can heal the broken heart,
Which, like the plants, that throw
Their fragrance from the wounded part,
Breathes sweetness out of woe.

"Then sorrow, touch'd by Him, grows bright
With more than rapture's ray—
As darkness shows us worlds of light
We never saw by day."

"So many great
Illustrious spirits have conversed with woe—
Have in her school been taught—as are enough
To consecrate Distress, and make Ambition
Even wish the frown beyond the smiles of Fortune."

Halcombe was just the kind of philanthropist that public opinion worships. Every widow who was in trouble came to him for help, and he never failed to extend it, although he never acknowledged love to God as the motive of his acts. His neighbors largely imposed on his seeming good-nature, and every day they would borrow his horses, his vehicles, his boats, and any movable thing he had, and return them very much abused. They would drive down to his plantation in large parties to be put over the river to Beaufort or Savannah, which entailed his sending in the fields for six oarmen and losing their work two days, giving him no equivalent whatsoever, as a South Carolina planter scorns asking *pay* for any such neighborly amiabilities. Every sick person, rich or poor, felt that it was impossible to recruit from typhoid-fever unless he spent a month at Palmetto Grove, to enjoy the salt air and the whole family of fish, oysters, clams, conchs, prawn, crab, turtle, terrapin, and shrimps. Every public benevolence, or public-spirited enterprise in the distriot, found Halcombe's name in the van, and Halcombe's energy in the performance. Every dying man looked to him as the most immaculate executor of his estate that could be appointed. He seemed to revel in the romantic idea of living for others, though he, of course, never neglected attending to his own personal interests too. His conduct to his step-mother and her children was the theme of admiration from Dan to Beersheba, and, perhaps, in the whole world around him, he was less interested in the welfare of his *own* two orphan sisters, Musidora and Britannia, than any human beings he had it in his power to patronize.

It is a singular fact, that a woman of genius is rarely, if ever, loved as a sister or a wife — never mind how consecrated she may be in her affections, or in the exact fulfilment of every domestic duty. Whether her husband, and brothers, and sisters, are envious of her talents, and feel humbled by their incompetency to patronize her, or whether everybody is offended that a *woman* can have logical reasons for her conduct or opinions, it is hard to divine; certain it is, however, that Halcombe loved his pretty weak-minded step-mother and her doll of a daughter (now growing up into her mother's beauty), much more than he did his *own* morally-magnificent and imposingly-talented orphan sisters, Britannia and Musidora, though these noble girls loved him with a fervor of appreciating love that his step-mother and her children were, by their very nature, incapable of.

Halcombe Wyndham may seem an unnatural character to those persons who have not deeply studied the human heart, but the Bible strikes at just such when it declares, "But if any provide not for his own, and especially for those of his own house, he hath denied the faith, and is worse than an infidel." The heart is so inexplicably subtle and cunning, that its deep sea of motive can only be sounded by the line and heavy plummet of God's Word; and probably those deluded heathen who threw themselves under the crushing car of Juggernaut, were not more profound in their idolatrous worship than are the idolators of *self* in this Christian land.

Musidora's noble, loyal, affectionate heart never allowed her to breathe to human being the slights or non-appreciation of her brother and the family; indeed, she was proud of his general disinterestedness of character, and never overlooked a single opportunity of trumpeting his praise to all her friends.

Halcombe would have been astonished if any one had taxed him with loving all the world better than his *own* high-souled, talented, loyal, devoted orphan sisters; or had detailed to him the injustice he had practised towards them in the division of their father's estate. He prided himself, above all things, in the exactitude of his justice in his dealings with men, and his universal beneficence. "But," says Lavater, "the generous who is always just, and the just who is always generous, may unannounced approach the throne of heaven;" and the great expounder of our Constitution — Daniel Webster — remarks, that "justice is the great interest of man on earth. It is the ligament which holds civilized beings and civilized nations together. Wherever her temple stands, and so long as it is *duly honored*, there is a foundation for social security, general happiness, and the improvement and progress of our race. And whoever labors on this edifice with usefulness and distinction, whoever clears its foundations, strengthens its pillars, adorns its entablatures, or contributes to raise its august dome still higher in the skies, connects himself in name, and fame, and character with that which is, and must be, as durable as the frame of human society;" and Colton wisely says, "If strict justice be not the rudder of all our other virtues, the faster we sail the farther we shall find ourselves from 'that haven where we would be.'"

CHAPTER XV.

"There is a glare about worldly success which is very apt to dazzle men's eyes," says a profound philosopher. "When we see a man rising in the world, thriving in business, successful in his speculations, if he be a man out of our line, who does not come into competition with us, so as to make us jealous of him, we are too apt to form a foolishly-high opinion of his merits. We are apt to say within ourselves—'What a wonderful man this must be, to rise so rapidly!' forgetting that dust, and straw, and feathers, things with neither weight nor value in them, rise the soonest and the easiest. In like manner, it is not the truly great and good man, generally speaking, who rises the most rapidly into wealth and notice. A man may be sharp, active, quick, dexterous, cunning—he may be ever on the watch for opportunities to push his fortunes,—a man of this kind can hardly fail of getting on in the world: yet with all this, he may not have a grain of real greatness about him. He may be all I have described, and yet have no greatness of mind, no greatness of soul. He may be utterly without sympathy and fellow-feeling for others—he may be utterly devoid of all true wisdom—he may be without piety, and without charity—without love—that is, either for God or man."

Musidora Wyndham, whose vigorous mind, untiring industry, and noble, elevating determination to give a good account of her stewardship, at the final reckoning, for every talent confided to her, morally, mentally, physically, or spiritually, by God, had kept her on the *qui vive* never to allow an opportunity of usefulness to her fellow-creatures to escape her enterprise, now devoted herself to the education, in its largest sense, of her step-mother's splendid-looking children; for Britannia had married a rich, very talented descendant of one of the Revolutionary heroes, and Mrs. Wyndham had not strength of mind enough to rear any child to be an honor to the high *moral* nobility of character that had distinguished the Wyndham family from their earliest settlement in Carolina.

Musidora's love for these children was as whole-souled, as the memory of her adored father, and the constant gazing into the realities of eternity for them hereafter, could elaborate in her religious heart and mellowed understanding. Every action of their lives was watched with argus eyes, in order truly to apprehend their varieties of character, so as to stimulate the right instinct, and depress the wrong. She taught them every day, by practical illustration, the hatefulness of higher law, selfishness. For, "healthy self-love, in a well-regulated breast, is as the steward of the household, superintending the expenditure, and seeing that benevolence herself should be prudential, in order to be permanent, by providing that the reservoir which feeds should also be fed."

Musidora taught these brothers the game of chess, as it was the only game she had ever excelled in; and she regarded it a means of training the mind to that inductiveness that perceives the consequential effects of all our moves on the great chess-board of life. She taught them gymnastics, instrumental music, singing, and dancing; and, after bathing them every night, and hearing their prayers, she very kindly explained what she thought had been amiss in their conduct throughout the day; so that these children grew up with as clearly-defined perceptions of moral right and wrong, as the oldest Bible Christians: whereas Musidora herself, having had no one to teach her in childhood, had learned every good thing at the point of the bayonet — that is, she had been scourged into all her knowledge by bitter experience of the miseries of error, and she was determined that by making these dear children bear the yoke in their youth, to prepare them for a manhood of tranquil moral happiness. Indeed, nothing brightens the intellect more than a Bible-instructed conscience, for then the human mind is housed in the pavilion of the Almighty, and not, therefore, drifting about the great ocean of life, without compass or pilot to steer the ship, that, driven by the winds of passion and prejudice, is in momentary danger of being wrecked on the rocks of self-confidence or despair. The man who is in the habit of listening to the voice of conscience, feels a delightful security about all his acts.* "If thine eye be single, thy whole body shall be full of light."

---

* "WASHINGTON'S RELIGION.—*Messrs. Editors:*—I have recently had the pleasure of reading a sermon preached in Newark, N. J., by the late Rev. Dr. MacWhorter, on the occasion of the death of General Washington. The lady of whom

Such loving, and morally elevating responsibilities, made Musidora feel rather a mother's, than a sister's anxiety, for these last, most promising children of her father's, who were named Pinckney, Cuthbert, Rutledge, and Gulielma. But experience proves continually, that you can teach no child successfully whose

---

I obtained it, now 95 years of age, was at the time a resident of Newark, and heard the sermon. I send you a note to it, which, if you think best, you can insert in the Observer.

"Very truly, ——

"NOTE.—General Washington was a uniform professor of religion. He steadily discountenanced vice; abhorred the principles of infidelity, and the practices of immorality. He was a constant and devout attendant upon divine worship. In the army he kept no chaplain of his own, but attended divine service with his brigades in rotation, as far as convenience would allow—probably to be an example to his officers, and encourage his soldiers to respect religion. He steadily attended the worship of God when President. He was not in this respect like too many, who practically declare themselves superior to honoring their Maker in the offices of religion. He firmly believed in the existence of God and his superintending providence. This appears in almost all his speeches and proclamations. He was educated in the Episcopal Church, and always continued a member thereof, and was an ornament to the same. He was truly of a catholic spirit, and considered the distinctions of the great denominations of Christians, rather as *shades* of difference, than anything substantial or essential to salvation. After President Washington's inauguration into his high office in New York, knowing the multiplicity of business to which he must attend, and that he must not be interrupted by continual visitants, 'he assigned every Tuesday and Friday, between the hours of two and three, for receiving visits, and that visits of compliment on other days, and *particularly on Sundays*, will not be agreeable to him.' I produce this quotation to show the great reverence he had for the Lord's day."

mother is working behind the scenes in antagonism, to undermine every day the structure of conscientiousness you are trying to build; so that many a righteous man has his grey hairs brought down in sorrow to the grave by his children, when he never dreams that their weak, sly mother, has, all their lives, weaned their loyalty and affection from him, and consequently destroyed the moral effect of his teachings. So that though Musidora had the delightful satisfaction of seeing these younger brothers grow up highly moral, still her heart was also sorely tried to find they had been all the while, by their narrow-minded mother, influenced against their elder sisters, though she had pretended great appreciation of Musidora's work of love, in training them to such dignified respectability. "Through wisdom is a house builded, and by understanding it is established."*

---

* A TRULY ROYAL FAMILY. — Some time since, we mentioned, says the New York Observer, under the head of "A Prince worth having," the noble conduct of Prince Alfred of England, in refusing to attend a celebration of the Olympic games at Athens, to which he had a special invitation, and which had been postponed on account of his expected arrival. The following will show how this royal family are brought up.

"A primary regard is paid to moral and religious duties. They rise early, breakfast at eight, and dine at two. Their various occupations are allotted out with almost military exactness. One hour finds them engaged in the study of the ancient, another of the modern authors, their acquaintanceship with the languages being first founded on a thorough knowledge of their grammatical construction, and afterwards familiarized and perfected by conversation. Next they are trained in those military exercises which give dignity and bearing. Another hour is agreeably filled up with the lighter accomplishments of music and dancing. Again the happy party assemble in the riding

Mrs. Wyndham was compelled to approve of Musidora's splendid disinterestedness, for God has left enough of Himself in the human mind, to force it to approve of the right, whether it practises it or not; but "Ordinary people regard a man of a certain force

---

school, where they may be seen deeply interested in the various evolutions of the menage. Thence — while drawing and the further exercise of music, and the lighter accomplishments, call off the attention of their sisters — the young princes proceed to busily engage themselves in a carpenter's shop, fitted expressly for them, at the wish of the royal consort, with a turning-lathe and other tools essential to a thorough knowledge of the craft. They thus become not only theoretically, but practically acquainted with the useful arts of life. A small laboratory is occasionally brought into requisition, at the instance also of their royal father, and the minds of the children are thus led from a contemplation of the curiosities of chemical science, and the wonders of nature, to an inquiry into their causes. This done, the young carpenters and students throw down their saws and axes, unbuckle their philosophy, and shoulder their miniature percussion guns—which they handle with the dexterity of practised sportsmen—for a shooting stroll through the royal gardens. The evening meal, the preparation of the morning lessons, and brief religious instruction, close the day.

"Rev. Mr. Wilson, late of Aberdeen, gives some additional information concerning the teachers and nurses selected for the royal children. He said, at a mission meeting in Leicester:

"'The monthly nurse in the queen's household was a member of Dr. Steane's (Baptist) Church, at Camberwell. The Princess Royal, now the Princess Frederick William, was awakened through reading a sermon of Adolphe Monod, and was led to give herself to God. When the last child was born, a Wesleyan was selected for nurse. The teacher of the Prince of Wales, Mr. Gibbs, was a Nonconformist. Previous to appointment, he was sent for twice, and for two hours was subjected to a severe questioning, by the Prince Consort and her Majesty, to test his knowledge. All the heads of departments about her

and inflexibility of character," says Merkel, "as they do a lion. They look at him with a sort of wonder — perhaps they admire him; but they will on no account house with him. The lap-dog who wags his tail, and licks the hand, and cringes at the nod of every stranger, is a much more acceptable companion to them."

Musidora, therefore, when afterwards she stood in need of the sympathy and friendship of her younger brothers and sisters, found that Rochefaucauld knew the human heart when he said, "We are always much better pleased to see those whom we have obliged, than those who have obliged us;" and that, although "almost every one takes a pleasure in requiting trifling obligations, and many people are grateful for moderate ones; still there is scarcely any one who does not show ingratitude for great ones;" and indeed with all politicians, we only experience their gratitude so long as we retain the power of rendering them service, and conferring favors.

The first Episcopal minister that took charge of the village of Iodilla, was a native of Charleston, South Carolina, together with his wife; and their fortune, their remarkable genius, their polished manners, their learning, and every excellent gift, had holiness to the Lord written upon it, so unequivocally, that they revo-

---

majesty were pious people. Every child that was born in the royal family was born amidst many prayers. The pious members of the household assembled themselves together and continued praying for the queen until the child was born, when they gave thanks. He thanked God for such a queen and such a court, and that under her, God was prospering Britain, as He had never prospered us before.'"

lutionized the whole community; and when this true man of God lay on his death-bed, he talked to his consecrated wife of heaven, as if he saw an innumerable throng of angels ready to convey him thither. This noble-minded couple had given a *seventh* of their income every year, to the advancement of religion and civilization among the poor and ignorant. They were Musidóra's friends, to whom her heart was transparent.

> Great souls by instinct to each other turn,
> Demand alliance, and in friendship burn."

The widow of this holy man still lives in Carolina, an eternal blessing to every human being that comes within the charmed circle of her religion.

Intense then was the grief of all who could appreciate such an apostle, to see his place supplied by a grey-haired man from Boston, a Mr. Ezekiel Sloper, who was more fitted for a small tradesman, than, like Uzza, to attempt to steady the ark of God. Many persons said he reminded them of the anecdote of the celebrated Dean Swift, who, when he heard that a tailor had set himself up for a new light in the theological department of wisdom, sent for him one day, and remarked that he had long wished to see him. The tailor, greatly flattered, awaited in self-adoring anxiety to hear the distinguished misanthrope, and learned divine, open the conversation. What was his dismay to find all his brilliant conceits overthrown, by the Dean remarking, that in Revelations, St. John says, "That he saw a mighty angel come down from heaven, clothed with a cloud, and a rainbow was upon his head, and his face was as it were the sun, and his feet as pillars of fire;

and he had in his hand a little book open; and he set his right foot upon the sea, and his left foot upon the earth, and cried with a loud voice as when a lion roareth." Now, my good friend, continued the Dean, I have sent for you to tell me how many yards of cloth it would take to make *thàt* angel a pair of breeches?

The negroes soon declared that they could not bear to hear Mr. Sloper preach, for they felt in their hearts that he did not care whether they had souls to be saved or not; whereas the Baptist* and Methodist preachers

---

* One of the Baptist ministers of South Carolina, whose paternal ancestor was the first pastor of that denomination that ever had a church in Charleston, had the following touching lines written on his tombstone by the poet William Grayson, who was his brother-in-law. His *name* was Benjamin Screven, and his *fame* was, "the Howard of the South."†

"Through faith triumphant, by affliction tried,
Christians alone can know how Screven died:
In death serene, without a doubt or fear,
His spirit seem'd of heaven while lingering here.
Teacher of truth, a lesson how to live
And die, his life and dying moments give;
Legate of Christ, with zeal untiring fraught,
He acted out the precepts that he taught:
Yet on his tomb bade partial friendship trace
No line but this—'A sinner saved by grace.'
Lamented and beloved, around thy bed
The grateful slave his tears of sorrow shed.
The widow mourn'd her hope of succor crost,
The orphan wept, a second father lost;
And pale with grief that cannot be express'd,
A wife's fond cheek his dying hand caress'd.
To thee the liveliest joys of earth were given,
Beloved in life, in death assured of heaven."

---

† The author's mother, when dying, gave her as an infant to this Mr. Benjamin Screven and his holy wife.

that came to Iodilla talked kindly with them, and instructed them so patiently, that they realized they had been helped a whole day's journey on to heaven, whenever they listened to their plain gospel sermons.

Mr. Ezekiel Sloper once undertook to visit the celebrated Mrs. Judge Heyward, at her ghostly big palace of White Hall; and after much conventional exhortation, he retired to rest, for the distance was too great to return home. But finding out that not a human being slept in this ancient house, save the old lady herself, he became so nervous lest he should be visited by the innumerable ancestral dead, who lay in a beautifully adorned grave-yard not very far off, that he rang his bell, and hired one of the black waiters to come and sleep with him in that elaborately large guest chamber, that the housekeeper had so respectfully prepared for him. "The wicked fleeth when no man pursueth, but the righteous is as bold as a lion." Mrs. Heyward heard the whole adventure the next morning, and amused her guests with the most sarcastic account of the eccentric clerical visit, declaring that Mr. Sloper might spare himself the tribulation of nerves necessary to his visitations of herself thereafter, for Southern ladies despise a man who is afraid of anything save crime and God.

The wife of said Mr. Ezekiel Sloper was perhaps twenty-five or thirty years younger than himself, and just such a languishing beauty as Byron delighted to describe. She was well educated, and a genius besides, but so daft that her house was kept like a pig-sty. The small congregation at the village of Iodilla gave him a thousand dollars a year, and at least five hundred more in presents, besides a comfortable parsonage and his horse-feed; and yet he was more needy of every temporality in housekeeping, than a Methodist circuit-rider who receives a salary of a hundred dollars per annum. His six children were such progressive outlaws, that not a member of his church could visit him without their bursting into the room with their besmattered garments, and their greasy mouths opened wide, to yell like Mohawks to mamma to give them some nice thing a neighbor had just sent. The want of everything like common sense, or thrift, made it seem impossible that she could have come from New England, where everybody has the reputation of being such utilitarians that not even the peel of a potato is lost, and their housewives are said to be remarkable for their order, and capacity to do all the work of their establishments themselves. Musidora came to the conclusion that clever, thrifty women were sprinkled about among all the States, and the Yankees did not raise any more of them than the Carolinians.

Episcopal ministers are generally remarkable for their wise and strict discipline over their children; indeed, the smallest child often has its memory stored with the truths of the gospel, taught orally long before it can read them for itself. Many strangers have been astonished, when they visited Mr. Joseph Walker, of Beaufort, South Carolina, to find that every young person in his vast congregation was as intellectually informed about the spiritual meaning and requirements of the whole word of God, as the oldest Christians. Mr. Walker is an Episcopal minister, who for more than two-score years has ministered to the same flock.

He has eminent talents, and so lovingly sympathizing with the character of Jesus Christ, that the mighty atonement is the burden of his every sermon. He does indeed preach nothing but Christ crucified; and it seems impossible not to love the Savior he so touchingly daguerreotypes.

But to return to our friend Mr. Sloper; he actually was so afraid of snakes that he never went to lecture at night without holding a lantern down to his feet every step he took to the church, and finally he got so demented with fright, lest the negroes should cut his throat,* (and this absurdity was always the phantom

---

* The Southern people never dream of any fear of their negroes any more than the sheep on the plantations. Ladies are left alone when their husbands are away on a journey for several consecutive weeks, and though there may be a hundred or two hundred negroes belonging to the establishment, she has no feeling of fear, but that the slaves are a perfect protection.†

---

† A rabid Abolition historian of the North, with refreshing naiveté, describes a scene he lately witnessed in Cuba, never seeming to dream that what was such a novelty to his prejudiced mind was to be seen every day on a Southern plantation. He remarks, that on the steamer "The prominent figures are two African nurses — Cuban slaves of Ethiopia's darkest hue." . . . "They each have a beautiful white child in their arms." . . . "A young gentleman and lady are talking and laughing with them very pleasantly, without the slightest recognition of color. Indeed, it is by no means improbable that both of them have nestled in the bosom of these ebon nurses, drawing from these breasts their nourishment." . . . "The love of the nurses for the children is manifestly hearty and sincere." . . . "Such honest smiles and caressings cannot be assumed." . . . "One of these beautiful infant children pats the cheek of her nurse, now one cheek, and now the other, and now placing a hand on each cheek, she presses her little ruby lip to the thick dark lip of her laughing attendant, and kisses her again and again, as lovingly as ever child embraced its mother."

After describing this affectionate scene, our Abolitionist becomes frantic

sitting on the mind of his wife, and her old mother too,) that they became the laughing-stock of the whole parish, and in six months he returned to Boston, and nothing was heard of him among the Iodillians until they saw his name as a prominent subscriber to the Sharpe's rifles that the anti-slavery latter-day saints had sent to Kansas to shoot everybody that did not believe that the *darkeys* were God's chosen people, and consequently the most noble race.

Musidora was now favorably known to the whole State of Carolina as the newly arisen Hannah More of the South. All the Episcopal clergy, with the Bishop of the diocese, were her earnestly appreciating friends. The Baptist ministers were deeply interested in her for her dead father's sake. The Methodists regarded her a living apostle of that Christian perfection, *that* their church believes in as an article of faith. The Presbyterians respectfully patronized her as a proselyte to their doctrine of the perseverance of the saints, and the impossibility of a real Christian ever falling from grace; and the Roman Catholic priests never passed through Iodilla that they did not call to converse with, and to strive to proselyte a person so capable of self-abnegating penance. No woman in the

---

against slavery, and mourns that the field negroes in the cotton and rice fields are none of them poets and philosophers—cannot be inspired by the eloquence of Mr. Everett, and have no libraries of recherche books in their cabins. And yet, dear reader, report says this man is not insane—not writing from a lunatic asylum. The *fact* is, he knows no more about slaves, or their masters, than he knows about the government of the people in the moon, and had better have given us another moon hoax, for that would at least have not stirred up the undying war he recommends between brethren, though he is a minister.

district commanded the moral influence that Musidora did. She had, year in and year out, waited on the sick, and consoled the afflicted among the poor and the rich. She had intróduced a practical mode of reforming vagrants, by giving them *well paid for* work; she had taught the wives of the poor how to adorn their houses with home-made comforts—and how to sew, and how to cut out their clothes and economize their little means. She had established schools to educate their children, and Sunday-schools to teach religion to the rising generation. She also taught *herself* a large Sunday-school that she had inaugurated many years lang syne in the village of Iodilla, for the negroes, and for all the children of her acquaintances and friends. She was never idle—for she collected all the plantation negroes at night to teach them, whenever she visited her brother Halcombe at Palmetto Grove. Whatsoever her hands found to do, she did it with all her might, feeling as if she was rushing into eternity, and must redeem and account for every moment of time.

"Cultivated women are as much an ornament and honor to a city or State as cultivated men. France has as much distinction from Madame de Staël as from the most brilliant of its philosophers. Fanny Burney (Madame d'Arblay), Mrs. Macauley, Agnes Strickland, and numerous other females, shed the highest lustre on England. The Irish boast of Miss Edgeworth, of the Porters, of Lady Morgan, and of Lady Blessington, with spirit indicative of the highest appreciation. Scotland, too, has gained in honor through the educated genius of more than one of its 'bonnie, bright-eyed lasses.' Every country in Europe has been benefited by talented women. So has our own grand America. Our female poets and fiction writers have done as much for our intellects, morals, tastes, and honor abroad, as our literary men. Miss Sally Bridges, Mrs. James Campbell, Mrs. Hale, Mrs. Sigourney, and scores of others, have written poems that America will be forever proud of. The nation whose women are cultivated cannot but be one of happy families, of the best and finest description of great men for all departments in its government, and of glorious, increasing, perpetual power and existence."

If ever a human being lived for the advancement of society by inculcating through her *actions* that unselfishness and nobility of purpose that only religion can impart, it was Musidora Wyndham; and yet she was the constant subject of detraction by the buzzing, gossipping women around her, who, convicted by her persevering zeal in always going about to do good to all within the circle of her influence, declared she was a monomaniac, or a wily hypocrite, or a self-righteous pharisee; and yet these very maligners would send their carriages for her as soon as they were sick, or crushed with grief at the loss of friends.

The great Aristotle says, "There is no distinguished genius altogether exempt from some infusion of madness;" and the wise *Seneca* agrees with him in this opinion too. Swift wittily remarks, "When a true genius appears in the world, you may know him by this sign, that the dunces are all in confederacy against him."

Musidora had a natural majesty of carriage that the women interpreted to mean conscious superiority and pride; and though she did not have that skulking bend in the neck, or that skulking, cunning pliability of mind that is often miscalled humility by those who wish everybody to be humble save themselves, she yet performed the most menial services for the sick. Indeed, the lowly negro cabin* as often found her sitting up all night, to encourage by prayer and exhortation a dying Christian African on his entrance into the dark valley of the shadow of death, as any of the rich aristocratic saints who are saved in spite of their wealth, yet so as by fire.

"He is good that does good to others. If he suffers for the good he does, he is better still; and if he suffers from them to whom he did good, he is arrived to that height of goodness that nothing but an increase of his sufferings can add to it; if it proves his death, his virtue is at the summit—it is heroism complete."

Strange to say, Musidora was the constant subject of bilious envy, though never standing in the sunlight of any of the fashionable women around her. "Envy is a certain grief of mind, conceived upon the sight of another's felicity, whether real or supposed; so that

* The before-mentioned Northern abolitionist describes with surprise the numerous temporalities for the comfort of the slaves on the Cuban plantations, that we all know are not so civilized as in the United States; for true religion is not faithfully taught them as it is by Southern masters here. He tells us, "At a little distance from the planter's house were to be seen almost invariably, in two parallel rows, the neat, whitewashed cabins of the negroes. . . . Some ladies at my side said, 'How pleasant these plantations look! How comfortably these servants are provided for! How *can* people say that the slaves are cruelly treated!'"

we see that it consists partly of hatred and partly of grief; both of them are hostile affections, and vexatious to the breast that harbors them. . . . Acts of love, indeed, naturally have something of pleasure still attending them, and please the mind while they proceed from it. But no man perfectly enjoys himself while he hates another, hatred being a quality that sours the whole soul, and puts all the faculties of it, as it were, in a posture of offence. . . . It is really war begun, and commonly so before it is proclaimed. . . . In a word, he lives in the fire, fighting and fencing; for hatred being too active and mercurial a passion to lie still, never takes up with the *theory* of mischief with sluggish thoughts and secret grudges, but, as opportunity serves, will certainly be up and doing; and till such opportunity falls in with it, (which frequently it does not,) it must needs afflict, grate, and feed upon the man himself, and make him as miserable as he wishes others."

"There may possibly be such a thing as an honest grief, hatred, fear, anger, and despair, but there can be no such thing in nature as an honest and a lawful *envy*. There is an original necessary disagreeableness between envy and the soul of man; for nothing can agree with this which consists not with innocence; and for a man to be envious and innocent too, is contradictory and impossible. . . . It is meat and drink to the envious man to see his superior starve; and his own clothes sit warmest upon him when he beholds others ready to perish with nakedness and cold. Like Ætna, never hotter than when surrounded with snow. . . . This temper if it comes also to be backed with interest and power, how grievous and intolerable it is to all persons of modesty and sobriety. . . . The envious man in high position lives in the world like a continual storm, blowing down all before him, and men *better* than himself must be willing to lie prostrate under his feet, and account it an honor forsooth to be trampled upon, and made a pedestal only for him to get up and ride."

"Nothing can satisfy envy but a man's utter confusion, and (if it were possible,) his very annihilation. It is not content only to asperse or defame a man, nor regards his infamy otherwise than as it is an instrument of his absolute and total ruin. No; it would see him begging at a grate, drawn upon a hurdle, and at length dying upon a gibbet. It would make him odious to his friends and despised by his enemies. Nothing short of death, clothed with all the circumstances of misery and disaster that human nature is capable of, can assuage the rage and fury of envy, which, in all its persecutions of a man, is as 'cruel as death, and as insatiable as the grave,' and the Bible says, 'Wrath is cruel, and anger is outrageous, but who can stand before envy?'"

After thus describing the Satanic character of *envy*, it must now be explained how the morally elevated Musidora came to be the provoker of it in its most rabid form.

Mr. Sloper was succeeded in the village of Iodilla by a clergyman from England, whose name was Iscariot Lauderdale. He was a man of most decided talents, but was proved, after several years, to have about as much religion as those Pharisees of old, to whom Jesus said, "Woe unto you, Scribes and Pharisees! for ye are as graves which appear not, and the men that walk over them are not aware of them." Though he was of humble birth, his character was precisely like that famous Lauderdale who belonged to the ever memorable cabal or cabinet of Charles II., who, though deeply concerned in the sale of Charles I. to the English Parliament, was now the chief instrument employed by the court in forcing episcopacy on his reluctant countrymen; nor did he in that cause shrink from the unsparing use of the sword, the halter, and the boot. Yet those who knew him, knew that thirty years had made no change in his real sentiments; that he still hated the memory of Charles the First; and that he still preferred the Presbyterian form of church government to every other.

But to return to the Rev. Iscariot Lauderdale. The Southern States had never then been secretly invaded by the blood-thirsty saints of higher-lawism, and therefore nobody dreamed that a minister of the gospel could be a person capable of sneaking, like a wolf in sheep's clothing, into the home-confidence of the generous frank Southern planters, to stir up their domestics to assassinate them in the midnight hour. But the negroes* were the first persons who became dissatisfied with Mr. Lauderdale; they declared that he had no more feeling for them than if they were dogs, that

---

* Returning to Slavery.—The Tecumseh yesterday took down a family of six persons—mulattoes—on their way to Helena, Arkansas, to enter again the service of their old master. They were manumitted about six years ago, since which time they have been living in New York, and now, strange as it may seem, having tasted of the sweets of liberty, voluntarily return to bondage.—*Cin. Com.*, 13*th*.

he would not talk kindly to them about their souls, and "dat us mausser need nebber fur to pay dat Buckra to ride ebery week fur to preach to dem at us plantation, fur dem's nebber gwinen fur to yeddy him wen nuff passon at de Euhaw Church lub de poe niggar, and nebber scown um, nun tall."

> "I venerate the man whose heart is warm,
> Whose hands are pure, whose doctrine and whose life,
> Coincident, exhibit lucid proof
> That he is honest in the sacred cause.
> To such I render more than mere respect,
> Whose actions say that they respect themselves.
> But loose in morals, and in manners vain,
> In conversation frivolous, in dress
> Extreme, at once rapacious and profuse —
> Frequent in park with lady at his side,
> Ambling and prattling scandal as he goes —
> But rare at home, and never at his books,
> Or with his pen, save when he scrawls a card —
> Constant at routs, familiar with a round
> Of ladyships, a stranger to the poor —
> Ambitious of preferment for its gold,
> And well prepared, by ignorance and sloth,
> By infidelity and love of world,
> To make God's work a sinecure; a slave
> To his own pleasures and his patrons' pride.
> From such apostles, O ye mitred heads,
> Preserve the Church! and lay not careless hands
> On skulls that cannot teach and will not learn."
>
> COWPER.

Mr. Lauderdale, when he left England, was engaged to be married, so Musidora was relieved of the constant jesting of the congregation, that she must become their pastor's wife. She went, critically, to listen to Mr. Lauderdale's sermons that were very learned and plausible; but she never had an opportunity, practically, to test the man till some three weeks after his arrival.

The village of Iodilla was equally divided between the politicians of the Union and Nullification stripe, and as the fire-eaters were the most wealthy and influential the oppositionists were very jealous and bilious against them, and even would not attend the Episcopal church in common with them. One of the ladies belonging to these rival cliques, who had for three years earnestly sought religion without a satisfying hope of heaven, was now dying of consumption. She was young and beautiful, and had one lovely child. She believed Musidora's conversations about the Bible could soothe her mind, and therefore sent her carriage for her. Musidora, most anxious to advance Mr. Lauderdale's clerical influence, begged the family to let her invite him to see the dying Mrs. Middleton, and out of their great respect for Musidora alone, they consented. She was deeply shocked to see the conduct of the minister at this solemn bedside of the dying penitent, for he held out no hope to the anxious sufferer, and when he left the room he talked with as much heartlessness of this interesting woman's soul as if it was the liver of a jackdaw or a cheweka. Just before she died she begged Musidora to sing that hymn, "Vital spark of heavenly flame," and joined in it herself with a voice that sounded like the ghostly echo from the tomb. As soon as the funeral invitations were forwarded to all the villagers, Musidora sent for Mr. Lauderdale, and privately begged him not to talk so imprudently about

Mrs. Middleton's going to hell, for he would destroy all his influence with the congregation.

He seemed to appreciate this frank kindness, and from thenceforth began to ask her opinions of every member of his congregation; which she gave truly, from no motive save the belief that, by knowing the peculiarities of each one, he would be better enabled to do them good; for she felt no dislike or enmity to a human being herself, though from girlhood she had had the eyes of Argus, and a habit of generalizing character, from every fact that came under her moral observation. Mr. Lauderdale seemed never happy, finally, out of Musidora's presence. He would visit her, on some pretence, three times a day, to the great amusement of her brothers. Indeed, he was a man to be pitied; for his health was very bad, and he lived entirely alone, with the exception of one old black servant-woman. Even Mrs. Wyndham was stimulated to tell him to come to her house to dine, as he said his cooking at home was so wretched that it almost killed him. So that a plate and chair were reserved for him every day at Mrs. Wyndham's dinner-table.

Musidora had horses, and a carriage, and a coachman of her own, that she kept to visit the poor for ten or twenty miles around. Mr. Lauderdale used this conveyance whenever he chose, for he had no horses himself; and, indeed, he became so entirely a member of the family, that all the household expressed their opinions and feelings before him, as if he was their brother.

He would write to Musidora three or four times a day about all his parochial hopes or difficulties; and, indeed, when she drove out in the morning to spend the day among the poor, she would find he had been running to the public road to watch for her return, almost like a sick child. "Love never fails to master what he finds."

"Love seizes on us suddenly, without giving warning, and our disposition or weakness favors the surprise: one look, one glance, from the fair, fixes and determines us. Friendship, on the contrary, is a long time in forming; it is of slow growth, through many trials and months of familiarity."

Did not, the question may be asked, did not Musidora know that this man was desperately in love with her, though engaged to be married to another lady in England? No, she did not; for it must be borne in mind that she was a simple village Christian — had spent all her early girlhood in roaming through the woods, and had had no mother to teach her anything. She had joined the church at the age of sixteen, and had read no novels; or else *these* would have given her some insight into the character of man. She had loved Mr. Fletcher with the most enthusiastic devotion; but the affection of a young girl for her first lover is as pure and innocent as an angel's. All her contemplations since his death had been sanctified by sorrow; and the thought of loving the unmanly, cold-hearted, unsentimental, ambiguous, abolition adventurer, Mr. Lauderdale, would have seemed an outrage upon her romance for the memory of her splendidly dignified, deceased lover. And not only so — her pure, religious mind regarded this minister as already married in the sight of God; and when he wrote her those despairing but non-committal letters, she would reply by pointing him to the consolations of the gospel to the afflicted from any cause.

One day, he began to talk to her about feeling so hopeless that he was tempted to commit suicide. Musidora looked straight at him; and his eye, blazing with passion, convinced her at last that he was madly in love with her.

"So love does raine
In stoutest minds, and make its monstrous warre:
He maketh warre, he maketh peace againe,
And yett his peace is but continuall jarre:
Oh miserable men that to him subject are!"

"What warre so cruel, or what siege so sore,
As that which strong affections do apply
Against the forte of reason evermore,
To bring the soul into captivity?
Their force is fiercer through infirmity
Of the fraile flesh, relenting to their rage,
And exercise most bitter tyranny."

"Mr. Lauderdale," said Musidora, solemnly and conscientiously, "never, so long as you live, talk to me in this strain again." And from that moment she could not restrain a feeling of disgust for his dishonesty to the woman to whom he was betrothed; so that her intimacy with this nondescript lover now began to wane from day to day. Indeed, she pitied from her very heart the woman who was destined to be his wife; who, if she had not touched his heart previous to his intention of leading her to the altar, "had scarcely a chance to charm it when possession and security turn their powerful arms against her."

Mr. Lauderdale was a man of great passion, but no heart; and as he possessed no adhesiveness, he could have passionately loved any woman with whom he was intimately acquainted; but if she returned his affection, he at once ceased to care for her. It seemed to be the pursuit, rather than the possession, that stimulated his enterprise; and there is no doubt that his frantic love for Musidora, was daily increased by the impossibility of getting her. Besides, all the congregation knew of his engagement to Miss Lillibridge, of England. These obstacles only made him more unreasonable in his affections, so that Musidora finally regarded him with prayerful pity, as no sensitive woman perhaps ever felt hatred for a man of genius who idolised her.

"The intelligence of affection is carried on by the eye only; good-breeding has made the tongue falsify the heart, and act a part of continual restraint, while nature has preserved the eyes to herself, that she may not be disguised, or misrepresented." . . . "To be in love, and at the same time to act wisely, is scarcely within the power of God." . . . "Oh, love, when thou gettest dominion over us, we may bid good-bye to prudence."

Perhaps a more intensely wretched man than Mr. Lauderdale, never lived; for he not only knew that Musidora never for a moment returned his affections, but his pride now began to scorch with fury, for all his parish knew how unprincipled his conduct had been to the woman to whom he was betrothed; and what was more terrible still, the whole year had passed, and the fixed time had arrived for him to fulfil his matrimonial engagement in England. We always dread the sight of the person we love, when we have been coquetting elsewhere. But Mr. Lauderdale had not the moral candor, or boldness, to write how he now felt, to the woman he had wronged; and he feared the criticism of society too much to let his actions correspond to the deepest emotions of his soul.

> "Fools not to know that love endures no tie,
> And Jove but laughs at lovers' perjury."

Musidora had had any number of clerical beaux, and often wondered at the arts they resorted to, to conceal their courtships; for surely affection for a charming woman is a perfectly orthodox alterative in a minister's life of severe, ghostly enterprise; and therefore they should not make love to a lady, as if they were ashamed of this natural impulse: or, as if they conferred everlasting obligation on the fair sex, in noticing them at all; whereas the fact is, no man on earth is so profoundly ignorant of the sinuosities of a woman's heart, as a clergyman; and no man is more easily captivated by a dimple, or a curl, for his mind is not diverted by hard friction with worldly business, that other men engage in every day; and moreover, this enterprise of courtship is the only recreation or amusement that conventionality thinks orthodox to his sacred vocation.

There is nothing that proves so conclusively how women worship moral worth, as the universal ease with which a minister can select whichever one he pleases among the girls, or widows, or old maids, of his congregation, and marry her. Not because he is handsome, or aristocratic in his family connexion, or particularly talented, or rich, for in most cases he has none of these advantages, but simply because he represents purity, and benevolence, truth, and honesty; and yet with this wide undisputed market from which to select the most gifted woman in the world, how rarely do ministers marry a help-mate indeed! how often is their influence curtailed by a wife whose weakness of mind, or whose gossiping propensities, are a scandal to the church. "I pity from my heart," says Osborne, "the unhappy man who has a bad wife. She is shackles on his feet, a palsy to his hands, a burden on his shoulders, smoke to his eyes, vinegar to his teeth, a thorn to his side, a dagger to his heart." The Bible speaking of a minister's family, says, "Even so must their wives be grave, not slanderers, sober, faithful in all things; discreet, chaste, keepers at home, obedient to their own husbands, that the word of God be not blasphemed."

No one could read the sermons written one or two hundred years ago, without being struck with the immense difference in the profundity of the thought-work eliminated *then*, from what is produced *now*. The Bible seems to have been studied with the most intense application of every power of the mind to comprehend its radical meaning; and no listener could have heard a Robert South, Barrow, Baxter, or John Howe, without bringing home with him from church, new and edifying thoughts of the mysterious boundless knowledge to be culminated from the study of God's word.

Surely the ministers of that day could not have visited their flocks, as incessantly as they do now, or it would not have been possible to concentrate their minds to the study of Bible truth, as they did then. General visiting of clergymen never has done any good among their congregations. He is to be set apart for a ghostly duty; and the human heart is so constituted, that a minister would command more confidence, if he lived more solitary in prayer and meditation in his study. No one in affliction of mind, body, or estate, but what would prefer to send for such an unworldly, sincere sympathizer, in their sorrows. We never dream of the gossiping and the gay, as suitable advisers, when our hearts are crushed with affliction.

> "Is not the care of souls a load sufficient;
> Are not your holy stipends paid for this?
> Were you not bred apart from worldly noise
> To study souls, their cures, and their diseases?
> The province of the soul is large enough
> To fill up every cranny of your time,
> And leave you much to answer if one wretch
> Be damn'd by your neglect."
>
> DRYDEN.

CHAPTER XVI.

"He that finds Truth," says Sir Philip Sidney, "without loving her, is like a bat; which, though it have eyes to discern that there is a sun, yet hath so evil eyes that it cannot delight in the sun."

The abolition, African reformers, do not respect the Bible enough to be governed by God's verdict of what constitutes moral right and moral wrong, and the question may appropriately be asked them in the words of an elegant pulpit orator, Mr. Ross: "What is sin as a mental state? Is it some quality—some concentrated essence—some elementary moral particle in the nature of things—something black, or red like crimson in the constitution of the soul and body amalgamated? No. Is it self-love? No. Is it selfishness? No. What is it? Just exactly *self-will*—just *that*. I, the creature, *will not submit* to thy will, God, the Creator. It is the *I Am*, created, who dares to defy and dishonor the I Am, *not* created—the Lord God, the Almighty, Holy, Eternal.

"That is sin, *per se*. And that is all of it—so help me God! (continues Mr. Ross.) Your child there—John—says to his father, 'I will *not submit* to your will.' 'Why not, John?' And he answers and says, 'Because I will not.' There, sir, John has revealed *all of sin* on earth, or in hell. Satan has never said—can never say—more. 'I, Satan, *will not*, because I will not *submit to Thee,* God; — *my will,* not *thine,* shall be.'"

This *I will not submit to God's institution of slavery,* as His appointed means for the civilization and Christianizing of heathen idolators, revealed in a hundred different verses in the Bible, is the whole Abolition doctrine from first to last. These New Lights in divinity, assume that they are more tender-hearted towards the African barbarian than God is, or rather *was,* when he inspired holy men to reveal his will in the Scriptures. The Black, Red, and Brown Republicans, have either dug up a new Revelation, like Joe Smith or Brigham Young; or they think the Bible was only intended for the primitive ages, when Abraham, Isaac, Moses, David, Jesus Christ, and his twelve Apostles, did not know half as much about the true spirit of sin, and of the law of God, as the higher-law party have eliminated ever since slavery ceased to be a *pecuniary* profit in New York, Boston, and the other Northern cities. There is no bitter irony in this statement of the rise of transcendental sensibility and infidel disrespect of the fact that the holy *God* himself ordered his chosen people to buy slaves with their money from among the heathen nations around them.

"I wonder," says the great Dr. Wayland, "that any should have the hardihood to deny so plain a matter of record. I should as soon deny the delivery of the ten commandments to Moses."

"Had we from the beginning been arrayed one State against another — had we disregarded our community of language and of interest, and fostered hatred and jealousies which we are *now* taught to cherish," the confederation of these United States could never have been formed. But history tells us that the Colonists found in their bosom at this time about seven hundred thousand slaves, and every one of the thirteen States declaring independence against Great Britain, were in favor of the slave-trade.*

---

* The following from a recent number of the *National Intelligencer*, (one among the oldest, most dignified newspapers in the Union), presents an accurate and clear view of an important part of our history in connection with this subject:

"THE CONSTITUTION AND SLAVERY.—The Journal of the Convention to frame the present Constitution of the United States, exhibits the following facts in connection with the subject of slavery.

"The first committee on the subject consisted of Rutledge, of South Carolina; Randolph, of Virginia; Wilson, of Pennsylvania; Gorham, of Massachusetts; and Ellsworth, of Connecticut; and they reported, as a section for the Constitution, 'that no tax or other duty should be laid on the migration or importation of such persons as the several States shall think proper to admit, nor shall such migration or importation *be prohibited*.

"This was the first action of the Convention on the slavery question; and it will be seen that a committee, the majority of which were from what are strong anti-slavery States, reported against any future prohibition of the African slave-trade, but were willing to legalize it perpetually.

"This section was subsequently referred to a committee selected by ballot, consisting of Langdon, of New Hampshire; King, of Massachusetts; Johnson, of Connecticut; Livingston, of New Jersey; Clymer, of Pennsylvania; Dickenson, of Delaware; Martin, of Maryland; Madison, of Virginia; Williamson, of North Carolina; Pinckney, of South Carolina; and Baldwin, of Georgia.

"This committee, a majority of which were from slave States (then and now) reported the clause, with authority to Congress to prohibit the slave-trade after the year 1800, and in the mean-

But it is affirmed by the pious abstractionists who aim to overturn the political institutions of the country, and clamor for the admission of the black race to all the political and social rights of the framers of the Constitution; that Northern opinions have established a higher standard of ethnological wisdom, philosophical truth, and Christian piety. How long, we may inquire, has this superlative standard been formed?

Governor Seymour, of New York, says, very pertinently, "How came slavery into these United States? Who brought the negro from Africa? The South never had ships. The men of New York, of Massachusetts, and the men of Rhode Island, were those who stole them from their homes and brought them over to the shambles here." . . . "Who laid the foundations of

---

time with authority to levy a tax on such importations." . . . "This section was afterwards modified and adopted as it now exists in the Constitution, extending the time before which Congress could prohibit the trade, until 1808.

"Massachusetts, New Hampshire, and Connecticut, free States, and Maryland, North and South Carolina, slave States, voting for the extension; New Jersey and Pennsylvania, free States, and Delaware and Virginia, slave States, voting against it." So that from the above historical record it appears —

"1. A committee, the majority of which were from free States, report in favor of denying to Congress the power at any period to prohibit the slave trade.

"2. That a subsequent committee, a majority of which were from the slave States, reported a new section authorizing Congress to abolish the trade after the year 1800.

"3. That this period was extended until the year 1808, thus giving eight additional years to the traffic, by the vote of New Hampshire, Massachusetts, and Connecticut, whilst the vote of Virginia was against it."

slavery which underlie the institutions of many of our States? The time was, when, over the whole length and breadth of this land of ours, the people did not recognise the black man as having any political rights. That is just as true of Massachusetts as of South Carolina, and Judge Taney, in so stating, merely stated a historical fact, and known to be so by every student of history." . . . "The other day (continues Governor Seymour) "in looking over papers which came into my hands, I found an original document, a bill of sale for a negro, from a man in Massachusetts to a man in New York, and that paper throws a remarkable light over the whole question of slavery.* It commenced thus:

* "Thus Massachusetts (says Mr. Wolfe), in 1786, passed a law similar to the Colonial one of which we have spoken. The law of 1786, like the law of 1705, forbids the marriage of any white person with any negro, Indian, or mulatto, and inflicts a penalty of fifty pounds upon any one who shall join them in marriage; and declares all such marriages null and void, and thus degrades the unhappy issue of the marriage by fixing upon it the stain of bastardy. And this mark of degradation was renewed, and again impressed upon the race, in the careful and deliberate preparation of their revised code, published in 1836. This code forbids any person from joining in marriage any white person with any Indian, negro, or mulatto, and subjects the party who shall offend in this respect, to imprisonment, not exceeding six months, in the common jail or to hard labor, and to a fine of not less than fifty, nor more than two hundred dollars: and like the law of 1786, it declares the marriage to be absolutely null and void. It will be seen that the punishment is increased by the code upon the person who shall marry them, by adding imprisonment to a pecuniary penalty." Reader, let us fall on our knees in devout thankfulness that God is not such a weathercock as these New England millennial perfectionists:

'To all Christian people to whom these presents may come, I, Mark Rose, sell my slave,' &c. The people of Massachusetts held that no persons were entitled to any political privileges unless they were Christians; and they went further than that — they held that no one was entitled to political privileges unless he was the right kind of a Christian. They held the views which laid the foundation of slavery in the theology of that time. They sold the Quakers into slavery — they sold the family of King Philip into slavery. These were the sentiments that existed in the North in our early days. When the Constitution of the United States was formed, and when the delegates from the different States met in convention, the question of slavery was there, and it was asked, 'When shall the slave-trade be put an end to?' Georgia says, 'Now;' Virginia says, 'Now;' South Carolina says, 'Not yet;' Connecticut, 'Not yet;' Massachusetts, 'Not yet;' Rhode Island, 'Not yet;' New Hampshire said, 'Not yet — the slave-trade is profitable.' If you will read Minot's History of Massachusetts, you will learn that the great business of New England was at one time the manufacture of rum — pure rum; and when they made rum, they took it to the coast of Africa and exchanged it for the slaves. The slavers landed their cargoes on some unfrequented shores of the Southern coast, and forthwith the entire South was charged with complicity in the slave-trade. But they do not at the

for, if He was, we could scarcely learn his will to-day, before to-morrow we would be accused of the sum of all villanies in not turning a somerset, and acting out exactly the contrary moral law to that eliminated from Almighty wisdom yesterday.

same time tell you, that the slave-ships are fitted out from New England ports — that they glide out to sea upon their nefarious voyages beneath the shades of Bunker Hill."

It must be remembered that at the adoption of the Constitution in 1798, the Northern States employed African slaves in their corn and wheat fields, and all economical labor, while, at the same time, cotton was hardly an item of export in the South; for, until the invention of the cotton-gin by Whitney, of New Haven, it was too expensive in its preparation for the market to be an article of commerce.

In 1786, there were but six bales of cotton exported from the South, whereas it is now the leading product of its agriculture and wealth. Not only England, not only France, Germany, and Italy, but the whole world uses its fabrics. Statisticians tell us that the cotton manufacturing interests of the world are estimated at $600,000,000. Taking the population of the world at 850,000,000, every man, woman, and child on the globe uses cotton goods annually to the value of seventy cents. Of the raw cotton produced, the United States supplies more than three-fourths, which, in 1859, was valued at $180,000,000; and this yearly sum of money, our heavenly-minded puritanical brethren, charging the culture of cotton by African slaves to be a sin *per se*, demand that the Southern States should instantly give up — *not*, be it remembered, to appease their *own* consciences, but that of a few sickly sentimentalists at the North, who say, constitution or no constitution, you must give up this highway to wealth.

For a moment let us look at the statistics of the

subject a little further. A member of Parliament said in 1860, "The loss of a single cotton crop would ruin England."

The average weekly consumption of cotton in Great Britain through last year was the largest ever known, being 44,120 bales per week, against 41,916, in 1858; 37,981 in 1857; and 43,520, in 1856. The crop of American cotton in 1856 (year ending September 1st) was 3,528,000 bales; in 1857, 2,640,000 bales; in 1858, 3,114,000 bales; in 1859, 3,851,000 bales; and the deliveries at the ports already show a sufficient increase to indicate a crop for the current year of not less than 4,400,000 bales—the largest crop yet known. The increase, however, over the preceding year has been exceeded in the years 1839–40, 1842–3, 1851–2, 1855–6, 1858–9; but placing the crop of the present year at the above figure, the increase for ten years will be about 1,300,000 bales, equal to the entire crop twenty-five years ago. England will take about 59 per cent. of the crop, our Northern manufacturers about 17 per cent.; and nearly all of the remaining 27 per cent. will be taken in the other countries of Europe.

A late number of the London Cotton Supply Reporter says:

"Upwards of 500,000 workers are now employed in our cotton factories, and it has been estimated that at least 4,000,000 persons in this country are dependent upon the cotton trade for subsistence. A century ago, Lancashire contained a population of only 300,000 persons; it now numbers 2,300,000. In the same period of time this enormous increase exceeds that on any other equal surface of the globe, and is entirely owing to the development of the cotton trade. In 1856, there were in the United Kingdom 2,210 factories, running 28,000,000 spindles and 299,000 looms, by 97,000 horse-power. Since that period, a considerable number of new mills have been erected, and extensive additions have been made to the spinning and weaving machinery of those previously in existence. The amount of actual capital invested in the cotton trade of this kingdom is estimated to be between £60,000,000 and £70,000,000 sterling.

"The quantity of cotton imported into this country in 1859 was 1,181¾ millions pounds' weight, the value of which, at 6d. per lb. is equal to £30,000,000 sterling. Out of 2,829,110 bales of cotton imported into Great Britain, America has supplied us with 2,086,341—that is, five-sixths of the whole. In other words, out of every 7 lbs. imported from all countries into Great Britain, America has supplied 5 lbs. India has sent us about 500,000 bales, Egypt, 100,000, South America, 124,000, and other countries between 8,000 and 9,000 bales. In 1859, the total value of the exports from Great Britain amounted to £130,503,185, of which £47.920,720 consisted of cotton goods and yarns. Thus, more than one-third, or £1 out of every £3 of our entire exports, consists of cotton. Add to this the proportion of cotton which forms part of the twelve millions more exported in the shape of mixed woollens, haberdashery, millinery, silks, apparel, and slops. Great Britain alone consumes twenty-four millions' worth of cotton goods.

"Two conclusions, therefore, may safely be drawn from the facts and figures now cited — first, that the interests of every cotton-worker are bound up with a gigantic trade which keeps in motion an enormous mass of capital, and this capital, machinery, and labor depend for five-sevenths of its employment upon the slave States of America for prosperity and continuance: secondly, that if a war should at any time break out between England and America, a general insurrection take place among the slaves, disease sweep off those slaves by death, the cotton crop fall short in quantity, whether from severe frosts, disease of the plant, or other possible causes — our mills would be stopped for want of cotton, employers would be ruined, and famine would stalk abroad among the hundreds and thousands of work-people who at present are fortunately well employed. Calculate the consequences for yourselves. Imagine a dearth of cotton; and you may picture the horrors of such a calamity from the scenes you may possibly have witnessed when the mills have only run on 'short time.' Count up all the trades that are kept going out of the wages of the working classes, independent of builders, mechanics, engineers, colliers, &c., employed by the mill-owners. Railways would cease to pay, and our ships would lie rotting in their ports, should a scarcity of the raw material for manufacture overtake us."

"Some idea of the importance of the cotton trade to the civilized world," says S. M. Wolfe, "may be obtained from the following graphic description of its influence, from the pen of the English historian, Macaulay:"—

"I see," says he, "in this country a great manufacturing population, drawing the materials of manufacture from a limited market. I see a great cotton trade carried on, which furnishes nearly two million people with food, clothes, and firing; and I say that if you shut out slave-grown cotton, you would produce a mass of misery among the people whom Providence has committed to your care, frightful to contemplate; you would introduce desolation into your richly-flourishing manufacturing districts; you would reduce hundreds on hundreds to beggary and destitution; you would risk the stability of your institutions; and when you had done all this, you would have great reason to doubt whether you had conferred any great benefits on the particular class for whom you made such a sacrifice."

After all these formidable statistical facts, England feeling jealous of the kingly power of cotton in the United States, and angry at her own anti-Bible sentimentality that betrayed her into the suicidal folly of abolitionizing her colonies, now feels like the fox who had lost his tail in a trap, and therefore the politicians of Exeter Hall come here, as that cunning old Reynard did of old, to convince all the Anglo-Saxons of the United States that it is morally fashionable to cut off this indispensable temporality to the perfection of the body politic.

This would close our schools of compulsory labor, ordained by God for the civilizing and Christianizing barbarians, that experience has proved, is the only system that can prevent the African from being a perfectly useless vagabond and expensive pauper* among us.

Mr. Clingman, a very distinguished and long-practised statesman of North Carolina, said in his last speech in the Senate of the United States (1860):—

"When, last spring, I landed in England, I found that country agitated with questions of reform. In the struggle, which was maintained on both sides with the greatest animation, there were constant references to the United States; and the force of our example was stimulating the liberals, and tending to the

* The Governor of New York says, in his Annual Message published in 1860, "It appears from the Report of the Secretary of State, that during the year 1858 relief was granted by the public in two hundred and sixty thousand one hundred and fifty-five cases, equal to seven and four-tenths per cent. of the entire population (of New York State), at an expense of one million four hundred and ninety dollars and twenty-eight cents." . . . "Of those relieved forty-one per cent. were natives of this country, and fifty-nine per cent. were foreigners." . . . "While in the twenty years, from 1831 to 1851, the population of the State increased only sixty per cent.; pauperism increased, in the same period, seven hundred and six per cent." . . . "In 1831 there was one person relieved to every one hundred and twenty-three inhabitants; in 1841, one to every thirty-nine; in 1851, one to every twenty-four; and in 1856, one to every seventeen."

overthrow of aristocratic and monarchic restrictions. Our institutions and our opinions were referred to only to be applauded, except by a small but influential aristocratic clique. That oligarchy cannot forget the Revolution of July, 1776, which deprived Britain of this magnificent western empire; and it sees, with even bitterer feelings, its own waning power and vanishing privileges under the inspiriting influences of our prosperity. It, however, is always ready to take by the hand any American of prominent position who habitually denounces and depreciates his own government, and labors for its overthrow.

"In this connection, I remember a statement made to me by the late American Minister at Paris, Mr. Mason. He spoke of having had a conversation with one whose name I do not feel at liberty to mention, but whose influence on the opinion of continental Europe is considerable, who admitted to him that there was nothing in fact wrong in our negro slavery; but who, nevertheless, declared that if the Union of our States continued, at no distant day we should control the world; and, therefore, as an European he felt it to be his duty to press anti-slavery views, as the only chance to divide us. I have other and many reasons to know that the monarchies of Europe, threatened with downfall from revolutionary movements, seek, through such channels as they control, to make similar impressions. A hundred times was the question asked me, 'Will you divide in America?' But never once was the inquiry made of me, 'Will slavery be abolished, will your country become more respectable in the eyes of the Abolitionists?'"

"The real issue," continues Mr. Clingman, "between the sentimental abolitionist and the practical sensible slave-holder is, whether or not the negro is the equal of the white man physically, intellectually, and morally? Though usually evaded in the discussion, this is the real question which lies at the foundation of the controversy. If the people of the Northern States should regard the negro as being the equal of the white man, then they will continue to feel a sympathy for him in slavery, and can be excited to efforts for his liberation. If, on the contrary, he be different in material respects from the white man, and also inferior, then his case must be decided on its own merits and not from any supposed analogy to that of the white man. It is not, as the Abolitionists in their silliness assert, a mere question of color or prejudice against a black skin. If the negro were in fact in all other respects like the white man, his blackness would have been of no more consequence than the difference between black and red hair or light and dark eyes. The feeling against him grows out of the fact that he is in all respects different from the white man and inferior. When I put the question to any one that I may meet here, the chances are that he will at once agree with me, in private conversation, and admit, in the language used some time ago by the Senator from Illinois (Mr. Trumbull), that Omnipotence has made a difference between the white man and the negro; and yet it is this very opposite view in favor of negro equality which gives its main force and vitality to the anti-slavery movement. When, sir, some twelve years ago, I, in discussion, threw out suggestions about the difference of races, I was denounced as one who attributed injustice to Almighty God in alleging that He had made the negroes inferior. Will any Senator on the other side of this chamber tell me why it is that Providence brings half the children that are born in New England into the world with constitutions so feeble that they cannot live until they are twenty-one years of age? Or will they, upon their views of His justice, explain why it is that in the same family one brother is provided with a good constitution and strong intellect, while a second has from his birth the seeds of debility and incurable disease, and a third is mentally imbecile or perhaps idiotic? Would the injustice to the feeble be greater if they were black men? Are we to refuse to believe the facts which nature constantly presents to us because they do not harmonize with our ideas of the justice of the Creator? The Bible itself does not explain to us why it is that, while ten talents are given to one man, to another but a single talent is given. For the inequality of the negro Providence is responsible, as He is for the entire creation which surround us. When human laws are in accordance with the system of nature, they are wise; but if in opposition to it, they are productive only of mischief. The question is significantly asked in the Scripture, 'Can the Ethiopian change his skin or the leopard his spots?' The ancients expressed their opinions on this subject in the fable which represented a black man as having been killed in an effort to wash him white."

Hegel's Philosophy of History, an imperishable monument of human genius, says — "The negro, as already observed, exhibits the natural man in his completely wild state." . . . "We must lay aside all thought of reverence and morality, all that we call feeling, if we would rightly comprehend him. There is nothing harmonious with humanity to be found in this type of character." — (Page 97).

"The undervaluing of humanity," Hegel continues, "among them reaches an incredible degree of intensity. Tyranny is no wrong, and cannibalism is looked upon as quite customary and proper." . . . "The devouring of human flesh is altogether consonant with the general principles of the African race. To the sensual negro, human flesh is but an object of sense — mere flesh." — (Pages 99–100.)

After describing many other characteristics, this author concludes — "Slavery to have been the occasion of *the increase* of human feeling among negroes. But thus existing in a state, slavery is itself a phase of advance from the merely isolated sensual existence, a phase of education, a mode of becoming participant in a higher morality and the culture connected with it."

"Now," says the Hon. L. Q. C. Lamar, "who will say that the hundred thousand negroes whose character is thus described by this German author, brought over to this continent, would ever have had their condition improved, or would ever have secured to themselves the benefits they now enjoy, had they been left in their 'natural condition?' At that time there were two barbarous races which came in contact upon this continent with the European. The one African, occupying the lowest point in the scale of human existence; the other was the noble Indian race, superior to the African in intelligence, in moral and physical development. Free as the wild bird of his native forests, bold as the stream which dashed down his mountain gorges, generous as the bounteous nature around him, the American Indian goes into history the poetic embodiment of savage life. What has been his fate, compared with that of the African? What, we repeat, has become of the Indian who occupied the Atlantic borders? Driven back by the advancing wave of European civilization to continually contracting circles, with diminished means of subsistence, into degradation, wretchedness, and extinction."

"The African, with all its foulness, with all its prosaic vulgarities, domesticated and disciplined, has been by that same wave borne up higher and higher, until now it furnishes inspiration for Northern song, heroes and heroines for Northern romances, and is invited by Northern statesmen into their charmed circle of political and social equality. He is still not your equal; and history proves that even when he has reached this point of civilization, if you take from under him the institution which has borne him up to it, he relapses into his pristine barbarism. This can be shown by detailed references to the French islands, the English Antilles, and other countries in which slavery has been abolished."

"In Hayti, where the negro was left with all the endowments of a civilization which vied with Rome in gorgeous magnificence, you see now nothing but poverty, vice, indolence, and all the other signs of a rapidly approaching barbarism. Anti-slavery authority shows that the British Antilles have disappointed every promise, and frustrated every hope that accompanied the act of emancipation." . . . "The condition of the free colored population in Peru, is exhibited by a most intelligent German traveller, Von Tschudi.

"But the Abolitionists sometimes say that, even if it be true that the negro is inferior, for that reason, namely, on account of his weakness, he ought not to be enslaved. Does this reasoning apply to children? The average of human life is less than forty years, and how can you justify depriving human beings of liberty for more than half that time? If children were the equals of adults, it would be wrong to control them. It is simply because they are inferior that we justify their subjection to the will of others. Upon these principles the negro, being, as compared with the white man, always a child, is benefited by the control to which he is subjected.

"There is no middle ground which can be maintained on this question. If the negro be your equal, why do you exclude him from your parlors? If he be unequal, your whole argument has in fact lost its foundation, and fails. If it once be admitted that the negro is inferior, then the entire edifice of Abolitionism falls to the ground, because it is intimately interwoven with, and owes its vitality to, the opposite belief. When pressed boldly on this issue, the Abolitionists of late are trying to evade it. It is a singular and striking fact, that when this issue has been made in the free States directly, and discussed before the people, they have decided the point against the negro. Such was the case in Connecticut and New York on the question of suffrage, and also in the States of Illinois and Indiana on the proposition to exclude free negroes from those States.

"Gentlemen of the North (representing the conservative element of the Abolition party) protest against the existence of a servile party at all in this blessed nineteenth century; so we must examine further this sophomoric assumption.

"Is the negro equal to the white man? the African to the Caucasian? 1st. Intellectually.—History, which is the record of the development of the human race in time and space, rather militates against such a conclusion. Optimism and philanthropy are both highly creditable to human nature, but neither the one nor the other can be considered to the exclusion of facts. It might be pertinently asked of those who avow their belief in the equality of the slave and his master, how the negro came to be his slave, when both races were equally endowed by nature? and *more Socratico*, he (the interrogator) might calmly inquire into the cause (which doubtless the Abolitionists would be able to assign) why it was that the negro was always a slave,—in India, Syria, and Egypt, three thousand years ago, as in Georgia, Louisiana, and Virginia to-day, with the same brain in the same proportion to the white races?—why, in the revolutions that have convulsed the nations under whom he lived a servant, has he not thrown off his fetters and become free? or rather, when undisturbed in the possession of those regions in which he attains his greatest physical perfection, and into which no invading army has ever penetrated, has he not, from the elaboration of those elements which he has in common with the Caucasians, rivalled in some degree his progress in arms, arts, and letters?

"Where are the obelisks of the Gold Coast, the pyramids of Guinea, the temples of Zanguebar? Gone! Where are their ruins? Why has no navigator of the early times mentioned their existence, or recorded their traditions in the unknown lands which recent enterprise has presented to us?

"In that delightful 'province of the sun,' explored by the English, where, generation after generation, age after age, the negro has lived secure from foreign invasion, why have no monuments of intellectual equality greeted the explorers, which would warrant us in believing in the doctrine? Not to elevate the standard too high, has the African ever equalled the Mongolian? Where, in the lands in which he has been domesticated, has he adopted the civilization around him, or preserved it when removed for any length of time from those who taught it?

"The elevated plateau of the Indo-Chinese world is scarcely more accessible, and has been little more open to foreign innovations, than Africa. Can any similarity be traced between them? Can any man in his senses compare one with the other? Yet the Mongul is not more superior to the negro than the Caucasian to him."

But it is affirmed that African slavery in the South is promotive of moral degradation; or that heathenism, and idolatry, and all savageness in Africa, is preferable to their Christian, but compulsory, condition in the Southern States, where the Sabbath is strictly observed, and Sunday-schools and churches maintained for their instruction in every kind of religious knowledge necessary to their fulfilling their every duty to God and man, and securing hereafter a heavenly reward. Or, in effect, that plenty, law, and labor, in America, are not preferable to starvation, free idleness, and crime, in Africa, or in the North.* The remedy proposed for

---

* "THE NEGROES IN CANADA.—*The Fruits of their Outrages appearing—the 'Poor Fugitives' banished from the township of Anderdon.*—The readers of the Free Press will remember the recent negro outrages in Canada, and particularly the affair in the township of Anderdon, a few miles from Windsor, where an elderly female was violated, and several males, who went to her assistance, were cruelly beaten, and left for dead on the floor of the house. Subsequently the perpetrators of the outrage were taken into custody, and, while being conducted to jail, were rescued by a band of their fellows. The exposure of this deed of violence in this paper brought down upon us the imprecations of the entire negro-worshipping press, not only of this city and country, but of Canada, who justified the outrage by insisting that the female was 'nothing but a squaw.' It is true that the woman whose home was assaulted, and upon whom the outrage was committed, was of mixed blood—French and Indian—but it is yet to be proved that the virtue even of an Indian woman is not as much to be respected as that of a white.

"It seems that the woman, though thus sneeringly spoken of by the negro sympathizers, is not without her friends, and her appeals for justice have not passed unheeded. The consequences of the outrage which the negro community sought to

sin, by the great founder of Christianity, was not the dissolution of the bonds that link people to their rulers, but the bonds that link them to sin—in the crimes of Sabbath-breaking, lying, stealing, adultery, covetousness, and all *personal* wickedness.

---

palliate, and the punishment due to the perpetrators whom their companions refused to surrender to justice, are to be visited upon the entire negro population. Their homes are to be sacrificed, and they are to be banished from the township.

"It seems that the greater part of the township of Anderdon is held under the Canadian laws as a reserve by the Wyandot Indians, who, by their local authorities, have entire control of their affairs. The authority is vested in a Council composed exclusively of the Indians. In consequence of this affair, the injuries resulting from which have befallen the Indians alone, a Council has recently been held, when the case was taken into consideration, and, after a full and dispassionate discussion, an order was issued, expelling all negro settlers from the lands embraced in the reserve immediately; at the same time a provision was made for the benefit of those having crops in the ground, giving them until the first of September next in which to remove. There are in this township between two and three hundred negroes, nearly all of whom are fugitives from American slavery. A few months since the entire body of them were presented by the Grand Jury of Essex county as a 'lazy, thriftless, thieving set,' and the government was importuned to interfere to prevent the increase of the nuisance. This was looked upon as an act of oppression and wrong towards an unfortunate and down-trodden race. It has never been urged that the acts committed by these fugitives towards their white and Indian neighbors, such as sheep-stealing, house-burning, robbery, violence to females, and even murder, were worthy of censure. These were to be considered as the pastimes of this much-abused class. The Grand Jury of the county thought differently, as do the Council of the Wyandot Indians."—*Detroit Free Press*, Feb. 14.

From the beginning to the end of the New Testament, there is not a syllable uttered by Christ or the evangelists, to break political bonds, or to induce servants to quit their masters, or to interfere at all with the civil laws or internal police of kingdoms or States. It is the regeneration of the human heart that is everywhere aimed at. Falsehood, hypocrisy, evil speaking, gluttony, wantonness, malice, anger, and hatred, are the evils to be extirpated. It was falsely asseverated by the Jews that Jesus interfered with the rights of Cæsar — he was in fact crucified on this falsehood. So far from its being true that the Son of God interfered with any of the civil laws of the land, we can prove by history that slavery, for instance, was perfectly satanic in its tyranny in our Lord's day; and that, although he taught maxims to regulate the conduct of husbands and wives, parents and children, masters and servants, he never once hinted at abolishing any of these institutions, and the Scriptures link them all together as equally binding.

"In Judea," at the advent of Christ, "both the food and the clothing of slaves were of the poorest description. All their earnings went to their masters. The maid-servants were employed in domestic concerns, though not unfrequently they were compelled to engage in those duties which, from their nature, were more befitting the other sex." . . . "They commonly had the consent of their masters to marry, or rather, to connect themselves with a woman in that way which is denominated by a Latin term, *contubernium*. (Cooper's Justinian thus explains it: '*Contubernium* was the matrimony of slaves, a permitted cohabitation; not partaking of lawful marriage, which they could not contract.') The children that proceeded from this sort of marriages were the property, not of the parents, but of their owners."—(*Jahn's Archæology*, pp. 180, 181.)

"In Rome, for slaves (says Adam's *Rom. Ant.*, pp. 48, 51), the lash was the common punishment; but for certain crimes they used to be branded on the forehead, and sometimes were forced to carry a piece of wood round their necks wherever they went." . . . "When slaves were beaten, they used to be suspended with a weight tied to their feet, that they might not move them. When punished capitally, they were commonly crucified.

"If a master was slain in his own house, and the murderer not discovered, all his domestic slaves were liable to be put to death. There was a continual market for slaves at Rome." . . . "The seller was bound to promise for the soundness of his slaves, and not to conceal their faults." . . . "Hence, they were commonly exposed to sale naked; and they carried a scroll hanging at their necks, on which their good and bad qualities were specified."

"In Greece, the condition of slaves appears to have been much the same as at Rome."—(*Potter's Gr. Ant.*, 1, 10.)

Jesus Christ and his apostles daily witnessed this tyranny, and yet they never attempted to abolitionize or sever the political or domestic bonds between masters and their slaves.

"The only cause of the difference between the legislation of Northern and Southern States on the subject of slavery is, that the negroes are not sufficient in number at the North to make it necessary to reduce them to the condition of domestic servitude, while with us that condition is indispensable to the good order and welfare of the whole society.* And it is demonstrable

---

* THE NEGRO DISTURBANCES IN CANADA.—*The Public Schools of Chatham taken in possession by several hundred negroes—school disturbances at Sandwich—the beauties of practical Abolitionism.*—The negro disturbances which were alluded to in our issue of yesterday, were not overrated in importance, as is confirmed by subsequent advices, while the extent of the agitation was much greater than was at the time surmised. In regard to the fiendish transaction enacted at Anderdon, half of the truth was not told. Officers are still in pursuit of the rescued criminals, and great indignation prevails throughout the whole vicinity, so that, if they are caught and delivered into the hands of the populace, they will be severely dealt with.

"At Chatham, forty miles from this city, a crowd composed of several hundred negroes took possession of the public schoolhouses early on Monday morning, and when the white teachers and scholars arrived, refused to allow them to enter or in any manner obtain possession of them. As there seemed to be a disposition to carry matters with a high hand, the authorities were called in, but, from the fact that the negroes inhabiting the town far outnumber the white citizens, there were no means available except those of conciliation. The Africans were headed by one Shadd, a negro, who has made himself prominent in that vicinity for some time, having been concerned in the forcible rescue case which occurred there two years ago. The mayor and councilmen assembled on the spot, accompanied by a majority of the citizens. The whole town was in an uproar in consequence of the warlike demonstrations of the negroes, and the crowd and excitement were consequently very great. The negroes demanded not only that the schools should be thrown open to them, but that they should be allowed to participate in their management, which, on account of their numbers, is equivalent to giving them the control. They have hitherto been

that the negro in the Southern States has reached a moral and intellectual development superior to his race in any other position in which he has been placed. That he contributes more in his present condition, to the good of mankind, their moral and intellectual pro-

---

allotted schools and teachers by themselves, the latter being drawn from their own race; but they declared that they were as good as the whites, if not better, and that they must be allowed to send their children to the white schools. It was not claimed that any superior advantages were to be gained by this arrangement, but the negroes considered it an indignity that they were not placed in immediate contact with the whites, and were determined to compel the latter to submit to their society, and that of their children. As the hatred entertained by the white citizens against the whole race is neither slight nor in any manner disguised, it may be imagined what their feelings were upon being coerced into compliance with such insolent demands. The conference continued some hours, the authorities maintaining a conciliatory and peaceful course, and the negroes asserting their claims with arrogance and violent demonstrations. They were finally quieted by the assurance that their claims should be taken into consideration, and such arrangements made as could with propriety be brought about. This means nothing, of course, as the demands of the negroes must be complied with or resisted. In case they are complied with, the town, and as a consequence, the surrounding country, will be under their rule, and if they are not, a conflict may be expected between the white and the black races, in which the former will have great difficulty in maintaining their ground, as they are in the minority. There are about 2,200 negroes in Chatham alone.

"At Sandwich, three miles below this city, there was a disturbance growing out of the same cause. The whites, in apportioning the school-tax, assessed themselves only, leaving the negro population out, in order that they might not control the cause of education by their votes at the ballot-box. The negroes were highly incensed at this, and went in a body to the polls on the occasion of the election of school officers, determined to

gress, than in any other position in which he has been placed. What was his condition when he was first brought here? Look at him upon his native continent. The most humane explorers of the African Continent tell us that they exist there without social or political order, without modesty or shame, some of the tribes not even reaching the civilization of the fig-leaf."

"The Southern planter is not the indolent, aristocratic nabob, which he has been represented to be. He

---

vote. They were resisted and driven away, and much ill-feeling and enmity engendered.

"It will be seen by all these indications that the negro population of our neighboring province is becoming organized and bold in its opposition to the legitimate institutions of the country, and overbearing and insolent toward its rightful citizens. We may safely say that the hatred with which they are regarded in return is not less violent or open than their own demonstrations. There are very few whites living on the borders, where this fugitive race must congregate, so fanatic as to close their eyes to the fact that their immigration is fast tending towards the demoralization of the country. As citizens they are worthless to the last degree, while crime prevails among them to an alarming extent, and swells the criminal calendars of the country with the most revolting offences—particularly with the violation of female chastity. With all this in return for the mistaken kindnesses which have been offered them, they are now becoming bold and violent, and have dared to resort to the high-handed measures which we have recorded, all of which, we repeat, are obviously the result of a concerted movement among the great body of negroes inhabiting this portion of the province. Canada has nursed a viper in its bosom, which is now preparing to turn upon it. The hordes of blacks which have for years poured into its border counties are beginning to feel their power, and, if we mistake not, will give infinite trouble before they are again crushed down to their proper level."—*Detroit Free Press, Jan.* 18.

is, in general, careful, patient, provident, industrious, forbearing, and yet firm and determined. It is these qualities which have enabled him to take a race of untamed savages, with no habits except such as inspire disgust, with no arts, no information, and out of such a people, to make the finest body of fixed laborers that the world has ever seen. England has imported Coolies, Chinese, natives from the African Coast, into her colonies, and yet she has been unable to compete with the Southern plantations. There is no product which requires such a constant and unremitting attention, such continuous labor, as the cotton plant. The great complaint in the British Colonies is, that the fruit of each year's effort is lost by the broken and irregular labor of the operatives. Now the Southern planter has secured continuity, consistency, and steadfastness, in the most indolent, inconsistent, and capricious of the human race. The Southern planter penetrates the dense forests, the tangled brake, the gloomy wilderness of our river swamps, where pestilence has its abode; and there, day by day, and year by year, amidst exposure, privation, and sickness, are his foresight, his prudence, his self-reliance, his adaptation of means to ends, called in requisition. In the communion with himself, — which his isolation makes indispensable, — and in the daily and yearly provision for a large body of domestics and dependants for whom he has to think, and whose labor he has to direct, he forms those qualities which enable him to emerge from his isolation to fill the county court, or to become a member of his State Legislature; to discharge the duties of the magistracy, or to take his place in the national councils."

"In confirmation of this fact, we have only to point to such communities as these, that a Washington, a Moultrie, a Marion, a Jackson, a Taylor, a Scott, a Twiggs, a Quitman, a Davis, a Lee, a Ringgold, a Bragg, a Butler, and a host of others, acquired those qualities which enabled them, in the positions in which their country placed them, to add such undying lustre to the American name. It was in such communities that such men as Jefferson, Madison, Monroe, Polk, Lowndes, Calhoun, Clay, Macon, Marshall, Taney, and a host of others, acquired those characteristics which their countrymen, North and South, instinctively discerned, whenever called upon to face some awful moment to which Heaven has joined great issues, good or bad, for human kind."

No person of intelligence and candor, who has visited Southern plantations, and seen the groups of orderly church-going slaves, can affirm that the effects of the gospel teaching are not as manifestly shown as among any of the common masses at the North.

In May, 1860, the Petersburg, Virginia, Express says that the number of colored persons baptized in the river there, on Sunday last, was 164; and that 1,000 colored people have professed religion within the last six weeks.

Dr. Nehemiah Adams, of *Boston*, Massachusetts, speaking of his late travels in the Southern States, says: —

"In Savannah, Georgia, in a population of several thousand blacks, more than one-third are church members. Three colored pastors, with salaries from eight hundred to a thousand dollars, are supported by subscriptions and pew-rents among their own members." . . . "More than one-third of the whole number of communicants reported by the Synod of South Carolina, are colored people." . . . "Of the 384,000 in that State, one-seventh, or more than 50,000, are professors of religion." . . . "In 1853, $15,000 were contributed by 5,000 slaves in Charleston, to benevolent objects." . . . "These statistics, which are a fair sample, might easily be multiplied, but it is unnecessary." . . . "Religion has gained a wonderful ascendency among these people.

"I went to their prayer-meetings. One of them will represent the rest." . . . "They met in the choir-part of the gallery in the evenings, once a week. A white brother presided, as the law requires, and read a portion of Scripture; but the slaves conducted the meeting." . . . "One of them stood up before the desk, and repeated a hymn, two lines at a time. At the singing of the last stanza in each hymn they all rose; and they invariably repeated the last two lines of a hymn. They prayed without being called upon. Such prayers I never heard. There was nothing during the week that I anticipated with so much pleasure as the return of that prayer-meeting." . . . "Earnestness in manner, overflowing love to God, compassion for their fellow-men everywhere, gratitude unbounded to Christ for his great love wherewith he loved them, a deep and touching sense of unworthiness, supplications for mercy and for grace to keep them from sin, all expressed in original, but frequently ungrammatical, yet sometimes beautiful and affecting terms, characterized all their prayers." . . . "I never perceived in their prayers anything that reminded me of their condition as slaves. They made no allusion to sorrows but those which are spiritual, and they chiefly dwelt upon their temptations. But the love of Christ and heaven, were the all-inspiring themes of their prayers and hymns." . . . "The pastor of a large colored church containing many free blacks, told me that he was never reminded by their respective prayers of their respective conditions, as bond or free.

"It is a sad contrast (continues Dr. Adams), a professor in a college for example, sitting silent for years in the devotional meetings of his church, and a poor slave who cannot pray grammatically, so wrestling with God in prayer as to make one say of him, 'As a prince hast thou power with God and with men.' Sometimes the ordinary low responses of fellow-worshippers in the Methodist prayer-meetings would be excited by seraphic expressions in the prayer of a slave brother to such a pitch, as to cause involuntary shoutings from the whole meeting, in which I almost wished to join; for the thoughts expressed were so awakening and elevating, that 'or ever I was aware, my soul made me like the chariots of Aminadab.'"

With regard to the religious, orderly, and social manners of the slaves, Dr. Adams remarks,

"A better-looking, happier, more courteous set of people, I had never seen, than those colored men, women, and children whom I met the first few days of my stay in Savannah. It had a singular effect on my spirits. They all seemed glad to see me. I was tempted with some vain feelings, as though they meant to pay me some special respect. It was all the more grateful, because for months sickness and death had covered almost everything, even the faces of friends at home, with sadness to my eye, and my spirits had drooped. But to be met and accosted with such extremely civil, benevolent looks, to see so many faces break into pleasing smiles on going by, made one feel that he was not alone in the world, even in a land of strangers.

"It was one of the pleasures of taking a walk, to be greeted by all my colored friends. I felt that I had taken a whole new race of my fellow-men by the hand. I took care to notice each of them, and get his full smile and salutation; many a time I would gladly have stopped and paid a good price for a certain 'good-morning' courtesy and bow; it was worth more than gold; its charm consisted in its being unbought, unconstrained; for I was an entire stranger. Timidity, a feeling of necessity, the leer of obliged deference, I nowhere saw; but the artless, free and easy manner which burdened spirits never wear.

"It was difficult to pass the colored people in the streets without a smile, awakened by the magnetism of their smiles

Let any one at the North, afflicted with depression of spirits, drop down among these negroes, walk these streets, form a passing acquaintance with some of them; and, unless he is a hopeless case, he will find himself in moods of cheerfulness never awakened, surely, by the countenances of the whites in any strange place."

The plantation negro feels highly respectable in his useful calling; and every master who is not a brute treats him always as one of the benefactors of mankind. And any listener can at harvest time hear these slaves complacently exulting over the large crops that their own labor has culminated. It is universal instinct to every mind to be wholesomely proud that it is useful in its day and generation; and, indeed, no poor retire to their rest at night with less of actual crime having been committed by them through the day; for they all feel the moral elevation of their beneficial labors.

"Come hither, ye that press your beds of down,
And sleep not: see him sweating o'er his bread
Before he eats it. 'Tis the primal curse,
But soften'd into mercy; made the pledge
Of cheerful days, and nights without a groan."

Of the political condition of the slave, the beforementioned Dr. Adams, in 1854, speaks thus:

"The conviction forces itself upon my mind, that at the South the most disastrous event to the colored people would be their emancipation, to live on the same soil with the whites." . . . "The two distinct races could not live together, except by the entire subordination of one to the other." . . . "Protection is now extended to the blacks; their interests are the interests of the owners." . . . "But, ceasing to be a protected class, they would fall a prey to avarice, suffer oppression and grievous wrongs, encounter the rivalry of white emigrants, which is an element in the question of emancipation here, and nowhere else." . . . "Antipathy to their color would not diminish; and being the feebler race, they would be subjected to great miseries."*

The negro of the South is indeed prone to be a religious being — a believer in the worship of God in his hypostasis of Jesus Christ, and an observer of the laws which surround his condition, when his mind is not poisoned by the miserable abstraction of Northern abolitionism. And it is a marvel that any law-abiding and order-loving citizen of the North — any person whose mind is indoctrinated by Divine teaching — should countenance, far less harbor, deluded, lawless fugitives.

"If one man," says Mr. Clingman, "out of every hundred, should be a thief, and the other ninety-nine should not restrain them by legislation or otherwise, this minority of thieves would be able to steal all the property in the community." . . . "If societies were formed in Massachusetts to steal property in Connecticut or New York, the Legislature and people of the State would doubtless take steps to restrain them. This is done even with reference to foreign countries, to prevent war between them. American citizens are punished for going into Canada to disturb that British community.

"If societies were formed in Canada for a similar purpose, and were, in fact, to steal an equal amount of property from New England, New York, Ohio, and other Northern States, to what is carried away by the abolitionists from the South, we should be involved in a war with Great Britain in less than six months. What would be the feeling of those border States if Canadian orators should boast that their societies had robbed them of $45,000,000 worth of their property, just as they now say they hold that value of Southern runaway slaves? But

* Dr. Nehemiah Adams's "*South Side View of Slavery.*"

men who combine to plunder the people of the Southern States, so far from being punished, are in many of the free States encouraged by the legislation there.

"During the last session of Congress, the Senator from New York introduced a proposition for additional legislation to prevent the foreign or African slave-trade to the United States. In 1808, Congress passed laws to prohibit that trade; and since that time, a period of more than fifty years, as far as I know, or have reason to believe, the law has been violated but in a single instance. What other law on your statute-book has been so well kept? I repeat, what law has Congress ever passed, which there was a temptation to violate, that has been so well observed? That it was not broken often, is not owing to any want of opportunity. Northern as well as foreign ships have been engaged in the trade, and the extent of the Southern coast affords much greater facilities for the introduction of slaves than does the island of Cuba, into which large numbers are annually carried. This law has not been broken simply because the people of the South *were not willing to violate it.* Now, sir, let me state a case for the consideration of the Senate. Suppose, instead of what has actually occurred, the State of Georgia, where some negroes were landed, and a number of other Southern States, had passed the strongest laws which could be devised to defeat the act of Congress forbidding the African slave-trade, and encouraging that traffic by all the means in their power. Suppose, further, that Southern Senators, and other prominent public men, had, in their speeches, earnestly recommended the violation of the law of Congress, and that all through the South money was subscribed and associations formed to defeat the law, and provide facilities by railroad or otherwise for the introduction of Africans, and mobs gotten up to overpower the United States marshals; could not a hundred negroes have been imported for every one that the abolitionists have stolen? Yes; with a shore-line of more than ten thousand miles, millions might have been imported. This proceeding would have been a violation of the laws of the United States, just like that which has occurred with reference to the fugitive-slave law. In the case supposed, however, the Southern men would have had greatly the advantage, on the score of both political economy and morality. They might have said, with truth, that the negroes imported from Africa added to the production and wealth of the United States, while those carried North by the abolitionists were generally converted into idle vagrants. It might also have been said that African savages were, by being brought to the United States, partially civilized, and not only made more intelligent and moral, but also Christianized in large numbers; while the negroes carried to the North become so worthless and so vicious, that many of the States there were seeking to exclude them by legislation, as communities do the plague and other contagious disorders. And the Senator from New York, who has declared that it is a religious duty of the people of the North to violate the fugitive-slave law, and urges them, instead of delivering up the runaway negroes, to protect and defend them as they do their paternal gods, stands up in the face of the American Senate and complains of violation of the laws against the African slave-trade! Was there ever such an exhibition? I repeat, was the like ever seen since the creation of the world?

"When we turn to the free negroes of the United States, what shall I say of them? Why, Northern as well as Southern men, and even Canadians, characterize them as the most worthless of the human race. Formerly, the abolitionists ascribed their degradation to the want of political and social privileges. But during the middle ages, in Europe, the Jews were not only without political privileges, but were, as a class, odious and severely persecuted; yet they were, nevertheless, intelligent, energetic, and wealthy. In point of fact, in some portions of the Northern States, the negro has been made a pet of, and, but for his native inferiority, must have thriven, and even become distinguished. On the other hand, it is an indisputable fact that the four million negroes who are held in slavery in the South, when their condition is considered with reference to their physical well-being and comfort, their productiveness as laborers, their intelligence, morality, and religion, stand superior to any other portion of their race. While the free negroes in the North, with fresh accessions from abroad, diminish in numbers, the slaves of the South increase as rapidly as the white race.

and upon the whole, perhaps, add as much to the wealth of the country in which they are located as any equal number of laborers in the world.

"What the abolitionists have to do is, to find or create a negro community which is superior to that of the slaves of the South. When they shall have done this, they will have laid some grounds for their appeals in behalf of emancipation. Hitherto, they have enlisted the sympathies and feelings of the North by falsely assuming that the negro and white man have in all respects the same nature. Let the inequality which the Creator has made be recognised, and their system falls to the ground."

Mr. Clingman, in the same speech, after enumerating some of the outrages of the abolitionists against the South, proceeds as follows:

"The second incident, which caused even a much stronger impression on the minds of the Southern people, was the manner in which the acts of John Brown are received in the North. Instead of the indignation and abhorrence which the atrociousness of his crimes ought naturally to have excited, there were manifestations of admiration and sympathy. Large meetings were held to express these feelings; sermons and prayers were made in his behalf; church-bells tolled, and cannon fired; and more significant than all these were the declarations of almost the entire Republican press, that his punishment would strengthen the anti-slavery cause. Yet Senators tell us that these things were done because of the courage Brown exhibited. But our people think you are mistaken. Though the mere thief may be, and usually is, a coward, yet it is well known that men who engage in robbery or piracy as a profession generally possess courage. Criminals have been executed frequently in New England who, both in the commission of their crimes and in their death, manifested as much courage as John Brown; and yet none of them called forth such feelings of sympathy. At a meeting in Boston, where thousands assembled, when Emerson, a literary man of eminence, proclaimed that Brown had made 'the gallows as glorious as the cross,' he was rapturously applauded. At the large meeting at Natick, where the Senator from Massachusetts was a spectator, the principal orator declared that the people of the North look upon 'Jesus Christ as a dead failure,' and hereafter will rely on 'John Brown, and him hanged.'

"In the Southern States, where old-fashioned Christian notions still prevail, it would be thought right to beat such blasphemers even out of a church, if they congregated there. We are told now that they were not interrupted because the people of Massachusetts are *law-abiding*, and in favor of the *liberty of speech*. But our constituents do not believe one word of this: because they know that, of all the people in the Union, the inhabitants of Massachusetts are the most excitable, and the most intolerant and overbearing. They know that men who dare to oppose the anti-slavery party there are persecuted with intense hatred; that mobs can be gotten up on the smallest occasions, and that ten thousand men can be assembled on the shortest notice to rescue a runaway negro from the custody of a United States marshal."

"The greatest friend of Truth," says a Christian philosopher, "is Time; her greatest enemy is Prejudice, and her constant companion is Humility."

The Rev. Mr. Ross, speaking of "Uncle Tom's Cabin," says, after complimenting the author's genius, "This book is bad in its theology, bad in its morality, bad in its temporary evil influence here in the North, in England, and on the continent of Europe; bad because her isolated cruelties will be taken as the general condition of Southern life, while her Shelbys, and St. Clairs, and Evas will be looked upon as angel visiters, lingering for a moment in that earthly hell." . . . "The *impression* made by the book is a falsehood."

CHAPTER XVII.

"A man's first care should be to avoid the reproaches of his own heart; his next, to escape the censures of the world. If the last interferes with the former, it ought to be entirely neglected; but otherwise there cannot be a greater satisfaction to an honest mind, than to see those approbations which it gives itself seconded by the applause of the public."—ADDISON.

THE Rev. Iscariot Lauderdale actually *did* make a flying trip to Europe, and there married the woman to whom he had been engaged, though his conscience thundered at such an unnatural union, when his heart was altogether consecrated in its affections to another.

He arrived at Iodilla one intensely cold morning, bringing his bride, and her sister, to a parsonage he had not as yet furnished; and therefore, leaving them in his house, he drove round to Mrs. Wyndham's to let Musidora know how he was situated. She instantly offered his wife and sister her own chamber for a week, and, whenever any persons from a distance visited them, they were hospitably entertained at Mrs. Wyndham's mansion, until arrangements could be completed for their comfort at the minister's own home. The first day that the bride made her appearance at church, the whole village were electrified by her form and face. She had a dark, bilious, stagnant-looking complexion—little, nondescript eyes, very near together—a perfectly flat nose — bulbous lips — and very large ears and mouth (that are said to be the sign of goodness of heart in men, but certainly are a misfortune to the looks of women.) Mrs. Lauderdale had also the high cheek-bones of our North American Indians, and a very broad face, made more prone to observation by her hair growing down so low on the forehead as almost to touch her bushy eyebrows — and her head was much more largely developed in the rear than in the front. She was partly hunch-backed — had a skulking bend in the neck — and a hesitating carriage, united with nearly six feet of height — and her hands and feet (that, in South Carolina, are extremities reckoned the greatest desideratum in the *tout ensemble* of a lady, and are universally small,) were as large as an Amazon's. But worse than all this, she had not been in the parish very long before it was discovered that she was subject to fits, or rather violent hysterics, that made her husband think she was dying, whenever she got excited from anger or jealousy — and how could such a woman be shielded from the darts of the green-eyed monster, when every glance into her mirror must have made the food he fed on.

The old Levitical law prohibited a priest to minister at the holy altar, who had a physical blemish of any sort — "A blind man, or a lame, or he that hath a flat nose, or anything superfluous;" or, "a man that is broken-footed, or broken-handed, or crook-backed, or a dwarf, or that had a blemish in his eye," etc., etc.; and he was commanded "not to marry a widow, or a divorced woman, or a profane; but he shall take a virgin of his own people to wife." Does not all this seem as if a minister's consort should be comely* in *person*, as well as in heart and mind? and it is very certain no men on earth admire beauty more than clergymen do.

"It is a very proper answer," says Clarendon, "to him who asked why any man should be delighted with beauty? that it was a question that none but a blind man could ask; since any beautiful object doth so much attract the sight of all men, that it is in no man's power not to be pleased with it."

How Mr. Iscariot Lauderdale became committed to marry such an unplausible helpmeet cannot be accounted for, except by the laws of propinquity, that some witty old croaker declared were so stringent—"that two broomsticks could not live together in the same house without getting married."

Musidora knew so little of the world that she never dreamed Mr. Lauderdale would hate her now, in exact proportion to his former unhallowed love, that had made him almost seek the alternative of suicide to relieve the torment of his passions. His wife, too, by intuition found out her husband's versatility of affection.

---

* The Washington "Evening Star," of April, 1860, says:—"Elder Kimball, of the Mormon Church, while preaching recently in Salt Lake City, Utah Territory, is said to have addressed some missionaries who were about starting on a proselyting tour, as follows: 'Brethren, I want you to understand that it is not to be as it has been heretofore. The brother missionaries have been in the habit of picking out the prettiest women for themselves before they got here, and bringing on the ugliest for us; hereafter you have to bring them all here before taking any of them, and let us all have a fair chance.'"

"But through the heart
Should jealousy its venom once diffuse,
'Tis then delightful misery no more,
But agony unmix'd, incessant gall,
Corroding every thought, and blasting all
Love's Paradise. Ye fairy prospects then,
Ye beds of roses, and ye bowers of joy,
Farewell! ye gleamings of departed peace,
Shine out your last! the yellow tingling plague
Internal vision taints, and in the night
Of vivid gloom Imagination wraps."

This ambiguously-united couple, in consequence of the aforesaid laws that govern the human heart in its now fallen state, had not been married one month before they both intensely hated the unconscious Musidora, who meanwhile was doing everything to advance their interests in the parish. Any praise extended to the noble life of Musidora was distorted by Mr. Lauderdale to reflect unfavorably on the unimposing, unenterprising minister's wife.

"And if she hapt of any good to heare,
That had to any happily betid,
Then would she inly fret, and grieve, and teare
Her flesh for felnesse, which she inward hid:
But if she heard of ill that any did,
Or harme that any had, then would she make
Great cheare, like unto a banquet bid;
And in another's losse great pleasure take,
As she had got thereby, and gayned a great stake."

Mr. Lauderdale became jealous, too, of Musidora's visitations among the poor, that, when he first knew her, had elicited his deepest, approving sympathy, and he had held her up everywhere as the most self-abnegating, elevated example to all his flock; but now he denounced her as a heretical Methodist, who was seeking salvation by works, and not by simple faith. Indeed, so angry was he at her success in establishing Sunday-schools among the poor, before he took charge of the parish, that one Sunday morning, when she was very earnestly teaching a large class of children, that for many years she had tenderly loved, he walked in, and dismissed the whole class, saying, "hereafter he would teach them himself." He had a sardonic, sneering laugh curling his lip, as he did this piece of rudeness, and Musidora thought of repeating to him—

> "Man, vain man! drest in a little brief authority,
> Plays such fantastic tricks before high heaven as make the angels weep."

But she remembered his holy calling, and said not a word, but employed her time in reading till the church service commenced. Mr. Lauderdale never taught these interesting children afterwards, and the school was broken up; so that when the Bishop visited the church, he rebuked severely the neglect of Sunday-schools in the parish.

After bearing all the disagreeableness and neglect of her pastor for a whole year, Musidora happened one day to mention it to one of Mr. Lauderdale's relatives, who answered: "Is it possible you don't know for what reason they both hate you? Why they heard you had written letters to the Rev. Mr. Knox, of Georgia, ridiculing Mrs. Lauderdale's want of handsomeness," etc., etc. Poor Musidora, instead of letting this tempest in a teapot boil over its useless froth, impulsively rushed home, seized her pen, and wrote to Mr. Lauderdale that she had just heard that one of the congregation, a Mrs. Fullsome, had told him she had disparaged his wife; and she declared, on the word of a Christian lady, that it was utterly *untrue;* and she urged him to cease his intimacy with a family who were regarded the greatest gossips in the whole community, and consequently inspired the natural opinion everywhere, that those who constantly sought their society were equal lovers of news-mongers, and detractionists of their neighbors; that those persons in the church who told him all that was said about him, were foes to his peace and his ghostly communion with his God, etc. "When will talkers refrain from evil-speaking? When listeners refrain from evil-hearing."

Mr. Lauderdale, in a great rage, charged Musidora with falsehood, and asserted that the family she had warned him about were the worthiest friends he had; and, indeed, that both Mr. and Mrs. Knox had told them personally how she had written against Mrs. Lauderdale, and they themselves were ready to testify to the fact. Musidora was now determined to put down such a scandal, so she wrote to Mr. Knox, and he replied that "he was astonished any one should presume to use his name in such a connection;" and he enclosed the only letter he had ever received from Musidora, which was written to forward him some money for his mission, and, in a postscript, she spoke kindly of her minister's wife, who had just arrived at Iodilla. Returning thanks to God for such a triumphant vindication of her Christian character, Musidora dispatched a courier to Mr. Lauderdale, with her own and Mr. Knox's letter.

It was naturally believed that when such infallible proof of her entire innocence of the malignity laid to her charge was produced, that a generous impulse would have induced this English abolitionist, who professed such nobility about striking down all tyranny from the earth, to fall down on his knees in penitence for his wicked suspicions and wicked patronage of scandal, and wicked insults to a lady of Musidora's magnificence of moral character. But Mr. Lauderdale belonged to that party of saints whose religion is bloodthirsty, malignant, and incapable, from its stubbornness, of being convinced of any fact it is not politic to believe.

> "He that's convinced against his will,
> Is of the same opinion still."

So this pitiable apology for a gentleman merely wrote on a scrap of paper "that he was glad to find that Miss Wyndham was correct in her estimate of the letter she had written to Mr. Knox." These few lines *in pencil* was all the concession made for accusing a Christian lady of falsehood — which savage higher-lawism, but for his clerical vocation, would have ensured Mr. Lauderdale's being sent out of the world by the insinuating enterprise of a "Kansas Sharpe's rifle," even in the law-abiding State of South Carolina.

"A Christian is God Almighty's gentleman. A gentleman, in the vulgar, superficial way of understanding the word, is the Devil's Christian. But to throw aside these polished and too current counterfeits for something valuable and sterling — the real gentleman should be gentle in everything, at least in everything that depends on himself — in carriage, temper, constructions, aims, desires. He ought, therefore, to be mild, calm, quiet, even, temperate—not hasty in judgment, not exorbitant in ambition, not overbearing, not proud, not rapacious, not oppressive; for these things are contrary to gentleness. Many such gentlemen are to be found, I trust, and many more would be, were the true meaning of the name borne in mind and duly inculcated."

Our overmuch righteous Pharisee, Mr. Lauderdale, had never, in all his life, heard that to confess and make atonement for any errors of judgment that have led us to injure an innocent person, is particularly the spirit enjoined in the Scriptures. "A man," says Pope, "should never be ashamed to own he has been in the wrong, which is but saying in other words, that he is wiser to-day than he was yesterday." Not so our hero, however, who came to the Southern States believing all the calumnies told in England, by traitors to their country, that slave-holders were savage ruffians. But he found in South Carolina, "young men greater, prouder, braver, and more generous than all those of his age. He found women so beautiful, so simple, so chaste, that they seemed fashioned from different clay — both walking as if upheld by the memory of their ancestors; and there is no doubt that they had in their blood globules of moral nobility" — for even tradition must ever confine them to those paths of honor and virtue that they have to tread, in memory of those august names they have inherited from the magnificent heroes of the Revolutionary War. Those apostles of progress who eliminated before the whole civilized world, the fact that the children of Japheth were, and ever will be, capable of self-government, for God has willed it so, and made the very father of Shem, Ham, and Japheth, prophesy this extraordinary inequality between his three sons, forever.

Mr. Lauderdale, though witnessing every day the utter absurdity of these abolitionists' scandals against the South, still was determined to believe them, like a certain Northern personage who undertook a journey to Cuba and some of the Southern States. Speaking of Mobile, he says, "The society I meet here is frank and agreeable. Indeed, it seems to me that there must be two classes of Southerners, as different from each other as light from darkness. I often wonder if our brethren at the South are bewildered by the same apparent diversity of character in our Northern men." . . . "The Southerners whom I meet at the South in social intercourse, to whom I am introduced at hotels, in steamboats, and at the fireside, are genial, friendly, courteous — gentlemen in tone, kind and polished in manners, ever recognizing the courtesies of refined society." . . . "But there is another class whom I never meet, whom I seek for in vain, but who are revealed to me in newspaper editorials, in convention-speeches, and in Congressional debates." . . . "It is difficult to account for the fact that one never meets any of those fierce creatures in his travels." . . . "I have not met a single one." . . . "I have seen, of course, some uncultivated men, some poor and debased, some profane men, but I have met with not a single specimen of this kind of character; and I can truly say that almost every Southerner whom I have thus far seen, has seemed to be a courteous, unassuming, kind-hearted gentleman." . . . "I expected to have caught a glimpse of some of those creatures, tearing over the hills like a locomotive under an attack of delirium-tremens." . . . "But thus far I have been disappointed. I have met with many who were truly genial companions, and whom any gentleman would love as intimate associates and neighbors, and friends." . . . "Do those fierce men who utter such terrible menaces, like lions, sleep in their lair by day, and never come out but by night?"

Would you believe it, dear reader, that this author-minister of the Gospel, who made the observations detailed above, in his diary while travelling in the South, where he received all the deference and kindness universally extended *there* to the clerical profession, went home and published the most abusive fanatical book that has ever been written against the Southern people, just to pander to the suicidal, unpatriotic, mawkish dementia of the anti-slavery party in the North. Can we be blamed for the strictest surveillance when these disorganizers of our Constitutional government hanker around our domestic hearths as *pre*-judging spies? dangerous indeed to our poor childish negroes, who know nothing of the miseries of those blacks in the North who have "gone masterless." *

" LUNACY AMONG NEGROES.—Statistics lately published, showing the prevalence of lunacy among the negroes of the various States of the Union, prove that mental disease is much more prevalent among the free blacks of the North than among the

Mr. Lauderdale was a fac-simile of this one idea bigoted abolitionist, and therefore Musidora did not hold him up as a paragon of inductive sense, chivalry, or manliness, much less of Bible religion; so she pityingly forgave his savage conduct and his Mohawk manners, the moment she obtained the proof of his littleness of mind in listening to tale-bearers, and her own triumphant vindication. But wishing to test an English abolitionist's interpretation of a minister's duty in the government of his church, she sent for Mr. Lauderdale, and remarked, "Now, my friend, you were so faithful in rebuking *my* sin as to order *me* from the communion-table, because you thought I had been guilty of falsehood; the Bible requires, as my innocence is proved, and Mrs. Fullsome's (the tale-bearer's) guilt is proved, that you prohibit *her* next Sunday, as you did myself from partaking of that sacrament of love." This Pharisee flew into a perfect rage, and said he would not rebuke Mrs. Fullsome at all, at all. Little did he know the power of Musidora's righteous indignation, when it was fairly roused against hypocrisy and villany.

Musidora put on her hat, and taking up Mr. Knox's letter, went immediately to see Mrs. Fullsome's brother-in-law, who was the most prominent vestryman in the church, and she explained to him her errand. He

slaves of the South. In Louisiana there is found only one lunatic in 2477 negroes; in South Carolina, one in 2999; while in Massachusetts there is one in 43, and in Maine one in 14. Such statistics go further than any argument or declamation to prove that the negro is better off in a state of slavery than in freedom. Unsuited by nature to endure the cares and anxieties incident to a condition in which he has to provide for himself, his weak brain gives way, and lunacy is the consequence."

nobly offered to go to his sister at once, and ask the meaning of such ambiguities; and she replied, "that never in her life had she breathed a word of the kind to Mr. Lauderdale, about Musidora." Here, then, this transcendental, nineteenth-century saint was caught in an unmitigated falsehood. "Lying lips are an abomination to the Lord." "God hateth a lying tongue." "All liars shall have their part in the lake that burns with fire and brimstone." "The devil is the father (the generator) of lies." So that when Musidora asked this true son of old Timothy Brimstone for an explanation, he contrived another falsehood,* and said,

---

* No Sin stands alone.—It is one of the appalling tendencies of sin to multiply itself, as the seed brings forth harvests a hundred-fold. One falsehood often leads inevitably to many others to hide the first; one fraud leads to successive peculations to recover lost ground, and every sin opens the way for numerous transgressions. This truth is well enforced in the following paragraphs:

Joseph's brethren envied him; that was a great sin; then they stripped him of his beautiful coat, and cast him into a pit; another sin; then they sold him to the Ishmaelites; still another; then, to hide these sins, they must add an act of falsehood and cruel deception; they dipped Joseph's coat in the blood of a kid, and carried it to their father, pretending that they had found it in the field. At the sight of it, Jacob's heart died within him. "An evil beast," said he, "hath devoured him; Joseph is without doubt rent in pieces." Now they must try to comfort him, and in so doing they were obliged to play the hypocrite. Then they must persist in their falsehood and deception during all the long years, at least twenty-two, that passed until Joseph made himself known to them in Egypt. What a chain of dreadful sins! Yes, what a chain! for all the wicked deeds were linked together. The first drew after it all the rest.

So Herod first did an unlawful deed in marrying Herodias,

perhaps he had made a mistake, and heard the story from Mrs. Fullsome's little daughter.

"Sir," said Musidora, "dare you to use your ghostly power to drive *me* from the church to which for ten or sixteen years I have consecrated every affection of my heart, and every enterprise of my mind, and then bring up an irresponsible child as your authority for an act so grave, that it involves a soul for time and eternity?"

Mr. Lauderdale actually shivered with alarm; not that he feared God, but the terrible vindication of man, that must follow such an *exposé* of his being a wolf in sheep's clothing. So the devil came to his rescue, and told him to go and read to Mrs. Fullsome

---

his brother Philip's wife; then, when John reproved him for this sin, he "added yet this above all, that he shut up John in prison." The first sin led to the second. But that was not the end. This same Herodias, whom he had unlawfully married, what did she do? When her daughter Salome danced before Herod and his lords, he was greatly delighted, and promised with an oath to give her whatsoever she would ask. This was both foolish and wicked. And now see how these two sins, that of marrying Herodias, and that of making this oath to Salome her daughter, united in producing another dreadful deed. At the mother's suggestion, who hated John for his faithfulness in reproving Herod, the daughter asked for the head of John the Baptist, and, for "the oath's sake," Herod sent and beheaded John in the prison.

Thus has it ever been, and thus will it always be. One sin leads to another, and so on without end. He who cheats is driven into lying; and he who tells one lie, must tell another to hide the first. Sabbath-breaking, disobedience to parents, and keeping company with the wicked, are all sins, and they lead to a great many more sins. When you take one wrong step, you know not whither it will carry you.

and her brother-in-law the letter Musidora had written, warning him against that lady; and he actually flew to carry this Satanic mischief into execution, so as to turn their wrath from himself upon Musidora. He then recalled every opinion of individuals in the community, that he had heard in Mrs. Wyndham's family, when he had been received there, during the first year of his ministry, with the confidence of a brother. These remarks he distorted and retailed everywhere, so that his whole parish were in a ferment of hatred against each other; and he actually made enmities in families, that never were healed during their whole lives.

> "From door to door you might have seen him speed,
> Or placed amid a group of gaping fools,
> And whispering in their ears with his foul lips.
> Peace fled the neighborhood in which he made
> His haunts."

Awful indeed is it that at this scandal-monger's ordination by the bishop, he had taken the solemn, ghostly vow propounded to deacons and priests in the Episcopal Church, namely: "Will you maintain and set forward, as much as lieth in you, quietness, peace, and love among all Christian people, and especially among them that are, or shall be, committed to your charge?" This monster of malignancy was so cunning, that he could distort any truth.

> "Skill'd by a touch to deepen scandal's tints,
> With all the kind mendacity of hints,
> While mingling truth with falsehood, sneers with smiles,
> A thread of candor with a web of wiles;

> A plain, blunt show of briefly-spoken seeming,
> To hide his bloodless heart's soul-hardened scheming;
> A lip of lies, a face form'd to conceal;
> And without feeling, mock at all who feel;
> With a vile mask the Gorgon would disown,
> A cheek of parchment, and an eye of stone."

Mr. Lauderdale was that whisperer that the Bible says "separateth chief friends." "He that uttereth a slander is a fool," says the wise King Solomon. "A prating fool shall fall." "A hypocrite with his mouth destroyeth his neighbor." "Pride and arrogancy and a froward mouth do I hate," says God. "The lip of truth shall be established forever, but a lying tongue is but for a moment." "An ungodly man diggeth up evil, and in his lips there is as a burning fire."

> "The shrug, the hum, or ha; these petty brands,
> That calumny doth use:—
> For calumny will sear
> Virtue itself:—these shrugs, these hums, and ha's,
> When you have said, 'She's goodly,' come between
> Ere you can say, 'She's honest.'"

Poor Musidora found that this whited sepulchre, that Jesus compared the Pharisees to, had deprived her, by these Satanic hints and whisperings, of friends whose esteem had been her choicest treasure. She at once wrote an elevated apology to Mrs. Fullsome for the letter, that was afterwards proved to be unjust, as that lady had not been guilty of the falsehood laid to her charge. This woman refused to accept any apology; and yet Mr. Lauderdale let her commune, against the rules of the church, for she was too rich for him to afford to offend her. She gave splendid dinners and suppers; she had monopolized Mr. Lauderdale and his family by constant invitations; she hired the most expensive pew, and she made him the most magnificent presents continually; how could he have the moral courage to rebuke the possessor of so many worldly goods? The Bible says, "Every one is a friend of him that giveth gifts," and that "a gift in secret pacifieth anger." The United States Government, indeed, is so much afraid of the ubiquitously corrupting influence of gifts, that its laws prohibit the President of the United States from accepting presents from foreign nations. Indeed, the church would be purer if every minister determined, as it was reported Mr. William Barnwell, of Charleston, did, as soon as he was ordained,—"that he would never receive a present from his congregation at all, lest his hands should be weakened in rebuking their sins, and lest the poor among them who could not afford to make these gifts too, should be offended or discouraged." Every people could prevent the necessity for such equivocal good, by giving their minister a sufficient salary.

Mr. Lauderdale not only thus broke Musidora's heart on the wheel of all her strongest friendships, but throughout the diocese he spread hints among the clergy that she was in love with him, though he was a married man. "Oppression driveth a wise man mad;" and now we again see the evil consequences of Musidora's having had no one to discipline her mind or heart in childhood; for the tremendous strength of her untamed will writhed in anguish to exterminate this man's fiendish influence.

"Have I not had my brain sear'd, my heart riven,
Hopes sapp'd, name blighted, life's life lied away;
And only not to desperation driven,
Because not altogether of such clay,
As rots into the souls of those whom I survey."

Musidora's intense abhorrence of this deep villain nearly drove her to that phrenzy of grief that had dethroned her reason when her lover became a madman. Few persons understand hatred; for when once this deep-toned passion takes possession of the mind and heart, it seems as if the world is not large enough to separate between yourself and your enemy; therefore you must exterminate him from off the face of the earth. It is, beyond a doubt, *madness*, for

"Revenge, at first though sweet,
Bitter, ere long, back on itself recoils."

"He that hateth his brother is a murderer, and no murderer hath eternal life abiding in him," says the Bible.

For six months Musidora never closed her eyes at night, but walked up and down her lonely chamber hopeless of life; for though she felt so sincere in living for the highest moral objects, that she often wished her heart could be transparent to the whole world, she could not, educated as lawlessly as she had been from childhood, refrain from the oft-repeated temptation of rebellion against God for allowing her thus to be tyrannized over by the wicked, when He knew her whole heart yearned to be holy in its every impulse. Two distinct spirits seemed to be contending for dominion over her; the one said, Curse God, and die;

the other softly and tenderly whispered of that Savior who had been scourged, and maligned, and spit upon, to save her soul from perdition, and to clothe her with that panoply of faith that would overcome the world, the flesh, and the devil, and would eventually restore the image of Jesus Christ in the soul of every human being who was willing to trust in no righteousness, save that purchased for them on the atoning, God-pacifying blood of the Cross that streamed from the thorn-crowned brow, and hands, and side, and feet of the crucified Redeemer.

The biography of the greatest Christians who have been the moral salt of the earth, invariably proclaims the fact, that not one of them has passed through their heaven-tracked sojourn in this world, who has not had their motives and character assailed by the asp-like tongue of detraction and envy; and we are told that that virago wife of the celebrated Reformer, John Wesley, was so jealous of him, lest he was visiting the pretty girls in his extensive missionary journeyings, that she would, with higher-law fury, rush at him and tear the hair from his august head, and sometimes secretly follow him a hundred miles to watch his whereabouts. And, finally, when the most dreadful reports were circulated against him, just as he was on the eve of another very distant journey, his distinguished ministerial friends, almost on their knees, begged him to contradict these calumnies. But he sublimely answered, "No; for that when he had given himself to God he had not excepted his *reputation*." God allowed the higher-law Mr. Lauderdale to be the instrument employed to put the proud Musidora into a furnace heated seven times; but that Savior whom she loved sat close by the crucible to watch the gold, and to remove it from the fire the moment he could see his *own* image in the purified metal, that demonstrated it was entirely separated from the dross.

Mr. Lauderdale's jealous, envious wife, and her sister, and their friends, all continued to circulate calumny after calumny against a woman that every one of those gossips in that parish secretly envied for her genius, her moral influence, and commanding goodness.

"If envy, like anger, did not burn itself in its own fire, and consume and destroy those persons it possesses before it can destroy those it wishes worst to, it would set the whole world on fire and leave the most excellent persons the most miserable."

Musidora's friends among the poor, to whom she had unweariedly ministered for ten or fifteen years, threatened to mob this petty Pope; and the gentlemen of the whole community declared "that were she their sister they would compel Mr. Lauderdale, from the pulpit, to confess his wickedness and beg Musidora's pardon before the whole congregation."

But what became of her brother Halcombe all this time? Mr. Lauderdale would have actually shivered before *his* righteous wrath. Why he was sitting down at home, canvassing whether it is ever right to resist evil;* whether the august Musidora *could* by any pos-

* A Noble Wife.—Many of our public men have been blessed with wives and mothers who were the ornaments of their sex, and their quiet and ennobling influence contributed largely to the subsequent greatness of their children and husbands. Mr. Parton tells the following story of General Jackson's wife:—

sibility be injured by an abolition adventurer; and no doubt he canvassed, too, the popularity or unpopularity

---

"When General Jackson was a candidate for the Presidency in 1828, not only did his political foes oppose him for his public acts, which, if unconstitutional or violent, were a legitimate subject of reprobation, but they defamed the character of his wife. On one occasion, a newspaper published in Nashville was laid upon the General's table. He glanced over it, and his eyes fell upon an article in which the character of Mrs. Jackson was violently assailed. So soon as he had read it, he sent for his trusty old servant Dunwoodie.

"'Saddle my horse,' said he to him in a whisper, 'and put my holsters on him.' Mrs. Jackson watched him, and though she heard not a word, she thought she saw *mischief in his eyes*. The General went out after a few moments, when she took up the paper and understood everything. She ran out to the south gate of the yard of the Hermitage by which the General would have to pass. She had not been there more than a few seconds before the General rode up with the countenance of a madman. She placed herself before his horse, and cried out,

"'O General, don't go to Nashville! Let that poor editor live! Let that poor editor live!'

"'Let me alone!' he replied; 'how came you to know what I am going for?'

"She answered, 'I saw it all in his paper after you went out: put up your horse and go back.'

"He replied, furiously, 'But I *will* go—get out of my way!"

"Instead of doing this she grasped his bridle with both hands.

"He cried to her, 'I say, let go my horse; I'll have his heart's blood; the villain that reviles my wife shall not live.'

"She grasped the reins but the tighter, and began to expostulate with him, saying that *she* was the one who ought to be angry, but that she forgave her persecutors from the bottom of her heart, and prayed for them; that he should forgive, if he hoped to be forgiven. At last, by her reasoning, her entreaties, and her tears, she so worked upon her husband that he seemed mollified to a certain extent. She wound up by

that might accrue to himself if he took the needful steps to cause the bishop to unfrock this disturber of the peace of all Christian people over whom he sacrilegiously dared to minister. Colton says "It was observed of the Jesuits, that they constantly inculcated a thorough contempt of worldly things in their doctrines, but eagerly grasped at them in their lives. They were 'wise in their generation,' for they cried down worldly things because they wanted to obtain them, and cried up spiritual things because they wanted to dispose of them."

Halcombe was also so unreasonable as to expect that his high-mettled, undisciplined sister, Musidora, would have treated with silent contempt a whisperer who had had the power to deprive her of friends she loved as her own soul. Such a silence would have dethroned her reason entirely; for who can bear or should bear the grossest injustice and tyranny in any church where religion itself requires us to demand a sufficient reason for excommunication.

Halcombe felt, too, that Mr. Lauderdale was too small to arouse his wrath. But did a fly ever know that it was his insignificance that enabled him to buzz around and annoy the ears of a lion? that he was too diminutive a little creature for that lordly beast to

---

saying, 'No, General, you *shall* not take the life of even my reviler; you dare not do it, for it is written, "Vengeance is *mine*, I will repay, saith the Lord!"'

"The iron-nerved hero gave way before the earnest pleading of his beloved wife, and replied,

"'I yield to you; but had it not been for you, and the words of the Almighty, the wretch should not have lived an hour.'"

expend his strength to annihilate him? even so Mr. Lauderdale, in his monstrous conceits, thought Halcombe was afraid of him.

Musidora's step-mother now revealed the jealousy that had hitherto only shown itself in petty tempests at home; she allowed Mr. Lauderdale, although she did not belong to his church, to visit her and speak against, and write to her sneeringly, about Musidora; and then her daughter, Gulielma, who was just grown up, contracted desperate intimacies with all Musidora's enemies, repeating, in her daftness, to them, every word exchanged between Halcombe and herself at home. Thus Mr. Lauderdale's fox-like cunning induced him to report to all the clergy in the State, that Musidora's family were all against her and in favor of himself.

Our characters in this world are really never injured by calumny if we are truly innocent; but poor human nature is too mercurial to believe this blessed fact when we feel ourselves in the blazing fire of wicked, envious women, or men's poisonous nimble tongues; so Musidora thought she had best write to every minister in the diocese, to defend herself from the innumerable scandals of Mr. Lauderdale — for be it borne in mind that her religious heart was so afraid of injuring the holy calling of the priesthood, that in all her anguish she had never said aught, except to her brethren and sisters in the Church of God; and she actually knew so little of the world that she thought St. Paul's injunction was an article of the 19th century religion, namely, "And whether one member suffer, all the members suffer with it; or one member be honored, all the members rejoice with it."

Musidora also believed that sarcasm was a gift that might be carefully used; for certain it is, that ridicule is often more pungent in showing vain people their absurdities, than the most philosophic reasoning or angular rebuke. She, therefore, with a pen dipped in irony, showed the clergy the absurdity of a married minister's thinking the girls in love with him. Mr. Lauderdale had one of these witty episodes sent to him by an enemy of Musidora's, and he jumped into a curricle, and actually ran his poor horse from Dan to Beersheba, proclaiming his purpose to issue immediately a bull of excommunication from the Church to her. Now she happened to care as much about passionate, malignant bulls of excommunication, as Napoleon Bonaparte did, for she felt innocent of any crime save that of self-defence. Her enemy soon perceived this, and therefore sent a letter to the vestry resigning the church, and assigning Miss Wyndham as the cause. This he did to overwhelm her, for he knew his congregation worshipped talent, and *he was*, indeed, a sparkling genius. The moment Musidora heard of this renewed cunning, she went personally to the vestry, and said, "Now, gentlemen, you know that the most prominent people in the State are my friends; therefore, if Mr. Lauderdale does not instantly recall this letter of resignation, I will write to let everybody know the *truth* which, from the very outset, has caused all this enterprising persecution for three years without cessation — namely, that I did not think the parson's wife a handsome woman." This presented the whole tempest in a teapot in such an irresistibly ludicrous light, that the resignation was immediately withdrawn from the vestry before it was communicated to the congregation; and afterwards Mr. Lauderdale gave up preaching the gospel as soon as a secular calling was offered to him that was more lucrative.

We may, however, hear of him again before this book closes, as skulking around the plantations and inciting the poor ignorant slaves to rise up at midnight and assassinate all the men, women, and children in South Carolina: and then the bells in Boston will peal in triumph over his angelic martyrdom, as they did about the Harper's Ferry massacre.

> "Then shall they seek to avail themselves of names,
> Places, and titles, and with these join
> Secular power, though feigning still to act
> By spiritual, to themselves appropriating
> The Spirit of God, promised alike and given
> To all believers; and from that pretence,
> Spiritual laws by carnal pow'r shall force
> On every conscience; laws which none shall find
> Left them enroll'd, or what the spirit within
> Shall on the heart engage."
>
> MILTON'S PARADISE LOST.

CHAPTER XVIII.

"A great, a good, and a right mind, is a kind of divinity lodged in flesh, and it may be the blessing of a slave, as well as of a prince; it came from heaven, and to heaven it must return, and it is a kind of heavenly felicity which a pure and virtuous mind enjoys, in some degree, even upon earth."

WE left young Edward Wyndham stationed at the theological seminary at New York; we now find him a deeply learned biblical scholar, and ordained minister, returned home to Iodilla; but he could not be happy with his step-mother, who most particularly disliked him, and subjected his temper to daily hourly irritations, more damaging to the patience of a saint, than the severest dispensations of Providence; "for in a great and sudden calamity, the religious mind rushes at once into the covert of submission to God's will, and has no fear of ultimate evil accruing therefrom;" for, "Like as a father pitieth his own children, so the Lord pitieth those that fear Him;" and *His* pity is omnipotent, to screen us from every harm. But when our fellow-creatures irritate us with their petty littleness every moment, we are sure, sooner or later, to forget the strength that enables us to overcome great hindrances to our pious equanimity. Christians may be ever so sincere in their religion, though their personal peculiarities may never be destroyed. For instance, a man of genius who has a mercurial temperament, will never have the temptations of a dunce, whose blood runs slowly as if surcharged with opium, while the other's is lively with mercury. The great activity of the brain, naturally produces irritability. But this temperament is perfectly consistent with amiability of sentiment, and Christian charity, in the heart. Generally persons who cannot feel indignant anger where there is a righteous cause, are too insensible to blush at their own disgraceful acts, and are indifferent to the esteem of the wise and good. "No man deserves to be praised for his goodness, unless he has strength of character to be wicked."

Edward Wyndham, like his talented sister Musidora, was constitutionally irritable, and though neither of them hated their feeble-minded, vexing, annoying stepmother, and were enthusiastic to advance the best interests of their idolized father's widow, and her children; still, when a minister is writing a deep treatise on the lost image of God in the soul of man, and its restoration to holiness under the new régime of forgiveness for sin, and faith in the finished complete righteousness of Christ,—whose satisfaction disarms justice, and whose payment on the Cross cancels the bond against us;—we repeat, when a minister of the gospel is writing out for the benefit of others this magnificent, sublime destiny of the vigilant enthusiastic seeker of Bible righteousness, he cannot bear to come down from his angelic flight into the third heaven of beatitude, to defend himself from a fretful, quarrelsome, grown-up baby, who is covetous lest he burned too much light in his study at night, which these unelevated utilitarians see no necessity for; or that my lady, who is "dying of a rose in aromatic pain," cannot sleep while anybody is awake in the house. Just as if her rest, when she has been engaged all day in expedients, merely to kill time, and drive off ennui, is of the least consequence in comparison with the mental labor that fires the enterprise of genius in eliminating god-like thought that can never die.

The great Adam Clarke had a landlady who was such a Bengal tiger, that when he was very poor, and yet thrilling with the fire of genius, and ravenous in his appetite for learning, she would not allow him a light to study by at night; and he used to make a dark tent in his room, with the bed-clothes and curtains, and hide his light underneath this miniature wigwam, so as to study linguistic learning, without her argus eyes finding him out. Indeed, it would be edifying and entertaining, if all the geniuses in the world had left a record of the almost insurmountable barriers that dunces have thrown in their path, during their courtship with the nine Muses. The exquisite rapture of constantly drawing from the brain, new and elevated moral thought, is quite out of the reach of language to describe. Oh, destiny, cries the professor of this divine gift, let the material, gold-loving world satisfied utilitarian carnality, have all the wealth of Crœsus; I shall envy not his gilded coach, or his marble palaces, or his high political, mercantile, or aristocratic position in society, provided I can have companionship with the mighty host of intellect, whose works live after their bodies have returned to their original dust.

One among the most captivating ideas held out in

the Bible is, that at the resurrection our souls will return to our veritable bodies again, that throughout our lives on earth had been so indissolubly united in interest and undying affection. For what sublime genius could bear the idea of having his soul housed for eternity, in any other than his own individual body? "Those many great improbabilities and unlikelihoods alleged against the resurrection of the same numerical body, are apt to give a mighty check to the mind of man in yielding its belief to it." . . . "For who could imagine or could conceive, that when a body, by continual fraction and dissipation, is crumbling into millions of little atoms, some portions of it into rarefied air, others sublimated into fire, and the rest changed into earth and water; the elements should, after all this, surrender back their spoils, and the several parts, after such a dispersion, should travel from all the four quarters of the world to meet together, and come to a mutual interview of one another, in one and the same individual body again?" . . . "That God should summon a part out of this fish, that fowl, that beast, that tree, and remand it to its former place, to unite into a new combination for the rebuilding of a fallen edifice, and restoring an old, broken, demolished carcase to itself once more? So that, by such a continual circulation of life and death following upon one another, the grave should become not so much a conclusion, as the interruption; not the period, but the parenthesis of our lives, a short interval between the present and the future, and only a passage to convey us from one life to another." . . . "These things, we must confess, are both difficult in the notion, and hard to our belief."

"For though indeed the word of truth has declared that 'all flesh is grass,' and man but as the flower of the field; yet the apprehensions of sense will hardly be brought to acknowledge that he therefore grows upon his own grave, or springs afresh out of the ground." "For can the jaws of death relent? or the grave (of all things) make restitution? Can filth and rottenness be the preparatives to glory, and dust and ashes the seed-plots of immortality." . . . "Is the sepulchre a place to dress ourselves in for heaven, the attiring-room for corruption to put on incorruption, and to fit us for the beatific vision?" Yes, the Christian believes all this—for God's word declares the fact; and the world has in it just as unfathomable mysteries, that science in its profoundest depths cannot explain. God, to keep our pride humble, forces us every day to acknowledge that we are an unfathomable mystery even to ourselves; and therefore why should we reject the resplendent idea of a glorified body, merely because we have not the infinite mind of Jehovah to comprehend how it can be solved?

"The doors of death were open'd, and in the dark
And loathsome vault, and silent charnel-house,
Moving were heard the moulder'd bones that sought
Their proper place. Instinctive, every soul
Flew to its clayey part: from grass-grown mould,
The nameless spirit took its ashes up,
Reanimate; and merging from beneath
The flattered marble, undistinguish'd rose
The great, nor heeded once the lavish rhyme
And costly pomp of sculptur'd marble vain.
Ye vainly wise! ye blind presumptuous! now
Confounded in the dust, adore that power
And wisdom oft arraign'd: see now the cause,

Why unassuming worth in secret lived,
And died neglected: why the good man's share
In life was gall and bitterness of soul:
Why the lone widow and her orphans pined
In starving solitude; while luxury
In palaces lay straining her low thoughts
To form unreal wants.

Edward, to relieve himself from petty annoyances, soon fancied himself in love with a widow who was a year older than himself, but who had a delightful home. No doubt many good people deceive themselves thus; for every lover believes that his marriage with his Hebe will increase his felicity; so that, if a poor genius sees even a *passée* lady, with all the surroundings of comfort that would enable him to spend the rest of his days in the beatitude of his library, it will not require a vast impulse of imagination for him to fancy himself sincerely in love with the possessor of so many avenues to the indulgence of cultivated taste. Certain it is, that Edward married the widow, though Sam Weller says a widow is equal to seventeen girls; and certain it is that she was not congenial, though she had *shoneau* enough to butter all his parsnips at dinner. He, however, had genius, and real religion; which, when united, command a store of felicity *within* that no enemy from without can ever deprive their possessor of.

Edward, having no temptation to idolise his fretful, passionate helpmeet, gave himself up entirely to the study of the voluminous world of sacred literature that he could now procure through this newly-opened purse; for it must be borne in mind that South Carolina is such an "old fogy," that all the ladies *there* are brought up to be obedient to their husbands; who are regarded so much the *head* of the house, that every temporality, even the purse, is under their direction; and never, since that State was settled by the chivalrous cavaliers of England, has such a progressiveness been thought of as "Woman's Rights Conventions.*

"But," says the Rev. Samuel Cox, "It takes Americans to know everything by instinct mainly; to teach without learning —especially in philosophy, politics, and religion; and to be

---

* "A Female Senate.—The movements among the 'strong-minded' women which modern times have developed, must have had their origin in the fact that very seldom has any share of legislation been allowed, in any country, or among any people, sect, or denomination, to the female sex. The 'lords of creation' usually take upon themselves the whole drudgery of making laws, as well as of executing them. The Quakers, however, are an exception to this rule; and, in the most perfectly republican manner, admit their women to an equal voice in managing the concerns of the Society.

"Heliogabalus, the most luxurious, as he was the most contemptible of the Roman emperors, established a Female Senate, and placed his mother at the head of it. But they had no voice in political affairs; their only business being the regulation of dress and fashion, and the determining who were 'qualified to keep a chariot or sumpter-horse; who should be allowed to ride on an ass; who should be drawn in a car by mules and oxen; what ladies should be allowed the flattering indulgence of being carried in a chair, and what sort of chairs they should use—whether leather, bone, ivory, or silver; and lastly, who should enjoy the envied distinction of wearing gold and jewels on their shoes.' This Senate expired with its founder, who was assassinated after a brief reign of four years."

'free' to do anything, especially if they are destitute of all qualifications for it.

"Lecturing is now degenerating, in our country, very fast. Charlatans of every stripe can make a flaming advertisement, get an auditory and a fee; and after that, a puff from some editor that loves 'equality,' and wants to encourage the aspirations of *promising* genius. So candidates are Amazonion, too. modest, shame-faced ladies, married and single, can man a rostrum, and inculcate a nostrum, as well as other substantives of doubtful gender — whose sphere seems as much an ambiguity as their sex: as to their wisdom, that is obvious."

Although the South Carolina ladies are not, and never can be, progressive enough to become public lecturers, yet no women on earth are more high-mettled and self-respecting, nor more honored by gentlemen, than they are; none are more frank and fearless in the expression of their feelings and opinions in the refined enclosure of the drawing-room; for, until Mr. and Mrs. Lauderdale made their advent into elevated society among them, such a barbarism as repeating private conversations to set their neighbors by the ears was never heard of.

In the Revolutionary War, mothers, sisters, and wives in Carolina buckled on the armor of their sons, brothers, and husbands; bidding them never to return except as triumphant victors from the conflict waged in defence of their just rights. And the descendants of these heroines are ready now to exercise the same patriotism, if the Northern abolitionist, instead of the British, attempts to invade the sacred rights of the Southern States under that Constitution framed by the virtuous wisdom of their high-born fathers.

The whole art of government, says a wise man, consists in the art of being honest. The South never, during her whole existence, has dreamed of interfering with the domestic policy of any of the Northern States. *She* has cheerfully and consistently fulfilled her every obligation under the compact of federation she entered into, and she is determined *now* to demand *rights*, not favors, from the North. The colonies in the Revolutionary War would not have submitted more willingly to a Benedict Arnold, than to a Lord Cornwallis. And now, when assailed by treason and midnight slaughter, by a blood-thirsty tool of the malcontent abolitionists, whose *secret* numbers are formidable indeed, every mother in the South will exclaim, as of old, "Had I a dozen sons, each in my love alike, I had rather have *eleven* die nobly for their country, than one voluptuously surfeit out of action."*

"He who maintains his country's laws
Alone is great; or he who dies in the good cause."

---

* LAFAYETTE AND WASHINGTON.—Lafayette, in his Memoirs, describes a review of Washington's army, which he witnessed:

"Eleven thousand men, but tolerably armed, and still worse clad, presented," he said, "a singular spectacle, in their particolored and often naked state; the best dresses were hunting-shirts of brown linen. Their tactics were equally singular. They were arranged without regard to size, excepting that the smallest were in the front rank; with all this, they were good-looking soldiers, conducted by zealous officers."

"We ought to feel embarrassed," said Washington to him, "in presenting ourselves before an officer just from the French army."

"It is to learn, not to instruct, that I came here," was Lafayette's apt and modest reply; and it gained him immediate popularity.

Edward Wyndham's retirement, then, to the peaceful society of books in his study, was the most plausible thing in the world; for these spiteful, enterprising women are often first-rate housekeepers — very industrious, and so exactly orthodox in all their fixings about the house, that they seem to be sure that everybody is wicked, whose happiness is impinged upon by the exceeding order of the whole establishment; though geniuses, who are always eccentric, believe that any refinements of housekeeping that make the family uncomfortable from their strictness, are perversions of that order that is Heaven's first law.

From the quickness with which Edward turned his back on a life of dissipation, to religion, at the death of his adored father, it must not be presumed that his heart had not been lacerated with conviction for his sins. Indeed, no man, not even King David himself, was a more heart-broken, contrite appreciator of the enormity of his youthful crimes; and in his excess of zeal to keep down those inward motions of evil that Satan injects, he would fast day after day. Sometimes his wife would find that he had fainted on his knees, from want of sustenance, and from long-continued supplication for that mind of Christ, that would enable him to roll back the flood of evil to others, that his example in college had germinated. He wrote the most powerful letters to all these young men, confessing his deep remorse for his numerous moral delinquencies; and, indeed, religion now sat enthroned as the sovereign queen of his ambition and every enterprise. A mind so set on one idea, is very apt to run into excesses, so that every now and then he would fly off into some new scheme for converting the world by a twist and a jerk; just like the anti-slavery saints, whose one idea is, that abolitionizing the negroes would at once blot all sin out of the Anglo-Saxon mind—for of course there are no sinners in the great progressive free States!

Edward had this advantage, however, over these one-idea "Northern lights;" and that was, that the smallest child could convict him by repeating Scripture antagonistic to what he was trying to accomplish. He bowed to the Bible as the only infallible teacher of what God would have him to do; and therefore could give an intelligent reason for the faith that was in him.

Sometimes his wife would vex him with her petty peculiarities, though she was a professor of religion; and his natural impetuosity would tempt him to be harsh. But then the Bible whispered, "Husbands, love your wives, and be not bitter against them." "Love your wives as Christ loves the church;" which surely is a long-suffering, hopeful love. In an instant the lion would become a lamb, and his mercurial wife would be melted to penitence by the godlike power of gentleness. Is it not, then, the best common sense to do what the Bible orders? Sometimes he was ready, with frantic zeal, to run off and become a vagrant street-preacher from one country to another, and desert his wife, and a family of children now growing up around him; but in this rhapsody of self-importance, he would find himself again held tight by the curb-rein of Scripture, so that in fact he wondered how any of those saints could have left their families starving at home, to run off far beyond Mason and Dixon's line,

39*

and contrive a general midnight assassination of unconscious men, women, and children, as a means of proving that the loving spirit of Jesus actuated this blood-thirsty enterprise.

> "Dark and unearthly is the scowl
> That glares beneath his dusky cowl:
> The flash of that dilating eye
> Reveals too much of times gone by."

"The weapons of our warfare," says St. Paul, "are not carnal, but mighty through God to the pulling down of strong-holds." "For we preach Christ crucified." "The word of God is quick and powerful, sharper than any two-edged sword, cutting to the dividing asunder of soul and spirit, and of the joints and marrow." Surely with such an all-conquering instrument as the Bible,* for convicting and converting men

---

* The "New York Observer," in its issue of April 26, 1860, contains the following query:

"WHO GIVE THE GOSPEL TO THE HEATHEN?—A writer in the Boston Recorder, in a series of articles on the causes of the debt of the American Board, and the decrease in the contributions to its treasury, in treating of the effect of the abolition excitement upon the churches, makes the following striking contrast: 'It has been recently published, that the Rev. Henry Ward Beecher's church — the church that contributed so liberally for Sharpe's rifles — the church that rents its pews for twenty-six thousand a year — the church that has ever been foremost in anti-slavery zeal—yet a church whose pastor gives his influence warmly in favor of the American Board, contributes only one hundred and fifty dollars a year for that Board. And most strikingly does this contrast with the fact, that the church whose pastor has been blamed so much for his "South-Side View" — a church whose number of worshippers probably is not one-fifth of the other, and whose aggregate ability is probato righteousness, no preacher of the gospel need recommend carnal, worldly weapons for this spiritual regeneration into the image of the Savior.

Nothing was more interesting to the moral observer than to witness, from day to day, this powerful man, mentally, morally, and physically—Edward Wyndham, whose natural will was hard and stubborn as iron—now acting out the gentle, teachable spirit of a little child, through his whole-souled love of God's word. But the fact is, "God is love;" and this meek, loving temper, seeking after those who had gone astray, made more converts to righteousness than a million of Sharpe's rifles could have accomplished. And he wondered what Jesus Christ or St. Paul would have thought, had they walked into that church where the bidding was so spirited to raise money to buy artillery, to shoot the poor misguided sinners or patriots of Kansas.

But we must leave this true epistle, known and read of all men, of the transforming power of New Testament Christianity—Edward Wyndham—and return to his much persecuted sister Musidora, who was now determined to leave the parish where Mr. Lauderdale preached; for though she had for three years never absented herself from the church where this man was stationed, because there was no other of the Episcopal denomination in Iodilla, still it is hard to listen to sermons from a priest whose life is directly antagonistic to his teachings. Dryden says:

---

bly in a like proportion—contributes over six thousand dollars. One swallow does not make a summer. But one contrast like this naturally puts us on the inquiry, how the facts in general tally with this.'"

"A fox full fraught with seeming sanctity,
That fear'd an oath, but like the devil would lie,
Who look'd like Lent, and had the holy leer,
And durst not sin before he said his prayer."

"Why should not conscience have vacation,
As well as other courts o' th' nation;
Have equal power to adjourn,
Appoint appearance and return."

BUTLER'S *Hudibras*.

Musidora had received pressing invitations to visit her step-mother's brilliantly talented, travelled brother, Dr. M'Elroy, who from her childhood had been Musidora's appreciating friend. So, taking advantage of her desire to forward her two half-brothers, Rutledge and Pinckney, to a far-off State where enterprise was opened to them, she accompanied them to Baltimore, where, leaving her with Dr. M'Elroy, they proceeded to their destination. After spending two months with him, he brought her to Washington to see the great world; and as he was obliged to return to his business, he left her in the care of a fashionable, highly respectable, private boarding-house keeper, where himself and family always sojourned whenever they visited the metropolis. Thus was this simple religious girl thrown into a mixed society, whose eccentricities she had never dreamed of before; and the ladies seemed astonished at the unconscious naturalness and independence of her expressions of opinion.

For the first time in her life, we find the gifted Musidora seven or eight hundred miles north, and in the ambiguous atmosphere of a democratic court. The celebrated divine, Dr. Young, says of court-life:

"See there he comes, th' exalted idol comes!
The circle 's form'd, and all his fawning slaves
Devoutly bow to earth; from every mouth
The nauseous flattery flows, which he returns
With promises which die as soon as born.
Vile intercourse, where virtue has no place!
Frown but the monarch, all his glories fade;
He mingles with the throng, outcast, undone,
The pageant of a day; without one friend
To soothe his tortured mind; all, all are fled:
For though they bask'd in his meridian ray,
The insects vanish as his beams decline."

Musidora, whose metaphysical mind had, in an unobtrusive country village, philosophized so wholesomely on the real objects of life that are alone worthy of every-day, practical illustration — namely, love to God and love to man—was suddenly thrown into the *omnium gatherum* of politicians, who regard disinterestedness of purpose a sure sign that you are a fool, or are moonstruck.

The first gentleman Musidora became acquainted with was the far-famed Professor Morse, and he asked her to accompany him to the President's levee. This great genius had just eliminated the "telegraph," and the whole world was in a blaze of wonder, and admiration, and thankfulness; so that, of course, he was the observed of all observers, and he introduced Musidora to all his friends. She was perfectly charmed with the modesty with which he received the ovations of society wherever he appeared, and, as she saw him every day, she had the best opportunity of testing his real worth. A long time afterwards they often joked together about the possibility of tender feelings having been exchanged, had he not been married to his new invention of the telegraph, with bonds that not even that irreverent little wretch, Cupid, could divorce.

Musidora's curiosity to make the acquaintance of Gov. Seward,* who, throughout the South, is regarded as the representative of the future overthrow of the United States Government, induced her immediately to call on his family, as the etiquette of Washington requires all strangers to make the first visit to the Senators and all the "powers that be." Her surprise was great indeed to find him a man of no arrogance of bearing, or speech, in private life; no expression of gratified notoriety in society; no assumption of superior intelligence that could be legitimately gathered from his unobtrusive, nay, almost hesitating, modesty of carriage, wherever he appeared; and, in his family, he was the embodiment of the most natural and consecrated affections. His wife, who is a devoted Christian, and so mellowed in her wise experiences of life that it is impossible to hear her converse without edification, Musidora admired more than any woman she almost ever knew in her whole life, and all her children are brought up with the same elegant naturalness of manner that distinguishes herself.

Musidora had many admirers, some of whom seriously proposed; but life had not been a romance to her, and she had never recovered the freshness of heart that she had possessed previous to her lover's death. No! the mind never is, never can be, the same

* Governor Seward's niece married the nephew of Henry R. Schoolcraft, the Indian historian.

after it has been ploughed up by some absorbing mental anguish.

One day she went to church, where she had been invited to sit in the pew of a friend. A very remarkable-looking gentleman arose from his seat, opened the door as she entered, and then seated himself by her side. He was perhaps fifty years of age, though his very long, waving, affluent, chestnut-colored hair, was scarcely tinged with envious grey; his features were large, his complexion florid, his eyes a brilliant blue, and his forehead was so white, broad, and high, that Musidora was on the tenter-hooks of curiosity to find out who the majestic stranger was. His height measured six feet; his hands were aristocratically small, and delicately white; while his dress indicated that he had no ambition to be a dandy, or worshipper of his own personal beauty. Musidora thought that, with the exception of her proud lover, Mr. Fletcher, she had never seen so noble, so lordly, so commanding a head, and she was reminded of a fancy sketch she had once seen, and greatly admired, of the god Jupiter. Impulsively she whispered to the ladies in the pew, and ascertained that he was the world-renowned scholar of England, Mr. Walsingham.

To her great surprise, this distinguished personage, who had merely been introduced, in passing out of the pew, to Musidora, called on her the next morning, and then the next, and the next—conversing a whole hour during each visit, with almost embarrassing intensity of interest. Indeed, he declared that he had often heard gifted women converse, but never in all his life had he listened to moral subjects canvassed with such sparkling truth and enthusiasm; and that, too, by a South Carolina lady, who is always represented by calumny to be almost oriental in the impractical, luxurious tendencies of her education. Of course, this enraptured genius called every morning and every evening, and planned walks in the Capitol grounds, and all places where curiosities were to be seen; and, indeed, he was so natural in his abstraction from every other object, save herself, on the avenue, that the gossips found out his whole secret long before he revealed it, by word of mouth, to Musidora herself.

Mr. Walsingham's father, though an Englishman, had been so enamoured of the lordly spirit of the American Colonies, that he actually came over to this country and enlisted under General Washington, and was killed in the storming of a fort occupied by the British. His wife, whom he had left in London, shared so deeply in her husband's enthusiasm, that, after his death, she reared her eight children with the greatest sympathy for the people of the United States.

Having been very unfortunate in his first matrimonial romance, Mr. Walsingham never expected to marry again, but to give himself up entirely to those researches that were so fascinating to his intellect. His meeting with Musidora Wyndham, that has been already detailed, was purely accidental. He was pleased with her noble person, bearing, and manners. Her figure was majestic, her carriage graceful and commanding; her air queenly, and her features classic. Her eyes liquid, dark, intellectual, and full of soul; her hair, like that of the Greeks, grew very low on the forehead, but phrenologically there was great height, breadth, and volume of brain.

But it was her extraordinary power of conversation that fascinated him. He listened to her with the intensely absorbed interest of a devotee. She had a natural flow of eloquence: moral sentences dropped from her lips with the naiveté of a child. She had read theology extensively; she was a critic of men and manners, and particularly acquainted with the eccentricities of clergymen, having known many of them intimately. She abounded in aphorisms, wise and witty; she was an excellent reasoner, her logic was most clear. Mr. Walsingham was perfectly charmed with her society, and very naturally was betrayed into the exposé of his feelings *nolens volens.*

"Corporeal charms may, indeed, gain admirers, but there must be mental ones to retain them; and Horace had a delicate feeling of this when he refused to restrict the pleasures of the lover merely to his eyes, but added those of the ear."

"Qui sedens identidem, te
Spectat et audit!"

The old maids* who sometimes feel very bilious against bachelors† for not appreciating their matri-

* It is said, that in Japan old maids are unheard of—do not exist. When the girls do not get married voluntarily in any reasonable time, the authorities hunt up husbands, and make them marry, willing or not willing. An exchange thinks that the Japanese know a thing or two even if they have been walled in for four centuries.

† The English Quarterly Review, in a sketch of the *personnel* of our old bachelor President, Mr. Buchanan, says: "He has

monial plausibility, were especially disturbed by Mr. Walsingham's devoted attentions to Musidora. One invented a calumny, and another circulated a scandal, and finally the very innocence and purity of Muidora's manners, were made use of against her; for she was thrown into a society so unlike any she had ever seen in Carolina, that it was an entirely new field of observation; and finally she was made so uncomfortable by unjust criticism, that she determined to remove to another house and board with another friend of Dr. M'Elroy's, as he was now very ill, and could not come for her. Here, again, she found the very same unaccountable prying into her affairs, and she determined that Washington was not congenial to her taste.

> "Courts can give nothing to the wise and good,
> But scorn of pomp, and love of solitude."

For courtiers and politicians in power are thus described by the poet *Young:*—

> "Who wrap destruction up in gentle words,
> And vows, and smiles more fatal than their swords:
> Who stifle nature and subsist on art:
> Who coin the face, and petrify the heart:
> All real kindness for the show discard,
> As marble polish'd, and as marble hard:

---

the habit that historians attribute to Alexander the Great, of holding his head somewhat inclined to one side, and sometimes partially closing one eye, as if to prove what was undoubtedly the case during his mission in this country, that he could see a vast deal more with half an eye than all our ministers when they opened both theirs to the fullest extent, as they had to do more than once, if all tales be true, during the course of their transaction of business with Mr. Buchanan."

Who do for gold what Christians do through grace,—
'With open arms their enemies embrace;'
Who give a nod when broken hearts repine,—
'The thinnest food on which a wretch can dine:'
Or, if they serve you, serve you disinclined:
And in their height of kindness are unkind."

This high-mettled widow lady's third son (Roland), the lover now of Musidora, stood high in the literary circles of England. His earliest celebrity arose from his popular essays, in which he proved his wonderful inductive powers of mind in tracing out the steady progress of England, in society, government, laws and literature, through the long line of dynasties from Henry VIII., to the final expulsion of the Stuarts. A series of bold and historical romances then issued from his nimble pen, denoting how a petty little kingdom had developed itself into a great representative Empire.

As a critic, a historian, a philosopher, a statist, an imaginative writer, and a poet, applauses greeted him wherever he sojourned. Mr. Walsingham's attachment to the principles of British liberty, as developed by long centuries of successful struggle between the Court and Commons of England, had induced him as a souvenir of his brave old father to visit the American shores. A limited monarchist, he had been an enthusiastic admirer of that heroic contest, for the equal position of power and taxation, which a feeble but united people, under the guidance of Washington, had triumphantly maintained in the American Revolution. In visiting the country, he had made himself familiar with its situation, geographical extent, and resources, having passed over the Alleghany mountains, visited the great valley of the West, and penetrated the great chain of American lakes; and from these various observations he indulged the highest anticipations of the future prosperity and glory of the country, and its final power and influence in the family of nations. Indeed, he confessed that England was beginning to realize the folly of her sickly sentimentality in abolishing slavery in her colonies, for experience had proved to them that there was not a single "respectable form of civilization that ever existed, which was not originally based on the institution of slavery."

"Mr. Bancroft," said Mr. Walsingham, "in the first volume of his History of the United States, gives an account of the early traffic of the Europeans in slaves. In the middle ages the Venetians purchased white men, Christians and others, and sold them to the Saracens in Sicily and Spain. In England the Anglo-Saxon nobility sold their servants as slaves to foreigners. The Portuguese first imported negro slaves from western Africa into Europe in 1442. Spain soon engaged in the traffic, and negro slaves abounded in some places of that kingdom. After America was discovered, the Indians of Hispaniola were imported into Spain and made slaves. The Spaniards visited the coast of North America and kidnapped thousands of the Indians, whom they transported into slavery in Europe and the West Indies. Columbus himself kidnapped 500 native Americans and sent them into Spain, that they might be publicly sold at Seville. The practice of selling North American Indians into bondage continued two centuries. Negro slavery was first introduced into America by Spanish slaveholders who emigrated with their negroes. A royal edict of Spain authorized negro slavery in America in 1518. King Ferdinand sent from Seville fifty slaves to labor in the mines. In 1531 the direct traffic in slaves between Africa and Hispaniola was enjoyed by royal ordinance. Las Casas, who saw the Indians vanishing away before the cruelty of the Spaniards, suggested that the negroes, who alone could endure severe toils, might be further employed. This was in 1518.

"Sir John Hawkins was the first Englishman that engaged in the slave-trade. In 1552 he transported a large cargo of slaves to Hispaniola. In 1557 another expedition was prepared, and Queen Elizabeth protected and shared in the traffic. Hawkins, in one of his expeditions, set fire to an African city, and out of the three thousand inhabitants succeeded in seizing two hundred and sixty.

"James Smith, of Boston, and Thomas Keyser first brought the colonies to participate in slavery. In 1654 they imported a cargo of negroes.

"In 1628 a Dutch ship entered James river and landed twenty negroes for sale. This was the epoch of the introduction of slavery into Virginia. For many years the Dutch were principally concerned in the slave-trade in the market of Virginia."

Only think, my friend, of the enormous expenses England, and the Northern States here,* are subjected

* "INCOMES OF LONDON CHARITIES.—There are in London twelve hospitals for general purposes, forty-six for special purposes, thirty-four dispensaries; giving relief to 365,956 persons every year. Ninety-two hospitals (income) £300,000; twelve societies for the preservation of life and health, benefiting 39,000, £40,000; seventeen penitentiaries and reformatories, £2,500; fifteen charities for the relief of the destitute, benefiting 150,000, £24,000; fourteen charities for debtors, widows, strangers, &c., £30,000; four Jewish charities, exclusive of twenty minor Jewish charities, £10,000; nineteen provident societies, £9,000; twenty-seven pension societies, benefiting 1,600, £58,968; thirty-three trade societies, of a purely charitable nature, exclusive of self-supporting societies, £113,407; a hundred and twenty-six asylums for the aged, benefiting 3,000, £87,630; nine charities for deaf, dumb, and blind, £25,000; twenty-one educational societies, £72,257; thirteen educational asylums, exclusive of schools supported by Government, 1,777 persons, £45,435; sixty home missions, many of which extend

to every year to sustain vagabond, useless, wicked paupers; whereas at the South there is no such degradation at all, for the oldest slaves, many of them over a hundred years of age, are supported by their masters

---

their operations beyond the metropolis, £400,000; five miscellaneous, not admitting classification, £3,252; seven Church of England foreign missions, £211,135. The above represent a total yearly income of £1,768,945. To these may be added five other societies not susceptible of classification, making a total of £1,682,197. If we separate the societies of a purely domestic character from those operations wholly or in part conducted in foreign lands, the result will be as follows: Home charities, £1,222,529; foreign missions, £459,668. The amount spent in foreign missions, therefore, is just one-third of that devoted to the relief, instruction, and reformation of the poor, the ignorant, the unfortunate, and the vicious of London."

The *New York Observer*, one of the most respectable and dignified *religious* newspapers in the world, remarks:

"In the city of New York the death-rate is very high, and has greatly increased within the last century. Compared with the death-rate of London, or with that of New York itself fifty years ago, there is a loss of 10,000 lives every year; that is, 10,000 persons die every year more than would die, were New York as healthy as it was fifty years ago, or as healthy as London now is. Correspondingly there has been, in this great city, a great increase of crime and pauperism; the latter having increased in the last twenty-nine years, in about a *tenfold* proportion above the increase of population. Every *seventh* person, in the entire population, is now a pauper and and supported at the public expense. Also, crime increased 25 per cent. in a single year, namely, the last year of which we have the Reports. And it is stated in the Report of the 'New York Juvenile Asylum,' that there are now in the city not less than '*forty thousand* delinquent and destitute children,' who are either already petty thieves and beggars, or else in a condition to become such, being 'homeless and neglected.' What a crop of social evil and

just as respectably and generously as when they were young — indeed, a centenarian is treated with a vast deal more of affectionate kindness by his owners.

Musidora was now invited by some of the members of Congress and their wives, from South Carolina, to join their party in spending two months at Point Comfort, and she determined to go with them, as the weather was intensely hot. As soon as Mr. Walsingham heard this arrangement, he instantly offered his hand to Musidora in marriage, which she accepted; for she had long since ascertained through his tell-tale eye, the intense devotion of his heart; and, moreover, she thoroughly admired the manly simplicity of his manners; the deep sincerity of his mellowed Christian philosophy, the brilliancy of his genius, and last, not least, the physical handsomeness of her lover; and, beside all these stimulants to affection, it must be borne in mind that her orphaned, nay widowed heart (for she had grieved as much for Mr. Fletcher as if she had been his wife) had long yearned for human sympathy.

True hope, too, is based on energy of character. A

---

misery is thus springing up to ripen into a harvest of crime and scatter the retributive seeds of turbulence, pauperism, and bloodshed throughout society!

"Judge Capron says that in this city there are 15,000 dram shops; 300,000 drinkers, each drinking two gills of liquor, being 600,000 gills, or 805 barrels per day—300,000 barrels per year. This would fill a reservoir 900 feet long, 50 feet wide, and 63 feet deep, and could float four large ships in full sail. At $30 per barrel it amounts to $9,000,000. Out of the 6,000 persons tried before the Court of Special Sessions during the last year, not more than 94 were sober when arrested. Paupers in the city cost $3,000,000 a year."

strong mind always hopes, and has always cause to hope, because it knows the mutability of human affairs, and how slight a circumstance may change the whole course of events. Such a spirit rests upon itself; it is not confined to partial views, or to one particular object. And if, at last, all should be lost, it has saved itself — its own integrity and worth. Hope awakens courage, while despondency is the last of all evils; it is the abandonment of good—the giving up of the battle of life with dead nothingness. He who can implant courage in the human soul is the best physician.

Mr. Walsingham was prevented from accompanying his lady-love, as he enthusiastically desired to do, by an imperative call from England, to attend to his children there, who had got into difficulties during his absence.

Musidora spent a month of exquisite enjoyment at the before-mentioned "watering place," where she met the most charming society, and was treated with distinguished consideration and friendship, so that she heard her own praises at every corner she turned in the hotel — for new hopes in life had inspired her remarkable conversational powers; and amiable and kind feelings to all around her, made her presence the signal of pleasure to every circle she approached — indeed, the landlord himself expressed his gratitude to her for having contributed so largely to the attractions of his house.

But in the midst of this refreshment to her mind and heart, she was hurried back to Carolina by the alarming illness of her sister Britannia, where, for seven months, she watched over her with one disease succeeding another, so that, finally, she was almost reduced herself to the same wretched condition that nervous fever had brought Britannia to—who now, however, began to convalesce, and Mr. Walsingham arrived from England to be married.

Mr. Lauderdale found out, to his deep chagrin, that all his atrocious calumnies and persecutions had, in the providence of God driven Musidora out of his parish only to return in conquering triumph; for now she was to be the honored wife of one of England's most resplendent geniuses, whose aristocratic descent and large fortune, and commanding moral and intellectual influence, would place her in the front rank of that noble society she was so fitted to grace.

Mr. Lauderdale immediately called on Mr. Walsingham, and also sent his wife to request Musidora to commune again in his church; for she had never been able to get the consent of her feelings to receive the sacrament from the hands of a person she regarded as an unmitigated villain. He also was very anxious to perform the marriage ceremony; but as no other Episcopal clergyman could be, with etiquette, invited without his consent into the parish, Musidora had already engaged a devotedly pious, gifted minister from another denomination.

> "For modes of faith let senseless zealots fight,
> His can't be *wrong* whose *life* is in the *right*."

Musidora's step-mother, though she received the distinguished Mr. Walsingham with obsequious politeness, never seemed to feel the slightest interest in her step-daughter's future destiny; and though her own daughter, Gulielma, together with herself, were experts at fine fancy work, and often made presents to young ladies who were going to be married at Iodilla, neither of them felt an instinct to embroider even a pin-cushion for the orphan Musidora, who was all the while fancying to herself the great pleasure she should have hereafter in inviting Gulielma and her mother to her house in London, where her husband's high position and wealth would contribute surely to Gulielma's advancement.

With enthusiastic sisterly affection, she had already succeeded in marrying her step-mother's eldest son to an heiress, who combined the most beautiful modesty with every other virtuous charm.

Halcombe had always felt Musidora his superior in talent and moral activity, and consequently had never patronized a sister whose independence of thought and purpose had made himself, and his step-mother and her children, all jealous of her. Halcombe never had a thought to dart into his mind to give Musidora a single thing, though he had loaded Gulielma with presents ever since her birth, and had it been *her* instead of his own orphan sister who was to immortalize the family by marrying a world-renowned genius, whose works could never die; had *Gulielma* been thus honored, Halcombe would have felt proud to expend his wealth in giving her an ample wardrobe, consistent with the conventionalities of society in which she was now to move in England.

On the morning that Musidora was to leave her home forever as a bride, she ascertained that her travelling-dress, sent from Savannah, did not fit at all, and she therefore begged Mrs. Wyndham to assist her to alter it. With that frown that had become chronic whenever her step-daughters wanted anything, she refused, so that, in the midst of the hurry and confusion of embarkation, Musidora had to arrange the dress herself. And this heartlessness was never forgotten, but haunted her like a vampire during her whole stormy passage to England.

Britannia, scarcely yet out of the bed of languishing illness, got up from her couch to see her orphan sister off. She threw herself on Musidora's neck, and wept so passionately, so inconsolably, that she fainted from exhaustion and excitement, and when she revived, she said she felt certain that this was a good-night! to her only sister whose good-morning! would be in heaven—*never*, never again on earth. And so it proved; for very shortly after their separation, Britannia, whose bodily sufferings had been the crucible that separated the pure gold from the dross of her character; Britannia, whose sainted mother's prayers had, throughout life, proved an unscalable wall against the escape of her children into the higher-law fascinations of progressive worldliness and sin; Britannia died, as her holy mother had died, in the triumphs of gospel faith; and though she had had ten children, every one of them preceded her to heaven.*

---

* "I HOLD STILL."

FROM THE GERMAN OF STURM.

"Pain's furnace heat within me quivers,
God's breath upon the flame doth blow
And all my heart in anguish shivers,
And trembles at the fiery glow;

Musidora, previous to leaving South Carolina for ever, — where all her ancestors had resided on that same Palmetto Grove, from generation to generation, and had never, by tradition, or even the malice of enemies, been accused of a disgraceful, lawless, or criminal act,—Musidora went to the family grave-yard, all embosomed among the centennial monarchs of the forest, to fall down on her knees, and to say farewell

---

And yet I whisper, 'as God will!'
And in its hottest fire hold still.

"He comes and lays my heart, all heated,
On the hard anvil, minded so
Into His own fair shape to heat it
With His great hammer, blow on blow,
And yet I whisper, 'as God will!'
And at His heaviest blows hold still.

"He takes my soften'd heart and beats it;
The sparks fly off at every blow;
He turns it o'er and o'er, and heats it,
And lets it cool and makes it glow;
And yet I whisper, 'as God will!'
And in His mighty hand hold still.

"Why should I murmur? for the sorrow
Thus only longer-lived would be;
Its end may come, and will to-morrow,
When God has done His work in me:
So I say, trusting, 'as God will!'
And trusting to the end, hold still.

"He kindles for my profit purely,
Affliction's glowing, fiery brand,
And all His heaviest blows are surely
Inflicted by a Master's hand:
So I say, praying, 'as God will!'
And hope in Him, and suffer still."

to the beloved dust of her father, her mother, her sisters, her brothers, her nephews, her nieces, and the long line of grandmothers and grandfathers, all sleeping in this sacred spot.

This venerable grave-yard had been Musidora's *sanctum sanctorum* from her earliest orphaned childhood. Here she had always repaired to refresh her spirits when loneliness, non-appreciation, and unkindness met her at every turn in her step-mother's house. Language cannot explain the intimate communion between her spirit and these noble dead. Often, very often, when despair placed in her hand that "bare bodkin" with which to make her quietus, the dead yet speaking voice of her mother would restore strength to bear the ills and tomb-like isolation of her destiny on earth. But now Musidora was to go off to a foreign land, and leave forever this mausoleum that contained the sacred remains of her angelic mother.

"Mother, dear mother! the feelings nurst
As I hung at thy bosom, *clung round thee first!*
'Twas the earliest link in love's warm chain,
'Tis the only one that will long remain;
And as, year by year, and day by day,
Some friend still trusted drops away,
Mother, dear mother! oh, dost thou not see
How the shorten'd chain brings me nearer to thee?"

Though none of the household of Musidora's step-mother cared at all at all what was to be her destiny with an utter stranger for a husband, Musidora still commanded the warm sympathy of hundreds of as humble, sincere hearts as ever throbbed in human breast;* for all the negroes on the plantations for twenty miles around Palmetto Grove had from her childhood been perfectly devoted to her; and now each one sent or came to bid her good-bye, as if she was their own loved child; to offer up prayers for her happiness as a wife, and to bring some tiny, uncostly thing as a present, that did not intrinsically exceed in value the two mites which the Bible tells us the poor widow cast into the treasury; but still, the said two mites were a splendid self-abnegation; for they were all the poor woman had — even her very living.

---

* Mr. Trollope, the Englishman, says sneeringly that "the negro loves his master as the dog does." Now, pray let us ask him if there is any faithfulness that surpasses that of your dog? If you are angry, he deprecatingly assumes humility of attitude. If you punish him, and lock him up, the moment you open his prison-door, he rushes to welcome you with every expression of blissful reconciliation. If you rave in hopeless grief, striding up and down your room all night, this faithful creature will keep awake, and finally wag his tail, and persuade you, by his mute but most expressive sympathy, that you need not blow your brains out in hopelessness while you have such an unchanging, consecrated friend as he is. In fine, there are, perhaps, few sensitive and sorrowful geniuses who have had to run the gauntlet of this selfish world, who will not, in the end, in perfect despair, turn to the pet dog, and feel in his inmost heart that *his* friendship and gratitude are more truly refreshing and pure than any he has ever experienced from those who are called rational creatures. The very worst men that have ever lived have had a *sanctum sanctorum* in their hearts still sacred to the love of their dog.

The slave can never be treated with the hardness of heart that poor white operatives are, because the fact of his being dependent makes his master love to patronize him.

"What," says Webster, "more tender, more solemnly affecting, more profoundly pathetic, than this charity, this offering to God, of a farthing? We know nothing of her name, her family, or her tribe. We only know that she was a poor woman, and a widow, of whom there is nothing left upon record but this sublimely simple story, that when the rich men came to cast their proud offerings into the treasury, this poor woman came also, and cast in her two mites, which made a farthing! And that example, thus made the subject of Divine commendation, has been read, and told, and has gone abroad everywhere, and sunk deep into a hundred million of hearts, since the commencement of the Christian era, and has done more good than could be accomplished by a thousand marble palaces; because it was charity mingled with true benevolence, given in the fear, the love, the service, and the honor of God; because it was charity that had its origin in religious feeling; because it was a gift to the honor of God."

The poor among the white people, whom Musidora had, from earliest girlhood, labored among as a missionary of progress in religion, civilized and useful arts, and education—yes, these people surrounded her now with heartfelt grief that nevermore would they be blessed with her experienced, wise ministrations of charity, in sickness, in health, in childhood, and old age; so that, although envy and detraction had pursued Musidora with their poisonous fangs in idle, gossiping, aristocratic society, the poor, the very poor and humble, had been her true friends; for she had improved their happiness by enlightening their minds and educating their hearts; therefore, with one voice they rose up and called her blessed.

"Two principles govern the moral and intellectual world. One is, perpetual progress; the other, necessary limitations to that progress. If the former alone prevailed, there would be nothing steadfast and endurable on earth, and the whole of social life would be the sport of winds and waves. If the latter had exclusive sway, or even if it obtained a mischievous preponderancy, everything would petrify or rot. The best ages of the world are always those in which these two principles are the most equally balanced. In such ages, every enlightened man ought to adopt both principles into his whole mind and conduct, and with one hand develop what he *can*, with the other restrain and uphold what he ought."

The moment had now arrived for Musidora to embark, and yet her step-mother would not allow her to leave her home forever without again wounding her feelings. Halcombe, seeing a few very fine nuts lying on the table, handed them to Musidora, to eat in the boat. But Mrs. Wyndham stepped up and said, "No: I wish them for my own daughter."

Musidora burst into tears; for she could not comprehend how any woman in the world could have proved so heartless to an orphan who had been in her care almost from infancy.

The black boatmen, gaily dressed, and very proud of the new member of the family, Mr. Walsingham, formed, as usual, a sedan-chair, by two strong men locking arms; and then kneeling, to allow the bride and groom to get seated, they passed over the mud with their burden, and deposited them safely in the boat; and, as the tide was beginning to ebb, and the wind was perfectly fair, the sails were spread, and in twelve or fourteen hours the bridal party safely landed in the town of Savannah, Georgia, from whence they expected to to take passage to Liverpool.

Finding that the ship would not leave Savannah for several days, Mr. Walsingham and his wife went to the

Pulaski House. But when Halcombe prepared to return home, and came into Musidora's chamber to bid her farewell (for her husband had walked out to examine the tremendously high bluff which introduces you into this pretty little city), Musidora threw herself into his arms, and implored him, for God's sake, not to leave her. She told him of the intense sisterly love that had been one of her life-long romances towards him — that she was now about to plunge into an unsounded sea — to give up every home tie, and follow a perfect stranger into a foreign land, where she could claim sympathy from no human being save her husband, in that London which Johnson has described so terribly:

> "Here malice, rapine, accident, conspire,
> And now a rabble rages, and now Fire;
> Their ambush here relentless ruffians lay,
> And here the fell attorney prowls for prey;
> Here falling houses thunder on your head,
> And here a female atheist talks you dead."*

Whether the mysterious, perhaps ubiquitous, spirit of Halcombe's dead mother now influenced his heart towards the orphan sister he had hitherto so unappreciated, and neglected, and ridiculed, and sustained his step-mother in persecuting with her puerile tyranny in her house, certain it is, he wept most tenderly over the heart-stirring emotion of Musidora; and he folded her

* According to Dr. Forbes Winslow, there are in London 16,000 children trained to crime, 5000 receivers of stolen goods, 15,000 gamblers, 25,000 beggars, 30,000 drunkards, 180,000 habitual gin-drinkers, 150,000 persons subsisting on profligacy, and 50,000 thieves.

in his great manly arms, and kissed her with as much affection as he had a thousand times done to Gulielma, his step-mother's daughter; so that the poor orphan whispered to herself, "Can it be possible that I have at last found the treasure of a true brother's love, just as I am about to be separated from him, perhaps for ever?"

Halcombe kept his boat at Savannah several days, until the steamer arrived on her way from Charleston. He then handed his sister on board, and stayed with her until the moment that the noisy steam-boat bell tolled her instant departure from the wharf.

"So fare thee well; and may th' indulgent gods
* * * * * grant thee every wish
Thy soul can form! Once more, farewell!"

"And now farewell! farewell! I dare not lengthen
These sweet, sad moments out. To gaze on thee
Is bliss indeed, yet it but serves to strengthen
The love that now amounts to agony.
This is our last farewell."

CHAPTER XIX.

"I love the sailor; his eventful life,
His generous spirit, his contempt of danger,
His firmness in the gale, the wreck, the strife;
And though a wild and reckless ocean ranger,
God grant he make the port, when life is o'er,
Where storms are hush'd, and billows break no more."

TAKING passage for England, Musidora and her husband found themselves ensconced in a comfortable stateroom, on board ship, where they had provided themselves with interesting books; for of course two such gifted, congenial lovers, did not need the society of the passengers, and therefore made arrangements (now that the hurry and bustle of the marriage-feasts and farewells were over) to spend their time quietly together; for hundreds of miles had separated them during their whole engagement. Musidora was on the tenter-hooks of curiosity to learn her husband's whole previous career in life, and therefore he commenced his narration by enumerating all the circumstances that determined his domestic history. A very rich talented nobleman, of England, he said, had, in a spirit of romantic adventure, extended his travels into the wild woods of America, in the year 1800. After canvassing almost this whole continent, in his antiquarian researches, he accidentally became acquainted with the far-famed Indian king, Skenandoah, whom the Indian Historian afterwards, in 1855, thus described. "Skenandoah early evinced the most active character as a hunter. Wise in the observation of the habits of animals, and skilful to track them in the forest, his agility was compared to that of a deer; and this is the idea embraced in the name of *Skenandoah.* In his person he was tall, brawny, erect, and dignified. His countenance was rather light for an Indian, his eye was grey (which is very unusual), his lips very pleasing, and expressive, his voice sonorous; and his whole air noble and commanding. In his youth, he had been a brave and intrepid warrior. In his riper years, he was one of the ablest counsellors. He possessed a strong and vigorous mind. He never gave way to violent passion. He calmly weighed every subject that was presented to him, and generally preserved a blandness of manner, which, without lowering his dignity, was very captivating.

"Few men have appeared among the aboriginal race, who are as well entitled to respect as Skenandoah. Few men in the narrow sphere of Indian action, had passed through such varied scenes; and still fewer have been spared to abide so many years on earth, for he was a hundred and ten years of age when he died. If so, he must have been born in the early part of the reign of Queen Anne, witnessing in the course of his long life, the reign of the line of Guelphs, from the First to the Third George, when the colonies assumed independence, and living on to the end of the Presidential octad, for he died at the close of Mr. Madison's term. In the revolutionary contest, his tribe (the Oneidas), and himself joined the colonists, and rendered essential services to the American arms; while the Mohawks, and other members of the celebrated and powerful Iroquois league, cast their lot with the cause of the mother country, and under the leadership of Brant, hung like a pestilence around the armies and settlements of the frontiers.

"At one of the treaties at Albany, he was betrayed into drunkenness (almost universal as a vice among Indians), and his pride revolted so much at this exposure, that when he found himself in the streets next morning, almost in a state of nudity, he saw in the clearest light the evils which threatened his tribe from this destructive practice, and he resolved from that moment never to indulge in it. This resolution he firmly kept for more than half a century, to the day of his death; and it was doubtless one of the leading causes of his advancement among the counsellors of his tribe.

"Through the preaching of a missionary, the Rev. Samuel Kirkland, Skenandoah had become a true Christian. Mr. Kirkland was a personal acquaintance and friend of Washington, and he often bore his counsels to the Indians. When the struggle of the revolutionary war assumed perhaps its lowest aspect in 1777, the Oneidas offered the struggling colonies two hundred and fifty men. They were not accepted for service in the field, but employed under the conduct of Skenandoah, and a chief called Lewis, as scouts and messengers. As such, they were usefully employed during the war, rendering signal service in announcing the progress of the enemy from Canada, under Sir John

Johnson, previous to and during the siege of Fort Stanwix.

"Skenandoah was so devoted to the missionary, Mr. Kirkland, that he often expressed a desire, and obtained from the family a promise, that he should be buried near the minister, his spiritual father (whom he survived several years), that, as he said, 'he might cling to the skirts of his garments, and go up with him at the great resurrection.' Skenandoah lived more than twenty years after the close of the war, and the triumph of the colonies. Its successful issue appears to have had the same effect on him, that it seems to have had on all the old soldiers of the revolution. It would seem by producing a pleasing serenity of mind, to have lengthened out their lives, for they all lived to a very old age.

"Skenandoah saw the wisdom of his policy in one respect, which he had probably never anticipated. All the land of the other cantons was legally confiscated; but the Oneidas retained theirs to the full. He saw the vast forests of the ancient Iroquois dominions settled with an industrious population. The plow was driven through valleys where he had before chased the deer; cattle, horses, and sheep, covered the banks of those beautiful lakes that once could boast little beyond the Indian canoe. What had been predicted by his teacher, Kirkland, now rose before his eyes, not in a vision, but in living towns, villages, and cities. It was not a dream interpreted, but a vision realized. Literally, 'the wilderness blossomed as the rose.'"

"Skenandoah became blind after passing his hundredth year. He was visited by all the great men of the country until he died; and on one occasion he made the following remarks to a large company who called to do him honor: 'I am an aged hemlock. The winds of a hundred winters have whistled through my branches. I am dead at top. The generation to which I belonged have run their course and left me. Why I live, the Great, Good Spirit only knows. Pray to my Jesus that I may have patience to await my appointed time to die.'" Honored chief! his prayer was answered; he was cheerful and resigned to the last. His body was buried near to that of his pastor, Mr. Kirkland, and a monument has been erected to Skenandoah at Hamilton College, New York.*

But to return to our young nobleman (the Earl of Nottingham), who, soon after his acquaintance with the renowned Indian chief, the above-described Skenandoah, fell madly in love with one of his idolized grand-daughters, and begged Skenandoah for her for a wife.

The proud old warrior, greatly flattered, replied—"Oh, yes! you can have Mud-wa-wa-ge-si-co-gua (my music of the heavens), provided you marry her as the pale-faces marry their wives."

---

* Is it not surprising that the abolitionists, who have such an overplus of sensibility for the savage negro of Africa, have expended none on the savage Indian in our own country, who is so very superior to the blacks, and whose homes we have ruthlessly driven them from, *only* because *we* were the stronger party! The sufferings of the poor faminishing Indians, are ten thousand fold greater than a plantation slave has ever dreamed of in his life. Indeed, we Anglo-Saxons of the United States, have already nearly extermated the red race by our cruelties and injustice.

The infatuated young man rashly consented to this dangerous amalgamation of races, so that the romance of one of England's proudest Anglo-Saxon sons — one of the descendants of Japheth whom divine prophecy had lifted far above his brothers, Shem and Ham, forever — we find this nobleman's aristocracy culminating in his marriage with a genuine North American Indian squaw, who was, of course, one of the immediate descendants of the *oldest* families in America. She was about fifteen years of age, very small, but perfectly formed. Her voice was as soft and permeating as a nightingale's; her hair was black and glossy as the raven's wing; and her eyes so tender that they seemed stealthily prying around, at all times, for something to love.

"And through her cheek
The blush would make its way, and all but speak;
The sun-born blood suffused her neck, and threw
O'er her clear nut-brown skin a lucid hue,
Like coral reddening through the darkened wave,
Which draws the diver to the crimson cave."

The manners of this wood-nymph were beautifully shame-faced, but she possessed that bird-like coquetry that poets call "a little streak of sin in woman;" but it is not—for the innocent birds, during the whole mating season, flit from tree to tree, and from branch to branch, and at times swinging so tremblingly on the tiniest flower-shrub, as if encouraging the pursuit of her lover by displaying her agility in running away from him. Proving that coquetry is the primitive instinct of the female heart, and that men would think her very tame and didactic without this piquant charm

Neither the aboriginal men nor women possess that arrogant unrefined impudence of manner that makes "young America" so offensive to people of dignity and sense. The *half-breed Indian*, however, has conceit enough to float a steamship like the "Great Eastern."

Our virtuous poetic nobleman took his bride with him to London, where, as a curiosity, she attracted universal notice in the most aristocratic circles; and he hired private tutors to instruct her, for she inherited all her grandfather's talent.

This Earl of Nottingham had six children by this extraordinary marriage, to all of whom he gave every possible advantage that his high station, wealth, and rich intellectual judgment could procure for them. His first child was a daughter of rare genius and accomplishments; all the rest were sons. As soon as this eccentric young lady took her place in society as a fascinating belle, Mr. Walsingham made her acquaintance, and his imagination became so electrified with the idea of another edition of the far-famed Pocahontas, that he visited this refined and gifted descendant of a native American king every day; charmed to discover that she not only wrote the tenderest wild poetry, but that pride of her race had excited her to perfect herself in the study of the Indian language. She was the very personation of her mother in her physique and in the modest charm of her bearing, but her mind had received the highest European polish and education.

Roland Walsingham, thrown into every-day propinquity with this unique young Hebe, of course fell desperately in love with her; and, obtaining her father's ready consent, he married her just as he had attained a world-wide reputation.

He had by this marriage two children, a son and daughter, that he named Leonora and Jefferson. No two children on the face of the earth were more unlike in looks and character, although they were both equally talented. The girl had a profusion of golden hair floating in ringlets over shoulders as white and transparent as wax-work. Her eyes were tender, intelligent, and blue as the sky; her limbs were moulded in faultless symmetry, although her stature was delicately unobtrusive.

The boy, on the contrary, was so entirely an Indian in the whole *tout ensemble* of face and form, and bearing, and character, that the most far-seeing ethnologist could not have discerned a single globule of Anglo-Saxon blood in his dark lowering physiognomy.

This Indian race is physically a marked type of mankind. The men are tall, well proportioned, and agile in all their movements, though in society they are as grave and dignified, and proudly self-respecting in their bearing, as the profoundest philosophers. The eye of the red-man is black and shining, like those of a snake; his head inclines to be conical, and is posteriorly developed; the cheek-bones are high, the face broad, and the features Jewish. The color of the skin a reddish cinnamon-brown, while the hair is very, very black, coarse, and profuse. This hair, under a powerful microscope, is perfectly round, while that of the white man is oval, and of the negro flat as a ribbon, making it kink up like wool, while a curl of any sort could not by any possibility be contrived from the stubborn locks of an Indian, whose soft tread in walking is so cat-like and cunning, that you are often reminded that this last characteristic is nature's advance-courier to warn you against the treacherous assassinating tomahawk and scalping-knife. He does not generally seem to have ever had one gleam of sensibility, and as nothing makes any one more self-possessed than an entire want of feeling, he never looks awkward. His intellect, nevertheless, is not deficient, though his moral perceptions are as dead as a stone. Conscience is an unknown guest.

"As monumental brass, unchanged his look:
A soul that pity touch'd, but never shook;
Train'd from his tree-rock'd cradle to his bier,
The fierce extremes of good and ill to brook
Impassive — fearing but the shame of fear —
A stoic of the woods — a man without a tear."

Mr. Walsingham idolized his Pocahontas wife with that patronage that a man feels for a woman who is a child in character and impulse, though he was, nevertheless often obliged to leave her, month after month, in his scientific explorations of various countries, and even when at home, he lived in his library fascinated with antiquarian and ethnological research; so that he only associated with his family at meals, and on the Sabbath, for no Puritan had ever been more exact than he in the observance of the Lord's day; * and he found,

* "When John Quincy Adams was Minister to the Court of Holland, he joined a society of learned men who met once a week for mutual improvement. Mr. Adams, though one of the youngest members, soon became a great favorite; his finely-toned mind and delightful conversation won him many friends,

in travelling in the woods, that his men were so recruited by this pious rest, that on Monday morning they could undergo double labor.

Mr. Walsingham's strong-minded mother had protested against his marriage with a descendant of the Indian race; and, indeed, her grief was so inconsolable that she died of a broken heart, for Roland had been her pride, her favorite son. The sequel proved how true were her parental instincts, for this amalgamation brought Mr. Walsingham's "grey hairs in sorrow to the grave."

After he had been married ten or fifteen years, and had enjoyed all the sweets of domestic love and harmony, he noticed that his wife's health became alarm-

---

and receiving as much enjoyment as he gave, he was always punctually present.

"On one occasion, however, the meeting was adjourned to Sabbath evening. Mr. Adams was not there. It was appointed on the next Sabbath evening. Mr. Adams was not there. His fellow-members noticed and regretted his absence. On the third Sabbath evening it met. Mr. Adams' chair was still vacant. Many were surprised that he, who was formerly so prompt and punctual, should thus suddenly break off. How did it happen? Press of business it was supposed. At last the meetings were returned to a week-day evening, and lo! there was Mr. Adams in his place, brilliant and delightful as ever. The members welcomed him back, and expressed their sorrow that press of business, or duties of his office, should have so long deprived them of his company. Did he let that go as the reason? 'No business engagements hindered me,' replied he; 'you met on the Lord's day — that is a day devoted to religious uses by me.' He then told them he had been brought up in a land where the Sabbath was strictly observed, and from all that he had felt and seen, he was convinced of the unspeakable advantages arising from the faithful observance of it."

ingly prostrated, and that she almost lived in bed. The best physicians were employed — the best nurses engaged — and her Indian mother never left her bedside. At last the horrible fact was elucidated that she had for years indulged excessively in the use of opium, until the habit had become the morbid passion of her every-day existence, and, to hide it from her trusting husband, she had educated her two children in every species of secrecy and cunning, to procure the drug for her without their father's knowledge. She had expended thousands upon thousands to gratify this insane craving for the fascinations of imagination that De Quincey, the opium-eater, has so glowingly described. So that this refined, gifted, plausible, gentle, interesting woman, was the hopeless victim of that accursedly-inebriating, poisonous weed, before her doting husband found it out. He tried every counter-stimulant to the nerves that the most scientific medical skill could culminate, but all in vain. For six years her brilliant mind continued to sink deeper and deeper into inanity; and then she died, leaving a daughter she had educated to regard her father a tyrant, because of his unending watchfulness in trying to prevent an access to his purse, that, in his previous generosity, had been the cause of the ruin of her mind, and the wreck of her body. She died, leaving a son to follow her example in the use of the soul-destroying stimulant of opium.

"The fathers have eaten sour grapes, and the children's teeth are set on edge." This quotation from Scripture is an expression in the form of a parable, meaning that we inherit diseases and infirmities from our parents. Their sins, or violations of nature's laws in relation to health, are the causes of many of our diseases.

Mr. Walsingham's only son, under the unhappy influence of his infatuated mother during his most imitative age, finally brought his father to the grave from remorse, that he had made so suicidal an experiment as to amalgamate in marriage with a race as inferior to his own as an ape is to a Napoleon Bonaparte, or a Skenandoah is to an African cannibal negro (Mumbo Jumbo.)

"Nature," observes Juvenal, "never says that which wisdom will contradict." Children who have had a mother that never punished, always indulged, and took their part right or wrong, never believe she can have any moral faults or weaknesses; so that, although Mr. Walsingham had sent his son and daughter away from home to distant schools, expressly because his wife was incapable, during the last six years of her life, of rearing them usefully, they taxed their memories with no souvenirs of their unfortunate mother, except that she had been an angel of kindness to them. So that *now* we find them, at the respective ages of seventeen and twenty, with little confidence in the love of a father whose wife had made so many concealments from him, and taught them the same want of frankness towards him. Indeed, when these two children heard he had married again, every spark of identity with his interests seemed banished from their sympathies, and their narrow-minded prejudices against a step-mother made them almost detest Musidora before they ever saw her face. And when, after all the horrors of a stormy voyage, she arrived in London, they received her with saturnine, freezing inhospitality.

Mr. Walsingham, from the time he became a widower, had broken up housekeeping, and taken a suite of rooms in a hotel; and, the morning after his arrival with his bride being Saturday, he ordered a coach, and took Musidora out on a shopping excursion to gratify his pride by purchasing innumerable costly presents for his majestic lady-love. He even selected a gem of a bridal bonnet, and all the belongings of a lady's tasteful toilet; and, on Sunday morning, observed to her that, as his new wife, she would be the observed of all observers, among his literary friends who frequented the church to which he belonged. "Now, then," continued he, "Ne-ne-mo-sha,* you must look your very prettiest to-day, as an illustration of my taste, in going all the way to the far-off sunny South to choose a ladye-love."

After her husband had dressed himself with more care than he had ever done in his life before (for literary men are proverbially abstracted about the clothes they put on,) Mr. Walsingham repaired to his private parlor, to read his Bible until Musidora was ready to accompany him to church. Just as she had progressed a little in arranging her toilet, she heard a rap at her door, and it proved to be her step-daughter, who wanted, she said, to warm her feet previous to going to church (though she was all dressed in furs.) Musidora very naturally said: "I am dressing, dear; won't you go to the parlor, where your father is, to warm

* Ne-ne-mo-sha means, in the Indian language, "my lover."

your feet, as there is a large fire there?" Little did Musidora dream that this was an unpardonable offence: but so it proved, for Leonora ran down stairs with the tears streaming from her eyes, and said she had been driven from her own father's chamber-door. Mr. Walsingham, with his feelings deeply hurt, rushed up stairs to know if it was possible that a woman he had married expressly to be a true mother to his children, should immediately have manifested such savage unkindness.

Poor Musidora almost fainted with astonishment, for her impulses were as guiltless as an angel's towards Leonora; and her proud heart hated to explain the truth, though her good sense finally triumphed, and she did so; but she could not restrain her tears the whole day in church, and never closed her eyes that night; for now she plainly perceived that no purity of intention, no high moral resolves to remove all the errors that the want of a mother's education of these children had engendered, and to strive every day for their happiness and best welfare for time and eternity, that she had vowed to her own heart should be her future vocation; she plainly perceived that such moral elevation would never be appreciated by themselves or their friends in a talented, accomplished step-mother; that her best feelings would be distorted, and all her exertions thrown away through sheer prejudice.

She therefore resolved to do what was right, and leave the judgment of her actions to God; but as her heart could not feel resigned to a thought ever darkening her *husband's* mind against her, she made *him* enter into a covenant with her, never to suspect her motives again as long as he lived; and this vow he kept most faithfully; and, perhaps, no husband and wife on this earth ever respected and appreciated each other more than they did ever afterwards.

Leonora was so angry at her father's marriage, that she refused to visit any of his friends, with his wife and himself. Indeed, she made an entire new set of acquaintances, with whom her parents had no congeniality or friendship. She went to a different church, she excluded herself from the society her father had always been the ornament of, and the prejudiced world at once said her step-mother forced her into the shades of retirement. While the fact was, that Musidora made her beautiful presents to betray her into adorning her person, and securing admiration for her talents and accomplishments in company; for she had real genius, highly cultivated by study of the most improving books, and a taste for music, of which she was very fond.

Musidora was delighted to see her attract the beaux of London, though, of course, she was very decided as to what circle of civilization they moved in. But nothing could reconcile Leonora to a step-mother, though Musidora pardoned her narrow-mindedness, knowing the natural instinct against such an anomalous relation to be almost ineradicable where the children of the first marriage are grown up before the father places over them a second mother. "Indeed, to divest one's self of some prejudices, would seem like taking off the skin to feel the better." And probably this wicked world does not contain more ineradicable prejudices than those experienced by step-children and the millennial reformer, the nineteenth century abolitionists, one of the latter of whom wrote a book, purporting to be historical, and declared "that, in his recent travels in the Southern States, he ascertained that the negroes were never allowed to leave the plantations, and no one allowed to visit them from any other plantation."*

The negro is the most gregarious animal on God's earth. At all their funerals, crowds of black people from the adjoining plantations attend, and though the planters (who hired a preacher to instruct them orally in religion,) attempted to build churches on the plantations, they found it perfectly useless, for the slaves would not attend the service, but voluntarily walked to a large Baptist or Methodist church, several miles off, where they could congregate with their innumerable friends on the Sabbath; and, during the Christmas holidays, any servant could obtain from his master a ticket to go where he pleased during that whole season.†

---

* The author was so grieved, so astounded that a minister of the gospel should write such a fiendish falsehood, that she here, in the presence of the all-seeing God, declares that she has lived all her life among thousands of negroes, and never heard even such a *suggestion* from a planter. On the contrary, the first time she ever attempted to write as a child, her father employed her every Saturday to write passes or tickets for the slaves to visit their friends till Monday morning. This is the universal practice in South Carolina, where the patrol is always out on the highway from Saturday till Monday morning.

† The author's father had a servant-man, named Henry, who, one Christmas, asked for a ticket to go to see his friends in the upper country, a hundred miles off. This request was granted, and exactly on the specified day Henry made his appearance again on the plantation of his master. At another time, a ser-

It is true, that since John Brown's anti-Bible, anti-slavery, and anti-Jesus Christ religion has been the overturning theology of the Northern mind, the planters have been obliged to keep a sharp look-out for Harper's Ferry insurgents, skulking around to incite the slaves to murder, rapine, and violence; consequently, a white man of undoubted integrity is present by *law* at all the numerous nocturnal gatherings of the negroes for prayer and praise; for these converted Africans can sit up to sing and pray till the dawn of morning; and they universally attend the services of the churches, and are so humble, so earnest, so child-like, so affectionate in their Christian faith, that it may be doubted whether the pride-hating, pharisee-abhorring God, looks down with more complacency on the worship of any of his creatures than these pious Africans command from the Great Spirit, who looketh through all disguises at the heart.

The negro firmly believes that God himself inaugurated slavery in the time of Moses, the great lawgiver of Israel; and he has been taught all the passages in the New Testament, showing that Jesus Christ and his apostles never found fault with the institution, but gave rules to the end of all time for the conduct of the master and the conduct of the slave. He is, therefore,

---

vant woman, named Louisa, begged to be allowed to go to Charleston to see her husband, who was a *free* mulatto, engaged with some captain of a ship to travel about with him. Charleston was a hundred miles off, and one of Louisa's husband's other wives, it was believed, poisoned her, for she has been under the care of physicians and nurses, prostrate in her bed, ever since, being nearly forty years.

perfectly resigned, nay, contented in that station to which God has called him; and, to secure respectability, he aims only at deserving it, where at the South he is sure to receive it. The fugitive slave is lazy and unprincipled, and, therefore, when he escapes North he is the most hopeless of beings; for he went there to get rid of work, and finds the alternative is starvation.

Mr. Walsingham's unpromising son, though only eighteen years of age, proved so morally hopeless in his character and dissipated habits, that his father procured for him a commission in the army, hoping thus to discipline him into regularity of tastes; but he passionately and stubbornly refused to accept the situation; and then his despairing father yielded to his earnest entreaty to become a merchant, and placed him with a great mercantile house in London.

In the meantime, Mr. Walsingham, like most literary men, had trusted all his money matters to agents, and he awoke one morning to learn that three hundred thousand dollars worth of property had been squandered by their breach of trust to him, so that he seemed inextricably ruined. A week or two, however, after this calamitous discovery, he received the most flattering offers of employment for his talents in the United States; and Musidora was delighted with his decision to accept the lucrative and honorable post assigned to him, for he had the warmest appreciators in America, where his noble father's blood had flowed in the last century in defence of the colonies.

We find him then, transferred to Washington, District of Columbia, and a perfect enthusiast in his literary labors. Musidora thought it best to board in some private house until their affairs were more plausible in the money market; but he would not consent. So she hired a house, and learning that ladies in Washington attended sales, her husband took her to one of them in a private house, hoping to find furniture suitable for a library. Musidora, in all her life in Carolina, had never heard of a lady attending an auction sale of furniture; so that this scene was so new, and the human heart laid so bare to the moral observer in the spirited bidding for all imaginable useless articles, that she forgot her own errand in the interest culminated to analyze the mysteries of the sin of covetousness. She was, indeed, so much entertained by watching the effect of gain or loss of any coveted prize in this unique lottery, that ever afterwards, when she got tired of studying the human heart in books of biography and history, she would forthwith accompany some appreciating lady to one of the said furniture, or book, or millinery, or flower sales, and bring home a fund of anecdote to amuse her grave, philosophic husband.

Ascertaining that it was also very fashionable for ladies to attend the markets and purchase their own edibles, she determined "while in Rome, to do as Rome did" in this respect, too, though in all her life in Carolina, she had never set foot in a market. Here, again, she often forgot to order the dinner until the last moment, so absorbed was she in the entertainment of watching that peculiarity so graphically described in holy writ, "It is naught, it is naught, saith the buyer, but when he goeth his way then he boasteth." She also made the acquaintance of the numerous poor who congregate in the city on market-days. Indeed, her husband got so expectant of her sallies of wit, when describing the lazaroni, and those who fancied *they* were the greatest people in the world, that whenever she came home, he made her retail all her adventures with the Washingtonians — small, smaller, smallest: great, greater, greatest — before he allowed her time even to take off her bonnet.

Musidora had one great trouble, however, as a housekeeper, and that was she could not tolerate the idea of white servants, whose manners were so rude, so unsympathetic, so unlike the kind, affectionate, well-trained, black house-servants of Carolina, that she could not bear them near her, and for the first time in her life determined to be without a maid at all in her chamber, rather than be annoyed by an inflated menial, who was so insolently careless of pleasing her or obeying her orders. Having hired an Irish cook, she found her so entirely divested of the least particle of knowledge of the culinary art (that all the *negroes* are born with) that she had to leave the delights of study with her husband, in his library, to go down to the kitchen to teach Biddy how to draw even a cup of coffee or tea, without allowing the aroma to escape; and one day, when she expected a large company to dinner, her gastronomic professor went to bed with the toothache just as the orthodox hour arrived for boiling, baking, and roasting the whole family of fish, flesh, and fowl; and she got up quite convalescent after Musidora had sent runners from Dan to Beersheba and obtained another Irish cook; and then, between the two contending daughters of Erin, her recherché dinner was sent up both burnt and raw.*

Musidora implored her husband to let her send to Carolina for her trained and most affectionate servants;

---

* "PLAINT OF AN EPICURE.—I am dying from irritability produced by eating raw mutton-chops, and indigestion produced by potato-bullets. My murderer is Betsy Jane, our cook. On my tombstone will be inscribed the words, 'Died from the effects of a very plain cook.' In vain I try to explain to her the chemistry of the first elements of cooking. She fries everything, and prefers that greasy, unwholesome, soaking mode of cooking, to the racy, chastened gridiron that gives to a chop such a healthy flavor; she prefers baking with its sodden steaming, to juicy roasting; and when she boils, she boils things so fast that they are hard, yet underdone; she has no forethought; she puts things down to roast too late, and then hurries them too much; she leaves the pot on the hob when it should be on the fire; and she boils at a jumping, pot-lid shaking canter, when she should simmer with a gentle, bubbling gurgle. In fact, musically speaking, she takes a joint at vivace when it should be allegro, and 2-4 when it should be 6-7. In fact, Betsy has no sense of the dignity of her art; no knowledge of the solemnity of her mission as the soother and nourisher of the human mind through the human stomach. She is always hot and cross, (cooking affects the liver and spoils the temper,) and is, in a word, a big-headed, irrational, insensate, miserable hireling, who turns potatoes into yellow tallow, meat into coke, and bread into soluble lead. I look on her as a perverter of the gifts of Providence, and, therefore, as an ally of Apollyon himself. The effect of fire on solids or fluids, the law of boiling, the nature of imprisoned juice, the science of condiment, are as unknown to my plain cook as the pleasures of dancing are to a hippopotamus, or the joys of pedestrianism to the great sea-serpent. She never thinks; she did not take my wages to think; she is only a walking plate-warmer, a portable ladle, a human cruet-stand; she would never kill herself, like the famous Vattel, because the woodcocks did not come in time for the dinner-party."

and he consented. So she wrote to her brother Halcombe to send by ship, her maid Phillis, who had been consecrated to her interests from her childhood. This excellent maid had, on her knees, implored Musidora to take her with her when she was married. She said she would give up father, mother, sisters, brothers, husband and children, to follow her beloved mistress to the ends of the earth; and, indeed, Musidora returned all this faithful creature's friendship, for she was a perfect gem of a servant. She was a complete pastry cook, an inimitable laundress, sempstress, and lady's maid (all ladies in South Carolina have a maid); but, above all, she had the most happy temper, and always when she received an order, flew to do it as if it was her most delightful service. Indeed, it was a standing joke among all the villagers of Iodilla, that Musidora must give Phillis to them when she was about to make her exit out of the world. Phillis was black, but very handsome; for everybody is fascinating who has a happy, contented, and yet industriously faithful disposition.

Phillis had twelve children; the first being born when she was fourteen years of age. So Musidora determined to leave eight of them with their grandfather and grandmother in Carolina, and bring the other four to Washington. Phillis's husband was a bad man, and had forsaken her and taken another wife. The four children, too, had had the measles and the whooping-cough, so that their constitutions were so much impaired that the Doctor thought a change to Washington might restore their health.

Musidora received her faithful servant with tears of gratitude to God, that she had thus been blessed with so faithful a friend in her first trial of housekeeping in Washington, and every temporality was rejuvenated in her new home by Phillis's untiring industry, and affectionate enterprise. Mr. Walsingham, and all his friends, thought they had never seen such an incomparable servant — for she was an example of what the Bible commands. "Let as many servants as are under the yoke, count their own masters as worthy of all honor, that the name of God and *his doctrine* be not blasphemed." "If any man (says St. Paul) teach otherwise, and consent not to wholesome words, even the words of our Lord Jesus Christ, and to the doctrine which is according to godliness." . . . "He is proud, knowing nothing, but doting about questions and strifes of words whereof cometh envy, strife, railings, evil surmisings, from such withdraw thyself" (oh! ye Southern people). . . . "But in a great house there are not only vessels of *gold* and silver, but also of *wood* and of earth; and some to honor, and some to dishonor." . . . "Servants, be subject to your masters with all fear; not only to the good and gentle, but also to the froward." . . . "Servants, obey in all things your masters according to the flesh, with fear and trembling, in singleness of your heart as unto Christ." . . . "Not with eye-service, as men-pleasers, but as the servants of Christ, doing the will of God from the heart." . . . "With good will, doing service as to the Lord and not men." . . . "Knowing that whatsoever good thing any man doeth, the same shall he receive of the Lord, whether he be bond or free." *

---

* "SLAVE LIFE PREFERRED BY NEGROES—THE RUSSELL COUNTY CASE.—A few days ago, says the *Montgomery* (Ala.) *Mail*, Ben.

A very brilliant, rich, aristocratic friend of Musidora's, now left South Carolina and took a house near Mr. Walsingham's, in Washington, where she meant hereafter to reside. About six months afterwards she rushed into Musidora's house, and said she had just found one of the greatest saints that had ever lived since the advent of the Savior on earth. That he was a missionary, of Scandinavian descent; that he had married a Southern heiress whose wealth consisted in

---

H. Baker, Esq., visited the city, and caused to be introduced a bill in the legislature, by which twelve free negroes are allowed to become slaves. The bill passed both Houses and was signed by the Governor, the speedy transaction of the affair being caused mainly by the entire confidence which members of both Houses (in which he has frequently served hitherto) have in the personal integrity of Mr. Baker. The facts are briefly these: The negroes, men, women and children, have been reared by Mr. Young Edwards, of Russell County, and have always lived with him, as servants. Lately some one informed these negroes that, being free, the Sheriff would be required to expel them, under a provision of the Code, within thirty days. At this they were greatly alarmed, and protested that they were unwilling to leave their master, and were perfectly willing to remain as his slaves, and in fact preferred it. Mr. Baker visited the negroes, explained to them their position and rights fully; and the up-shot was they induced him to come and lay their case before the Legislature, asking it to allow them to become the slaves of Mr. Edwards. The bill was accordingly passed. It provides that the Probate Court of Russell shall have the negroes brought before it, and diligently take testimony to ascertain if any undue influence has been used to obtain their consent to become slaves; and upon being satisfied that they wittingly, and with full knowledge of their rights, desire to enter a state of servitude, shall decree them to be the slaves of the person they may choose to be their owner."

negroes; that from pure principle he had given them all their freedom twenty years ago—paid all their expenses to Africa, and supported them there a year; that he had then taken his penniless wife to the South Sea Islands, where, as missionaries, they had spent fifteen years in constant dread that the savages would eat them up (for we have heard that a nice bit of a cold clergyman, who has been eaten smoking *hot* the day before, is considered a decidedly refreshing breakfast by these cannibal epicures), and even after laboring fifteen years, and Mr. Jellabee was rewarded, as he hoped, by the conversion to Christianity of one old South Sea Islander, who was an aged woman; she declared to him in the confessional, that there was such a fat, plump baby of her daughter's in the house, that Satan was always tempting her with the idea of what a delightful relish its tender fingers would be for her supper.

These two unrivalled missionaries were named Menomone and Nicodemus Jellabee. (Menomone means, in Indian, wild-rice makers.) Mr. and Mrs. Jellabee not only had lived through the long martyrdom of fear of being eaten up by the savages, but at times they were themselves almost reduced to starvation; and who can tell, with famine staring them in the face, whether they had not been tempted sometimes by the devil to believe, in that far-off wilderness, that a fat, oil-fed South Sea Islander might be profitably cured of unrighteousness by boiling him up into a nourishing jelly, that would last the famished missionaries a whole month?

Musidora's wildly romantic South Carolina friend

continued her narration of the unearthly disinterestedness of these missionaries, by telling her that, after all this self-abnegation,—which of course gave them liver complaint, and every other disease that flesh is heir to when stimulated every moment by mortal dread of being eaten up alive, or dying of starvation among these outside barbarians, whose country did not furnish the kind of food necessary to keep a Christian's soul and body together,—Mr. and Mrs. Jellabee, though they firmly believed that all men, even those who prey on human flesh, were born free and equal, determined to give the South Sea Islanders up to the devil, as they themselves must return home to the United States to die. They were as jealous about the land where their bare bones were to be buried, as Abraham, the father of the faithful, was; for he had no idea of allowing his dust to enrich the soil of Egypt, but had it carried far away into the Cave of Machpelah, in the promised land; which was certainly very pious, and very sensible. For the above-named reasons, Mr. and Mrs. Jellabee had selected the District of Columbia, and the neighborhood of the Congressional burying-ground, for their bodies to turn to their original dust.

In the meantime, however, while these abolition saints were patiently awaiting the caprices of grim Death to hurry them to that heaven they thought they had purchased by living fifteen years among the devilish South Sea Islanders, Mr. Jellabee had taken a little box of a church in Washington, where he thought he might, with his blazing talents, attract even members of Congress to righteousness, and to the knowledge that the great ubiquitous eye of God spies out all their morals, and the "recording angel" writes down all their motives and acts of "bribery and corruption."* Mr. Jellabee proposed, too, as a more hopeful enterprise, to "preach the gospel to the poor."

Musidora's Southern romance and religious enthusiasm were so nervously irritated, that she determined

---

* TAKING BRIBES.—With his rugged, fearless honesty, the good Bishop Latimer, in three several sermons, when preaching before his youthful sovereign, Edward the Sixth, denounced the judges who loved gifts and took bribes. He cited what seems to have been with him a favorite incident, the story of the Persian ruler, Cambyses, who having convicted one of his law-dispensers of being the recipient of such bribery, ordered his being flayed alive, and commanded that the skin of the offender should be stretched on the judgment-seat, there to remain under all future occupants of the place, that coming judges might be reminded at what cost they would themselves cherish an itching palm. Describing the culprit as "a briber, a gift-taker, a gratifier of rich men," the faithful preacher, who was to be so heroic a martyr, exclaimed in a burst of indignant uprightness, "Surely it was a goodly sign, a goodly monument, the sign of the judge's skin. I pray God we may once see the sign of the skin in England!" And again, in the last sermon which this stern chaplain delivered in the same august presence, "in his Court at Westminster," Latimer took occasion to shame some juridical offender in this fashion: "He that took the silver basin and ewer for a bribe, thinketh that it will never come out; but he may now know that I know it; and I know it not alone, there be more beside me that know it. * * I can never believe that he that is a briber shall be a good justice. *It will never be merry in England, till we have the skins of such.*" Three centuries have since rolled by. The Bench of Britain has been long free from the imputation of similar corruption. But perchance its modern exemption from such suspicions even, may in part be traced to the quaint fearlessness of the pulpit, when filled by worthies so earnest and dauntless as good Hugh Latimer.—*Examiner.*

to join this man's humble little church; for of all things, her heart craved to be instructed by one whose mind was energized every day by the pure flame of communion with the Holy Spirit of God, that makes the whole body full of light. Besides, in all her life in the South, she had never seen nor heard of an abolitionist who had the loving spirit of Jesus — who was willing to preach (*only*) Christ crucified, as the radical panacea provided by Omnipotence for the regeneration to holiness of the human heart. The gifted lawyer-statesman of New York, George Wood, in his political letter of 1860, says:

"These men, deeply imbued with a spirit of religious fanaticism, have already discovered that slavery is a sin in itself, and is not to be tolerated for a moment. Hence, without any delicacy or regard to the feelings of their brethren in the South, they disseminate libellous and incendiary pamphlets, through their agents, encouraging the slaves to rebel against their masters — the natural tendency of which is to violate all law and order, and to spread a scene of devastation and ruin. And, strange to say, some clergymen, whom we are accustomed to look upon as shining lights to lead mankind in their pathway to another world, have been very conspicuous in those efforts of mischief. Such a scene as this a few years ago would not have been witnessed. And to what are we to trace the causes of such a wonderful change, but to that spirit of religious fanaticism to which I have already alluded? This is an extraordinary state of the human mind, which is but imperfectly understood as yet, and has not been thoroughly analyzed. It insensibly undermines the vital principle of virtue. The man who is subject to it becomes a bundle of contradictions and contrasts — he is credulous, and at the same time crafty — he is philanthropic, and at the same time vindictive and cruel — he is devout, and at the same time marked with a spirit of vengeance. That spirit, when once it takes possession of the human mind, will convert an angel of light into a demon of destruction. Its bad qualities are not all exhibited at once — they require development by time, but their development is rapid — *viris acquirit eundo.* The fanatic is the most presumptuous of men. He stops at no obstructions in his path, and does not wait to consider the impracticabilities of his schemes. Knowledge and learning and experience are set at naught, and he has no respect for those who possess them. Placed on a lofty eminence of sacred law, he looks down from his eagle-height with indignant scorn upon mere human enactments. Constitutions and laws, framed with the utmost care, are set at defiance by the presumptuous fanatic.

"As he advances in his career, he becomes more hardened in cruelty; and that which at first he would look upon with horror, becomes easy and familiar to his mind. It is not surprising, therefore, that some men who were very conscientious and respectable in former days, when they become deeply imbued with this spirit, should recommend to a slave to kill his master, unless he would instantly allow him to go free. When the Emperor Charles the Fifth made captive the great Reformer of that day, in a generous and manly spirit he set him free. But as he advanced in life, and became possessed of the fanatical spirit, it became a source of deep regret to him that he had not taken the life of Luther. When he retired from the cares of the empire, and, in the spirit of a devotee, secluded himself within the walls of a cloister, he regretted that he had to chaunt his praises to the God of mercy without having dyed his hands in human gore. To the same spirit must be traced the infuriated massacre of St. Bartholomew.

"But we need not resort to history for melancholy examples of this spirit. The scenes recently enacted at Harper's Ferry are enough for our purpose. We are told that the leader in that diabolical transaction was once generous and brave; but mark the change. With deep dissimulation and with apparent friendship he gains the confidence of that unsuspecting community. Of a sudden, and in the midnight hour, their peaceful and quiet abode was changed to a scene of slaughter. After his execution, a convention was held in New York to approve of his proceedings, at which clergymen, highly respectable attended, and joined in the approbation."

But let us not forget our romantic religionist Musidora, who, on the following Sabbath, accompanied her friend to the far-off little meeting-house to hear Mr. Jellabee, the *practical* abolitionist, preach. A little mite of a man ascended the pulpit. He looked, indeed, as if he had been half-starved. His complexion was bilious and wilted; his hair a nondescript, yellowish, sun-burnt brown; his cheeks so sunk and emaciated that you might have anatomized every bone in his wiry, lean-looking face. He would not have weighed more than ninety pounds, while he was afflicted with that undignified, jeremy-go-jingle briskness of carriage and deportment, so peculiarly unfortunate in Lilliputian men. He wore an old faded, snuff-colored coat, the seams and cut of which testified to its antiquity. Indeed, had Musidora heard nothing about him, she would have judged from his eye and his sermon, that no mortal man had so mistaken his calling, as he did when he took to preaching; for his whole *tout ensemble* looked so daft, that an irresistible smile was the sure impulse of your mind, if you watched his nimble, jimmy movements; and he preached exactly as if the audience were South Sea Islanders, who had never heard of the Bible before. He had no more imagination than a stone, though he was reputed to have learned thoroughly the language of the barbarians, — which of course could be of no use in Washington, except among the members of Congress.

Is it not surprising that men who have not talent enough to preach at home, should be sent for instance to be missionaries among the Indians, who are cavellers, though they believe in innumerable spiritual influences. Colonel Creesy remarks, that "while travelling in 1831, in Mississippi, I often met squads of the Choctaws, and wondered at their apparent want of curiosity; sometimes I doubted their descension from mother Eve, for nothing whatever seemed to interest them but *whiskey;* and if they ever heard of Eve's eating the apple, contrary to Divine command, they would have said her punishment was *deserved*, for not making cider of the apples, and brandy of the cider, instead of greedily munching the fruit. Upon two occasions, however, I heard a few words in addition to the eternal '*Ugh!*'

"At a camp-meeting near Shongalo, Carroll County, the first I understood ever held in that region, there were present perhaps thirty Choctaws, and a crowd of white persons; where *from*, no one (who had rode through the forests, in their native wilds, as I had, without meeting with a single located democrat, sometimes in a whole day's ride) could imagine; but there they were, several hundred of them, with a goodly number of females, and no less than five of those untiring circuit-riders, or missionaries, of the economical and enthusiastic society of Methodists, who rival the primitive Christians in the earnestness and simplicity of their devotions, and never-exhausted exertions to make converts. Their labors and privations, their poverty and perseverance, deserve success. They surpass the early Catholic missionaries who accompanied Cortez, Pizarro, and other Spanish conquerors to the New World, at whose head stands the great, the good, the pious Las Casas. The world at large knows not the value and importance to the human race of the labor of these holy men. May heaven's blessing rest on them.

"The preaching commenced quite early on the day I happened to be a spectator, as well as the poor Indians; and about twelve o'clock, under the ranting of a fluent, if not an eloquent preacher, a number of those influenced became greatly excited, particularly the females. Many of them shouted loudly, clapped their hands, tumbled down, rolled over, jumped up, and were apparently frantic. I turned from the exhibition to the Choctaws, who had repeatedly grunted 'Ugh! Ugh!' very near me; when one of them, with more feathers and paint on him than any other, looked at me rather cunningly for a Choctaw, turned his head back, opened his mouth, raised his hand up to it as if drinking, and to my astonishment, said audibly and distinctly: 'Hoxie heep whiskee too much.' My risibles were so strongly excited by the naïve remark, that I felt it my duty to leave the ground, being compelled to admit that a simple-minded Indian could come to no other conclusion.

"Subsequently, I happened on a Sabbath to be near where a Baptist meeting was to be held in Yazoo County, and with several acquaintances, went to see the baptism of new converts in a well-known stream, called Wallokchebogue. On our way we overtook a small party of Choctaws, who had been hunting, and their squaws picking out cotton for some time in the neighborhood, also bound to witness the immersion, of which they understood nothing. We were a little too late for the first scene, one of the converts having been already baptized, and the preacher and his followers singing. One of the Choctaws who spoke English enough to be understood tolerably well, inquired, with a little semblance of curiosity, the meaning of the ceremony, seeing several persons standing in the water, and one thoroughly wet; when a member (I believe he was a clergyman), with much earnestness and patience, endeavored to explain it. The Indian at last appeared to understand that the belief was, that on being dipped, or covered all over in the water, the believer was made perfect and holy; would sin no more, and could appear before his God, in the land of spirits, without fear of punishment; for all his crimes, and evil deeds, and thoughts, were thus washed out, and he would be the companion and brother of Jesus Christ, the Savior of mankind.

"'Ugh! ugh!' said the Indian, 'me know, undestan, me bobbashela, too.'

"At this moment, another convert was led into the water. The clergyman, after the usual exhortations and blessings, plunged him under, and as he did so, the now enlightened Choctaw threw off his blanket, sprang head-foremost into the stream, very near the baptized man, swam under the water until he reached the opposite side (about thirty feet), shook himself like a water-dog, plunged in again, and rose alongside of the clergyman, gave another shake, and exclaimed aloud, looking up and raising his extended hands above his head,

"'Hell *exchow!*' Hell exchow! Jesus Christ and me bobbashela, now. Ugh! Ugh!'"

"Exchow," is Choctaw for "gone," or "lost," or "done over," and "bobbashela" is "brother."

Musidora was so disappointed at the preaching of Mr. Jellabee, that all her friend's enthusiasm could not reconcile her to the idea of a saint like that. Her conscience, however, triumphed over prejudice, and she said to herself, indeed, indeed, the Holy Spirit of God *can* live in even such a homely temple as Mr. Jellabee's assuredly is; besides, had he not impoverished himself to the verge of starvation, to give his hundred slaves their freedom; which, though foolish to the last degree, for these slaves had no doubt turned back to heathen barbarism in Africa; still, he had lived out his abolition doctrine to the immolation of all his *own* selfish interests, therefore his fanaticism was not cheap, but morally respectable.

Musidora from her very heart, believing all this absurd 19th century romance, determined to divide her whole earthly portion with these true saints. For could there be a greater honor than to have all her worldly goods used in common with the most heavenly-minded friends of Jesus, who had ever appeared on this earth since His crucifixion.

Although Mr. Walsingham was an Englishman, he was not an abolitionist, for his long experience of the history of nations, their rise and progress, and the utter destruction to all enterprise and prosperity in the British West India Islands, since the abolition of slavery had opened his eyes (though the government had paid the planters for their negro property, previous to this suicidal act.) Mr. Walsingham had been to Jamaica,* and with sorrow had analyzed the awful mistake England had made in abolishing compulsory labor; for now the plantations that formerly yielded a hun-

* The New York Herald, in a criticism on the recent work of Mr. Trollope, an Englishman, who was sent to Jamaica on public business, thus describes that gentleman's opinions of the freed negroes there.

"In these illustrations of character the chief thing to be noticed is that there is little self-sustaining power and no sense of the future in the negro — facts that are all important in determining the question of labor in the West Indies. A servile race, peculiarly fitted by nature for the hardest physical work in a burning climate, the negro has no desire for property strong enough to induce him to labor with sustained power. He lives from hand to mouth. In order that he may have his dinner, and some small finery, he will work a little, but after that he is content to lie in the sun. This in Jamaica he can very easily do, for emancipation and free trade have combined to throw enormous tracts of land out of cultivation, and on these the negro squats, getting all that he wants with very little trouble, and sinking in the most resolute fashion back to the savage state. Lying under his cotton-tree, he refuses to work after ten o'clock in the morning. 'No, tankee, massa, me tired now; me no want more money.' Or, by way of variety, he may say, 'No; workee no more; money no 'nuff; workee no pay.' And so the planter must see his canes foul with weeds because he cannot prevail on Sambo to earn a second shilling by going into the cane-fields. He calls him a lazy nigger, and threatens him with starvation. The answer is—'No, massa; no starve now; God send plenty yam.' These yams, be it observed, on which Sambo relies, and on the strength of which he declines to work, are grown on the planter's own ground, and probably planted at his expense, and Mr. Trollope suggests an inquiry into the feelings of an English farmer if our laborers were to refuse work on the plea that there is plenty of potatoes and bacon to be had —the potatoes and bacon being the produce of the farmer's own fields. There lies the shiny, oily, odorous negro under his mango

dred thousand dollars per annum, could not command that many coppers, for they had sunk into ruin and decay. The free negro never will work *consecutively*;

---

tree, eating the luscious fruit in the sun. 'He sends his black urchin up for a breadfruit, and, behold,' says Mr. Trollope, 'the family table is spread. He pierces a cocoanut, and, lo! there is his beverage. He lies on the ground, surrounded by oranges, bananas, and pine-apples. Why should he work? Let Sambo himself reply. 'No, massa, me weak in me belly; me no workee to-day; me no like workee just 'em little moment.' Mr. Trollope saw a gang of ten or twelve negro girls in a cane-piece, lying idle on the ground, waiting to commence their week's labor. They had not been to work on the Monday; this was Tuesday morning, and they were lying with their hoes beside them, meditating whether they would measure out their work or not. The planter happened to be with Mr. Trollope, and they immediately attacked him. 'No, massa, me no workee; money no 'nuff,' said one. 'Four bits no pay! No pay at all,' said another. 'Five bits, massa, and we 'gin morrow 'arly.' The demand was refused, and the planter observed to Mr. Trollope, 'They will measure their work to-morrow; on Thursday they will begin, and on Friday they will finish for the week.' 'But will they not look elsewhere for other work?' it was asked. 'Of course they will, and occupy a whole day in looking for it, but others cannot pay better than I do, and the end will be as I tell you.'

"As it is, we find that continually fewer Europeans now turn to the West Indies in quest of fortune, and very few indeed think of remaining there permanently. As far as Jamaica is concerned, what is there to tempt the Englishman? It is a fact that half the sugar estates, and more than half the coffee plantations have gone back into a state of bush, and a great portion of those who are now growing canes in Jamaica, are persons who have lately bought the estates 'for the value of the copper in the sugar-boilers, and of the metal in the rum-stills.' The Anti-Slavery Society will scarcely believe in the poverty and ruin of the planter, because they hear wonderful accounts of

and without *this*, neither cotton, rice, or sugar, can be grown. In Jamaica they would not even pick up the coffee on the ground, but lounged about in abandon childishness and vice; so that every Christian philosopher returns home from visiting Africa, and then the abolitionized West India Islands, with the conviction that nothing short of omnipotent wisdom, could have devised such a scheme for making these degraded wretches useful in their day and generation,* as the compulsory labor system, and to convert heathens to the knowledge of the true God, by bringing them into the living, acting, neighborhood of Christianity; where as *property* to the white man, the poor ignorant barbarians become an element of the most vital interest —

---

his hospitality. 'We send word to the people at home that we are very poor,' say the planters. 'They don't believe us, and send out somebody to see. For this somebody we kill the fatted calf and bring out a bottle or two of our best. He goes home and reports that these Jamaica planters are princes who swim in claret and champagne.' The planter accordingly makes the complaint, 'This is rather hard, seeing that our common fare is salt fish and rum and water.'

* W. H. Seward's Testimony concerning Africa. — In the extracts from some letters of W. H. Seward, published in the Albany Journal, giving his observations as a traveller abroad, we perceive that he exclaims, on leaving Egypt for the Holy Land:—"Farewell, Egypt! long sought for, seen at last. Farewell, Africa! the only region in the world which Providence seems to have fortified against civilization. And why fortified? Is it on account of the African soil or climate, or the African race?" The subject is an interesting one, and we hope that Mr. Seward, on his return home, will avail himself of the first occasion to explain why he thinks Africa "the only region in the world which Providence seems to have fortified against civilization." — *N. Y. Herald.*

an interest as permeating in the body politic, as any fundamental, ineradicable instinct, in the heart of man, which is to take increasing care of his own property. Mr. Walsingham never dreamed therefore of the cruelty of giving freedom to *his* wife's negroes, who were perfectly happy, and enjoyed every comfort, and the proper degree of respectability, as *Africans.*

Musidora, as all Washington was on the tenter-hooks of admiration of Mr. Jellabee's godlike disinterestedness, now called on his wife. She was a very tall, angularly-boned, square-shaped woman, perhaps forty years of age; she held her shoulders high up against her ears, like persons do who have an excruciating pain in the side, from liver complaint; her hair was ambiguously yellow and red; her eyes a greenish-grey; her complexion was the color of saffron, though the skin was *thin*, like a blonde. But what terrified Musidora more than all her other peculiarities, was that skulking bend in the neck, that she always associated with treachery and cunning.

Musidora thought that, in all her life, she had never met with such an unfortunately unprepossessing couple. But although the two looked enough alike to be brother and sister, still their minds and character were perfectly diverse.

Mr. Jellabee had no fixed opinions on any subject that could be reached by a single practical illustration. He had lived among barbarians until his feeble, undisciplined mind, had lost the line that separates sin from holiness in the human heart, or rather conscience. He was so conservative, that everybody who talked to him about politics, infidelity, Unitarianism, Universalism, Calvinism, Arminianism, Roman Catholicism, or Old or New School Presbyterianism, believed he was of their opinion. His wife, on the contrary, was as angular as a meat-axe in all she said or did. Her intercourse with this wicked world had destroyed all trust in her fellow-creatures; so that Talleyrand himself was not less *frank*, or more *politic*. She was not intellectual; had read few books of genius or information; and she had no conversational powers: but her mind was as sharp as a needle about her own or her children's interest. As to her innocent, unsentimental, fence-man husband, she seemed to regard his daftness with motherly patronage. Musidora wondered whether she had not been born in Iceland, rather than, as her biographers asserted, in Florida.

This cunning woman gave Musidora such a heart-rending account of their poverty, and want of every comfort in their tiny house, that she went among the congregation of Mr. Jellabee, and so excited their enthusiasm that they sent their pastor a whole wagon-load of groceries of every description, even a "little wine for their stomachs' sake, and often infirmities." They also sent them all their wood and coal every year, and the ladies vied with each other in giving them the various kinds of dry-goods. Musidora betrayed Mr. Jellabee into a clothing-store, where she fitted him out with a clerical suit of black broadcloth, so that the unorthodox, snuff-colored remnant of antiquity, that he had worn as an apology for a coat, might be transferred to some poor street-beggar. Perhaps God was never more sincerely honored than He was by the gifts presented to these missionaries, for every offering was for Christ's sake. Nobody loved Mr. and Mrs. Jellabee personally at all, except so far as they regarded them as the true friends of the Savior.

Musidora had been persuaded by many that he was a great genius in the impenetrable disguise of a conservatism, that made him as changeable as a weathercock. So *she*, wishing to patronize this said humble genius into a knowledge of his transcendent intellectual gifts, wrote to the President of the United States about the immaculate saint, who had just made his advent into Washington. She wrote to Mr. Webster, Mr. Clay, Gov. Seward, Judge McLean, and all the lions, together with the Cabinet of the President, and she aroused such an enthusiasm in their minds for goodness, that they furnished money to enlarge Mr. Jellabee's little church. Musidora, indeed, became so fanatical about these missionaries, that she dared not buy a fat turkey, or old sugar-cured ham, for her own table, without procuring an exact duplicate for Mr. Jellabee's too; for she said to herself, "Why should I, an erring sinner, pamper my body with luscious food, while that representative of Jesus upon this earth is so denuded of all his fatness and muscularity, from pious, self-imposed penury?"

Musidora, fearing some mistake about their giving freedom to so many negroes, carried one or two of her brilliant letters, stating these facts, to *Mrs*. Jellabee to read, and she smiled proudly, but did not contradict one word of it. Judge, then, Musidora's amazement when, three years afterwards, she happening to be walking with Mr. Jellabee, he unconsciously let out the truth that he had *sold!*—yes, SOLD!—yes, I repeat, SOLD!—*all* of his Southern wife's negroes, except one single family that were so old, and sentimentally attached to his wife and her sister, that they gave them their freedom, after ascertaining that they would cost three hundred dollars to maintain them in a town in Florida, for they were too old to support themselves; and as some missionaries were about to sail for Africa, old aunt Jane, and the other liberated, useless slaves, went along with them to Liberia.

Musidora actually wept with godly sorrow, that the only abolitionist saint she had ever heard of, who was willing to drain his *own* purse to carry out his own eccentric principles, that "all men are born free and equal," should have proved a man getting fame on false pretences, and getting presents on false pretences (for the fact leaked out that his table was more recherché than that of all his neighbors, and his children more expensively clothed and educated.) When the truth became incontrovertible, that this cunning, skulking, deceiving woman (for her husband had not character enough to be wicked,) had obtained so much praise and so much money that she never deserved, Musidora perfectly despised her, and said to herself: Why, when Mrs. Harriet Beecher Stowe has energized her naturally mercurial imagination to depict the most fiendish cruelties practised on an invaluable slave (Uncle Tom,) and should have published to the world that Southern plantations are a hell upon this earth, and slaveholders the representatives of Satan in the United States, should I allow these abolition deceivers, these whited sepulchres, Mr. and Mrs. Jellabee, to escape the laceration of public opinion? But this man was a preacher, and she felt afraid to strike a blow that must immolate him in Washington society; still, she could not resist the racy, irritating temptation, to send a richly-flavored account of Mr. and Mrs. Jellabee's great financial prudence in giving freedom to their slaves, to the renowned abolitionists of Boston.

Musidora now began to feel deeply grieved about her dearly loved maid, Phillis, for she seemed so changed in heart, in mind, and in body, that her own mother would not have known her. All her sleek rotundity of figure, all her merry friendly laughter, all her prompt and loving obedience, and confidingness, and industry, was gone. She was so discontented and miserable that Musidora feared to ask her to do a single thing, for she seemed so uninterested, so abstracted, and was constantly asking for twenty-five cents to take a ride. Musidora never denied her anything, and took care of her sickly children during her long absence in the mornings. Finally a high principled neighbor stept over to Mr. Walsingham's house, and told him he had heard the whole arrangement between Phillis and an abolitionist, to run away with her; and as he was a poor devil, and could intend nothing, except to sell her somewhere, they came to warn Musidora about her deluded maid's folly.

As usual, Phillis came again for money to ride out the next morning, and her mistress gave it to her, but employed a policeman to follow her in another hack, and ascertain *who* she visited. He came back in an hour or two, and reported that he had followed her in the direction of the Navy Yard, and there ascertained that the abolitionists congregated in a blacksmith's shop, *there* to lecture * to the negroes about the new light-edifying religion, that requires these poor children, in

---

* "Our system of lectures in these days, appears to have become quite an institution. Through all our country, it seems to be either progressive or ascendant. It exerts a powerful influence. It is formative, educational, characteristic. It is also American. Would to God it were equally safe, good, true; or, all in a word, equally Christian! But this is not the case. Some lecturers have no good principles, and are almost incapable of a good motive. They are flashy, trashy, crashy, and ridiculous. They are unsound; they insinuate error, and folly, and poison. They are often ignorant, with no apprehension of how much they know — not! As say the Latins, and as Christians may say, more emphatically: *Duplicem ignorantiam jactes: nil scis te nil scire:* which some one — I recollect not who, just now — thus not inaptly renders :—

'A double ignorance thou may'st boast:
Thou know'st not — that thou nothing know'st.'

But as here we are 'all born free and equal;' — are all opposed to monopoly, aristocracy, and superior attainments—in others; and as we are all peers of the realm, in erudition, good manners, refinement, and modesty: so, we can all teach, all preach, all lecture; and any man of us seems liable to be made President — especially this year! Hence the system of lecturing, like a cheap omnibus, is ready to break down with passengers. Well, what then? Why, persiflage apart, it is obvious that —

The system needs to be guarded, vigilantly, from all kinds of abuse! to be defended against insidious perversions, and resulting mischiefs, in which all that is good might otherwise suffer, or die, in our social communities. If not good—it is bad.

The doctrine of 'equality' is often currently perverse; as a sheer, yet proud and vaporing hallucination. *Égalité* was a great word, electric and full of mendacity, in revolutionary France. It would seem to import that all men — especially boys, are six feet high, at least; are about forty or more years

character and intellect, to cut their master's throats — to assassinate their only practical friend who has had all the trouble of educating them to usefulness in the great hive of the world's industry. Yes, these sanguinary illuminated lecturers persuade the poor credulous uninductive negro, that the blessed Savior would receive them into the mansions of holiness in heaven, if they came there with their hands reeking with the blood of their best friends, from their cradle to their graves. Musidora threw herself on her knees to pray for these disorganizing, blood-thirsty, sanguinary traitors to the Bible, and traitors to that "Constitution" they had sworn to support, kissing the Word of God before men and unseen angels who surround us in all our walk through this world. As to Phillis's treachery she pardoned it; for the poor negro has no idea of the misery of the African fugitive at the cold North; but she felt such remorse for having brought this happy, useful, respectable servant into such a snare of the devil, as Washington is to the colored people, that she wept unconsolably for two weeks. Poor Phillis guessed the cause of her grief, and told her *all* the steps that led to her foolishness. She said, that the abolition men had constantly visited her, to talk to her about

old; all healthy, rich, strong, and remarkable for good and great qualities; all learned, experienced, travelled, and knowing, alike; and are all instructed, against the old Catechism, in reference to the fifth commandment, where our relative duties are treated, 'to superiors, inferiors, and equals,' that of late we have no 'superiors;' and if any 'inferiors,' which is of no consideration as fact or fiction, we have no 'duties' to them! no duties at all, only—'rights.'"—*Rev. Samuel Hanson Cox, D. D.*

slavery, in her chamber at night,* as it was a basement-room fronting on the street; that they betrayed her into other crimes that had destroyed her health, grieved her conscience, and broke her heart; that to relieve the anguish of her mind, she had determined to run away with Mr. Vode, and leave her children; for she knew her Misses would mind them better than she could; as vice had wrecked her bodily health, and that now she must die, for she could not bear to be exposed. Musidora wrote immediately to her brother, Halcombe, to come and take Phillis back to her mother and father in Carolina, as the change might save her life. In the meantime she went to the richest abolitionist in Congress, stated Phillis's case in all its enormity of hopelessness, and begged him to buy her, and give her freedom, for the poor creature had heard so much of the higher law, that all her Bible religion had vanished, and she was left just on that sea that has no shore—for it is not bounded either by the laws of God or man. Mr. Fox, of course, refused to spend a single dollar for the cause of freedom, though he had preached that the Southern people, to gratify the conscience of the North (not their own convictions of duty, mind ye), must give up every cent of property they had on this earth, and see their wives and children (and slaves, too) famish for the sake of a romantic abstraction of

* "The devil's in the moon for mischief; they
Who call'd her chaste, methinks, began too soon
Their nomenclature: there is not a day,
The longest, not the twenty-first of June,
Sees half the business in a wicked way
On which three single hours of moonshine smile—
And then she looks so modest on the while."
BYRON.

the Northern Lights—the abolition politicians who are famishing for the loaves and fishes, that come along in shoals, with every new President inaugurated into the White House.

Surely every Southern man, woman, or child in the United States would join themselves as a nation to England or France rather than be any longer subjected to the insult, injury, and injustice which they have borne from crack-brained abolitionists in power, for nearly a quarter of a century. We never received near the injuries from our mother country, England, that we have patiently borne from our Northern brethren because family pride has sustained us; knowing that "a brother offended is harder to be won than a strong city;" and that family quarrels, when once publicly proclaimed, weaken all the family influence in society, as it has already done in making this Republic an object of hissing and a byword to all the kingly governments of Europe. Fie, fie upon you, suicidal abolitionists!

Halcombe hurried to Washington; for Musidora had not let Phillis know that she had written for him. He armed himself, so as to resist any attempts of Phillis's abolition beaux to "rescue her," as they ironically term it, "from her only true, sympathizing friends."

Getting on board of a steamer, he arrived in South Carolina without let or hindrance; and Phillis, once more inhaling the rejuvenating salt air of Palmetto Grove, gradually, under the care of skilful physicians, recovered her health, as she had begged Musidora to keep her troublesome children in Washington till she herself was again able to take care of them.

A very good-looking negro man, who said he was born in New York, and had been *free* all his life, came to Walsingham's after Phillis was gone, to hire himself as a dining-room servant. Musidora thought it a blessed providence to get an educated free African to wait in her house (for the man said he had been to school seven years); so she forthwith hired Henry Bradley, as he called himself, and in a few days afterwards a black woman named Sarah, an acquaintance of his, offered her services as a cook; and she, too, declared she had been free from her birth.

One day, Musidora, seeing how capable Sarah was, sent her to market to purchase the dinner; for she was a great judge of tender meats. She returned with such abominable-looking spoiled chickens, that they had to be thrown away; and all day there was something strange in her manner, which excited Musidora's fears.

About twelve o'clock that night, seeing from her chamber-window a blazing reflection of light in the kitchen, Musidora got up out of bed, and went down to the basement; where the gas was sputtering from being turned on to its greatest extent, and there lay Sarah, apparently dead, on the kitchen floor. Musidora almost fainted with fright, and she rushed to her servant-man's door, to wake him up; which feat she accomplished, after alarming nearly the whole neighborhood, by the energy of her blows against the outside of his chamber-door. With real sympathy in Musidora's alarm, however, he repaired to the kitchen, and after examining the prostrate Sarah, pronounced her indeed to be a corpse. In a few moments afterwards, however, he found a large jug of whiskey, and then he declared that she was only dead drunk. Indeed the next morning she developed symptoms of *mania a potu*; and Musidora, after watching over the poor creature several days, had to dismiss her; for she discovered, through her own private confessions, that she had become a hopeless drunkard from having had her voluntary abode as a hired servant in a house of *ill-fame* ever since she was fourteen years of age.

Musidora was now compelled to send her black waiting-man, Henry, into the kitchen to cook until she could procure another servant; and then, going to her husband's library, to converse with him on the wickedness of ever giving negroes their freedom in this country, she was suddenly startled by Henry bursting unceremoniously into the room, trembling in every joint, and begging her for God's sake to say that his name was *not* Henry Bradley.

Before she could comprehend what he meant, she heard a loud rap at the door, and there stood a constable, ready to arrest Henry. Musidora delivered him up to the officer of the *law* instantly, though she could not divine what was the matter. In about an hour, Henry returned, accompanied by the constable, and implored Mr. Walsingham to stand his bail for a hundred dollars for three days; which was cheerfully done.

Musidora now understood that he was arrested for stealing the clothes of a gentleman who lived in a hotel where he had hired himself as a dining-room servant.

It seemed impossible that this should be true; for when Henry had hired himself to Mrs. Walsingham, he was so destitute of every orthodox garment for a house-servant, that she, out of charity for the poor negro, had given him twenty dollars' worth of clothes —coat, vest, pants, shoes, and shirts.

Finding that the prosecutor was a Virginia gentleman, she visited him repeatedly, until he finally agreed to let the poor fellow off, as imprisonment produces no moral effect at all on the negro, and Henry promised that all his wages for a year should be faithfully handed to the merciful Virginia gentleman who had pardoned him, together with Musidora and her husband, who knew too much of the African to expect *him* to be an honest or high-minded representative of humanity. The return for all this blotting out of his transgressions was, that in two weeks he stole nearly a hundred dollars' worth of property out of Mr. Walsingham's house, and then scampered off, and never was heard of afterwards.

Thus ended the experiment of employing one of the *free*, educated, black *gentlemen* of the Northern States.

CHAPTER XX.

Mr. Walsingham now received letters so appalling as to the career of his talented son, whom he had left in a mercantile house in London, that he requested a friend who was returning to the United States after a long absence abroad, to bring Jefferson Walsingham along with him. Oh! how the father's heart was wrung when the unfortunate young man arrived in Washington—for intemperance, debauchery, and gambling had left their usual stereotyped mark on his wrecked form and withered countenance. Soon letters arrived from Europe that he had used his father's honored name to obtain fabulous sums of money from the most prominent persons of Mr. Walsingham's acquaintance. It was indeed wonderful how this irresponsible young spendthrift had been able to deceive the most practical business men, so as to realise the largest drafts on the strength of innumerable false pretences. But his Indian dignity and modesty of bearing, and his imperturbability of countenance, presented an effectual shield against suspecting so highly educated a gentleman.

Indeed, he often boasted of his extraordinary talents in this respect, and confessed that with many common people, he had obtained moneyed sympathy by abusing his step-mother — and then, again, praising her when conversing with the most refined and morally elevated whom he intended to take a *toll* from, on account of their great respect for his father.

Musidora's pride was so tortured (for it was impossible to refund the enormous sums of money thus swindled out of her husband's most appreciating friends) that she shut herself up in her chamber three days and three nights, in an anguish of mind, too intolerable for any consolation—for this insane gambler was her husband's only son, and bore his father's venerated name. Fasting and praying to God for help in this dire calamity, she besieged heaven to sustain her poor hopeless husband, whose intensely absorbing grief brought on a derangement of the whole nervous system, and in one week he was struck down with paralysis that no medical skill could reach.

Jefferson, who daily witnessed the misery he had brought upon the whole family, was still not in the least weaned from his darling vices. Indeed, he seemed as insensible as a marble statue to every interest save that of selfish indulgence. Conscience never appeared to speak loud enough to arrest his attention even for a moment.

Perhaps the chronic selfishness of young spendthrifts of this description is the most faithful miniature of that of Satan, who "goeth about as a roaring lion, seeking whom he may devour."

> "The cloyed will,
> (That satiate yet unsatisfied desire,
> That tub both filled and running) ravening first
> The lamb, longs after for the garbage."

Jefferson, while his noble father lay helpless and prostrate on his bed, waiting for death, Jefferson Walsingham still kept running around and inventing new schemes for obtaining money from the friends of Musidora and her now imprisoned husband; while these said friends respected them too much to publicly prosecute this infatuated member of their family.

Musidora knew that no power on this earth could reach that young man. But she also knew that the love of Jesus could regenerate any human being, without reference to the type of his moral diseases, from the day that He was promised as a Savior in the garden of Eden, after our first parents had eaten of the forbidden fruit, and proved that they possessed the germs of that higher-law disobedience that thrust Lucifer, star of the morning, out of heaven.

Musidora thoroughly believed in the expulsive power of a new affection in the heart of man, so she not only prayed and fasted before God, night and day, for the regeneration of her miserable step-son; but she also determined to wean him from vice by expending every energy on making his home pleasant to him. Whenever she could leave her helpless husband, she would run out and purchase presents so as to secure a recherché wardrobe for Jefferson, "for *dress* has a moral effect upon the conduct of mankind. Let any gentleman find himself with dirty boots, old surtout, soiled neckcloth, and a general negligence of dress, he will in all probability find a corresponding disposition by negligence of address."

Musidora furnished a delightful chamber, and innumerable books and writing materials, and encouraged this morally sick patient to write criticisms of new works, that at one time he was very gifted in analyzing. She invited young ladies to stay with her to amuse him in the evenings, and she bought games for them to play with him, and taught him *chess* as the most interesting of them all. She required from her servants the most scrupulous deference to his orders, even to the neglect of her own. She sent for the best physicians to consult together about the propriety of carrying this not only morally, but physically, diseased young man, through a course of mercury, as an alterative to his shattered constitution. But the end of all these godlike exertions to rescue this poor fellow from the bottomless pit of infamy in this world and the next, was, that Jefferson Walsingham broke open the safe where all his father's gold was deposited, and then ran away with the accumulated treasure from the sale of his works of the patient industry of Mr. Walsingham; leaving him hopelessly paralyzed, with no means of recruiting his scattered fortune. Musidora and her husband never heard of him afterwards. Thus was Mr. Walsingham's wise mother's prescience of the danger of amalgamation with a different race * from

* "THE BRIDGEPORT AMALGAMATION CASE.—The Hartford 'Press,' states that Mrs. Beach, the wealthy and handsome Bridgeport widow, who married George W. Francis, a black man, gave to her friends as one reason for her conduct, that she had received communications from her deceased husband in the spirit world, advising her to marry Francis, and stating that since he had left this vale of tears he had been conjugally united to the spirit of a colored damsel. The marriage ceremony was performed by Rev. Mr. Millet, in the evening, when the lady was so much disguised by 'frizzing' her hair, &c., that he did not suspect she was a white American woman. Francis once gained some notoriety as the supposed nephew of Soulouque, the Emperor of Hayti."

his own, brought home to him in his advancing years with the arbitrariness of prophecy.

The half-breed Indian is a fine-looking man physically, but he has no more idea of conscience than the rock of Gibraltar. He has none of the redeeming traits of the full-blooded Indian, and none of the virtues of the white man. He is mentally very bright, and cunning as a fox. He can acquire any amount of learning, but it is of no earthly use to him—for "unstable as water" is written indelibly upon every enterprise he attempts. He is almost as sure to be a drunkard as that he is able to procure ardent spirits. He is intensely conceited, but seems incapable of that pride that fears and scorns to be disgraced in public opinion, and yet, with his cultivated intellect, he will sit down and reason by the hour on the meanness and wickedness of his neighbors, who are as far superior to him in virtue as daylight is to darkness. His moral vision never turns inward, but like the Pharisee, he is ever on the qui vive to pull the mote out of his brother's eye, when his *own* is blinded with an ineradicable beam. He has so much imagination that it is next to impossible for him to speak the truth. His *facts* are *poetical* licenses. He is therefore the most to be pitied of all God's rational creation—for he seems constitutionally incapable of excelling in anything; he has no adhesiveness, no sensibility, and very little hope or enterprise—no accumulativeness, no providing for to-morrow. The white man sins against the laws of Nature, when he intermarries with the Indian or the African, for no doubt all hybrids are subject to the same fixed laws of moral deterioration that the half-breed Indian man almost universally develops, either in youth or advancing years.

It is a remarkable fact, that the red man's divestment from every species of covetousness has been the greatest drawback to his civilization; and the moment you can succeed in interesting a savage in the orthodox accumulation of *property*, he takes a respectable place in the ranks of civilization and Christianity in America. The slave who ran away from his master, and took refuge with an Indian protector, taught him the use of the plow, and from hence arose the progressiveness of the Creeks, the Choctaws, and the Cherokees. The institution of slavery among these aborigines made them gentlemen.

Jefferson Walsingham only developed in his eccentric conformation of mind, and utter want of inductive moral perception, the same fixed characteristics that any ethnological or philosophic observer can easily detect in the career of all half-breed Indian *men* — whereas the women (who are always short-lived,) are, of course, from conventional requirements, not able to act out their instincts as the males do, and therefore *their* peculiarities are not so manifest.

Mr. Walsingham, in spite of his mother's superior age and experience, warning him against amalgamation with other races in marriage, thought the union of the American aborigines with the noble Anglo-Saxon would produce the highest specimen of humanity; and, with ethnological enthusiasm, he had given Leonora and Jefferson every advantage that education, travel, and the best society could germinate. But you cannot make Shem or Ham equal to Japheth, for God predestinated their inequality forever and forever; and, indeed, what is most remarkable, is the fact that the *own* father of these three races of men, who was inspired to prophesy their inequality in all their posterity, seems to have been so much more satisfied with the will of God respecting his own offspring than the abolitionists, six thousand years afterwards, are about those with whom they have no blood or national ties. Why don't the 19th century saints, through their inspired spiritual mediums, call up Noah, and wrangle with, and lecture against, and burn *him* in effigy, as the embodiment of the "sum of all villanies," for his pusillanimity in not fighting with God Almighty before the flood, when he might, with his *created* moral, and *created* physical strength, have fought gloriously, sensibly, and victoriously, against *uncreated* wisdom and omnipotence, that chose of his own free will to decree inequality throughout his dominions, throughout this earth, and throughout the heavenly bodies too? Who made a fly and an elephant, a lion and a humming-bird? Who finally said: "Let us make man in our own image, after our likeness, and breathe *our* breath into his nostrils; and *let* him have dominion over *all* the earth, and over the fish of the sea, and over the fowls of the air, and over the cattle, and over every creeping thing that creepeth upon the earth?" Gracious God! what a magnificent king this Adam was ordained to be! Why, everything on the earth and in the sea bowed to his nod. The lion and the panther crouched respectfully, and hung down their heads, and the anaconda moved deferentially out of the path where this godlike genius appeared. And yet, after all this sovereignty conferred upon him so lavishly, Adam was not happy — none of these creations of God gave him a home for his affections on earth, as well as in heaven. Therefore God said: "It is not good for man to be alone; I will make a help-meet for him. And the Lord God caused a deep sleep to fall upon Adam, and he took one of his ribs, and closed up the flesh thereof; and the rib which he had taken from man made he a woman, and brought her unto the man. And Adam said, This is now bone of my bone, and flesh of my flesh, and she shall be called woman, because she was taken out of man."

"How hard it is for natural reason to discover a creation before revealed, or, being revealed, to believe it, the strange opinions of the old philosophers, and the infidelity of modern atheists, is too sad a demonstration. To run the world back to its first original infancy, and, as it were, to view nature in the cradle, and trace the outgoings of the Ancient of Days in the first instance and specimen of his creative power, is a research too great for any mortal inquiry; and we might continue our scrutiny to the end of the world, before natural reason would be able to find out when it began."

Of course, Eve, being made not as Adam was, in the image of God, but out of one of the small ribs of her husband, was entirely his inferior, and altogether subject to him. But God, in his mercy, to protect her weakness against his strength, instilled into his most radical affections the love of patronizing the helpless, and the love of the waving curls, and dimples, and smiles, and romantic adhesiveness of woman: and this passionate love of beauty was so permeating and softening to his rugged, gigantic mind and heart, that he actually obeyed this frail, ruby-lipped, flaxen-haired Hebe, the very first moment she offered him a temptation to disobey the great Creator of the universe. Perhaps, when Adam lost one of his ribs, he was not as perfect in the image of God as at first, and therefore this bereavement might have caused the breaking-down place in his primitive perfectibility.

Rochefoucault says that "when a woman thinks alone, she always thinks evil;" and therefore, Milton, whose wife's "incompatibility of temper" was very vexing to him, pretends, in Paradise Lost, that Eve had wandered off by herself, when the devil (who must have been an eloquent pulpit-orator, or stump-speaker,) tempted her. But this is not true. Adam was with her, the Bible says; and no doubt, though his *curiosity* was not as great as that of the ladies generally is, he connived at the disobedience, when knowledge was the bait held out by old Timothy Brimstone. Certain it is, he made no objection to eating the tempting apple that her *curiosity*, and courageous enterprise, had so rashly plucked. "The receiver is as bad as the thief."

Let us weep for poor Eve. Think of the change, from a lordly, godlike, sovereign king, to love, honor, and obey, as a husband—one who was God's great vicegerent of the universe, who ordered the sea, and all that was therein, and the earth's inhabitants too, and gave all his subject-creatures their names. Who would slap in the mouth the lion and the tiger, if they even growled too loud to interfere with the harmonious music of creation, that was entirely subject to his almightiness, was now by *sin* so miserable a coward that ever since he will run from a spider or a tiny wasp, and tremble at the musical notes of a mosquito buzzing around his couch at night. And yet we poor, unfortunate ladies, who so admire a man who fears nothing save God — we high-mettled ladies are still required to bow as *inferiors* to this fallen representative of the magnificent Adam. Oh! Eve! Eve! Eve! why did you so lawlessly experiment on the taste of that apple? Truly, idle curiosity is the weakness that made us from the very first betray our great inferiority to the male sex, who, however, with all their superior *caution*, will rush into any mischief, if we only march in the van of battle. There is no doubt that the higher-law party, whose leader was the devil (for this party always makes use of their smartest man as a mere cat's-paw), there is no doubt, we repeat, that Satan promised Eve that, if she disobeyed God, she would in the end become as wise and independent of *Him* as the abolitionists of Anno Domini 1860. This ambition that all should be free and equal, built up the superstructure called *Hell*. *That* was the fiery prison erected for the first archangel who proclaimed the higher-law doctrine of "equality" in heaven. And it can be proved that all those infidels who are wise above what is written in the Bible about slavery, marriage, governments, obedience to the magistrates of the civil law of the land, or any other institution of God's contrivance, will finally find themselves in that thronged place that burns with fire and brimstone; for, says St. John, "I testify unto every man that heareth the words of the prophecy of this book: if any man shall add unto these things, God shall add unto him the plagues that are written in this book. And if any man shall take away from the words of the prophecy of this book, God shall take away his part out of the book of life, and out of the holy city, and from the things that are written in this book." . . . "Woe to the inhabiters of the earth, and the sea (and the United States,) for the devil is come down unto you in great wrath, because he knoweth that he hath but a short time." *

What, for God's sake, would become of the civilized world if all the ladies were to become converts to higher-lawism? These boys in men's clothes that have been palmed on us, with few exceptions, for husbands, ever since Adam lost his godlike, manly dignity, have

* There is a flying rumor that the abolitionists, who are the Don Quixotes of the 19th century, are so enraged at the Japanese Embassadors, now on a visit of great national importance to the President of the United States, from the Emperor of Japan; it is rumored, we repeat, that the above higher-law, levelling party, are so enraged that the servants of these august Embassadors *kneel*, in 1860, when they approach their superiors, that they have been skulking around Willard's Hotel (where the "Embassy" is now sojourning,) to persuade the said servants to assassinate their masters, and then take to their heels, and run to Boston, where the nigger-worshippers will receive them with open arms, as their skins are yellow. It is devoutly to be hoped this rumor is true, for then we should be involved in a bloody war with the Emperor of Japan, which would be an outlet for all the sanguinary biliousness of our Northern New-Lights, whom we would *force* into the *front* ranks of our attacking army, as they are so mercurial, and thus get the uneasy spirits killed off, who so trouble the United States with their pugnaciousness.

(though we feel ourselves superior to them in morals, and practical sense, and adhesive beautiful affections,) been treated with the most ghostly respect. Why? Because the Bible commands us to do so. God orders the wife to be obedient to her own husband, to honor and love him. But the moment we ladies get wiser than our Creator, that moment we will assert our independence; and instead of ruling the men with our dimples, and our curls, and our smiles, and our moral loveliness, and refined dependence on them to vote for us, and work for us, and fight for us, and let us stay at home to enjoy the magnificent privilege of teaching the young idea how to shoot; instead of this sublime destiny for mothers and wives, we should have a race of coarse, ugly Amazons, scratching and biting all who oppose them of the masculine, or feminine, or neuter gender; instead of Venuses, and Hebes, and gentle, loving Marys, like her who was the humble mother of Jesus Christ, we should have anomalous creatures, fresh from the women's rights conventions, elbowing their way through mobs of greasy, half-nude Republicans, pistol in hand, to cast their vote to make some Jezebel President of the Dis-United States.

These higher-law furiosos would enter into the marriage relation, not reverentially as God's ordinance, but as a mercantile speculation, and as soon as the *firm* got tired of each other, from *any* cause, it would dissolve partnership, as dry-goods or wholesale shipping merchants do every day; and then what is to be the destiny of the children of the establishment? Where is the domestic altar around which *they* are to be reared for moral usefulness in this world and beatitude in the next?

St. Paul says, by the authority of inspiration, "I suffer not a woman to (preach) teach, or to usurp authority over the man." Let us then, dear ladies, not aspire to be captains of steamboats, or boatswains on board a man-of-war. No! no! no! let us stay at home, love our husbands, love our children, govern our servants in righteousness, and bring up our sons and daughters with such reverence for the Bible and the civil law that God has ordained, that they will, in the course of time, have that appropriating faith in Christ that will restore to them *his* image.

Our masterly inactivity, dear ladies, hitherto, in the affairs of State, has surely procured for us all the power we crave, which is power over the human *heart*. The men venerate us for preparing their children for usefulness in their day and generation. The husbands of to-day, it is true, are not such respectable, august fellows as Adam was before he was thrust out of Paradise, but our beauty, and dependence on their superior strength, and our high *moral* fealty to them, are just as powerful to bring them chivalrously to our feet *now* as they were when the august monarch of the universe of God, even the man Adam, made in the image of his Creator, and endowed with more power and dominion than any human being has ever been honored with since—even *he* bowed chivalrously before the beauty and *personal* loveliness of Eve, though she had not yet tasted of the tree of knowledge, and, consequently, had not *our* privilege of a cultivated intellect, refreshing conversational powers, and sparkling, innocent wit, to charm our husbands, even after the sere and yellow leaf of autumnal age renders our physical attractions *passée*. Remember, the Bible does not allow us to marry a man at all, except "for richer, for poorer, for better, for worse, until death us do part," and, therefore, it is not orthodox or refined to run off to Kansas for a divorce. The first year of our marriage is, of course, the most difficult, for it is the transition state between having a knight of chivalry swearing that he loves you—loves you to distraction—loves the very ground you walk upon; that he dreams of you all night, and sighs for you all day—and that, without your love, existence will be a burden, and the very sky darkness; that every flower of the earth will wither and lose its fragrance to him—and, indeed, that your eyes alone are the stars of the sky, your love the only solace of his life. We repeat that the transition state from listening to all that soft nonsense in a lover, and then as a husband, seeing his character, and temper, in dishabille, and hearing his savage complaints about the dinner if it is not exactly orthodox in *time*, quality, and preparation, *is* a trial to a high-mettled wife. But the best catholicon for a husband's ill-humor is to kiss him lovingly when you find he is getting displeased or unreasonable, and humbly, and without martyrdom or affectation, say to him, with our original mother Eve,

> "What thou bid'st
> *Unargued* I obey; so God ordains;
> God is *thy* law; *thou mine:* to know no more
> Is Woman's happiest knowledge, and her praise."
>
> MILTON.

CHAPTER XXI.

"She has all
That would ensure an angel's fall,
But there's a cool, collected look,
As if her pulses beat by book—
A measured tone, a cold reply,
A management of voice and eye,
A calm, possess'd, authentic air,
That leaves a doubt of softness there,
Till —— look and worship as I may,
My fever'd thoughts will pass away."

MUSIDORA, being settled in Washington as her home, now carried out her affectionate desire of introducing her step-mother's only daughter, Gulielma, into the court atmosphere of the grand metropolis of the United States. She therefore sent to Carolina for this beautiful half-sister to come and live with her, and Mr. Walsingham was delighted with the arrangement; for, said he, "all Gulielma's influence, as a companion for my daughter, will, of course, be directed towards making Leonora love you." Little did he dream that Gulielma had, from her birth, been brought up with no sympathies for her elder half-sisters; so that the very first impulse of this girl was selfishly to pave the way to Leonora's heart, by sneering secretly at Musidora in all the harassing perplexities of her daily life, after her husband had been struck down with paralysis.

Leonora, strange to say, though not half so beautiful as Gulielma, had a great many more beaux and lovers; for though mentally stoical as a philosopher, there was a sort of physical, impromptu nervousness of manner, that had all the pleasing effect of child-like frankness and artlessness. Though a poetic genius, there was no conceit, no arrogance, or didactic assumption of wisdom in her modestly-expressed opinions in company, so nobody envied or wished to see her put down, as they did her apparently towering, though, in fact, experimentally and religiously humble step-mother. All the gossiping, idle, fashionable women hated the very sight of Musidora's unbending, self-respecting, majestic bearing in every society she moved in; and yet her manners were the legitimate result of her orphaned, unsympathized-with childhood, that had thrown her completely on her own resources; and, perhaps, the whole District of Columbia did not contain a human being whose heart was more entirely humbled before God, or more anxious to befriend and elevate her fellow-creatures. Man judgeth according to appearance, but God judgeth the attitude of the spirit.

Mr. Walsingham idolized his queenly looking wife; for her inner graces of affection, and sensibility for the whole brotherhood of the world, were transparent at all times to his morally appreciating glance. Not so, however, did she appear to outside barbarians,—to envious, calumnizing gossips,—who troubled themselves night and day to dive into the daily domesticities of her household; which idle curiosity into your neighbors' most private concernments, is a sure sign that you are seeking to do him some shrewd evil turn.

"Envy makes a man think another of greater facul-ties, only a continual blemish to himself. He thinks his candle cannot shine in the presence of the other's sun; that is, in truth, he is angry with God for not making him better and wiser and stronger. He expatiates on the supposed injuries of his creation, and questions his Maker for not coming up to his measures. For while envy spits its venom directly at men, much of it falls obliquely upon God himself; and while it quarrels with the effects of his goodness towards others, does by consequence blaspheme the cause."

Poor Musidora seemed to stand in the sunlight of these weak, unelevated gossips, though her whole mind was set on one absorbing idea, and that was to employ every gift she possessed in contriving amusements out of the library for her long-imprisoned husband, who was a constant wonder to her, from the Christian philosophy with which he sat down, chained to his seat, every day for ten or twelve years, without a murmur, though his brain was clear as the sunlight, his body without a pain, and his high-mettled spirit as vaulting as ever in its interest in politics, patriotism, literature, and everything worthy of a genial philosopher's consideration. No man would have revelled more wholesomely than he in his former extraordinary powers of locomotion. And yet when that gift, so common to all men, was hopelessly withdrawn from him, he seemed to be so content as almost to demonstrate gratitude that God, who had given him so many blessings, should *only* have visited him with painless *bodily* disability. Such a manly, dignified, edifying Christian philosophy, under such a tantalizing bereavement of locomotive energy, made the morally appreciating Musidora venerate him as Eve did her husband, before he was stripped of his godlike attributes. Musidora coveted, therefore, no society, no admiration, no approbation, but *his*. How, then, could she stand in the sunlight of any woman at this Republican Court, when her every ambition and sympathy centred in the deep privacy of home?

Leonora was now engaged to be married to a man of renown in the literary world; but the very week before the bridal ceremony was to take place, he died; and Musidora, fearing the effect of this disappointment, induced Gulielma to visit Carolina, and take Leonora along with her for six months. "Love, like fire, cannot subsist without continual movement; as soon as it ceases to hope and fear, it ceases to exist." Even so, in an incredibly short time, Leonora had captivated another beau; and through the infallible expulsive power of a new affection, she felt it very plausible to marry him. "Some boys have the complaint of love favorably, and gently. Others, when they get the fever, are sick unto death with it; or, recovering, carry the marks of the malady down with them to the grave, or to remotest age. Suppose," says Thackeray, "one is in love with a woman twice as old as himself: have we not all read of the young gentleman who committed suicide in consequence of his fatal passion for Mademoiselle Ninon de L'Enclos, who turned out to be his grandmother? Kick and abuse him, you who have never brayed; but bear with him, all honest fellow-cardophagi; long-eared messmates, recognize a brother donkey."

And who do you think, dear reader, was Leonora's affianced? Why actually the most idolized and youngest brother of Musidora herself; so that she was now to be placed in the droll position of mother and sister to her step-daughter, and mother and sister to a handsome brother she had been devoted to from his birth. She did not like the contradictory consanguinity that Cupid had so suddenly culminated; but as her husband was delighted with the match, she sent to Carolina for her mercurial pet brother, a month after Leonora had returned home to Washington.

In order to frustrate this young lover in his arrangements for going off to California to make a fortune, and then to return in three years, bringing twenty hundred pounds of gold dust to lay on the altar of Hymen — or rather, *then* to get married, and go to housekeeping; for Prentice says, in one of his witty *feuilletons*: "It takes, in America, three to make a pair; *he*, *she*, and a hired girl. Had Adam been a modern, there would have been a hired girl to look after little Abel, and raise Cain." Musidora determined to get the magnificent, gigantic, Adonis lover a place under the Government; but she reckoned without her host, if she imagined a proud, sophomoric South Carolinian would dance attendance on any power on earth, to get an office. Her dear, darling brother Rutledge refused even to make a call with her on the powers that be in Washington, for he said he had never in his whole life paid attention to people in order to get favors out of them.

Musidora, therefore, as there were six hundred applicants for the place she desired for Rutledge, had to run to Congressmen, and visit the Cabinet of the President of the Dis-United States, and write letters every day to convince the Secretaries that without the help of her Adonis brother as the fifth wheel to the wagon of State, the whole Government would be smashed all to pieces. After six months of extraordinary exertions to bring the Executive officers to this orthodox conclusion, Musidora's romantic enthusiasm was crowned with success, and Rutledge received a plausible office. His sister, soon to be his mamma, now got all the et-ceteras ready for the wedding; and though she thoroughly despised Mr. and Mrs. Jellabee, the hypocritical abolitionists, Leonora insisted that *he* should be the officiating clergyman. In a week after the bride and groom had been united in marriage, Mrs. Jellabee influenced Leonora and her husband to leave Mr. Walsingham's large, elegantly furnished house, and go to board with a private family who were the enemies of her father and Musidora; for though the said Jellabees had run off twenty thousand miles, perhaps, to teach religion to the heathen, they came back to a Christian land to teach the children of pious parents to disobey, and not honor, their father and mother. Previous to this mischief-making in Mr. Walsingham's household, Mrs. Jellabee had induced an undying feud in the family of Musidora's South Carolina friend, who had so nobly and generously expended all her *shoneau* and influence in Washington to advance the before-mentioned abolition missionaries, the transcendently sublime, disinterested Jellabees. They succeeded, it is true, in their revenge against Musidora and her husband, who could not at all hold intercourse with Leonora and her husband, while they lived *voluntarily* with the enemies of their parents.

But God, after three or four years, allowed such a storm of indignation to arise in the popular mind of Washington against Mr. Jellabee's folly, that every man of any importance or judgment left his church. The ministers of his own denomination ceased all intercourse with him; his church was sold, and torn down to its very foundations, and even the name blotted out of the records. Mr. Jellabee gave up preaching the moment a more lucrative trade was offered to him, and afterwards his daughters, who had been reared to the higher-law doctrines of the equality of Ham with the descendants of Japheth, ran away with several fugitive slaves from South Carolina, and were married to these black gentlemen in Boston.

Thus ended the history of the most famous abolitionist that ever made his advent into Washington. Thus ended the career of Mrs. Jellabee, who was one of the women who always swelled herself to the size of an ox, in her conceit that the gifted, talented, generous, frank-hearted, and most morally elevated Musidora Walsingham, stood in *her* sun-light, just because she received unbounded praise for staying at home with her paralyzed, interesting husband, instead of being a street hack, to accompany Mrs. Jellabee in what she was pleased to term her philanthropic enterprises, hither and yon, among the poor; not one of which loved this inveterate, gossiping, abolitionizing missionary, who was the very embodiment of envy.

"Envy is a weed that grows in all soils and climates, and is no less luxuriant in the country than in the court; it is not confined to any rank of men, or extent of fortune, but rages in the breasts of all degrees. Alexander was not prouder than Diogenes; and it may be if we would endeavor to surprise it in its most gaudy dress and attire, and in the exercise of its full empire and tyranny, we should find it in schoolmasters and scholars, or in some country lady, or the knight her husband; all which ranks of people more despise their neighbors, than all the degrees of honor in which courts abound; and it rages as much in a sordid affected dress, as in all the silks and embroideries which the excess of the age, and the folly of youth, delight to be adorned with. Since, then, it keeps all sorts of company, and wriggles itself into the likings of the most contrary natures and dispositions, and yet carries so much poison and venom with it, that it alienates the affections from heaven, and raises rebellion against God himself, it is worth our utmost care to watch it in all its disguises and approaches, that we may discover its first entrance, and dislodge it before it procures a shelter or retiring place to lodge and conceal itself."

In all Musidora's trials, God had spared her one, that she shuddered even to think of; her husband's brain was not in the least affected by his paralysis of body; indeed he seemed brighter in his intellect than ever, and the physician told her that a man who had the gout, or any ailment of his extremities, would be clearer and stronger in his head. She therefore became his amanuensis, and thus enabled him to publish works that will immortalize him forever. Poor fellow, he was so proud of his South Carolina wife, and her romantic adhesiveness to him, for better, for worse, for richer, for poorer, in sickness, and in health, that he found at the bottom of that ancient Pandora's box of evils, that blessed gift of hope, that seemed to circumvent every dart aimed at his heart, even by the grim tyrant Death. He would send out and buy the most dashing bonnets, shawls, and gowns, for his incomparable ladye love; and she would wear all his gifts, though the gossips thought it a crime for a Christian, but particularly for Musidora, to wear a white silk bonnet trimmed with flowers, or feathers, and a blue, brown, or green silk dress. Just as if God has not adorned the flowers of the field with every magnificence of hue, though apparently for no other purpose than to refine the human heart, by making it feel the sublime charm of the beautiful. Has the Bible taught us what is the orthodox religious color of the clothes, that those who love God should wear? Is not the rainbow, that emblem of God's covenant with man, embellished with every glorious tinge of beauty, and variety of color? Does not even God's word assure us, that "nothing from without defileth a man, but those inward thoughts of malevolence that all harsh judgers of their neighbor's private affairs indulge in, are the fruitful causes of sin." Musidora was watched in all her actions, as if she was the antagonist of all the gossiping women around her. But the fact was, that her only offence consisted in the splendid moral elevation that governed what society was pleased to call her eccentricities; surely then it was very eccentric to have lived for the advancement of the poor, to have performed all the duties of a true daughter to her parents, a sister to her brothers, a kind mistress to her numerous servants, a consecrated wife to her afflicted husband, and an elevated Christian mother to his unloving, ungrateful, undutiful children.

"Nothing, however, stirs up envy more than the despair of being what the envied person is, and that despair is founded upon a man's consciousness of his not being able to reach the same pitch of perfection; and this consciousness sticks so close to the mind, that for all a man's flattering himself, and his boasting to others, yet he can neither boast nor flatter it away; but that it is a perpetual check to his spirit, and will be sure to keep him under in the inmost judgment he passes on himself. Some have observed that there is no creature whatsoever, but by a kind of natural instinct, knows its match; and no doubt by consequence its superior and over-match too. And when a man knows this by an impartial comparison of himself with his rival (the inward apprehensions of the soul being generally impartial and true, what disguise soever they may put on in men's carriage and expressions), upon such a comparison he sinks and sneaks inwardly; and weighing himself in the balance with the other, quickly sees which scale rises, and which falls."

"Envy, in fact, is always stimulated by something either good or great; for no man is envied for his failures, but his perfections. Envy sucks poison out of the fairest and sweetest flowers, and like an ill stomach, converts the best nutriment into the worst and rankest humors. So that if we would give in an exact catalogue of all the motives of envy, we must reckon up all the several virtues, ornaments and perfections, both internal and external, that the nature of man is capable of being ennobled with."

CHAPTER XXII.

"Man oft is right, yet if or wrong, or tame,
He is himself alone, not God to blame."

The fat and the lean kine, the full and the blasted sheaves of wheat, did not more truly prefigure the seasons of plenty, followed by those of famine, than did that long, perverse, disloyal course of teaching of the popular mind — that an inferior race, morally, politically, and socially, was equal to, and should be instanter invested with, all the privileges of the superior and ruling race. That the Anglo-Saxon mind, the highest type of the world's progress, in laws, government, inventions, letters, and civilization, and its boast in philosophy, and poetry, should be reduced and confined to the low, servile, unchristian barbarous standard of the Ethiopian. In other words, that this degraded class should be made to impose tasks, where it had before served, and to assume the mace of sovereignty, before it had given the least evidence of capacity for self-control.

This fountain of bitter waters was first opened by the fierce political struggle for the admission of Missouri, in 1820. Clever boys and girls, in the schools and seminaries at the North, had read that false political apothegm brought forward in the Declaration of

Independence,* a declaration made primarily to vindicate rebellion in the mind of Europe, and secondly, to throw dust in its eyes, that "All men are born free and equal;" a phrase which is most completely disproved by the history of every State in Europe, from despotic Russia and Austria, to the liberty-exalted shores of England. Indeed, the framers of the Constitution in 1798, when they came to adopt a *practical* Government, could make no use of so fallacious a declaration; but proceeded to fix a great political equatorial boundary line, North of which, African slavery should be abolished, and South of which, it should continue legally to exist.

The discussions of 1820, thirty-two years after the adoption of this Constitution, arose from an effort to fix new boundaries to the *slave* State area, to limit it, and to enlarge that of the free States. The bitter fountains of Jericho were sweetened by casting in the branch of healing; but no such divine virtues flowed from the great compromises of 1820 and 1850, which

* History tells us that Thomas Jefferson, an *infidel*, and the author of the Declaration of Independence, that the abolitionists cite as their authority for the mad enterprise of emancipation—History, we repeat, tells us "that Jefferson was married on the 1st of January, 1772, to Mrs. Martha Skelton, widow of Bathhurst Skelton, and daughter of John Wayles, an influential lawyer of Charles City." This lady, then twenty-three years of age, and remarkable for the beauty of her person, and the grace of her manners, brought him a very considerable fortune. She had inherited 135 *slaves*, and 40,000 acres of land, the value of the whole being about equal, we are informed, to Jefferson's *own* patrimony. The two combined formed an ample estate, and Jefferson's practice as a lawyer, added largely to his income.

politically shook the land. What was bitter before became more bitter; the poisoned fountains rose to a flood, and overflowed the country. The daily, the monthly, the quarterly press of the North never ceased to agitate the subject, and generally with the highest degree of zeal where there was the lowest degree of knowledge. The United States, it was affirmed, was certainly right in setting up a great Federal Republic for the human race, where universal equality should predominate. No matter whether our fathers set up such a government or not. God himself was an "old fogy," *He* did not see that the command to enslave heathen nations two thousand years before the Savior was born, would continue this institution in the same heathen class of men two thousand years *after He* was crucified. There was no progress in this, *He* could not see the end from the beginning; Wendelili, Agarison, and Cheeveri knew better. The American Constitution was but "leather or prunella." It ought to be torn up. There was a *higher law* than any contained in the Pentateuch or New Testament, even "strong-minded women" could read it. Lucera was superior to the prophetess Deborah of old. It was not only the diurnal and periodical press that kept up the quixotical agitation—every element of Red Republicanism from Europe added to it. The political madcaps of France and Germany, the very jail-birds of Austria, joined in this agrarian cry of equality. Every foreign tongue wagged in this contest; and, for every single voice, a newspaper sheet spoke a thousand tongues.

In the forty years that it had taken for abolitionism to culminate, the population had increased from a little over nine millions to thirty millions; the number of States had risen to thirty-three. Fifteen of these were slave States, and eighteen free States. What further use, said the disorganizers, to parley? We will put weapons in the hands of the Africans; we will supply them with torches, swords, and pikes, instead of Bibles.

Such were the acts and actors, and such were the means used in the contest which had now reached the year of its culmination. Arise, said the above-named disorganizing levellers, the era of the equality of all races is come. The Anglo-Saxons have filled the measure of their iniquities. The reign of the Anglo-Africans approaches. The odor of the poppy is to be substituted for that of the rose; the cornus-florida for the lily and the violet; and the black sons of Ham, from the Niger and the Congo, are to lead to the altar of Hymen the fair and beautiful daughters of Japheth; and so reverse the word of prophetic inspiration, that the descendants of Ham should be the servants of Japheth's *forever*.

The eighteenth Presidential term had now arrived, and after a long and stormy contest, success crowned the Ethiopian equality party. They elected a President who was inaugurated at the Capitol, and took possession of the "White House." But the hour of triumph is often the hour of trial. Before he could communicate his first message to Congress, or take any definite, public, official action, an extensive insurrection of the negroes broke out, from the waters of the Chesapeake to those of the Apalachicola. The great outbreak of the French Revolution, in 1798, was not more sudden, desolating, and bloody. From Delaware to Louisiana and Texas, the negroes, led on by the most rabidly fanatic of the abolitionists, rose up in a secret and well-concerted plot against their masters. Not a Southern State was exempted from the horrible calamity. Masters and their families were ruthlessly and brutally murdered. Fire, massacre, and barbarian cruelty and treachery, marked every plantation; and for a season the extermination of the white race seemed inevitable.

San Domingo fiendish cruelty gloated itself with blood on the first outbreak of this servile war. But with its usual want of induction and power of combination, the negro failed. The high spirit of the old cavaliers and gentry was roused. Men who had defeated armies in the Revolutionary struggle of 1776, at King's Mountain, Eutaw, Camden, Cowpens, and Yorktown, were not slow in marshalling squadrons to the field; and hecatombs of blacks were sacrificed in every village and city of the South. Streams of African blood, borne down by their affluents, swelled the currents of the Perdido, the Mobile, the Coosauhatchie, the Altamahah, and the Savannah, the Rappahannock and Potomac, and tinged the mighty tides of the Mississippi and Missouri. In a few months a *million* of negroes were put to the sword. The party who had by their writings and orations fomented this insurrection found themselves in a miserable dilemma.

The popular voice, which is always greatly influenced by success, and steady in nothing but fluctuations, turned strongly against the negroists. A Congress was elected, before whom the recommendations of the President were nothing, and the whole abolition effort proved that he who is a traitor to his country is sure to pay the penalty of his misdeeds by disappointment and universal contempt.

The lever to lift the world, which Archimedes sought, was found in the 14th century, in the printing-press. Its power shook the condition and history of States and kingdoms, and is yet destined to produce the most powerful changes, revolutions, and reforms in human society.

What other power broke up the icy sea of religious error, and scattered, as with the volcanic force of truth, the lights of the Reformation in the 16th century? What other power, fired by the match of the American Revolution, burst up the platform of continental despotism, and inaugurated the French Revolution of 1798? — a revolution, not ended as Burke and the great statesmen of the age supposed, but is yet in full, but sure and slow, progress at this day, after a smouldering action of seventy-two years. And now, in 1860, we behold it in its very worst and most unfixed state — a military despotism.

If liberty, if knowledge, if religious truth, have ever had free scope, and been advanced to their utmost point, it has been through the influence of the press. And this great agent has had, and will ever have, the property of being the *antidote* as well as the *poison* to the human mind. No sooner are errors produced by it than they are destroyed by it. "*Cheats*," says the great English moralist, Dr. Johnson, "cannot long stand against *truth*."

It has been shown, in the preceding pages, that

every form of the typographical art — the newspaper, the magazine, and the review—were employed to prove that Almighty God was partial and unjust in granting freedom to one set of his creatures, and imposing servitude on the other; and that no equitable distribution of social privileges, no right reasoning, no sound philosophy, could approve or tolerate this eccentricity. In season and out of season, in Congress and out of Congress, in every village, town, and city, this insane conclusion was drawn and frantically proclaimed, and the doctrine of universal emancipation announced as *ab initio.*

Not only were these dogmas urged in all the forms of printing and writing, but they were preached from the pulpit. Not only did the Iscariot Lauderdales and Nicodemus Jellabees skulkingly assert it; but three thousand clergymen of the North, banded together, put their names to a declaration that the retention of the hereditary servants of the South was a sin *per se*, and that God's word did not sustain it. This doctrine of abolitionism was laid down with as much arrogance as if it was the eleventh commandment. Surely the tenth commandment, which interdicts the covetousness of taking away a man-servant and a maid-servant must have been intended *for*, and is binding *only* upon, the barbarous age of the world. Surely it could not relate to the men of the nineteenth century, with whom wisdom is to die! Surely the omniscient Jehovah is a little mistaken *here!*

The Southern States had been so long badgered with these and such like sentiments, and had received such remarkable illustrations of the undying energy and bigotry of fanaticism, by the negro insurrection, that they determined to sever themselves from the Union of 1790, which had proved *to them* utterly fallacious. They rose up, in the majesty of their constitutional panoply, and, basing their appeal on those ungranted and prescriptive rights which were guaranteed to each State,—namely, the management of their internal laws and domestic institutions in their own way, uncontrolled by a central and centralized government,—they united in a Southern confederacy, for the original purposes recited in the great constitutional charter of liberty: namely, "to form a more perfect union, establish justice, insure domestic tranquillity, provide for the common defence, promote the general welfare, and secure the blessings of liberty to ourselves and our posterity."

By this continued crusade of the Northern upon the Southern States, they demanded, in fact, the surrender of four thousand millions of property, in opposition to common sense, in opposition to their own Bible-instructed consciences, and in opposition to the commercial interests of the whole world; and all of these sacrifices to be offered *only* to gratify the cheap philanthropy of the North. And this demand, too, was made in the self-righteous effrontery of the highwayman, who not only required the travellers' purses, and that quickly, but bade them thank God for sparing their lives.

In this confederation, the South gave up no principle for which it had contended in the Revolution—no principle for which its eloquent orators had contended in the Congress at Washington. It loved the country, it approved free trade, it hated inequalities in tariffs, it loved its rights, it loved liberty, and aspired after national glory. It had surrendered none of its faith in the *principles* of the Constitution of 1790.

Its new organization proved the prosperity of the State. A single year's loss of the Southern cotton crop, during the horrors of the before-mentioned insurrection, had stopped the cotton-mills of New and Old England. An alliance with the latter power, and a treaty of peace and commerce, immediately followed. Others, with France, Holland, Germany, and Spain, succeeded. It furnished Europe with cotton, rice, and sugar. It prospered greatly at home, it prospered abroad. The political differences in the nomenclature of the Republics, and their treaties and negotiations, was only that of the United States South, and the United States North.

Musidora and her husband, through the earnest entreaty of Baron Bunsen, had visited the far-famed medicinal springs of Germany, and Mr. Walsingham, after a few months' trial of these *naturally* tepid baths, was entirely cured of his paralysis.

Leonora and Rutledge, having lost many children, now became true penitents for their folly in listening to Mrs. Jellabee's advice, and forsaking their renowned father, Mr. Walsingham, in his severe bodily helplessness; and now, profiting by all the elevated examples of Musidora, and her unwearied efforts to instil proper sentiments into their hearts and minds, they became most excellent Christians, and a comfort ever afterwards to their pious parents.

The beautiful but statuesque Gulielma lived and died

an old maid. Halcombe and Edward, awakening to the superior moral worth of their long-neglected orphan sister, Musidora, now concentrated all their affections upon her, and she and her husband returned to live in the flourishing State of South Carolina.

Edward Wyndham's wife had died; Halcombe had never married; so now we see the three remaining children of the sainted Mrs. Wyndham, reunited in the bonds of undying affection, spending the remnant of their days together at the venerable Palmetto Grove; where, every Sabbath morning, at the rising of the sun, Edward, Halcombe, and Musidora repaired to the grave of their dead mother and father, to enter into a renewed covenant with their glorified spirits to consecrate themselves to the service of that God who had so abundantly rewarded the faith and prayers of their Christian parents. And the whole of this noble family now directed all their energies to the missionary work of converting the African slaves in their midst to civilization and Christianity; and the recording angel, at the judgment-day, will read out before the assembled universe the secret love to God that all the family of the Wyndhams had been governed by throughout their journey in life. And when their separate names shall be called in the reading of the above-named scroll of reckoning, each one of these slave-holders will approach the throne of God bringing thousands of redeemed African heathen in their train; and every one of them, masters and servants, will receive the plaudit, "Well done, good and faithful servant; enter thou into the joys of thy Lord."

THE END.

CPSIA information can be obtained
at www.ICGtesting.com
Printed in the USA
LVHW032029220323
742311LV00010B/714